INTRODUCTION TO COMPUTER SCIENCE

INTRODUCTION
TO COMPUTER
SCIENCE

HARRY KATZAN, Jr.

Chairman, Computer Science Department
Pratt Institute

 PETROCELLI/CHARTER   NEW YORK 1975

First Printing
Second Printing
Printed in the United States of America

Library of Congress Cataloging in Publication Data

Katzan, Harry.
    Introduction to computer science.

    Includes bibliographies.
    1. Electronic digital computers. 2. Electronic data processing. I. Title.
QA76.5.K374   001.6'4   75-5751
ISBN 0-88405-309-1

CONTENTS

v

CHAPTER 7.   COMPUTER SYSTEMS ARCHITECTURE

CHAPTER 8.   INPUT AND OUTPUT

Part III. COMPUTER SOFTWARE

CHAPTER 9.   ASSEMBLER, MACRO, AND PROGRAMMING LANGUAGES

PART IV. TOPICS IN COMPUTER SCIENCE

PREFACE

Recent advances in computer technology have created the need for a modern up-to-date introduction to computer science that reflects the field as it exists today and is expected to exist in the predictable future. The objective of the book is to present an introduction to the subject matter without being an introduction to programming and problem solving. To be sure, programming and algorithmic processes are covered in the book, but they are placed in perspective. There is much more to computer science than programming, and that point of view has been adopted for this book.

The book covers topics taught in most computer science programs that are omitted in most introductory textbooks that are oriented towards programming and problem solving. Typical examples are introductions to automata theory, computer systems architecture, language processors, and operating systems, and a chapter on computers and society. However, the book does highlight recent advances in programming methodology, including:

Structured programming
Top-down development
Group programming methods
HIPO design and documentation techniques
Virtual storage

It must be emphasized that the newer topics are not included at the expense of the conventional subjects, such as introduction to computing, algorithmic processes, computer hardware, data structures, and numerical analysis. They are all covered in full detail.

The book is composed of the following parts:

I. Fundamental Concepts
II. Computer Systems
III. Computer Software
IV. Topics in Computer Science

Part I is intended to provide a background for the study of computer science and covers: the scope of computer science; an introduction to computing; program and systems development; number systems; and basic data and computation structures. Part II is designed to familiarize the student with computing machines and presents: an introduction to computer hardware; computer systems architecture; and input and output. Part III deals with a popular topic that students want to know about early in their studies. Topics covered are: assembler, macro, and programming languages; language processor methodology; and operating system technology. Part IV is designed to acquaint the student with some of the areas that are part of computer science and surveys the following topics: structured programming, data structures, numeric computing, automata theory, and computers and society.

In effective computer science education, it is important that principles are taught; this point cannot be overemphasized. *Introduction to Computer Science* is relevant to this need because it permits the scope of computer science to be covered in the first course, so that the remaining courses in the computer science curriculum can be placed in proper perspective.

It is a pleasure to acknowledge the valuable comments and suggestions of the reviewers, the help of Mr. Kenneth Antolak of Honeywell Information Systems, and the assistance of my wife Margaret, who typed and helped with the preparation of the manuscript.

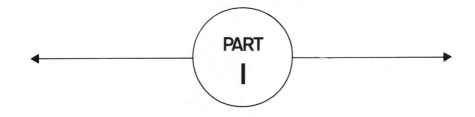

PART

I

FUNDAMENTAL
CONCEPTS

1

SCOPE OF COMPUTER SCIENCE

1.1 INTRODUCTORY REMARKS

Welcome to the world of computer science. By most standards, it is a new field. In terms of years, however, its short history is misleading, since the field is the product of advanced technological innovation built on a solid foundation of mathematical and engineering principles.

Computer science is one of the most recent disciplines to be developed, but is currently very popular because of the widespread use of computers in everyday affairs. Computers are used in business, government, education, and research. Although most computer utilization involves organizations, there have been remarkable achievements in the areas of personal computers, computers in the home, and in recreational computing. In fact, one of the better stories is about the college professor who programmed a minicomputer to play a variety of board games, such as tick-tack-toe, and to store a large collection of party jokes classified as G, GP, R, and X. In response to a request for an "X joke," for example, the computer would select an X-rated joke at random and display it on the computer's output unit. The portable computer that used ordinary house electrical current was intended to be used for demonstrations and at parties. After one particularly joyful evening, the following report was received: "The computer performed well all evening and was an instant success. The only problem occurred when a happy celebrant poured his cocktail into the computer. Needless to say, the computer reacted violently."

Most applications of computers are complicated, as are the computer systems themselves. In fact, the humorous episode given in the previous paragraph actually represents a nontrivial application of computers. Some applications are complicated because a sophisticated

3

computational process is involved. Other applications are complicated because of the volume of data involved and the manner in which it must be managed. It is the computer scientist's job to design and build computers, systems, and languages to facilitate the use of computers.

Computer science cannot be studied in a vacuum and it is well for the prospective computer scientist to obtain as wide a background as possible in other academic areas. While it is true that most fields now use computers as a tool for increased productivity, the interdependence of computer science and other fields is much stronger. For example, computers are designed and built by electrical engineers; computational processes require a mathematical background; studies of the similarity of computers and the brain require a training in biology; artificial intelligence requires an exposure to psychology and logic; and optimization and simulation techniques require a knowledge of business operations and modeling methods. Computer science differs from other scientific areas such as physics and chemistry; it is not a natural science established to study a class of natural phenomena but rather an "artificial science"—the study of something that man has created.

Computer science is generally regarded as an applied science, which means that it is a discipline encompassing principles for "doing things" and for measuring how well they are done. People with a background in computer science can apply their knowledge to computer programming, systems analysis, computer design, management, and so forth. However, computer science is much more than a way of doing things. There are theories of programs, abstract machines, data structures and languages —to name only a few. In short, computer science is also an academic discipline, and many students continue their formal education in computer science and go into teaching and research.

1.2 THE NATURE OF COMPUTER SCIENCE

The word *computer* in computer science implies that a computer is involved, in one way or another. This is basically true. Computer science is concerned with the process of using the computer, with the applications of computers, with the manner in which information is stored in the computer, with the theory of computers, and so forth. Therefore, a good knowledge of the computer and how to make it work is necessary. *It is important to recognize that computer science is considerably more inclusive than simply a study of computers and how to program them.** There

* A computer program is a series of instructions that tells the computer what to do. The process of developing a program is termed programming. Programs and programming are covered in considerable detail in later chapters.

is a definite orientation in computer science toward the computational process in whatever form it may take. The remainder of this chapter, except for a brief excursion into the history of computers, is concerned with the various areas of computer science and the major applications of computers.

It is important to recognize that no topic introduced in this book is covered completely. (The word *introduction* in the title is to be taken literally.) Most topics covered correspond to other courses in the computer science curriculum. Gaining an appreciation for computer science is desirable and the reader should make full use of the Selected Readings given at the end of each chapter to gain perspective on the field.

1.3 A VERY BRIEF HISTORY

The processing of information is present in almost every activity of our lives and takes place whenever two or more persons or systems interact. Throughout history, many devices have been developed to aid in this information (or data) processing. One of the first aids was the *notched stick* that served as an aid to counting and remembering. The first machine, per se, was the *abacus* developed by the Romans in ancient times. A more popular version, the Chinese abacus, was developed in the 12th century and is still used in China today.

The next major advance in computing machines was the *slide rule* invented in 1621 by William Oughtred, an Englishman. Since that date, many improvements have been made to the slide rule for both general and special-purpose applications. The first adding machine (1642) is credited to Blaise Pascal, the famous French mathematician. This gear-toothed machine was followed in 1673 by a machine that performed multiplication by repeated additions and was developed by the mathematician G. W. Leibnitz. The machines of Pascal and Leibnitz are the forerunners of modern desk calculators.

The modern era in computing began in 1804, when Joseph Marie Jacquard invented a loom in which the weaving operations were controlled by punched cards. The first automatic computer was designed by Charles Babbage in 1822; it could perform numerical calculations. The machine, called the *automatic difference engine*, was originally proposed by J. H. Mueller in 1786 and finally built in Sweden by George Scheutz in 1853. Another of Babbage's machines, the *analytical engine* was designed in 1833 but was never built. It is the forerunner of today's stored-program computers.

The punched card and related processing equipment were developed in the 1880s for use in the U.S. census. As it turned out, the development of the punched card became one of the most significant events in the widespread use and acceptance of computers and data processing equipment.

The first automatic computer was completed by Harvard College and IBM in 1944. This machine, called the Mark I, was constructed from mechanical components and handled 23-decimal-digit words. The inherent slowness of the Mark I resulted in the design and development of the first electronic computer, the ENIAC, at the Moore School of Engineering at the University of Pennsylvania in 1946. Modern computers are an outgrowth of this pioneering research of the middle 1940s.

Every advance in computing machines was associated with an actual need. For example, ancient cavemen and shepherds needed the notched stick to count their flocks (or wives, as the case may be). Similarly, the adding machine resulted from tax computations in France; Babbage's computers resulted from a need for difference tables; and the Mark I and ENIAC efforts were largely influenced by World War II.

The current computer explosion, which we are now witnessing, is not simply the result of a new invention or a new technique—although a multiplicity of technological innovations have been made in the last 25 years in the computer field. Other factors have contributed to this widespread growth.

In the area of science and technology, computers have played a major role in many significant technological advances, and as a result of these advances, computer use has snowballed. Concrete examples in this area are missile guidance, simulation studies, and computer control systems, in addition to the traditional scientific problem solving. In general, scientific computing has received its fair share of publicity.

Computers play an equally important role in business and government, although the glamour seems to be lacking for various reasons. The volume of business and governmental data processing has grown enormously along with the growth in size of businesses and the expanding scope of government. The use of computers for diverse operations, such as check processing, has given rise to a variety of advanced input, output, and mass-storage devices. Many management problems created by geographical locations and distances are presently relieved through the use of telecommunications facilities* that permit information to be transmitted between remote locations at electronic speeds. Here again, reasonable success in using the computer to reduce

---

* Telecommunications facilities involve the use of ordinary telephone equipment for the transmission of information between locations.

the volume of clerical operations has caused the use of computers to snowball. Another important factor in the growth of computer utilization is that we are now more adept at identifying computer applications and at applying the computer to those applications.

In the computer field, it seems as though success breeds success. To summarize, the computer era is the result of three major advances:

1. The development of the punched card and card processing equipment
2. The development of the automatic electronic digital computer
3. The development of telecommunications facilities for transmitting computer data between remote locations

Each of these major advances utilizes its own technology and has contributed in its own way to the vigorous growth, at home and abroad, of computer science.

1.4 APPLICATIONS OF COMPUTERS

Organizations, such as businesses, governmental agencies, and schools, are the primary users of computers. Moreover, most computers are fairly expensive and computer people are reasonably well paid. The computer applications necessary to justify this expense are varied and substantial. This section contains a general survey of the various computer applications grouped into the following classes: data processing, problem solving, modeling and simulation, feedback and control systems, on-line and real-time systems, information systems, and artificial intelligence. Some applications are presently more useful to society than others. For example, data processing is more useful to more organizations than is artificial intelligence. On the other hand, artificial intelligence is academically more interesting to computer scientists than is data processing. In the following paragraphs, no emphasis is placed on the relative importance of the various areas, which is a matter of individual judgment.

One final note is necessary. Complete comprehension of the following descriptions of the various computer applications is not required. Only a general familiarity is needed; however, this familiarity goes a long way in helping to make the study of computer science relevant and interesting. It is a good practice to constantly try to relate the methodology of computer science to the classes of applications given here.

Data Processing

Data processing involves the storage, processing, and reporting of information. Although data processing is definitely related to the record-keeping activities of an organization, it is not restricted to those activities and usually encompasses many clerical and time-consuming functions.

One of the more useful applications of data processing is customer billing in a utility-type company. Each customer has a record on a customer file that reflects his name, address, billing rate, credit status, cumulative usage, previous meter reading, and service category. Each month the customer's meter is read by a "meter reader" and the current use is recorded in books. Subsequently, each customer's reading is keypunched, so that each customer's use is reflected in a single card. To the data processing program, each of these cards is referred to as a *transaction*. At the end of the billing period, all transaction cards are sorted by customer's account number and placed on magnetic tape. This is referred to as "batching," since it would be inefficient to run the program separately for each customer.* The billing program can now be run using the "old" customer file and the transaction tape as input, as depicted in Figure 1.1. The program processes the customer file and the transaction tape sequentially and a bill for each customer is computed. Output from the billing program is a "new" customer file containing "updated" records, a set of customer bills, and a report that summarizes the processing that was performed. The "old" customer file and the transaction tape are saved for emergency purposes. The "new" customer file will be used in the next month's run of the billing program.

Data processing often combines several operations:

1. transaction processing
2. record keeping
3. bill preparation
4. management reporting

and almost always involves at least the following input and output files: old master file, transaction file, new master file, and the report file. Other common data processing applications are:

1. Accounts receivable
2. Accounts payable
3. Inventory control
4. Payroll

---

* The term *batch* is also used with operating systems technology, wherein a set of jobs to be run on the computer is collected on an input medium. This is covered later.

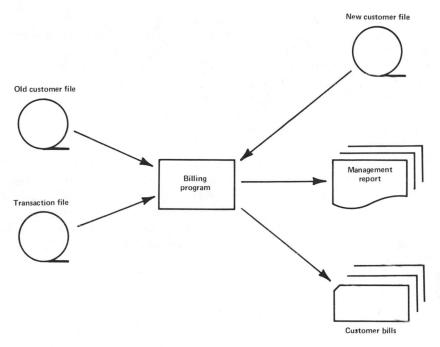

Figure 1.1   Typical data processing application—a billing program.

In fact, any high-volume operation that must be performed on a periodic basis lends itself to data processing methods. The input operation may vary in data processing; for example, check processing in a bank involves a magnetic ink character reader and inventory processing in many department stores requires special merchandise ticket readers.

Problem Solving

The earliest use of computers took place in the areas of scientific and engineering problem solving. This was a normal consequence of the fact that computers were invented and developed by scientifically trained persons who were keenly interested in the computational processes of the computer. The concern for data management and the problems of business and government came later.

Currently, problem solving activities with the aid of the computer are not restricted to science and engineering and now encompass business, education, and many other disciplines, such as architecture, medicine, and the humanities. In fact, many problems in this category do not solve a problem, per se, but perform a task that lends itself to computers, such as the calculation of a space trajectory or the statistical analysis of a set of data values.

A typical engineering problem would be the computation of design parameters for a bridge or a road. Important here is the time factor and the accuracy level. Obviously, engineers have designed and constructed bridges and roads for centuries without the use of computers. With the use of computers, however, the computations can be performed in a very short period of time, allowing different design alternatives to be evaluated. Contrary to "semipopular" opinion, computers are extremely accurate,* so that the need for an engineering aid to check calculations is not usually necessary. Accuracy also reduces the amount of redesign that is necessary after construction has begun.

A problem that falls into this category characteristically requires a small amount of input, performs a relatively large number of calculations, and outputs a small number of results. Problems range from simple calculations to complex iterative procedures. A simple problem might be the calculation of compound interest as described by the formula

$$V = P(1 + \frac{r}{n})^n$$

where

P is the principal
r is the interest rate per time period
n is the number of time periods
V is the value of P after n time periods

Similar calculations might be to compute the yield of a bond issue or the predicted size of a herd of cattle after a given number of years.

Another common example might be the calculation of the roots of a quadratic equation of the form

$$ax^2 + bx + c = 0$$

The roots r of this equation can be computed using the quadratic formula

$$r = \frac{-b \pm \sqrt{b^2 - 4ac}}{2a}$$

---

*Most modern computers include error checking circuitry to detect errors that occur during computation.

Although these examples represent trivial applications of the computer, they both demonstrate cases where the use of a mathematical concept can be made more practical with the aid of an appropriate computer program.

Although textbook problems are usually well defined and the value, V, to be solved for is readily available, as in

$$v = f(x,z)$$

many problems in science, engineering, and business take the form

$$v = f(x,y,v)$$

where the variable to be solved for exists on both sides of the equation and an iterative solution is needed. A common example is van der Waal's equation for the molar volume of a gas when the temperature and pressure are known:

$$P + \frac{a}{v^2}(V - b) = RT$$

where

> P is the pressure
> T is the absolute temperature
> V is the molar volume—the desired variable
> R is the ideal gas constant (0.08205 atm/T)
> a and b are constants for the particular gas

This problem requires an iterative solution; that is, successive values of V are calculated until a value that satisfies the equation is found.

The quadratic formula was given in the preceding paragraph for computing the roots of a quadratic equation. Not all equations that we wish to find the root of have well-defined solutions. Figure 1.2 depicts an equation that is assumed not to have a well-defined solution. The root of an equation of this type requires an iterative solution known as "interval bisection." The root of the equation is given by the point at which the equation $f(x)$ intersects the x axis. The method of solution successively halves the interval while ensuring that $f(L_i)$ and $f(U_i)$ have different signs until a solution with the desired accuracy is reached.

Problems in this category vary in scope and magnitude. Computer programs are used to calculate the trajectory of a space vehicle from an

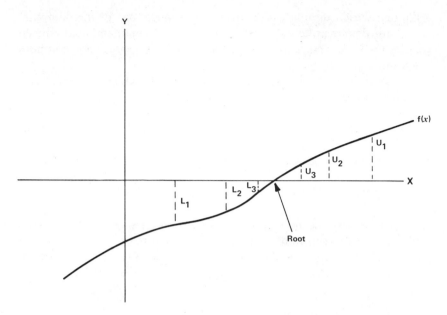

Figure 1.2   The iterative method of interval bisection can be used to calculate
the root of an equation.

earth orbit to a moon orbit; in this case there is considerable output for
very little input. Data analysis programs, such as those used with the
U.S. census, generate a relatively small amount of output in the form of
summarized data in response to a tremendous amount of input. In fact,
computer programs have been written for practically any type of
problem for which a solution is known. Programs have been used to
calculate the exact ingredients of sausage and to prepare an index for a
book. Most of us have even received mail addressed by computer and
letters written by computer.

The dividing line between data processing and problem solving is a
fine one. Data processing is characterized by periodic computer runs
involving large amounts of data. Problem solving is characterized by
nonperiodic runs and a predominance of machine computation. As it
turns out, there is no defining characteristic for either category.

Models and Simulation

A *model* is defined as an abstraction of a real-life situation from
which we can draw conclusions or make predictions about the future. In
a sense, a model is a duplication of a system or subsystem with an

emphasis on aspects of interest. Once a model is developed, it is usually more convenient to manipulate the model than to work with the actual system. Typical models are a road map and an aerodynamic model used in a wind tunnel.

Models are classified as iconic, analog, and symbolic. An *iconic model* physically resembles the system it represents; examples are the aerodynamic model, a globe of the world, a photograph, and a blueprint. An *analog model* establishes a correspondence between a system, subsystem, or variable of a system and an analogous variable in the model. Examples are the bar chart in a sales graph, a schematic, and an electrical analog. A *symbolic model* uses logic, mathematics, and empirical generalizations (i.e., laws of nature) to establish a set of assumptions about a real-life phenomenon, from which conclusions can be deduced. Symbolic models are frequently referred to as *mathematical models*, which are the kind used in computer applications.

A familiar mathematical model describes the fall of an object in a vacuum. This law of nature, proposed by Galileo, gives the relationship between distance fallen d and time t as follows:

$$d = 16t^2$$

If the object is dropped from a height of 10 feet, we can conclude from the model that after 0.5 second, the object will have fallen 4 feet, or be 6 feet from the ground.

When models are constructed, the determination of the element of the system that needs to be abstracted—or modeled, as they say—is of prime importance. Once a model is developed, its *validity* becomes of immediate concern. In short, it is necessary to know how well the model represents the system being studied.

Simulation is the use of models to attain the essence of a system without having to develop and test it. One of the most familiar forms of simulation is the "trainer" used to train pilots and astronauts. The objective of such devices is to give the participant experience in a realistic operational environment. A *computer simulation* is a computer model of a real situation; a computer model uses mathematical models, as discussed above, and computational procedures to achieve a realistic description of a system.

Typical computer simulations involve the description and flow of traffic in a major city, the number of checkout counters needed in a supermarket, and the design specifications of a digital computer. Computer simulation is widely used because of the simple fact that many processes or systems cannot be described by mathematical equations.

However, these same processes or systems can be described with flow diagrams, so that a computer program can be written to simulate them. Running the program with various parameters is analogous to the operation of the real system. Thus, a system can be analyzed without having to experiment with real-life situations. Traffic flow in a city is a reasonably good example. In prior years, the traffic commission would establish one-way streets on a trial basis. After a period of time, the change would be evaluated. In the event of a poor design, people have to suffer during the period in which it is being evaluated. With simulation, the traffic flow can be simulated; when a good design is achieved, then the physical implementation can be made.

Feedback and Control Systems

The terms *feedback* and *control* are almost self-explanatory. The most common example of a feedback and control system is the combination of automobile and driver. The output of the system is the path of the automobile; the driver provides the objective of the system and receives "road information" as input. The driver provides control signals to the automobile as required. Another common example of a feedback and control system is the heating system found in most homes. The thermostat serves as the control mechanism. The output of the system is the heat produced by the furnace. The automobile-driver system is referred to as an *open system* because of the driver in the feedback loop. The heating system is referred to as a *closed system* because it can operate without human intervention.

In computer control systems, the computer serves as the control mechanism. A typical application might be the control of temperature, among other things, in a chemical process. The chemical processing equipment contains sensing devices that send signals to an analog-to-digital converter, which serves as an input device to the computer. The computer is programmed to sample the input signals on a periodic basis and compare the values against prescribed limits. If the temperature is too high or too low, the computer generates appropriate output signals to achieve the desired result. The output signal is converted to analog form and serves as input to a control mechanism that is part of the chemical process. The above process is depicted conceptually in Figure 1.3. In actual applications, the monitoring of hundreds of input signals is not unusual. This application of computers is referred to as *process control*; the technology is widely used in applications that range from control of space vehicles to control of a sewage disposal plant.

Computers are also used in manufacturing processes through a concept known as *numerical control*. Using conventional machining

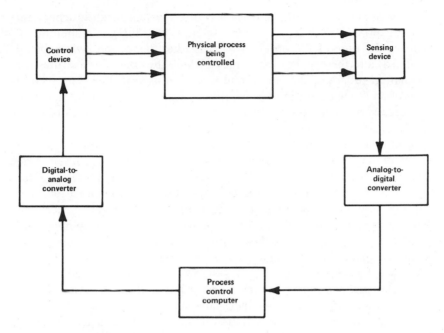

Figure 1.3   Feedback and control system using a digital computer as a control mechanism.

techniques, the production of a precision part is a time-consuming and costly process. Moreover, successive pieces produced by the same machinist vary in precision, within given tolerance limits, due to human limitations. When using numerical control, a machinist/mathematician, known as a part programmer, describes the piece to be machined in a computer-oriented language. The description of the piece in that language is known as a part program. The machine tool used to machine the part is directed by a control system that accepts signals from the computer and guides the machine tool accordingly. There are two modes of operation. In the on-line mode, the computer is connected directly to the control system. In the off-line mode, a punched tape is produced by the computer and the tape is read by the control system to guide the machine tool.

On-Line and Real-Time Systems

An on-line system is one in which the computer communicates directly with a component external to the computer—regardless of whether that component is a person using a terminal device via telecommunications facilities or is a control system of an independent physical process. The term *real time* refers to two things. In simulation, there is the time of the problem (that is, the time in the system being modeled) and there is the clock time in which the computer executes the simulation program; the clock time is known as real time. The second kind of real time occurs in physical processes or on-line systems in which it is necessary for the computer to respond within time limits in order for the results to be useful in the real world.

Two common examples of on-line real-time systems are the airline reservation system and the savings bank system. In an airline reservation system, a central computer records passenger reservation information for scheduled flights. When a customer requests space accommodations, the central computer is queried via a specially built terminal device and telecommunications facilities to determine if the requested facilities are available. If the customer makes a reservation, the amount of remaining available space on the aircraft is reduced and the customer's data are recorded. In a system of this type, the requirements are such that the computer must respond within a specified period (e.g., 10 seconds or less) in order to ensure customer satisfaction. Flight records, which change dynamically as reservations are made and cancelled, must be stored on mass storage devices in order to meet the real-time requirements of the application.

In a savings bank system, customer records are stored on main storage devices at a central computer. Teller stations (that is, input/output terminal devices) are located in each branch of the bank. As deposits, withdrawals, and other transactions are made, each transaction is recorded in the customer's records at the time of transaction. As a result, banking facilities are available at all times to all customers at all bank branches.

Information Systems

An *information system* is a set of hardware, software, and informational facilities that permit the accumulation, classification, storage, and retrieval of large amounts of information. An information system not only stores data, but also provides facilities for assigning meaning to data, and hence, provides information. The scope and complexity of information systems vary from a deck of punched cards to comprehensive library retrieval systems.

An information system consists of three major components:

1. A large repository for data—called a data base
2. A means of accessing the data
3. A means of processing the data for analysis and reports

A *data base* is defined as a collection of physical data that are related to each other in a prescribed manner. For example, a data base may be the total collection of data known to be in a business, or it may be a central record of all known criminals in a major city. The key point is that all pertinent data is available through a central facility and that access to the facility provides the latest up-to-date information.

The manner in which data are organized in an information system is dependent upon the needs of the computer applications that use the system. For example, an information system may contain documents that are retrieved by author, title, or key words; or it may contain customer data (for a data processing application) that are accessed sequentially or by account number.

Information systems are frequently accessed by people who are not computer professionals. Sometimes a query language is used so that an informational request of the form

IN FILE ALPHA-3
IF AGE>30 AND MALE AND MARRIED
LIST NAME,ADDRESS,EMPLOYEE-NO,YEARS-OF-SERVICE

is entered to retrieve information from the system. Usually, an input request with this general form is interpreted by a special computer program written for that purpose. The program scans the input lines, determines the information required, retrieves the information, and displays it for the user. This is an example of the current trend in information systems. An experienced group of systems analysts and programmers develops a system and a language that can be used by nonprofessional people. The language is frequently "made up" to suit the needs of *that* particular application. The implications, of course, are wide-reaching. Once a system is developed, practically anyone can use it—and with ease.

Artificial Intelligence

The question, "Can a machine think?" is one that has been debated for some time now and is not likely to be answered in this book. However, the subject is fruitful from the point of view of "what the computer can do."

There are various opinions on the subject. Some say that thinking is an activity that is peculiar to human beings; therefore, machines cannot think. Although thought as something unique to humans may have been in the minds of philosophers when they first considered the subject of thinking and intelligence, this definition gets us nowhere. Others maintain that a machine is thinking when it is performing activities that normally require thought when performed by human beings. Thus, adding 2 and 2 must be considered a form of thinking. To continue, some psychologists have defined intelligence in the following simple way: "Intelligence is what an intelligence test measures." In light of the preceding section on information systems, all we need to do is feed enough information into an information system and develop an appropriate query language and we have an intelligent machine. This line of reasoning also gets us nowhere. Perhaps we are wasting our time, but the fact remains that computers are doing some amazing things, such as playing chess, guiding robots, controlling space vehicles, recognizing patterns, proving theorems, and answering questions, and that these applications require much more than the conventional computer program.

Hamming* gives a definition of *intelligent behavior* that is useful to our needs:

> The ability to act in suitable ways when presented with a class of situations that have not been exhaustively analyzed in advance, but which require rather different combinations of responses if the result in many specific cases is to be acceptable.

The importance of the subject lies in the direction in which society seems to be going. Currently, we use machines for two reasons: (1) The job cannot be done by a human being; (2) the job can be done more economically by machine. To this list, we must add another reason. Some jobs are simply too dull to be done by humans, and it is desirable from a social point of view to have such jobs done by machine. For this, we require more "intelligent" machines, since we seem to be moving outward on a continuum of what we consider to be dull and routine behavior.

1.5 NOTES ON THE REMAINDER OF THE BOOK

It is important to recognize that computer science is an independent academic discipline and is neither mathematics, electrical engineering, logic, nor any other field. Computer science draws from various other disciplines but has an identity of its own.

The applications of computers given in the preceding section are

* Hamming, R. W., *Computers and Society*, McGraw-Hill, New York, 1972, p. 267.

included to give some perspective on how computers are used. The study of computer science does not include every possible application of computers, just as the study of mechanical engineering does not include every possible machine that can be built. The objective is to study principles, interlaced with practical considerations, so that a person's knowledge can be applied to a wide range of situations.

There is probably some truth to the assertion that every professor who teaches an introductory course or every author who writes a book on the subject views the various topics differently and classifies them accordingly. The organization of this book is intended to give an overall grasp of computer science to the reader as quickly as possible.

Part I, entitled Fundamental Concepts, is concerned with important topics necessary for an understanding of computer operations and basic computational processes. The use of the term *fundamental concepts* implies basic knowledge and not theory and includes the following topics: introduction to computing concepts, the processes of program and systems development, number systems, and basic data and computation structures.

Part II, entitled Computer Systems, is an introduction to computer hardware, computer systems organization, and input and output media and devices. This area of computer science is more closely related to electrical engineering than other areas of computer science; fortunately, one does not have to know how to design and build a computer to use one effectively. However, a basic knowledge of computer operations is essential to effective computer utilization.

Part III, entitled Computer Software, involves concepts and associated programs that aid in using and operating the computer. This area is concerned with languages for programming the computer, translator programs that translate programs written in a language to an equivalent computational form that can be executed by the computer, loader programs for placing translated programs in main storage for execution, and operating system programs that are used to operate the computer efficiently.

Part IV, entitled Topics in Computer Science, includes theoretical and practical topics that are usually contained in the computer science curriculum. Obviously, a value judgment is required here because of the diversity of subjects that can be included. The topics emphasized in this book are: structured programming, data structures, numeric computing, automata theory, and computers and society.

It should be emphasized that the various areas that constitute the field of computer science are related. As knowledge is gained in one area, it affects the understanding of related areas.

QUESTION SET

Using the Selected Readings that follow, prepare a short one- or two-page report on a computer application of interest. The emphasis in the report should be on the "whys" and "hows" of that application.

SELECTED READINGS

Cole, R. W., *Introduction to Computing*, McGraw-Hill, New York, 1969.

Dorf, R. C., *Introduction to Computers and Computer Science*, Boyd and Fraser, San Francisco, 1972.

Feigenbaum, E. A., and J. Feldman (eds.), *Computers and Thought*, McGraw-Hill, New York, 1963.

Feldzamen, A. N., *The Intelligent Man's Easy Guide to Computers*, David McKay, New York, 1971.

Hamming, R. W., *Computers and Society*, McGraw-Hill, New York, 1972.

Katzan, H., *Information Technology: The Human Use of Computers*, Petrocelli/ Charter, New York, 1974.

Sanders, D. H., *Computers in Society*, McGraw-Hill, New York, 1973.

Squire, E., *The Computer: An Everyday Machine*, Addison-Wesley, Reading, Mass., 1972.

2

INTRODUCTION TO COMPUTING

2.1 KEY TO UNDERSTANDING

Understanding computers is like understanding many aspects of the physical universe. On the surface, an event or a physical entity may appear to be too complex to describe or understand. Once the event or entity is broken down into its component parts and basic laws or principles are applied, the complete system becomes understandable and is frequently manageable, as well. The same kind of thinking also applies to computers. Some typically complex computer applications are:

1. An on-line information retrieval system. The user has a remote terminal that is connected to the computer via telecommunications facilities. The user is allowed to query the system to satisfy his informational needs and is normally provided with the requested information within seconds.
2. A computer is used to guide an airborne missile. The precise location of the missile and the target are obtained from radar units, electronically, and converted to computer numbers. A precise direction for the missile is computed and that control information is sent to the missile via radio devices. There is no human intervention in the process.

Obviously, these applications are complicated—even for the most experienced computer professionals. Yet, each application can be analyzed in terms of its component parts and easily understood. The same concept applies to the computer. The precise operations that the computer performs and the manner in which they are performed can be analyzed as discrete functions. Each function executed by the computer

21

is implemented through electronic circuitry; that function is well defined and is easily understood by the designers and builders of the computer. In fact, any reader of this chapter could understand the electrical properties of the computer—if he were interested enough and wanted to go through the trouble of learning them.

The following key point must be emphasized: *As in the case of the automobile and the airplane, a person need not be capable of designing and building a computer in order to effectively study and use one.* While it is true that you will know considerably more about computers when you finish this book and subsequent computer science courses, you need not know how the "add" operation of the computer works before you can talk about it. The same reasoning holds true for other computer operations and for the various computer components. In other words, you can talk at a "higher level," recognizing, of course, that eventually each circuit of the computer must be developed and each computational procedure must be specified exactly.

2.2 THE CONCEPT OF AN ALGORITHM

One of the most important aspects of using the computer as an aid in problem solving is that a precise description of the problem must exist. Normally, the problem description is followed by a list of the procedures that must be followed to solve the given problem. Many sets of procedures exist in everyday life; however, computer procedures are a little different. A specific procedure that gives the solution to a problem is termed an *algorithm*. More formally:

> An *algorithm* is a list of instructions specifying a sequence of operations that guarantees the answer to a problem of a given type.

The notion of an algorithm has been known since antiquity, even though in modern times the term is most frequently used with computers. As an example of an algorithm, consider a simple procedure for adding two signed numbers, a and b, that is, for finding the number $a + b$:

1. If a and b have the same sign, add the magnitude of b to the magnitude of a and affix the sign of either a or b.
2. If a and b have different signs, subtract the smaller magnitude from the larger and affix the sign of the larger magnitude.

Thus, for example, $(-3) + (-2) = -5$, $(-3) + (+2) = -1$, and $(+3) + (-2) = +1$. Before we discuss the properties (or characteristics) of an algorithm, it is well to note that the simple procedure just given is slightly more general than is ordinarily used for computer solution. The following algorithm for the same procedure is more detailed:

1. If a and b have the same sign, go to step 5. (Otherwise continue with step 2.)
2. (By default, a and b must have different signs.) Subtract the smaller magnitude from the larger magnitude. (Continue with step 3.)
3. Affix the sign of the larger magnitude to the result. (Continue with step 4.)
4. Stop.
5. Add the magnitude of b to the magnitude of a. (Continue with step 6.)
6. Affix the sign of a to the result. (Continue with step 7.)
7. Stop.

Now, several of the characteristics of this algorithm (and algorithms in general) can be given:

1. The algorithm consists of a finite number of steps.
2. The instructions are precise.
3. The instructions are unambiguous.
4. The procedure will work for any two numbers, a and b.

The fourth characteristic is significant, and it must be stated that some people never quite get the "hang" of it. An algorithm to operate on any two numbers is different (and usually more complicated) than a procedure to operate on two specific numbers. For example, a procedure to compute $(-3) + (+2)$ is

1. Subtract 2 from 3.
2. Affix a minus sign to the result.

In fact, the latter procedure usually is not even referred to as an algorithm.

As another example, consider the Euclidean algorithm for the following problem:

Given two positive integers *a* and *b*, find their greatest common divisor.

In light of the above discussion, there are as many problems of this type as there are pairs of positive integers *a* and *b*. The algorithm involves the construction of a descending sequence of numbers: the first is the larger of the two numbers; the second is the smaller; the third is the remainder from dividing the first by the second; the fourth is the remainder from dividing the second by the third; and so on. The process ends when there is a zero remainder. The greatest common divisor is the last divisor in the sequence. For example, the descending sequence of numbers for the greatest common divisor of 44 and 28 is: 44, 28, 16, 12, 4, 0. The last divisor is 4, which is the result. The algorithm can be summarized in the following list of instructions:

1. Write down *a* and *b*.
2. If *b* is greater than *a*, exchange them.
3. Divide *a* by *b*, giving the remainder *r*.
4. If *r* is equal to zero, stop. *b* is the greatest common divisor.
5. Replace *a* by *b*; that is, $b \rightarrow a$.
6. Replace *b* by *r*; that is, $r \rightarrow b$.
7. Go to step 3.

The actual calculations can be listed as follows:

GCD of 44 and 28:   GCD of 10 and 8:

a	*b*	*r*
44	28	16
28	16	12
16	12	4
12	4	0

Result is 4.

a	*b*	*r*
10	8	2
8	2	0

Result is 2.

The Euclidean algorithm demonstrates another important characteristic of an algorithm. The number of operations that are actually performed in solving a particular problem is not known beforehand; it depends upon the input data and is discovered only during the course of computation. This may appear to be a contradiction, but it is not. The number of instructions in an algorithm *is* finite; however, some instructions may be executed more than once and others may not be executed at all.

The concept of an algorithm can be summarized with two defining characteristics:*

The deterministic nature of an algorithm. An algorithm must be given in the form of a finite list of instructions giving the exact procedure to be followed at each step of the calculation. Thus, the calculation does not depend on the calculator; it is a deterministic process which can be repeated successfully at any time and by anyone.

The generality of an algorithm. An algorithm is a single list of instructions defining a calculation which may be carried out on any initial data (in its domain) and which, in each case, gives the correct result. In other words, an algorithm tells how to solve not just one particular problem, but a whole class of similar problems.

2.3 DESCRIPTIVE TECHNIQUES

When algorithms are complex, a list of instructions, like those given in the preceding section, is hard to follow. A similar situation is encountered when asking for directions in a strange city. If only a few directions are involved, such as:

1. Go to the second traffic light and turn left.
2. Go four blocks and turn right.
3. The building is on the left.

then a simple list is usually sufficient. When the directions get much more complicated, a map is usually preferred. Here's the key point! The list of instructions is just as good (if they can be remembered or are written down), but a map is much more convenient and enables the onlooker to grasp a substantial amount of information at a glance. (A picture is worth a thousand words.)

In the computer field, people use flow diagrams, or flowcharts, as they are usually called, to describe a complex process. A *flowchart* is a graphical picture of the steps that must be performed to accomplish a given job; it is used for planning a program or system, for development,

* Katzan, H., *APL Programming and Computer Techniques*, Van Nostrand-Reinhold, New York, 1970, p. 23.

and for documentation. Figure 2.1 gives a simple flowchart of the algorithm for adding two signed numbers given in Section 2.2. In general, a flowchart can take *any* form and a "lousy" flowchart is better than no flowchart at all. However, the computer industry has adopted standard flowcharting symbols to facilitate the exchange of information. The following conventions have been established (see Figure 2.2):

The *flow direction* symbol represents the direction of processing flow. The usual flow is top to bottom and left to right. Flow lines should not cross each other and arrowheads are usually used on all lines; an arrowhead should be placed at the point of entry to a connector or function symbol. (In actual practice, the

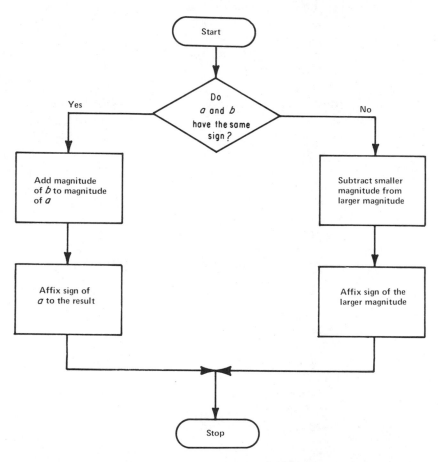

Figure 2.1   Flowchart of the algorithm for adding two signed numbers.

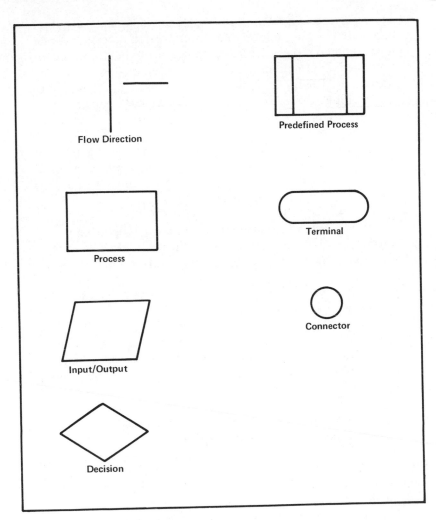

Figure 2.2 Flowcharting symbols.

conventions on the use of the flow direction symbol are relaxed and flow lines occasionally cross each other and flow sometimes goes right to left and bottom to top, depending upon the algorithm being depicted.)

The *process* symbol is used to represent a computer operation or a group of computer operations. The process symbol is also used to represent computer operations not represented by other flowcharting symbols.

The *input/output* symbol is used to denote any input or output operation. Making information available for processing is an input function (i.e., the read operation). The recording of processed information is an output function (i.e., the write operation). The input/output symbol is also used to represent input/output control operations, such as backspacing or rewinding a tape, positioning of a disk device, and so on.

The *decision* symbol is used to specify a point in an algorithm at which a branch to one of two (or more) alternate paths is possible. The basis on which the choice is made (i.e., the test) should be clearly indicated.

The *predefined process* symbol represents a function not outlined in detail on the flowchart. (A typical predefined process is a library subprogram, such as a square root routine.)

A *terminal* symbol denotes any point where an algorithm originates or terminates.

A *connector* symbol specifies an entry to or an exit from the flowchart. A set of two connector symbols is used to indicate continued flow when the use of a flow direction symbol would not be practical.

Computer specialists use other flowcharting symbols; however, the symbols given here suffice for most applications.

Figure 2.3 depicts a flowchart for the Euclidean algorithm. It is slightly more complicated than the addition algorithm and includes a loop, wherein the same steps in the algorithm are executed more than once depending upon the input data.

It is no surprise by now that a computer program is a computer-oriented representation of an algorithmic process. (In fact, a program is implied in the flowchart of Figure 2.3 that includes "read" and "print" denotations.) It is usually suggested that beginning programmers draw a flowchart of the method of problem solution before the program is written to ensure that they have the logic of the problem in good order. For large programs, flowcharts are almost mandatory—even for experienced programmers. In spite of their usefulness, however, the use of a flowchart has its disadvantages. First, a flowchart can easily become a "bushy mess," especially for a program in which the internal logic is complex. Second, the use of a flowchart essentially requires that the programmer describe his problem and develop his program at the same time.

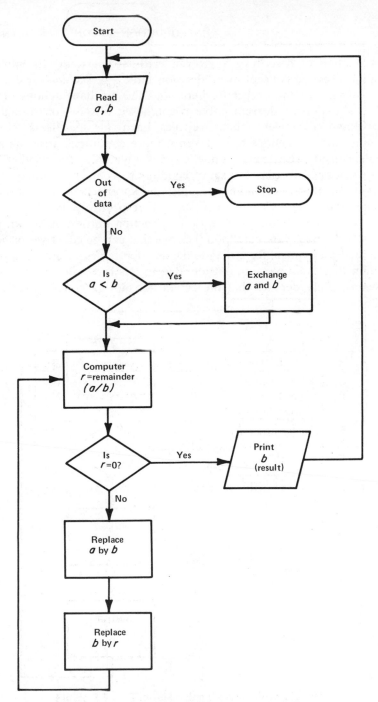

Figure 2.3　　Flowchart for the Euclidean algorithm.

A method of describing a problem without specifying its implementation uses the concept of a "decision table." A *decision table* is a tabular display of the decision criteria and the resultant actions of a problem situation. A decision table is composed of a set of mutually exclusive and collectively exhaustive rules. Each rule specifies a set of conditions and the actions to be taken if those conditions arise. As an example, consider the decision table, given in Figure 2.4, for whether or not to carry an umbrella. The set of conditions occupies the upper left quadrant and the set of actions occupies the lower left quadrant; they are called the *condition stub* and *action stub*, respectively. Each vertical rule is composed of condition entries and action entries, as shown in Figure 2.5. An irrelevant condition (i.e., one that can be either yes or no) is denoted by a hyphen. Returning to the decision table in Figure 2.4, the condition that it is not rainy outside, that rain is forecast, but that the weather is sunny denotes that the action "do not carry an umbrella" should be taken.

		Rule			
	Umbrella Table	*1*	*2*	*3*	*4*
Conditions	Raining outside	Y	N	N	N
	Rain forecast	-	Y	Y	N
	Sunny outside	-	Y	N	-
Action	Carry umbrella	X		X	
	Do not carry umbrella		X		X

Figure 2.4 Decision table for deciding whether to carry an umbrella.

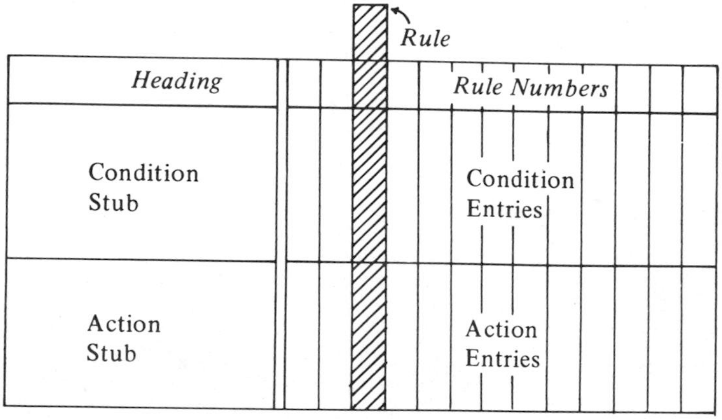

Figure 2.5 Format of a decision table.

As a realistic example, consider the problem of who should file a U.S. tax return and whether to use Form 1040 (long form) or 1040A (short form). An individual must file a return if one or more of the following conditions hold:

1. Citizen or resident of the United States
2. Earned $600 or more if under 65 years of age
3. Earned $1200 or more income if 65 years of age or older
4. A tax refund is desired

An individual is permitted to use the short form (1040A) if all of the following conditions hold:

1. Income is less than $10,000.
2. Income consists of wages subject to withholding and not more than $200 total of other wages, interest, and dividends.
3. The taxpayer wishes to use the tax table or take the standard deduction instead of itemizing deductions.

This problem is conveniently described (see Figure 2.6) in two decision tables: the first to determine if a return should be filed and the second to determine which form should be used.

The use of decision tables is particularly appropriate when it is necessary that all possible conditions that can occur be accounted for. In fact, many students have commented that a decision table would be useful in many legal contracts.

2.4 COMPUTER FUNDAMENTALS

A computer can be viewed as a "numerical transformation machine," as depicted in Figure 2.7. The process of computing involves three "basic" steps:

1. *Input*, whereby data on which the computer is to operate are entered into the machine.
2. *Computing*, whereby the data are transformed to meet the needs of a given application.
3. *Output*, whereby the results are made available for subsequent use.

The notion of computing in this sense is certainly not new. For example, an ordinary mathematical operation, such as addition, uses a similar concept, shown as follows:

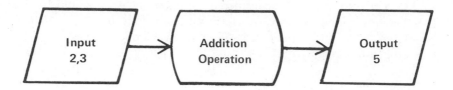

In general, the computer can be viewed as a device that performs a "well-defined" function on the input data and that produces appropriate output data. Input and output are symbolic processes that can have descriptive as well as numeric connotations.

If the computer is to be viewed as a "black box," then it must be capable of operating automatically without human intervention—at least between elementary operations such as addition or division. This is, in fact, the precise manner in which it does operate.

As a means of introducing the concept of computing, it is useful to outline the steps that a person follows when solving a computational problem with the aid of a pencil, paper, and a desk calculator, slide rule, or ordinary adding machine. The human calculator usually has a list of instructions he is to follow and a set of input data. The process by which the calculations are performed is summarized as follows:

1. *Information is stored* by writing the list of instructions, as well as input data, on the piece of paper. During the course of performing the calculations, intermediate results are also written on the paper; however, the person frequently keeps some information in his brain while using charts and tables, and other information is held temporarily in the calculating device.

2. *Information is processed* by utilizing the computing device—that is, the slide rule, desk calculator, or adding machine—to perform the elementary calculations required by the computational process. Each operation is performed by taking data values (i.e., operands) from one place on the paper, performing the specified operation, and recording the result in a definite place elsewhere on the paper.

3. *The computational process is controlled* by the human calculator by referring to the list of instructions and by carrying each instruction out in a specified order. Each instruction is read, interpreted, and executed by the person performing the calculations and the execution of an instruction is completed before the next is begun.

Although this is indeed an oversimplified analogy to the functional structure of a computer, hardware components that correspond to the piece of paper and the human calculator and his computing device exist; they are covered in the next section together with representative input and output devices.

	Return Table	*1*	*2*	*3*	*4*	*5*	*6*	*7*
Conditions	Citizen or resident of U.S.	Y	Y	Y	Y	Y	Y	N
	Age less than 65	Y	Y	Y	N	N	N	-
	Earned $600 or more	Y	N	N	-	-	-	-
	Earned $1200 or more	-	-	-	Y	N	N	-
	Refund desired	-	Y	N	-	Y	N	Y
Action	File return (go to form table)	X	X		X	X		X
	Do not file return			X			X	

	Form Table	*1*	*2*	*3*	*4*
Conditions	Income less than $10,000	Y	Y	Y	N
	Not more than $200 of other wages, interest, etc.	Y	Y	N	-
	Tax table or standard deductions	Y	N	-	-
Action	Use Form 1040 (long)		X	X	X
	Use Form 1040A (short)	X			

Figure 2.6   A set of decision tables for filing income tax.

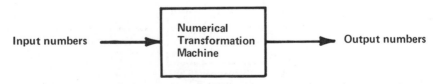

Figure 2.7   The computer can be viewed as a numerical transformation machine.

2.5 OVERVIEW OF A COMPUTER SYSTEM

The major hardware units in a computer system, (shown in Figure 2.8), are main storage, the processing unit, and input/output units. *Main storage* is analogous to the "piece of paper," mentioned in the previous section, and is used to hold computer instructions and data. The *processing unit* is analogous to the human calculator and his computing device and consists of a control unit and an arithmetic/logic unit. The *control unit* is the means by which the computer can operate automatically. The control unit reads an instruction from main storage, decodes it, and sets up the circuitry necessary to have the instruction executed. When the execution of an instruction is completed, the control unit reads the next instruction and the preceding steps are repeated. The *arithmetic/logic unit* contains the circuitry necessary to perform the arithmetic and logic operations of the computer. The arithmetic/logic unit normally includes a limited amount of high-speed storage, called *registers*,* for holding the values used during computer operations.

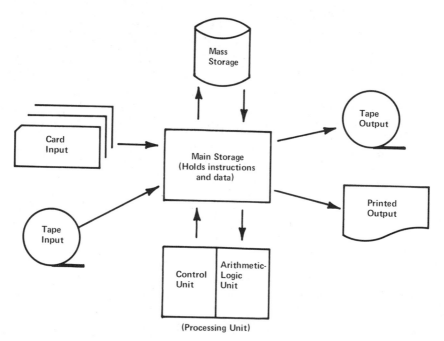

Figure 2.8   Functional structure of a computer system (simplified).

---

* Registers are analogous to the accumulator in a desk calculator or adding machine.

Input and output units are necessarily related to a specific recording medium. The most frequently used input and output devices are briefly summarized, as follows:

1. *Card readers* and *card punches* are used to read punched cards and to punch them.
2. *Magnetic* and *punched tape units* are used to read and write magnetic and punched tape. Tape is used for both mass storage and conventional input and output.
3. *Direct-access devices*, such as magnetic disk or drum, are used for mass storage and allow data to be accessed directly without having to pass over preceding information, as is the case with tape devices.
4. *Terminal devices* are used to communicate with the computer via telecommunications facilities. Terminal devices are usually similar to an ordinary typewriter or utilize a visual display along with a suitable keyboard.

The principal parts of a computer, then, are: a processing unit for performing computer operations, a storage unit for holding instructions and data during computation, and input and output units for placing data into main storage, so that it can be used by the processing unit, and taking data from main storage and placing it on a recording media for future use. One of the most obvious recording (output) media is the printed page, which enables humans to read the output. Two obvious input media are the punched card and the computer terminal.

2.6 STORAGE, INSTRUCTIONS, AND DATA

Storage

The purpose of the main storage unit of a computer is to hold instructions, data, and computed results that may be needed while a set of computations is being performed. Main storage is *not* used for long-term storage of instructions and data for several reasons:

1. Main storage is relatively expensive.
2. Only a limited amount of main storage can be attached to a computer.
3. Main storage is not portable.
4. Main storage may be volatile, which means that when electric power is turned off, the information contained in main storage is lost.

For long-term storage of instructions and data, mass storage devices such as tape or disk are used. Information is also stored on punched cards, although the use of cards for storing large amounts of information is declining because of the sheer bulk involved. However, punched cards continue to be the primary input medium.

Conceptually, main storage is organized somewhat like a group of numbered mail boxes in a post office. Each box is identified and is located by its number, which is termed a physical address. In the computer, main storage is organized in much the same manner into a set of locations. Each location can be used to hold a specific unit of data—such as a character, a digit, a series of characters, or a number, depending upon the structure of the computing system. To insert or remove data at a location, the address must be known.

When data enter a location, they replace the previous contents of that location. When data are taken from a location, however, the contents of the location remain unchanged, so that the same data may be used many times.

Registers

A *register* is a high-speed storage location that is used by the processing unit. Different computers have different registers. For example, some computers have several accumulators and others have a single accumulator. The question of "how many?" is one of basic design philosophy and is governed, to some extent, by the applications for which the computer is intended. Three basic registers are found in most computers; briefly, they are:

1. The *accumulator register*. The accumulator register is used for performing arithmetic. Temporary results are frequently left in the accumulator for the next arithmetic operation. When more than one accumulator is used, they are usually identified by number.
2. The *current address register*. The current address register contains the address in main storage of the location containing the instruction currently being executed. (The significance of this register will become obvious later.)
3. The *instruction register*. The instruction register holds the current instruction during execution.

Of the three registers, the only register that is used explicitly by the user is the accumulator.

Instructions and Data

One of the reasons that modern computers utilize the concept of a stored program is that the processing unit has access to instructions and data at electronic speeds, rather than having to retrieve each instruction and data item individually for processing from an electromechanical input/output device. What this means is that both instructions and data are held in main storage and that care must be taken not to interchange the two. Instructions and data are usually coded in the same form —usually binary—and are both regarded as a series of bits.* However, it is important to note that instructions and data differ because of the interpretation placed on their format and numeric content, even though each is a sequence of bits.

The format of a computer instruction varies between computers; however, all formats require, as a bare minimum, three items:

1. An *operation field* that denotes what operation the computer is to perform.
2. At least one *operand field* that denotes the data on which the computer should execute the operation (specified in the operation field).
3. *Modifier fields* that augment the operation field or the operand field.

A typical computer instruction might be:

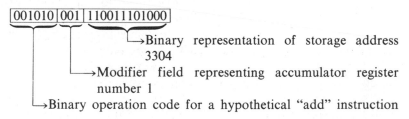

              →Binary representation of storage address 3304

        →Modifier field representing accumulator register number 1

  →Binary operation code for a hypothetical "add" instruction

For simplicity, this instruction is represented symbolically as:

| ADD | 1 | 3304 |

It is important to realize that an instruction occupies a storage location in the same way that data do.

The form of computer data is governed by a particular application,

---

* The term *bit* is an abbreviation for binary digit.

the nature of the information to be stored, and the computer involved. As an example, the "fixed-point" value* +37 might be stored as:

```
0 | 00000000000000100101
```

└→Binary representation of the value 37
└→Sign position (0 denotes +, 1 denotes −)

For simplicity, again, the above number is represented as:

```
+ | 0000037
```

A numeric data item occupies a location in main storage.

2.7 OPERATION OF THE COMPUTER

The preceding discussion is leading up to a brief discussion of how the computer operates. We know, essentially, the general form of instructions and data and the fact that the instructions and data are held in main storage when the computer operates.

All computer instructions are executed in precise units of time that are governed by pulses emitted from an electronic clock, which is a part of the computer's control circuitry. A fixed number of these pulses is termed a *machine cycle*. In a machine cycle, the computer can execute one or more microsteps that are combined to form conventional computer instructions, such as ADD or MULTIPLY. The exact number of microsteps that constitutes a given computer instruction is governed by the nature of the instruction itself and the data involved.

The processing unit operates in a prescribed sequence when executing instructions. Two cycles are involved: the "instruction" cycle and the "execution" cycle. The *instruction cycle* (referred to as the I-cycle) comes first and involves the fetching of the next instruction from main storage and the decoding of it to determine the operation to be executed. The following functions are performed during the I-cycle:

1. The address of the current instruction in main storage is obtained from the current address register.
2. The instruction is fetched from main storage and held in the instruction register of the central processing unit.
3. The instruction is decoded.

---

* The term *fixed point* refers to a format where the location of the decimal point is fixed.

4. The current address register is updated to point to the next instruction.

5. Control signals are sent to the processing unit to have the specified operation executed.

The current address register is usually set initially to the first instruction in a prescribed set of instructions. Normally, instructions are executed sequentially so that the current address register is updated with the address of the next instruction during the I-cycle. Most computers incorporate a "branch" instruction that discontinues sequential execution and permits execution to continue from a specified location. Usually, a branch instruction simply alters the contents of the current address register.

The *execution cycle* (referred to as the E-cycle) follows the I-cycle and involves the execution of the prescribed operation. If an arithmetic operation is involved, the operand is fetched from main storage using the address portion of the current instruction and the operation is performed using the specified operands. The length of the E-cycle depends upon the instruction to be executed. Other computer instructions include input and output, loading, storing, branching, shifting, testing—to name only a few.

Figure 2.9 depicts the execution of three instructions in a hypothetical computer. The *first instruction* is located at main storage address 4050. This fact is denoted by the contents of the "before" current address register. The instruction in storage location 4050 appears as follows:

| LOAD | 1 | 7384 |

It tells the computer to load the "contents" of storage location 7384 into accumulator register number 1. (The previous contents of accumulator register number 1 are simply replaced.) The current address register is updated to contain the address of the next sequential instruction (i.e., 4051). The *second instruction* is located at main storage address 4051 and is as follows:

| ADD | 1 | 9123 |

It tells the computer to add the "contents" of storage location 9123 to the "contents" of accumulator register number 1. Accumulator register number 1 contained + 123 and storage location 9123 contains + 14; the result is placed in accumulator register number 1, so that it now contains + 137. The contents of storage location 9123 remain unchanged. The contents of the current address register are updated to contain 4052. The

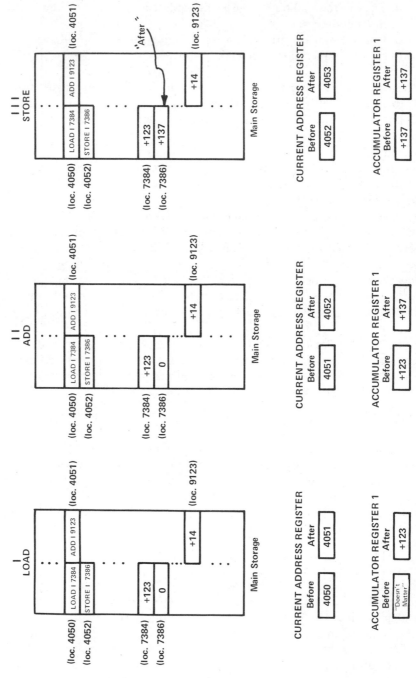

Figure 2.9 Execution of three instructions, LOAD, ADD, and STORE, in a hypothetical computer.

40

third instruction is located in the main storage location numbered 4052
and is:

$$\boxed{\text{STORE}}\;\boxed{1}\;\boxed{7386}$$

It directs that the current "contents" of accumulator register number 1
should be placed (i.e., should be "stored") in the main storage location
numbered 7386. The contents of the accumulator remain unchanged,
and the current address register is updated to contain 4053.

Even though the above example is oversimplified, it effectively
demonstrates three important points: (1) The computer executes discrete
instructions; (2) both instructions and data are held in main storage; and
(3) everything the computer does must be broken down into individual
steps.

QUESTION SET

1. Prepare a flowchart to input five numbers and find the maximum
   value.
2. Prepare a flowchart of the procedure necessary for dropping or
   adding a course at your school.
3. Prepare a flowchart of the logic for "making change."
4. Prepare a decision table of the procedure for "making change."
5. Write a flowchart to tell a robot how to find a door in an L-shaped
   room and open it. The starting point and the position of the door(s)
   are not known. Initially, the robot faces parallel to some wall. The
   doors slide open to the left. The computer in the robot has a stored
   program. The robot can accept the following commands:

   1. *Move* straight ahead until you either bump something or sense the
      crack on the right of a door. The crack cannot be sensed unless the
      wall is directly to the robot's right, and the sensing mechanism is
      unreliable and should be given three chances to find a crack.
   2. *Turn* 90° to the left.
   3. *Insert* hand in crack.
   4. *Ring* buzzer—to be done if crack cannot be found.

   The computer receives the following feedback:

   1. Whether the robot has stopped moving
   2. Whether it was stopped by a wall or a crack
   3. Whether there is a wall on the robot's right

6. To some degree, the preceding chapter treats the units of a computer system as though they are "black boxes." Try to name ten other devices and/or units that are usually treated in a similar manner.
7. Distinguish between a main storage location and a register.
8. Here is a brief but interesting research problem: Most computers store and process information in binary form. Why is this so? (Ask any computer scientist or electrical engineer.)
9. How does the computer, as described here, relate to information, as you know it?
10. Some computer scientists have even discussed the possibility of a "household" computer to help around the house. What tasks could it perform? Would it be as useful as a robot? What about in the year 2000?

SELECTED READINGS

Bohl, M., *Flowcharting Techniques*, Science Research Associates, Chicago, 1971, pp. 1–45.

Calingaert, P., *Principles of Computation*, Addison-Wesley, Reading, Mass., 1965.

Cole, R. W., *Introduction to Computing*, McGraw-Hill, New York, 1969.

Crowley, T. H., *Understanding Computers*, McGraw-Hill, New York, 1967.

Feldzamen, A. N., *The Intelligent Man's Easy Guide to Computers*, David McKay, New York, 1971.

Katzan, H., *Advanced Programming: Programming and Operating Systems*, Van Nostrand-Reinhold, New York, 1970, chap. 9.

Maurer, W. D., *Programming: An Introduction to Computer Techniques*, Holden-Day, San Francisco, 1972.

Squire, E., *The Computer: An Everyday Machine*, Addison-Wesley, Reading, Mass., 1972.

3

PROGRAM AND SYSTEMS DEVELOPMENT

3.1 THE CONCEPT OF A COMPUTER PROGRAM

There is a certain similarity between an algorithm, as defined in the previous chapter, and a list of computer instructions. The similarity is not a coincidence, and most, but not all, computer programs originate as algorithmic processes. In the short history* of computers, hundreds of thousands of algorithms have been developed by mathematicians, engineers, analysts, researchers, and students. Most of these algorithms have resulted in computer programs. Actually, anyone with a problem that lends itself to computer solution, in one way or another, can develop an algorithm and a corresponding computer program.

A meaningful sequence of computer instructions is referred to as a *program*, and the process of writing a program is called *programming*. Because it is cumbersome to discuss computer instructions in their binary form, it is customary to refer to operation codes symbolically and to represent numeric operands in decimal notation. The reader will recall that we represented the "add" instruction in Chapter 2 in the following convenient form:

| ADD | 1 | 9123 |

The process of programming requires that a program be entered into the computer in an established format, and a commonly used convention is to distinguish between the various components of an instruction, as in the following representation of the "add" instruction given above:

* It is only a little over 20 years since computers were first applied to practical problems.

43

Location	Operation	Operand
4051	ADD	1,9123

Thus the sample program in Figure 2.9 could be expressed as:

Location	Operation	Operand
4050	LOAD	1,7384
4051	ADD	1,9123
4052	STORE	1,7386

where the "location" column denotes the address of the location the instruction is to occupy.

Obviously, the three instructions LOAD, ADD, and STORE are not sufficient to write a program and most computers contain a large number of different instructions. Table 3.1 describes a set of useful instructions that are used in subsequent examples. We are going to use a simple computer that contains three accumulator registers (numbered 1, 2, and 3), contains a main storage unit with 100 locations, and is designed to execute the instructions given in Table 3.1. Lastly, we assume that the program may not be placed before location 10 in main storage because locations 1 through 9 are used for special purposes by the computer.

As an example of computer program, consider the following problem:

Given: Three numbers, A_1, A_2, and A_3
Compute: The average sum of the squares of these numbers, that is,

$$\frac{1}{N} \sum_{i=1}^{3} A_i^2$$

Considerations: If $A_i = 0$, skip it and do not count it in the average; the counter is N and it is not increased in this case.

There are several ways of writing the program. A straightforward method is given in Figure 3.1; it operates as follows:

1. The three numbers are read into main storage (at locations 41, 42, and 43).
2. The numbers are squared and placed in main storage (at locations 44, 45, and 46).
3. The sum of the squares is computed and a count is made of nonzero values.

4. The average is computed and the result is written to an output device.
5. The program stops.

It should be noticed in the program that storage areas, that is, locations 41 through 50, must be established for data values and constants. The program does the job and if a suitable computer existed, the program would work.* A key question is, "What would happen if there were 100 numbers?" The technique would result in a fairly long program. The solution to the problem is to use a program "loop." A *loop* is a series of instructions that are executed repeatedly, each time with different data.

To demonstrate a loop, let us modify the problem slightly. Suppose that in this case, we wish to compute the average of several values—the exact number of values is not known when the program is written. All we know is that the last number is zero. The problem is stated as follows:

Given: *n* numbers
Compute: The average sum of the squares of these numbers, that is,

$$\frac{1}{N} \sum_{i=1}^{n} A_i^2$$

Considerations: The exact number of values is not known beforehand. The *last* number is zero.

A short program to perform these calculations, using a program loop, is given in Figure 3.2. The program would work for any number of input values, even though the program requires only 20 storage locations.

The concept of using the same instructions with different data, as demonstrated in Figure 3.2, is a frequently used technique in computing. It reduces the storage requirements of a program and allows a program to be developed that can operate on different sets of data.

3.2 PROGRAMMING AND LANGUAGES

There was a time, in the early 1950s, when programs were actually written in internal form—that is, in binary notation or whatever the representation the machine used—and the programmer had to use actual operation codes and real computer addresses (as in the preceding

---

* This comment is for computer experts. The program is written as it is to prove a point. It is acknowledged that the program makes inefficient use of main storage.

Table 3.1
Typical computer instructions

Instruction	Format	Description
Load	LOAD m, n	Place the contents of storage location n into accumulator register m. The contents of n remain unchanged.
Add	ADD m, n	Add the contents of storage location n to the contents of accumulator register m; the result is placed in accumulator register m. The contexts of n remain unchanged.
Multiply	MULTIPLY m, n	Multiply the contents of accumulator register m by the contents of storage location n; the result is placed in accumulator register m. The contents of n remain unchanged.
Subtract	SUBTRACT m, n	Subtract the contents of storage location n from the contents of accumulator register m; the result is placed in accumulator m. The contents of n remain unchanged.
Divide	DIVIDE m, n	Divide the contents of accumulator register m by the contents of storage location n; the result is placed in accumulator register m. The contents of n remain unchanged.
Store	STORE m, n	The contents of accumulator register m are placed in storage location n. The previous contents of n are lost. The contents of accumulator register m remain unchanged.
Branch	BRANCH n	The computer takes the next instruction from storage location n and sequential execution continues from that point.
Test and branch	BZERO m, n	The contents of accumulator register m are tested. If the value is less than or equal to 0, then the next instruction is taken from storage location n and sequential execution continues from that point. Otherwise, the next sequential instruction is executed.
Read	READ n	The next value is read from the input and is placed in storage location n. The previous contents of n are lost.
Write	WRITE n	The contents of storage location n are written to the output unit. The contents of n remain unchanged.
Stop	STOP	The execution of the program terminates.
Constant	CONST v	The constant value v is placed in the storage location specified in the "location" column when the program is "loaded" into the computer for execution.
End	END	The END card denotes the physical end of the program. (The computer does not contain an END instruction.)

Location	Operation	Operand	Comment
10	READ	41	Read and store A_1
11	READ	42	Read and store A_2
12	READ	43	Read and store A_3
13	LOAD	1, 41	Load register 1 with A_1
14	MULT	1, 41	Mult register 1 by A_1
15	STORE	1, 44	Store $A_1{}^2$
16	LOAD	1, 42	Load register 1 with A_2
17	MULT	1, 42	Mult by A_2
18	STORE	1, 45	Store $A_2{}^2$
19	LOAD	1, 43	Load A_3
20	MULT	1, 43	Mult by A_3
21	STORE	1, 46	Store $A_3{}^2$
22	LOAD	1, 47	Sum (initially zero)
23	LOAD	2, 47	Count
24	LOAD	3, 44	$A_1{}^2$
25	BZERO	3, 28	Test $A_1{}^2$
26	ADD	1, 44	Add $A_1{}^2$ to Sum
27	ADD	2, 48	Add 1 to Count
28	LOAD	3, 45	$A_2{}^2$
29	BZERO	3, 32	Test $A_2{}^2$
30	ADD	1, 45	Add $A_2{}^2$ to Sum
31	ADD	2, 48	Add 1 to Count
32	LOAD	3, 46	$A_3{}^2$
33	BZERO	3, 36	Test $A_3{}^2$
34	ADD	1, 46	Add $A_3{}^2$ to Sum
35	ADD	2, 48	Add 1 to Count
36	STORE	2, 49	Store Count
37	DIVIDE	1, 49	Divide Sum by Count
38	STORE	1, 50	Store result
39	WRITE	50	Print result
40	STOP		Stop program
41	CONST	0	A_1
42	CONST	0	A_2
43	CONST	0	A_3
44	CONST	0	$A_1{}^2$
45	CONST	0	$A_2{}^2$
46	CONST	0	$A_3{}^2$
47	CONST	0	Value 0
48	CONST	1	Value 1
49	CONST	0	Count
50	CONST	0	Result
	END		

Figure 3.1 A straightforward program that computes $\dfrac{1}{N}\sum\limits_{i=1}^{3} A_i^3$ for a maximum of three values. (See Figure 3.2.)

Location	Operation	Operand	Comment
10	LOAD	1,25	Sum (initially zero)
11	LOAD	2,25	Count (initially zero)
12	READ	27	Read A_i
13	LOAD	3,27	Load A_i
14	BZERO	3,20	Test and branch (if zero) to compute Average
15	MULT	3,27	Compute A_i^2
16	STORE	3,27	Store A_i^2
17	ADD	1,27	Add A_i^2 to Sum
18	ADD	2,26	Add one to Count
19	BRANCH	12	Loop to read another value
20	STORE	2,28	Store Count for DIVIDE
21	DIVIDE	1,28	Compute Average
22	STORE	1,29	Store result
23	WRITE	29	Print result
24	STOP		Stop program
25	CONST	0	Constant zero
26	CONST	1	Constant one
27	CONST	0	Storage for A_i and A_i^2
28	CONST	0	Temp storage for Const
29	CONST	0	Result
	END		

Figure 3.2 Program demonstrating a loop that computes

$$\frac{1}{N}\sum_{i=1}^{n} A_i^2 \text{ for } n \text{ values.}$$

examples) instead of symbolic equivalents, such as ADD or STORE. It is sufficient to say that there were many problems involved with writing programs in this way and programming was a costly and time-consuming business. Then someone thought of using symbolic operation codes and symbolic names for data, somewhat as follows:

Location	Operation	Operand	Comment
	LOAD	1,ZERO	Sum (initially zero)
	LOAD	2,ZERO	Count (initially zero)
LOOP	READ	A	READ A_i
	LOAD	3,A	Load A_i in register 3.
	BZERO	3,AVER	Test and branch (if zero) to compute average.

Location	Operation	Operand	Comment
	MULT	3,A	Compute A_i^2
	STORE	3,A	Store A_i^2
	ADD	1,A	Add A_i^2 to Sum
	ADD	2,ONE	Add one to Count
	BRANCH	LOOP	Loop to read another value
AVER	STORE	2,COUNT	Store Count for DIVIDE
	DIVIDE	1,COUNT	Compute Average
	STORE	1,RESULT	Store Result
	WRITE	RESULT	Print Result
	STOP		Stop program
ZERO	CONST	0	Constant zero
ONE	CONST	1	Constant one
A	CONST	0	Storage for A_i and A_i^2
COUNT	CONST	0	Temporary storage for Count
RESULT	CONST	0	Result
	END		

This symbolic program computes

$$\frac{1}{N}\sum_{i=1}^{n} A_i^2.$$

The program looks like a program, but is not in an internal form. It is punched into cards—one line per card—and read into a computer program called an *assembler program*. The assembler program essentially translates the symbolic form of the program into a corresponding internal form. Thus, the computer is used as an aid in preparing its own program. A set of conventions for programming in this way is referred to as an assembler language—a language close to the language of the machine—or symbolic machine language.

The form of symbolic programming was a substantial improvement over the old method, but it wasn't good enough. Most people who programmed in assembler language were professional programmers who had to be trained to utilize the computer effectively. A typical problem-solving sequence, at that time, existed somewhat as follows:

1. A scientist, engineer, analyst, or the like has an idea that a particular computer program might be useful for a problem of some kind that he is involved with.
2. The problem originator meets with a programming manager to discuss the feasibility of having a program written.
3. If a computer program seems desirable, a professional programmer is called in and he meets with the problem originator

and the programming manager to discuss the scope of the project.
4. The problem originator and the programmer decide on the details (such as input and output specifications) of the program, as well as the main processing requirements.
5. The programmer writes the program, as specified.
6. The problem originator verifies that the program satisfies requirements and that results are correct. (Frequently, specifications are changed at this point and steps five and six are repeated.)

Obviously, there are serious disadvantages to this way of doing business. First, the process is cumbersome and communication problems frequently arise. Second, the process is time-consuming and many programs that need to be developed are never written because of the time factor. Lastly, the growth of the computer field and the computer industry is limited by the supply of professional programmers.

As a result of these problems, it seemed desirable to develop a language, of some kind or other, that could be used to communicate with the computer. The English language was ruled out because of its verbosity and because of ambiguities that arise in everyday usage. One of the characteristics of a language that would facilitate programming is that it should be meaningful to the intended user. Thus, a language for engineers and scientists should be mathematically oriented, and so forth. The main idea was that a mathematician, engineer, analyst, or student could develop his own programs and both the computer industry and the users would benefit.

After several pilot projects and research efforts by various computer groups, IBM finally came out with the first commercially available programming language in 1957. It was named FORTRAN, which is an acronym for FORmula TRANslation. FORTRAN was designed for scientific computer programming and it caught on very quickly because many computer applications involve numerical calculations of a scientific nature. With the use of FORTRAN, a person could write his own programs, since a notation familiar to his kind of work is involved. For example, a simple FORTRAN program to compute $r = (-b + \sqrt{b^2 - 4ac})/2a$ for several values of a, b, and c is given as Figure 3.3. As with assembler language, a program in the FORTRAN language is converted to internal computer language with a computer program known as a *compiler*.

The popularity and success of FORTRAN gave rise to the widespread use of other programming languages. Some well-known programming languages are:

1. The algorithmic language ALGOL for scientific computing
2. The business-oriented language COBOL for data processing applications
3. The multipurpose programming language PL/1 for scientific and business applications and for applications that include characteristics of both areas
4. The easy-to-use language BASIC for problem solving in a time-sharing environment*

Because programming languages are an important part of computer science, the subject matter is introduced in Part III of the book so that the reader can become reasonably familiar with the concepts without becoming committed to any particular languages.

One of the easiest languages to learn is the BASIC language, developed at Dartmouth College to enable students and faculty to utilize the computer there for problem solving and research work without having to make a significant investment in learning time. A BASIC version of the "root" program of Figure 3.3 is given in Figure 3.4. In fact, the BASIC program in Figure 3.4 can be simplified further, as shown in Figure 3.5.

How and why are programming languages so effective? The answer is inherent in the following discussion. Consider a computation that involves multiplying A − B by C and storing the result in the location that is given the symbolic name D. In assembler language, suitable

```
2   READ (5,8)A,B,C
    IF(A .EQ. 0.0) GOTO 3
    ROOT = (−B+SQRT(B**2−4*A*C) ) /(2. *A)
    WRITE (6,9)A,B,C,ROOT
    GOTO 2
3   STOP
8   FORMAT(3F6.2)
9   FORMAT(1X,3F6.2,F9.3)
    END
```

Figure 3.3   FORTRAN program to compute $(-b +\sqrt{b^2 - 4ac})/2a$ for several values of a, b, and c.

* Time sharing refers to the remote use of the computer via telecommunications facilities and computer terminals. It is discussed later.

```
10   READ A,B,C
20   IF A=0 THEN 60
30   R=(-B+SQR(B↑2-4*A*C))/ (2*A)
40   PRINT A,B,C,R
50   GOTO 10
60   STOP
70   DATA 1, -1, -6, 8, -2, -3, 0, 0, 0
80   END
```

Output:

```
1 -1 -6 3
8 -2 -3 0.75
```

Figure 3.4   BASIC program to compute $(-b +\sqrt{b^2 - 4ac})/2a$ for several values of a, b, and c.

```
10   READ A,B,C
20   PRINT A,B,C,(-B+SQR (B↑2-4*A*C))/(2*A)
30   GOTO 10
40   DATA 1,-1,-6,8,-2 -3
50   END
```

Output:

```
1 -1 -6 3
8 -2 -3 0.75
OUT OF DATA IN 10
```

Figure 3.5   Simplified form of the BASIC program given in Figure 3.8.

machine instructions would be:

```
LOAD    1,A
SUB     1,B
MULT    1,C
STORE   1,D
```

and a statement in a programming language would be:

$$D = (A - B)*C$$

(where ∗ denotes multiplication and = denotes replacement.) In this case, the programming language is only slightly more convenient than assembler language. Next consider a more complicated computation such as the calculation of $a/[b/(c - d) + e]$ and the replacement of w with the result. In assembler language, a suitable set of machine instructions would be:

```
LOAD     1,C
SUB      1,D
STORE    1,TEMP
LOAD     1,B
DIV      1,TEMP
ADD      1,E
STORE    1,TEMP
LOAD     1,A
DIV      1,TEMP
STORE    1,W
```

and a corresponding statement in a programming language would be

$$W = A/(B/(C - D) + E)$$

where / denotes division. The convenience of a programming language in this example is more obvious. Another important advantage of a programming language is that it reduces the number of errors that arise, since it uses a notation similar to mathematics and is easy for a human to use. Assembler language, on the other hand, is generally unfamiliar, in addition to being more detailed; the use of assembler language is more likely to result in programming errors that have to be identified and corrected.

To sum up, the use of a programming language subordinates the details of "machine-level" programming to a computer program called a compiler, as summarized in Figure 3.6. Another important advantage of most programming languages is that they are machine-independent. This means that a program written for one computer, let's say an IBM machine, can be used with another computer, for example, a UNIVAC machine. All a user need do is to recompile the program on the second computer. This is a very significant concept. All we need to learn is a single programming language, such as FORTRAN. We can use this programming language with any computer that has a FORTRAN compiler. In a sense, therefore, the compiler provides the key link

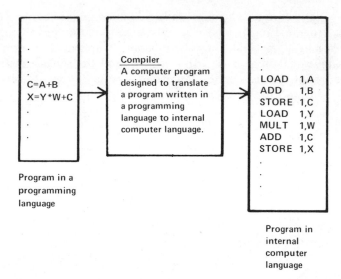

Figure 3.6   Conceptual view of the translation of a program written in a programming language to internal computer language using a compiler program.

between the programming language and the computer.* Computer manufacturers usually provide compilers for "standardized" programming languages, such as COBOL and FORTRAN. (Standardized activity is currently underway for the BASIC and PL/1 languages.)

Programming languages have become the key link between man and the computer, and the topic of programming languages has become a bona fide field of study. To a great extent, the growth of the computer industry is dependent on programming languages, since they provide for machine-independence, they facilitate programming, and they provide a means of describing a computational process in an unambiguous manner.

3.3 STRUCTURE OF A COMPUTER PROGRAM

In its most common form, a computer program is composed of a collection of machine instructions and data. A program normally occupies contiguous locations in main storage; however, this is not a

---

*It is important to recognize that computers differ. They have different system configurations and they have different instruction repertoires. Moreover, operating conventions and basic design philosophy also differ between computer manufacturers and between distinct computer models from the same manufacturer.

defining characteristic and some programs use storage that is allocated in noncontiguous blocks.

A program is usually expressed (or regarded) as a series of program statements that are executed sequentially until a statement is executed that transfers control to another part of the program, where execution continues. Structurally, however, very few programs exist as a simple set of statements. The reason is that ordinary mathematical functions such as the square root or the trigonometric sine need to be used and it would not be feasible for every programmer to prepare his own routine. In fact, the simple program of Figure 3.5 uses the square root routine. (See statement 20; SQR denotes a reference to the square root routine.) A structure that allows the execution of identical kinds of computation with different data is referred to as a "subprogram."

Most executable programs are composed of a *main program* and one or more subprograms, as depicted conceptually in Figure 3.7. A subprogram is either prepared by the programmer or stored in a library maintained by the computer installation. When a main program is loaded into the computer for execution, the needed subprograms are loaded along with it. Program control is passed to a subprogram and subsequently returned to the calling program with an instruction sequence referred to as "linkage." Thus, a trade-off is made between the extra time necessary for using a subprogram and the extra storage that would be needed for providing the instructions for executing that function each time it is needed in the program. In a typical set of

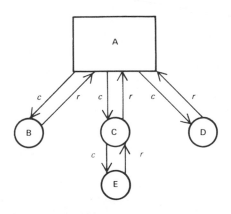

A denotes a main program
B,C,D,E denote a subprogram
c denotes a reference to a subprogram
r denotes a return to the main program

Figure 3.7   Conceptual description of program structure.

engineering calculations, a square root subprogram, for example, might be used hundreds of times.

In some cases, the "linkage" instructions to invoke a subprogram are not justified by space savings. This would be the case with a very small subprogram. For these cases, it is judicious to simply insert the necessary computer instructions directly into the program at each place it is used. A subprogram of this type is called an *open* (or in-line) *subprogram*, as contrasted with a *closed* (or out-of-line) *subprogram*, where only one copy of a given subprogram is used during program execution. Closed and open subprograms are depicted in Figure 3.8.

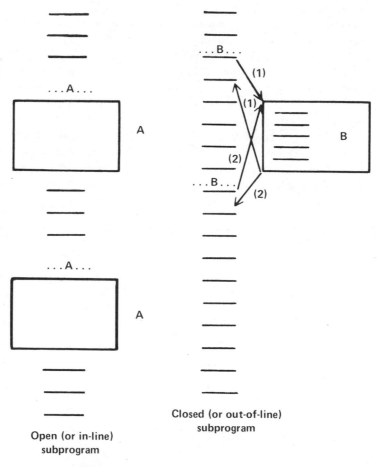

Open (or in-line) subprogram

Closed (or out-of-line) subprogram

Figure 3.8   Open and closed subprograms.

3.4 PROGRAM DEVELOPMENT PROCESS

All of the necessary tasks in program preparation have been covered: problem definition and analysis, algorithm development and description, and programming. Sounds easy, doesn't it? Actually, program preparation is a relatively straightforward process, provided that each task is clearly understood. Each of the tasks just given, however, is relatively broad and should be expanded into its component parts. The various steps in preparing a program, therefore, are usually listed as follows:

Problem definition
Systems analysis
Algorithm development
Programming
Compilation or assembly
Debugging and testing
Documentation
Systems implementation or production

Each step is discussed separately in the following text.

At first glance, *problem definition* would hardly seem to be worth considering. (This is especially true of students who have programs assigned by an instructor.) In the real world, however, a problem is manifested by a need of some sort. Examples are the need to process test data within 24 hours or the need to test a hypothesis or theory on an extensive set of test cases. On a larger scale, a banking need might be the keeping of up-to-date banking records through a network of teller terminals. Frequently, the person who recognizes the need and who is in the position to do something about it is limited in several ways:

1. He is not exactly sure of what he wants.
2. He is not certain that his needs can be satisfied.
3. He does not know how his needs can be fulfilled.
4. He is not certain that he can justify the computer application.
5. He is uncertain of how a system satisfying his needs would fit in the total organization.

Usually, the person or group originating the computer application is advised to state the proposed idea clearly, giving all relevant facts that might require further study. The key point is that the problem originator may not be experienced in computer technology.

The proposed computer application then goes through a *systems analysis* cycle in which an experienced person in both computer applications and in computer technology studies the problem to determine the following:

1. If the proposed application can be done
2. The "general" methodology to be employed
3. If the proposed application can be effectively integrated into the total organization

For cases in which a proposed application is considered to be a viable project for the organization involved, the systems analysis cycle continues with a detailed flow analysis of the program or system, and a precise specification of inputs and outputs. This is the stage at which flowcharts and decision tables are used.

Depending upon the computer application, *algorithm development* may be a part of systems analysis, programming, or a separate phase of the development cycle. Algorithm development involves the precise specification of the procedures the computer is to follow and may require mathematical analysis, heuristic reasoning, or the simple formulation of a list of steps. For example, if the computer application is to compute the trajectory a space vehicle should follow to a distant planet, then algorithm development would involve the specification and solution of complicated mathematical equations. Similarly, if the application is to perform a statistical analysis of experimental test data, then algorithm development involves the selection of appropriate statistical formulas and a specification of how they should be applied. For a payroll program, algorithm development would involve the methods for computing overtime, withholding tax, FICA, insurance, pension contributions, and so on. For a chess-playing program, algorithm development would involve a means of representing board positions in the computer and a procedure for move selection.

Programming is the process of writing the statements that comprise the computer program. Sometimes, the selection of an appropriate programming language is done during systems analysis or algorithm development. In other cases, the programmer chooses the programming language to be used. The same holds true for the development of the flowchart that describes the program. Sometimes the programmer develops it and sometimes he does not. When assembler language is used, programming is a complicated process. When a programming language is used, programming is easier, but it is never a trivial process. Assembler language is used when a suitable programming language is not available for the given program or when special circumstances prevent the use of a programming language.

Compilation or *assembly* involves the conversion of a program written in a programming language or in assembler language to machine language for execution on the computer. (Recall here that compilers and assemblers are also computer programs.) A program is usually written on a "coding form" or simply a sheet of paper and then punched on cards or entered at a computer terminal on a line-by-line basis. Not all programs compile or assemble correctly the first time; in fact, most of them do not. The process of removing errors from programs is referred to as "debugging and testing," which is covered next. The manner in which a program is actually executed is covered in Chapter 6.

Errors can occur in programs in several ways:

1. The algorithm is incorrect or inappropriate.
2. One or more statements of the program have syntax errors in them—that is, they are written incorrectly.
3. The logic of the program is incorrect.
4. The program is correct but applies only to a limited subset of data that must be processed.
5. The systems analysis is faulty and the program does not serve its intended purpose.

The recognition and removal of program errors is referred to as *debugging*. The process of ensuring that the program computes correctly is referred to as testing. Debugging and testing can occur at several stages, as follows:

1. The correctness of the algorithm can be determined by applying it to test cases, manually.
2. The program can be desk-checked to locate syntactical errors and detect obvious logic errors.
3. During compilation or assembly, the computer checks for syntactical errors and a "clean" compilation or assembly is not obtained until errors of this type have been removed. The program cannot be executed until it is syntactically correct. However, the compiler or assembler does not verify the logical correctness of a program.
4. The logic of the program is tested by running it against a set of test data—frequently referred to as a test deck.
5. Lastly, the program is run with actual data, which may involve running in parallel with the "old" method.

An important consideration is this: When a program error is uncovered at any of the above stages, except obviously the first, a change is made in the program and it must be recompiled or reassembled. Sometimes, the process of correcting one error creates others. When a program is modified, therefore, it must be retested to ensure it is correct. The practice of retesting a program after modification is frequently referred to as *regression testing*.

Documentation has two meanings. It refers to the process of describing a program or a data processing system and it refers to the description itself. There are three major forms of documentation: a system or program document, an operator's document, and a user's document. The *system* or *program document* includes introductory and descriptive material, decision tables, flowcharts, and a listing of the programs. For most student assignments, this level of documentation is sufficient. For nonacademic programs or systems, programs are frequently developed for use by several people. Therefore, the *operator's manual* tells the computer operator how to run the program and the *user's manual* tells a prospective user what the program does and how he can use it. In the latter case, a precise description of the required input data is mandatory.

Documentation is very important, especially in business and governmental organizations that make a substantial investment in computer programming. Personnel are transferred, promoted, or resign, and a new person frequently has to work with another person's programs. In cases such as these, adequate documentation is an absolute necessity.

Systems implementation or *production* refers to what happens to programs after they are written. Many programs are "one-shot" jobs. Student, scientific, or engineering programs frequently, but not always, fall into this category. The name *one-shot* implies that the program is written, tested, debugged, documented, and answers are obtained and that afterwards the program is very likely to remain unused. At the opposite extreme are programs, such as a company payroll program, that are used for many years—often going through change cycles to meet the needs of the times. Sets of programs that are useful to a wide range of users are called *applications packages* and are now sold as any other commodity. In the last few years, companies have emerged that deal exclusively in the development of applications packages.

Computer programs are frequently a component in a larger system, such as a billing system, an accounts receivable system, or an inventory control system. Programs used in this way sometimes replace similar procedures done manually and require a high level of testing and verification. Similarly, computer-based systems require verification to ensure that all conditions that can arise are accounted for in the systems design. Many of the difficulties that ordinary citizens have with computer-based systems, as with billing procedures with charge accounts and up-to-date record keeping, are the result of a poor systems design rather than an incorrect computer program. The systems analysis innocently neglected to take cognizance of a possible case that could occur.

3.5 SYSTEMS DESIGN AND DOCUMENTATION USING THE HIPO METHOD

As the preceding discussion implies, the processes of systems design and program development are not well defined; they are more of an "art" at this stage than a "science." It is within the realm of computer science to establish tools and techniques to facilitate the design and development of systems and programs.

The use of flow diagrams is only a partial solution to the problem because a flow diagram exhibits structure and implementation rather than function. Thus, the process of flow diagramming a system or a program utilizes "implementation-dependent thinking" and is directly analogous to the programming of that application. As a result, documentation of a system or program does not help the designer or the implementator and frequently lags behind the current state of the project. Stated in another manner, it is useful to know what a system or program does—that is, its function—prior to design and development. The use of decision tables lies at the opposite extreme, since a decision table is concerned with problem description and reflects neither the functions performed in a system or by a program, nor the inputs and the outputs. Another problem is that many systems and programs are designed and developed in a "bottom-to-top" sequence. Briefly, this means that an effort begins at the unit level, resulting in false starts and interface changes due to poor organization.

HIPO—Hierarchy plus Input, Process, Output

What is needed, therefore, is a structural framework for assisting the designer/developer in the design/implementation processes and that produces meaningful and useful documentation as a byproduct. A design aid and documentation tool that serves this need is HIPO, a diagram language for describing systems and programs.

HIPO is an acronym for *H*ierarchy plus *I*nput, *P*rocess, *O*utput. The

HIPO system is a technique for documenting the design of a program through the following states of development: design, implementation, testing, and maintenance. The description of a system or program using HIPO is referred to as a *HIPO package* and consists of the following components:

1. A visual table of contents
2. Overview diagrams
3. Detail diagrams with extended descriptions

The general form and relationship of these components is given in Figure 3.9. Compared with organization and logic that are described with other techniques, a HIPO package shows function and answers the question, "what does it do?"

The *visual table of contents* looks like an organization chart and gives the hierarchical structure of the functions that comprise a system or program. *Overview diagrams* provide the inputs, processes, and outputs for the major functions performed in an application. *Detail diagrams* with extended descriptions specify actual data processing functions and optionally indicate routines that perform associated operations.

The HIPO design aid and documentation tool is introduced through a familiar computer application: an inventory processing and billing operation. Each component of a HIPO package is introduced and the corresponding entries for the inventory problem are given.

Visual Table of Contents

The objective of the visual table of contents is to delineate functional structure at every level of detail. Each box in the *hierarchy diagram* corresponds to a HIPO diagram that describes the corresponding function. Thus, a person using a HIPO package has access to a functional description at varying degrees of detail by following the chain from the functional overview through one or more subfunctions. Collectively, the visual table of contents contains three parts:

1. A hierarchy diagram
2. A legend
3. A description section

The *legend* gives the symbols used in the HIPO package, and the *description section* provides additional information on each box in the hierarchy diagram. Figure 3.10 gives the visual table of contents for the inventory problem.

The hierarchy diagram of the visual table of contents should be read

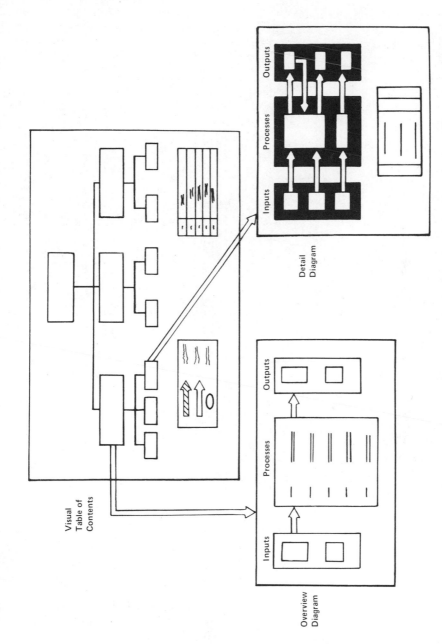

Visual
Table of
Contents

Outputs

Processes

Inputs

Detail
Diagram

Outputs

Processes

Inputs

Overview
Diagram

Figure 3.9   General form and relationship of the components of a HIPO package.

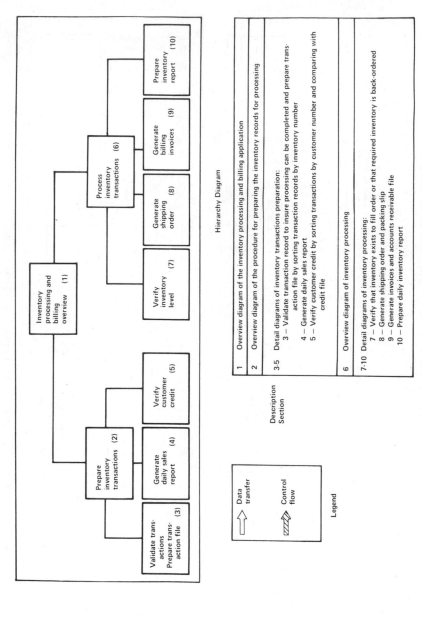

Figure 3.10 Visual table of contents for the inventory problem.

from left to right at any level of detail. If it is necessary to obtain additional information on a particular function, the user of the hierarchy diagram should then drop down successive levels until the desired level of detail is reached.

Overview Diagrams

The purpose of a HIPO diagram is to describe function at each level of detail. Each box in the hierarchy corresponds to a HIPO diagram, so that if a description of a particular function is needed, the reader need only reference the particular HIPO diagram that describes the function in which he is interested. However, the hierarchy diagram is also used to demonstrate how the various functions relate to one another.

HIPO diagrams are relatively easy to understand because the same structure and format are used. Inputs are listed on the left and outputs are listed on the right. The process block is in the center and it describes what functions are performed, but does not describe how they are performed.

The objective of an *overview diagram* is to provide an overall idea of the function to be performed. No indication is given of where the inputs are used and from which process the outputs are generated. The process block shows the major subfunctional units and the numbers of the diagrams that describe them in detail. It should be noted that the subfunctional units that are listed in the process block correspond to corresponding subfunctions in the hierarchy diagram of the visual table of contents.

Overview diagrams are shown in Figures 3.11, 3.12, and 3.13. The subfunctions in the process block of Figure 3.11, the overview diagram corresponding to the "highest" block in the hierarchy diagram, lists subfunctions that correspond to the overview diagrams of Figures 3.12 and 3.13. In neither of these diagrams is the specific manner shown in which the inputs are used. This is desirable because, at the general level, only an overview of the function is needed. If more detail is needed, then the next lower hierarchical level can be used.

Overview diagrams can exist at several levels, and there is no rule stating how many levels should exist in the hierarchy.

Detail Diagrams

The objectives of a detail diagram are threefold:

1. To describe where the inputs are used
2. To describe where the outputs are generated
3. To establish a relationship between the functional diagram and implementation structures, such as flow diagrams and module names

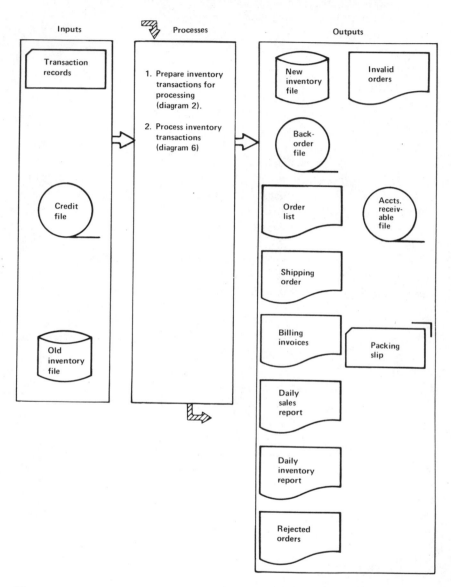

Figure 3.11 Overview diagram (highest level) for the inventory problem. (Diagram 1)

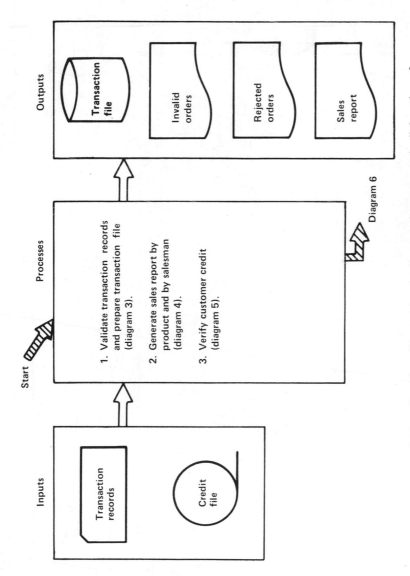

Figure 3.12 Overview diagram for the "transaction preparation" function of the inventory problem. (Diagram 2)

67

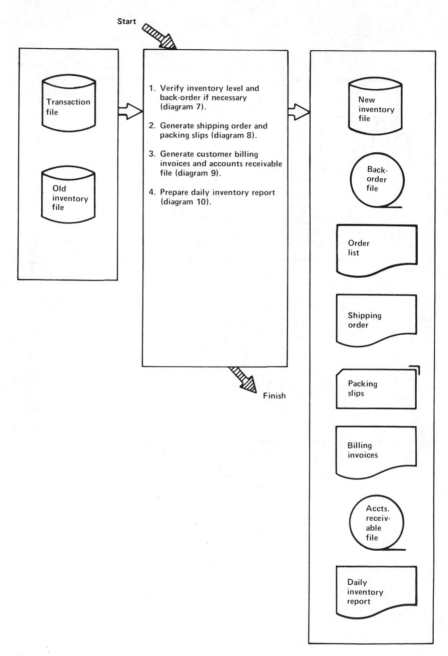

Figure 3.13 Overview diagram for the "inventory processing" function of the inventory problem. (Diagram 6)

A *detail diagram* consists of two components:

1. An input, process, and output diagram
2. An extended description that further describes the subfunctions described in the process block

An example of a detail diagram is given in Figure 3.14. Here, the specific inputs are associated with processes, and processes are associated with outputs. Specific details, such as field names or flow diagrams, can be identified in the extended description.

HIPO diagrams go "from the general to the specific," so that as much detail as is necessary can be added. Ordinarily, details that are machine- or implementation-dependent are recorded in separate tables, lists, or charts that are identified in the extended description. However, because a HIPO package shows function and not implementation, its validity is not dependent upon variables that can change with time.

A Final Remark

The preceding examples have reflected a data processing environment for the use of the HIPO concept. The techniques are applicable to any process, ranging from industrial data acquisition and control to sophisticated systems programming. Clearly, an input or output can be a field in a control block or a signal from a digital-to-analog converter in the same manner that files and records are used in the examples.

Lastly, a system need not utilize the computer to lend itself to a HIPO package; any process-oriented system can be described in terms of the functions that it performs.

3.6 GROUP PROGRAMMING METHODS

The classical stereotype of the programmer is a rather introverted individual who seemingly sustains a weird lifestyle and enjoys working at a level of detail deemed intolerable by most human beings. In the days when programmers were at a premium, they were frequently referred to as "prima donnas," regardless of the circumstances. If the above description *were* ever true, it is definitely not true today. Programmers and analysts work on teams in relative harmony to produce large and complicated systems. There exist several ways of organizing a programming project and Figure 3.15 gives two of them.* In spite of

---

* Weinberg, G. M., *The Psychology of Computer Programming*, Van Nostrand-Reinhold, New York, 1971, pp. 67–94.

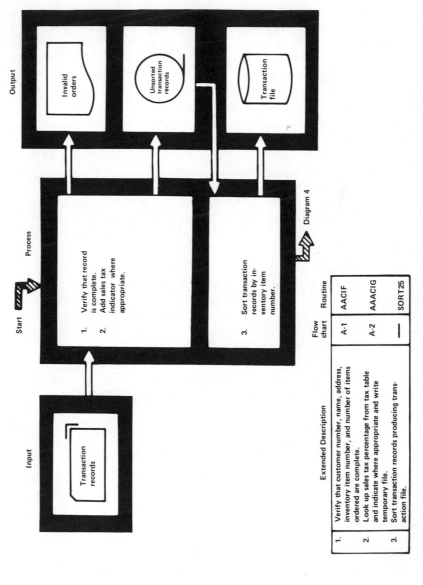

Figure 3.14 Detail diagram of the function that "validates transaction records and prepares transaction files" for the inventory problem. (Diagram 3)

70

advances that have been made in project organization, one significant statistic prevails: "Including all overhead, five to ten debugged instructions are coded per man-day on a large production programming project."* The implication is that programmers spend their remaining time on debugging and reworking. Several operational techniques have been applied to the problem, including having team members inspect each other's code and having dynamic walkthroughs, where a group of team members actually works through computer programs. In short, it is generally felt that thinking errors, rather than coding errors, are the cause of poor programming productivity.

Two concepts are involved: top-down programming and the chief programmer team concept. Both topics are introduced briefly.

Top-Down Programming

Programming has evolved as a bottom-to-top process, wherein the lowest level processing programs are coded and tested in preparation for integration into the total system. Bottom-to-top development is suggested in Figure 3.16. The difficulties in the process are that module interfaces must be established simultaneously and by more than one person, and that driver programs must be written to test modules as they are written. Also, the integration of the total system is "error prone" because of the large number of interfaces and modules involved.

Top-down programming is said to alleviate these problems because systems are developed in a natural order, that is, from the control structures downward. Top-down development is suggested in Figure 3.17. The development process starts at the highest hierarchical level and proceeds downward in a natural order until the system is complete. The concept of a "stub" is employed to test interfaces. In most cases, a stub module simply displays a message indicating that control flow reaches a certain point and then returns to the calling program. One of the advantages of top-down development is that the system is always operable, so that a backlog of errors does not appear toward the end of the system-development life cycle.

Chief Programmer Team Concept

Closely related to top-down programming is a method of group programming known as the "chief programmer team" concept. A *chief programmer team* is a small group of personnel organized to work

---

*Baker, F. T., and H. D. Mills, "Chief programmer teams," *Datamation* **19**, No. 12 (Dec. 1973), p. 58.

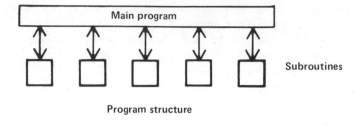

Program structure

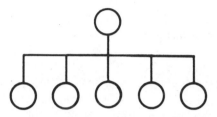

Project organization

(A) Programming project organization with one experienced programmer and five less experienced programmers.

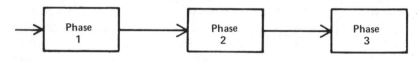

Program structure

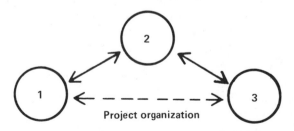

Project organization

(B) Programming project organization with three programmers with the same experience.

Figure 3.15   Two methods of organizing a programming project.

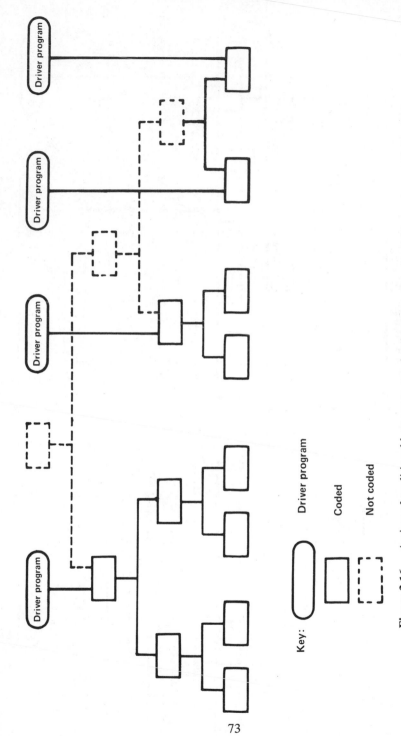

Figure 3.16 A view of traditional bottom-to-top development, showing "driver programs" for testing.

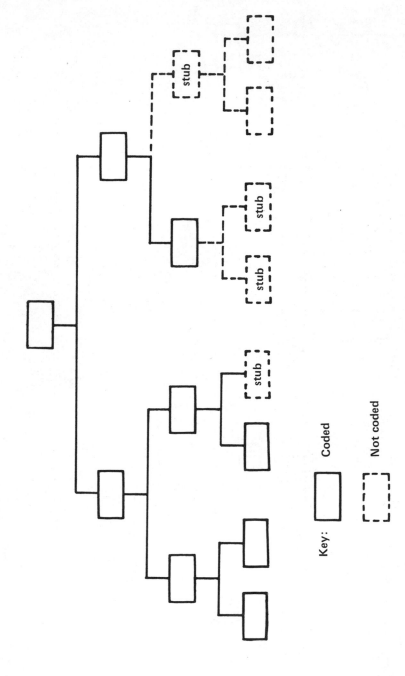

Figure 3.17 A view of top-down development, showing "stub modules" for testing.

Key: ▢ Coded   ⌐ ⌐ Not coded

effectively as a programming unit.* The team consists of the following:

1. A chief programmer
2. A backup programmer
3. A program librarian
4. Three to five production programmers, depending upon the project

The *chief programmer* is a senior position with overall project responsibility. The chief programmer, even though he performs technical management functions, participates in the development process and codes critical segments. Through top-down development, the chief programmer can maintain project responsibility. The *backup programmer* serves as research assistant and system designer, and participates in the coding effort. He is involved in every aspect of the project and can assume project responsibility at any time. The *program librarian's* prime function is to maintain programs, test data, and a development library. *Production programmers* exist at varying levels of experience and report to the chief programmer. Collectively, the chief programmer team can be viewed as a "super programmer" operating as a single agent in a project.

HIPOs, Top-Down Programming, and Chief Programmer Teams

HIPOs, top-down programming, and the chief programmer team constitute more than a managerial approach to development. They exist as a development methodology that can be applied to any programming project. One aspect of development remains: the techniques for actually producing code. A programming technique known as "structured programming" is used, which reduces program structure to a few meaningful concepts and further enhances the development process. Structured programming is introduced in Part IV.

QUESTION SET

1. Using the computer instructions given in Table 3.1, write computer programs to do the following:
    (a) Read three numbers a, b, and c. Find the largest value, that is,

$$r = \text{maximum } (a, b, c)$$

    Print the result r.

* "Chief programmer teams: principles and procedures" (Form number FSC71–5108), IBM, Federal Systems Division, Gaithersburg, Md., June 1971, p. 1.

(b) Read two numbers a and b. Divide a by b, that is,

$$r = a/b$$

Print the result r.
(Easy? Not quite. Check for division by zero since the computer, like a desk calculator, does not permit it.)
(c) Read two numbers a and n. Compute a to the nth power, that is,

$$r = a^n$$

Print the result. (Note: $a^0 = 1$)
(d) Read two numbers *hours* and *rate*. Compute *totalpay* as follows:

If *hours* is less than or equal to 40, then compute the total pay as

$$totalpay = hours \times rate$$

However, if *hours* is greater than 40, then also pay overtime as follows:

$$totalpay = (40 \times rate) + (hours - 40) \times (rate \times 1.5)$$

(That is, time and one-half for overtime.)

Print *totalpay*.
Loop back to read two more values. If *hours* is equal to zero, stop the program.
(e) Modify the preceding program to include an employee number as identification. The calculations are the same. For output, print employee number, hours, rate, and total pay.
2. Have you had enough programming? Well, you can take pleasure in knowing that you have just been through the most difficult part of computer programming. Here's the question: If you could do anything in the whole world to make programming easier, what would it be? Obviously, there is no right or wrong answer to this question, so let your imagination wander.
3. Complete the HIPO package for the inventory problem given in the chapter. Make any necessary assumptions but utilize the given inputs and outputs.
4. Construct a complete flow diagram of the inventory problem given in the chapter and in question 3. What aspects of the problem lend

themselves to HIPOs and what aspects lend themselves to flow diagrams? Where could decision tables be used?

5. Give the similarities and differences between HIPO diagrams, top-down development, and the chief programmer team concept.

SELECTED READINGS

Baker, F. T., "Chief programmer team management of production programming," *IBM Systems Journal* **11**, No. 1 (1972), 56–73.

Baker, F. T., and H. D. Mills, "Chief programmer teams," *Datamation* **19**, No. 12 (Dec. 1973), 58–61.

Cole, R. W., *Introduction to Computing*, McGraw-Hill, New York, 1969.

Katzan, H., *Introduction to Programming Languages,* Petrocelli/Charter, New York, 1973.

Maurer, W. D., *Programming: An Introduction to Computer Techniques*, Holden-Day, San Francisco, 1972.

Weinberg, G. M., *The Psychology of Computer Programming*, Van Nostrand-Reinhold, New York, 1971.

Wilde, D. U., *An Introduction to Computing*, Prentice-Hall, Englewood Cliffs, N.J., 1973.

HIPO: Design Aid and Documentation Tool, (Form No. SR20–9413 Audio education package), IBM, White Plains, N.Y., 1973.

4

NUMBER SYSTEMS

4.1 INTRODUCTION

Computers are designed to process data in two principal forms: numeric and nonnumeric (or descriptive). A numeric data item is 123; a nonnumeric data item is "TEA FOR TWO." Even though the two data items are usually stored in the computer in a similar manner, the difference between the two is substantial. The number 123 means more than the characters "1," "2," and "3" written next to each other. The form of the number 123 implies the Arabic number system, so that 123 is interpreted as:

$$1 \times 10^2 + 2 \times 10^1 + 3 \times 10^0$$

where 10^2 means 10×10, 10^3 means $10 \times 10 \times 10$, 10^n means $\underbrace{10 \times 10 \times \ldots \times 10}_{n \text{ tens}}$, and $10^0 = 1$.) The Arabic system is frequently referred to as the positional number system; we all know it but usually take it for granted in everyday arithmetic. A nonnumeric data item means just what is written; thus, "TEA FOR TWO" means just that and no more.

Related to the subject of data are the ways that it is used, the manner in which it is organized, and the manner in which it is stored and referenced. This necessarily requires that variables, operators, expressions, and arrays be covered. The key point is that a basic knowledge of number systems, conversion, and data representation is needed in computer science. Once these concepts are known, however, they are usually subordinated to a more intensive study of systems, languages, and theoretical topics.

4.2 BASIC CONCEPTS

When discussing number systems, two items are of importance: the radix and the radix point. The *radix* is the base to which a number is taken. Normally, we deal with base-10 numbers in everyday affairs. Most computers use base-2 numbers. Most people say that we use base-10 because we have ten fingers and toes; base-2 is frequently used in computers because two states, on and off, are easily implemented. This is discussed later. The *radix point* (for example, the decimal point) tells where the integer portion of a number ends and where the fraction starts. More specifically, the radix point implicitly gives the magnitude of each numeral in the number. For example, the number 215 means

$$2 \times 10^2 + 1 \times 10^1 + 5 \times 10^0$$

while the number 21.5 means

$$2 \times 10^1 + 1 \times 10^0 + 5 \times 10^{-1}$$

Normally, the decimal number system is used by people for calculations when dealing with calculators and manual processes. The three number systems that are widely used in computer systems are binary, octal, and hexadecimal. The *binary system* is a base-2 system; the *octal system* is a base-8 system; and the *hexadecimal system* is a base-16 system.

Every number system has a set of symbols that represents the numerals of that number system. The decimal system has the ten symbols: 0, 1, 2, 3, 4, 5, 6, 7, 8, and 9. Accordingly, a base-*n* system uses *n* symbols. The rules of arithmetic are the same for all number systems, but different arithmetic tables are used. For example, the following *addition table* is used for the decimal system:

+	0	1	2	3	4	5	6	7	8	9
0	0	1	2	3	4	5	6	7	8	9
1	1	2	3	4	5	6	7	8	9	0*
2	2	3	4	5	6	7	8	9	0*	1*
3	3	4	5	6	7	8	9	0*	1*	2*
4	4	5	6	7	8	9	0*	1*	2*	3*
5	5	6	7	8	9	0*	1*	2*	3*	4*
6	6	7	8	9	0*	1*	2*	3*	4*	5*
7	7	8	9	0*	1*	2*	3*	4*	5*	6*
8	8	9	0*	1*	2*	3*	4*	5*	6*	7*
9	9	0*	1*	2*	3*	4*	5*	6*	7*	8*

where the asterisk denotes a carry of 1 into the next place.

4.3 THE BINARY SYSTEM

The binary number system is a base-2 system that uses the symbols 0 and 1. The binary number 101, for example, is evaluated in decimal as:

$$
\begin{aligned}
(101)_2 &= 1 \times 2^2 + 0 \times 2^1 + 1 \times 2^0 \\
&= 1 \times 4 + 0 \times 2 + 1 \times 1 \\
&= 4 + 0 + 1 \\
&= (5)_{10}
\end{aligned}
$$

(Remember, we are doing our own calculating to the base 10.) In the preceding example, the subscript denotes the base; for example, $(101)_2$ means the number 101 to the base 2, and $(5)_{10}$ means the number 5 to the base 10. When dealing with different number systems, it is important to state the base, since a number can be meaningful to more than one base.

The use of a binary point is demonstrated in the following decinal expansion for the binary number 1011.1:

$$
\begin{aligned}
(1011.1)_2 &= 1 \times 2^3 + 0 \times 2^2 + 1 \times 2^1 + 1 \times 2^0 + 1 \times 2^{-1} \\
&= 1 \times 8 + 0 \times 4 + 1 \times 2 + 1 \times 1 + 1 \times \tfrac{1}{2} \\
&= 8 + 0 + 2 + 1 + \tfrac{1}{2} \\
&= (11\tfrac{1}{2})_{10} = (11.5)_{10}
\end{aligned}
$$

Recall that a negative exponent means, "take the reciprocal." Thus 10^{-1} means $1/10^1$, 2^{-4} means $1/2^4$, and m^{-n} means $1/m^n$.

The addition table for binary addition is

+	0	1
0	0	1
1	1	0*

where the asterisk denotes a carry of 1 into the next place. Thus, for example,

```
    101                    1011
  + 10                   + 101
  ------        (Carry)   1 1 1
    111         (Sum)    10000
```

4.4 THE OCTAL SYSTEM

The octal number system is a base-8 system that uses the symbols 0, 1, 2, 3, 4, 5, 6, and 7. The octal number 375, for example, is evaluated in decimal as follows:

$$(375)_8 = 3 \times 8^2 + 7 \times 8^1 + 5 \times 8^0$$
$$= 3 \times 64 + 7 \times 8 + 5 \times 1$$
$$= 192 + 56 + 5$$
$$= (253)_{10}$$

The octal system uses an *octal point*, as in the following example:

$$(24.5)_8 = 2 \times 8^1 + 4 \times 8^0 + 5 \times 8^{-1}$$
$$= 2 \times 8 + 4 \times 1 + 5 \times \tfrac{1}{8}$$
$$= 16 + 4 + \tfrac{5}{8}$$
$$= (20\tfrac{5}{8})_{10} = (20.625)_{10}$$

The addition table for octal addition is

+	0	1	2	3	4	5	6	7
0	0	1	2	3	4	5	6	7
1	1	2	3	4	5	6	7	0*
2	2	3	4	5	6	7	0*	1*
3	3	4	5	6	7	0*	1*	2*
4	4	5	6	7	0*	1*	2*	3*
5	5	6	7	0*	1*	2*	3*	4*
6	6	7	0*	1*	2*	3*	4*	5*
7	7	0*	1*	2*	3*	4*	5*	6*

where the asterisk denotes a carry of 1 into the next position. Thus, for example,

```
        425                 136
      +  31               +  45
      ─────    (Carry)      1 1
        456    (Sum)        203
```

The identity $2^3 = 8$ gives us a clue to a useful relationship between binary and octal numbers. The identity implies that an octal numeral can be represented "exactly" by three binary digits (or bits, as they are called), as demonstrated in the following table:

Decimal	Octal	Binary	Decimal	Octal	Binary
0	0	000	5	5	101
1	1	001	6	6	110
2	2	010	7	7	111
3	3	011	8	10	1000
4	4	100	9	11	1001

As a result, a long sequence of binary digits can be written more conveniently as octal digits by replacing each sequence of three binary digits by an equivalent octal digit from the preceding table. Thus, a series of bits such as

$\boxed{101001011010111001}$

is expressed simply as 513271 in octal. The forms are equivalent, as suggested in the following additions:

Binary	Octal	Decimal
010011	23	19
+011101	+35	+29
110000	60	48

4.5   THE HEXADECIMAL SYSTEM

The hexadecimal number system is a base-16 system that uses the symbols 0, 1, 2, 3, 4, 5, 6, 7, 8, 9, A, B, C, D, E, and F. The various symbols have the following decimal equivalents:

Hexadecimal Symbol	Decimal Equivalent
0	0
1	1
2	2
3	3
4	4
5	5
6	6
7	7
8	8
9	9
A	10
B	11
C	12
D	13
E	14
F	15

The hexadecimal number 2B7, for example, is evaluated in decimal as

$$(2B7)_{16} = 2 \times 16^2 + B \times 16^1 + 7 \times 16^0$$
$$= 2 \times 256 + 11 \times 16 + 7 \times 1$$
$$= 512 + 176 + 7$$
$$= (695)_{10}$$

Use of a hexadecimal radix point is seen in the following example:

$$(1A.C)_{16} = 1 \times 16^1 + A \times 16^0 + C \times 16^{-1}$$
$$= 1 \times 16 + 10 \times 1 + 12 \times {}^1\!/_{16}$$
$$= 16 + 10 + \tfrac{3}{4}$$
$$= (26.75)_{10}$$

The development of an addition table for hexadecimal addition is left as an exercise for the student. Examples of hexadecimal addition are

```
     6A2              A6C
  +   4B               47
  ---------       ---------
             (Carry)    1
     6ED    (Sum)    AB3
```

A useful relationship also exists between binary and hexadecimal numbers, since $2^4 = 16$. A hexadecimal numeral can be represented "exactly" by four binary digits, or bits, as demonstrated in the following table:

Decimal	Hexadecimal	Binary
0	0	0000
1	1	0001
2	2	0010
3	3	0011
4	4	0100
5	5	0101
6	6	0110
7	7	0111
8	8	1000
9	9	1001
10	A	1010
11	B	1011
12	C	1100
13	D	1101
14	E	1110
15	F	1111

As a result, a long sequence of binary digits can be written more conveniently as hexadecimal digits by replacing each sequence of four binary digits by an equivalent hexadecimal digit from the preceding table. Thus, a series of bits such as

$$\boxed{1000101100010110111000101 1001101}$$

is expressed more simply as 8B16E2CD in hexadecimal. The forms are equivalent, as suggested in the following additions:

Binary	Hexadecimal	Decimal
00100011	23	35
+01001101	+4D	+ 77
01110000	70	112

4.6 CONVERSION BETWEEN DIFFERENT NUMBER SYSTEMS

The method given previously for converting numbers from binary, octal, and hexadecimal to decimal is known as "literal expansion." In general, *literal expansion* of a base-r number consists of the evaluation of the following mathematical identity:

$$\begin{aligned}(A_{n-1}A_{n-2}\cdots A_1 A_0.A_{-1}A_{-2}\cdots A_{-m})_r \\ = A_{n-1}r^{n-1} + A_{n-2}r^{n-2} + \cdots + A_1 r^1 + A_0 r^0 + A_{-1}r^{-1} \\ + A_{-2}r^{-2} + \cdots + A_{-m}r^{-m}\end{aligned}$$

in the number system *into* which the conversion is being made. The method works well for conversions *into* decimal, since we are familiar with decimal calculations. However, the following conversion from decimal to hexadecimal:

$$\begin{aligned}(286)_{10} &= 2\times A^2 + 8\times A^1 + 6\times A^0 \\ &= 2\times 64 + 8\times A + 6 \\ &= C8 + 50 + 6 \\ &= (11E)_{16}\end{aligned}$$

where the calculations are performed using hexadecimal arithmetic, shows the inconvenience and confusion that can result from performing calculations in a base other than decimal.

Conversion to Decimal. As stated immediately above, literal evaluation is the most straightforward method, as demonstrated in the following examples:

Binary-to-decimal
$$(11101010.1)_2 = 1 \times 2^7 + 1 \times 2^6 + 1 \times 2^5 + 0 \times 2^4 + 1 \times 2^3 + 0 \times 2^2$$
$$+ 1 \times 2^1 + 0 \times 2^0 + 1 \times 2^{-1}$$
$$= 128 + 64 + 32 + 8 + 2 + 0.5$$
$$= (234.5)_{10}$$

Octal-to-decimal
$$(352.4)_8 = 3 \times 8^2 + 5 \times 8^1 + 2 \times 8^0 + 4 \times 8^{-1}$$
$$= 192 + 40 + 2 + 0.5$$
$$= (234.5)_{10}$$

Hexadecimal-to-decimal
$$(EA.8)_{16} = E \times 16^1 + A \times 16^0 + 8 \times 16^{-1}$$
$$= 14 \times 16 + 10 \times 1 + 8 \times \tfrac{1}{16}$$
$$= 224 + 10 + 0.5$$
$$= (234.5)_{10}$$

Obviously, the integer and fractional parts can be converted separately, and a "short-cut" method is known for evaluating the integer part. Consider the decimal expansion of $(352)_8$ expressed as follows:

$$3 \times 8^2 + 5 \times 8^1 + 2 \times 8^0$$

This expression can be rewritten as follows:

$$(8(8 \times 3 + 5)) + 2$$

and is referred to as "nested multiplication." This process is summarized as follows:

> Multiply the leftmost digit by the radix n and add it to the next digit, progressing to the right. Multiply this sum by the radix n and add it to the next digit. Repeat this process until the rightmost digit has been added. The resulting sum is the decimal equivalent of the given base-n number.

For example, $(1101010)_2$ is evaluated as

$$(2(2(2(2(2(2 \times 1) + 1) + 0) + 1) + 0) + 1) + 0 = 234$$

Conversion from Decimal. Conversion from decimal to any base is most frequently performed by treating the integer and fractional parts separately. As an example, the decimal integer 7361 is converted to octal by successively dividing the number by 8 until a quotient of 0 is obtained. The successive remainders form the equivalent octal number beginning with the rightmost digit:

$$
\left.
\begin{array}{rl}
0 & \text{r.1} \\
8)\overline{1} & \text{r.6} \\
8)\overline{14} & \text{r.3} \\
8)\overline{115} & \text{r.0} \\
8)\overline{920} & \text{r.1} \\
8)\overline{7361} &
\end{array}
\right\} \quad 16301
$$

Remainders

Thus, $(7361)_{10} = (16301)_8$. The process is summarized as follows:

Repeatedly divide the decimal integer by the radix n of the target base, saving the remainders until a quotient of 0 is obtained. The equivalent base-n number is formed from the remainders, where the first remainder is the rightmost digit and the last remainder is the leftmost digit.

The following examples depict the process for binary and hexadecimal integer conversions:

$$
\left.
\begin{array}{rl}
0 & \text{r.1} \\
2)\overline{1} & \text{r.0} \\
2)\overline{2} & \text{r.0} \\
2)\overline{4} & \text{r.1} \\
2)\overline{9} & \text{r.0} \\
2)\overline{18} & \text{r.1} \\
2)\overline{37} &
\end{array}
\right\} \quad 100101
\qquad
\left.
\begin{array}{rl}
0 & \text{r.2} \\
16)\overline{2} & \text{r.0} \\
16)\overline{32} & \text{r.4} \\
16)\overline{516} & \text{r.13} \\
16)\overline{8269} &
\end{array}
\right\} \quad 204D
$$

$$(37)_{10} = (100101)_2 \qquad\qquad (8269)_{10} = (204D)_{16}$$

The conversion of a fraction from decimal to another number system is essentially the inverse of integer conversion. Whereas an integer is converted by a process of successive divisions, the fraction is converted by a process of successive multiplications. As an example, the decimal fraction 0.8125 is converted to a binary fraction by successively multiplying the fraction by 2; the integer parts of the products are the successive digits of the binary fraction starting with the most significant digit. After the first multiplication, the integer part is ignored in the next multiplication; the process continues until the fraction has been reduced to zero or the required number of binary places is generated. For example,

Decimal Fraction	Product		Integer Part	
0.8125	×2 =	1.625	1	(most significant digit)
0.625	×2 =	1.250	1	
0.250	×2 =	0.5	0	
0.5	×2 =	1.0	1	(least significant digit)

Thus, $(0.8125)_{10} = (0.1101)_2$. The process is summarized as follows:

Repeatedly multiply the decimal fraction by the radix n of the target base, saving the integer parts of the products as the digits of the target fraction. The multiplication is repeated using only the fractional result of the previous multiplication. The first integer obtained is the most significant digit (i.e., leftmost) of the fraction, and so forth. The process is continued until a zero fraction or the desired accuracy is generated.

The following examples depict the process for octal and hexadecimal fraction conversions:

Decimal Fraction	Product		Integer Part	
0.8125	×8 =	6.5	6	(most significant digit)
0.5	×8 =	4.0	4	(least significant digit)

$(0.8125)_{10} = (0.64)_8$

Decimal Fraction	Product	Integer Part	Hexadecimal Digit
0.8125 × 16 =	13.0	13	D

$(0.8125)_{10} = (0.D)_{16}$

Decimal Fraction	Product	Integer Part	Hexadecimal Digit	
0.78125 × 16 =	12.5	12	C	(most significant digit)
0.5 × 16 =	8.0	8	8	(least significant digit)

$(0.78125)_{10} = (0.C8)_{16}$

Number conversions are usually lengthy and tedious when dealing with actual computer numbers and self-explanatory tables are frequently used to lessen the chore. In general, however, a basic understanding of the process is all that is normally needed in computer science.

4.7 COMPLEMENTS AND SUBTRACTION

One of the topics that is conspicuous by its absence thus far is subtraction. As the inverse operation to addition, the concept of subtraction is well understood. Binary subtraction is presented as an example. Binary addition takes the form:

$$0 + 0 = 0$$
$$0 + 1 = 1$$
$$1 + 0 = 1$$
$$1 + 1 = 10$$

so that its inverse operation, subtraction, takes the form:

$$0 - 0 = 0$$
$$1 - 0 = 1$$
$$1 - 1 = 0$$
$$10 - 1 = 1$$

The case $0 - 1$ is handled by borrowing from the next position, similar to the manner in which borrowing is done in decimal subtraction. The following example of binary subtraction requires no borrowing:

Binary Form		Decimal Equivalent
	Borrowing	₁₁₁
10101		2̸1̸
− 100		− 4
10001		17

The following example does depict borrowing:

	Binary Form		Decimal Equivalent
	0 10 0 10	Borrowing	
	1̸0̸1̸0̸1		21
	− 1010		− 10
	1011		11

Similar conventions exist for octal and hexadecimal subtraction.

Another method for representing negative numbers and for performing subtraction is to use complement arithmetic. Consider, for example, the expression

$$684 - 435 = 249$$

The subtraction operation can also be expressed by using the ten's complement of the subtrahend, as follows:

$$684 + (1000 - 435) - 1000 = 249$$

The term $(1000 - 435)$ is referred to as the *ten's complement* of 435, which evaluates to

$$
\begin{array}{r}
1000 \\
- \ 435 \\
\hline
565
\end{array}
$$

The ten's complement of a number can be developed by inspection. (Each digit is subtracted from 9 and a 1 is added to the low-order digit.) The difference is then computed by adding the complement of the subtrahend to the minuend:*

$$
\begin{array}{r}
684 \\
565 \\
\hline
1249
\end{array}
$$

Lastly, the 1000 is subtracted by dropping the high-order 1. Later, we will see that when fixed-length arithmetic registers are used, the high-order digit is dropped automatically.

The *complement* of a number N (or more specifically, a *radix complement*) is defined as follows:

$$\text{Complement of } N = b^n - N$$

where b is the radix (or base) and n is the number of digits in N. Actually, $b^n - 1$ is the largest number that can be defined with n digits, so that b^n is one more than the largest possible number. Thus, the ten's

---

* The terminology is: MINUEND − SUBTRAHEND = DIFFERENCE.

complement of 435 is 565 and the two's complement of 1010 is 0110.

In the computer, numbers are stored in "fixed-length" storage locations or are held in fixed-length arithmetic registers during arithmetic calculations. Although computers vary, the leftmost digit of a "computer" number is used to represent the arithmetic sign. Thus, the following 16-digit binary word:

$$\boxed{0000000000000101}$$

represents the value $+5$ in decimal, where the high-order 0 (i.e., the leftmost digit) represents the plus sign; similarly, a 1 bit is used to represent a minus sign. Negative numbers are generally represented in two ways. In the first method, the value is stored in true form with a negative-sign bit, as in the following binary representation of -5:

$$\boxed{1000000000000101}$$

The second method involves storing a number in complement form, so that the binary representation of -5 is

$$\boxed{1111111111111011}$$

The second method has several distinct advantages. First, it is relatively simple to find the two's complement of a binary number. It is performed as follows: Convert all 0's to 1's, all 1's to 0's, and add 1 to the result.* Thus, for example,

Binary number	0000101100101011
Bits inverted	1111010011010100
Add 1	$+1$
Two's complement	1111010011010101

The two's complement is easily implemented in computer circuitry. The second advantage is that arithmetic operations can be executed in a straightforward manner without regard to the sign of the operands. For addition, numbers are simply added as follows:

---

* The process of converting all 1's to 0's and all 0's to 1's is referred to as the *one's complement*.

	Binary	*Decimal*	
	0000000000000101	(5)	
+	0000000000001101	+ (13)	
	0000000000010010	18	(result)
	1111111111111011	(−5)	
+	0000000000001101	+(13)	
1	0000000000001000	8	(result)

↑
└— discarded

	Binary	*Decimal*	
	0000000000000101	(5)	
+	1111111111110011	+(−13)	
	1111111111111000	−8	(result)
	1111111111111011	(−5)	
+	1111111111110011	+(−13)	
	1111111111101110	−18	(result)

The simplicity of the above technique should be compared with the conventional method, listed as follows:

1. If the numbers to be added have like signs, add the magnitude of the numbers and give the sum the common sign.
2. If the numbers to be added have unlike signs, compute the difference of the numbers and give it the sign of the number with the largest magnitude.

Complement arithmetic has similar advantages for subtraction; it is performed by taking the two's complement of the subtrahend and adding it to the minuend, as demonstrated in the following examples:

Binary	*Decimal*
`0000000000001101`	13
− `0000000000000101`	− 5

becomes

	`0000000000001101`	(13)
+	`1111111111111011`	+ (− 5)
	`0000000000001000`	8 (result)
	`0000000000000101`	(5)
−	`1111111111111011`	− (13)

becomes

	`0000000000000101`	(5)
+	`1111111111110011`	+ (− 13)
	`1111111111111000`	− 8 (result)
	`0000000000000101`	(5)
−	`1111111111110011`	− (− 13)

becomes

	`0000000000000101`	(5)
+	`0000000000001101`	+ (13)
	`0000000000010010`	18 (result)
	`1111111111111011`	(− 5)
−	`1111111111110011`	− (− 13)

becomes

$$\boxed{111111111111011} \qquad (-5)$$
$$+ \ \boxed{0000000000001101} \qquad +(13)$$

$$\boxed{0000000000001000} \qquad 8 \quad \text{(result)}$$

The above technique is very similar to the conventional manual method of inverting the subtrahend and adding it to the minuend.

The primary advantage of complement arithmetic for a computer lies in the simplicity of the arithmetic unit—it uses the adder for both addition and subtraction. When complement arithmetic is used in a computer in the above fashion, negative numbers are normally stored in two's complement form.

QUESTION SET

1. Develop a multiplication table for hexadecimal multiplication.
2. Convert the following decimal integers to binary, octal, and hexa-decimal:

396	64
16	32,768
100	0

3. Convert the following binary integers to decimal:

101
1011
1100110101101

4. Convert the following octal integers to decimal:

10
64
777
6432

5. Convert the following hexadecimal integers to decimal:

E3
3FF
ABC
9D31

6. Show that $10 \times 10 = 100$ in any number system.
7. Convert the following decimal fractions to binary, octal, and hexadecimal:

   0.75
   0.934125
   0.628125

8. Convert the following binary fractions to decimal:

   0.101
   0.0001101
   0.1101

9. Convert the following octal fractions to decimal:

   0.101
   0.6371
   0.0574

10. Convert the following hexadecimal fractions to decimal:

    0.101
    0.FF2B
    0.ABC
    0.828125

11. Convert the following decimal numbers to binary, octal, and hexadecimal:

    15.345   10.1101
    697.21   77.777

12. Convert the following numbers to decimal:

    $(10.1101)_2$ $(16.572)_8$ $(3F.DC)_{16}$
    $(11101.1011)_2$ $(641.2335)_8$ $(A39.7304)_{16}$
    $(11.11)_2$ $(77.77)_8$ $(FF.FF)_{16}$

13. Find the ten's complement of the following:

     634   18   137   999   5

14. Find the two's complement of the following:

     11011   1   1001   11111110   1011

15. Show that the two's complement of the two's complement of N equals N.

16. Using 16-bit words, perform the following calculations and show all work:

$$
\begin{array}{cccc}
(137) & (634) & (-57) & (-163) \\
+\ (94) & -(791) & -(119) & +\quad(85)
\end{array}
$$

(Remember, the operands must be converted to binary words before the arithmetic operation is performed.)

SELECTED READINGS

Awad, E. M., *Business Data Processing*, chap. 8, Prentice-Hall, Englewood Cliffs, N.J., 1971.

5

BASIC DATA AND COMPUTATION STRUCTURES

5.1 ARITHMETIC DATA

The preceding chapter gives the meaning of numeric data along with some idea of how it is stored in the computer. This chapter relates these concepts to the data we ordinarily use to solve problems.

Fixed-Point Data

In everyday arithmetic, calculations are performed on numbers represented as sequences of decimal digits, possibly a decimal point, and possibly an algebraic sign. A number of this type is called a *fixed-point* number. More specifically, a fixed-point number x is represented by an expression of the form:

$$x = n + 0.d_1d_2d_3 \ldots$$

where n is a signed or unsigned whole number and the d_i's are digits in the range 0 to 9. The following constants are fixed-point numbers:

17	0.00936	-1.234
-134	57.148	0

The exact manner in which a fixed-point constant is entered into the computer depends upon the computer language used. In general, however, unneeded constituents are not written.

When a fixed-point number is stored in the computer, the radix point is not present and its position is implicitly understood by the programmer. (Although most computers store data in binary form, decimal is used here to simplify the description.) Thus, the number 1.5, for example, could be stored in several positions in a computer word, including the following:

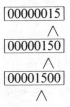

When this datum is used, the computer must be programmed to keep track of the decimal point, indicated by a caret here. This topic is discussed in Section 5.2, "Arithmetic Operations."

Integer Data

A fixed-point number without a fraction is an *integer*. Integer arithmetic has some characteristic properties. When integers are added, subtracted, multiplied, or divided, the result is an integer. Thus, if division of a by b is defined by

$$a = q{\cdot}b + r \qquad \text{where } r < b$$

then the result is the quotient q and the remainder r is lost. Thus, when integer arithmetic is used, 5 divided by 2 (that is, 5/2) gives the result 2 and (3/2)*4 gives a result of 4. (The asterisk in the preceding expression denotes multiplication.)

As with fixed-point data, the implied radix point of an integer datum can be anywhere in a computer word. Usually, it is placed to the right of the low-order digit (that is, the rightmost digit). The integer 25, for example, would normally be stored as

$\boxed{00000025}$
$\wedge$

Integer operations are covered with fixed-point operations in the next section.

Floating-Point Data

When the magnitude and precision of data vary in mathematically oriented calculations, engineers and scientists frequently use a form for representing numbers that is referred to as *floating-point* (or scientific)

notation. A floating-point number is a fraction multiplied by a power of ten, as shown in the following representation of 3000000:

$$0.3 \times 10^7$$

The use of floating-point notation eliminates the problem of keeping track of the radix point and the need for carrying unneeded digits. Normally, the most significant digits of a number plus a two- or three-digit exponent are maintained, as demonstrated in the following floating-point representation of -0.00000825336:

$$-0.825336 \times 10^{-5}$$

Representation of a floating-point number in the computer requires a special format because the fraction and exponent fields of the number must be recognized. In addition, the problem of two signs—one for the number and one for the exponent—must be handled. Normally, only one sign is associated with a word in computer storage. In most modern computers, the problem is solved by adding a positive base value to the exponent, called a *bias*. Using a bias of 50, the floating-point number 0.3×10^7 would be stored as

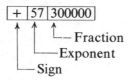

and the number -0.825336×10^{-5} would be stored as

$$\boxed{-}\ \boxed{45}\ \boxed{825336}$$

In these examples, the exponent denotes a power of 10.

Decimal notation has been used to introduce the concept of floating-point data. Except in very special cases, floating-point numbers are stored in binary form. As an example of binary format, consider the following 16-bit floating-point word:

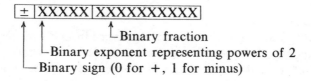

Next,

$$(11.5)_{10} = (1011.1)_2 = (0.10111 \times 10^{100})_2$$

Note that in the rightmost representation, all constituents are in binary. The number would be stored in binary floating format as follows, using a bias of 10000 for the exponent:

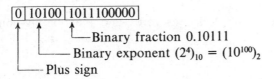

Similarly, the number

$$(-0.171875)_{10} = (-0.001011)_2 = (-0.1011 \times 10^{-10})_2$$

is stored in binary as

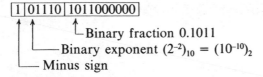

Note that the following are numerically equivalent:

| 1 | 01110 | 1011000000 |

| 1 | 01111 | 0101100000 |

| 1 | 10000 | 0010110000 |

A floating-point datum in which the leftmost bit of the *fraction* is 1 is referred to as a *normalized number*. Since the size of a floating-point word is fixed, it is common practice to store a floating point number in normalized form, since the maximum number of digits of precision can be maintained. It should be noted here that the number of bits in the fraction field determines the amount of accuracy a number can have and the number of bits in the exponent field determines the magnitude a number can have. For example, consider the following floating-point number

$$\boxed{0}\ \boxed{11101}\ \boxed{1000000000}$$

The actual exponent is 1101 (after removing the bias) which places the binary point outside of the fraction, as follows:

0.1000000000XXX,

Actual binary point

The low-order bits are simply taken as zeros and the floating-point number is evaluated as

1000000000000.

which is equal to 2^{12}, or 4096, in decimal.

Another method of managing the binary exponent that gives a greater range to the number is to interpret the exponent as a power of 16 corresponding to four bits of the fraction. Using this technique (referred to as a *hexadecimal* exponent), the 32-bit floating-point number (using an exponent bias of 100000)

$$\boxed{0}\ \boxed{1000001}\ \boxed{0101\ 0000\ 0000\ 0000\ 0000\ 0000}$$

is evaluated as

.01010000 0000 0000 0000 0000

Actual binary point

which equals 5 in decimal. It follows that the fraction is normalized in groups of four bits, thus sacrificing precision for range. In computers that use a hexadecimal exponent, an optional extended-precision format is usually available for use in cases where high precision is needed.

5.2 ARITHMETIC OPERATIONS

The basic arithmetic operations in computing are addition, subtraction, multiplication, and division; these functions are usually built into the computer and are available for use with a single computer instruction. Arithmetic operations were introduced in the previous chapter and this section is intended to extend those concepts through the recognition of fixed- and floating-point data.

Fixed-point addition and subtraction operations and all floating-point arithmetic operations are normally performed in an accumulator register designed for that purpose. Fixed-point multiplication and division use an accumulator and an extension to it, frequently referred to as the multiplier/quotient register.* In computers with multiple accumulator registers, the registers are usually numbered for identification, and odd/even numbered pairs of fixed-point registers correspond to the accumulator and multiplier/quotient registers, respectively; floating-point arithmetic is performed in floating-point registers.

Arithmetic operations typically operate as follows (addition is used as an example):

1. The addend is placed in an accumulator register.
2. The arithmetic operation is performed with an augend (to be added to the addend) from main storage.
3. The result is placed in the accumulator register, replacing the addend, for use in a subsequent computer operation.

In the description of fixed- and floating-point arithmetic operations that follows, fixed-point registers are numbered 1 and 2, depicted as follows:

| Register 1 | Register 2 |

These registers are used for fixed-point arithmetic. Floating-point register 2, denoted by

| Floating-Point Register 2 |

is used for floating-point arithmetic. Fixed-point register 2 is regarded as a right-hand extension to fixed-point register 1. Decimal numbers are used in the following sections.

Fixed-Point Operations

The following sequence of computer instructions, in symbolic form, constitutes a simple add operation:†

```
L    1,1000
A    1,1570
ST   1,2634
```

---

* The use of double registers is explained under "Fixed-Point Operations."

† We mentioned earlier that symbolic operation codes would become more abbreviated. Operation codes, in actual practice, are normally as abbreviated as possible.

The meaning of the instruction is

1. *Load* fixed-point register 1 with the contents of memory location 1000.
2. *Add* to fixed-point register 1 the contents of memory location 1570.
3. *Store* the result of the addition in memory location 2634. (Fixed-point register 1 contains the result after the store operation is complete.)

What about the implied decimal points? Fixed-point operations blindly "go about their business" as though all quantities were integers. The programmer must ensure that the decimal points are aligned for additive operations. Consider the following values:

Memory Address	Value
6380	000153
	∧ Implied decimal point
5124	000241
	∧ Implied decimal point

The instructions

    L   1,6380
    A   1,5124

would produce the following result:

    000394   Fixed-Point Register 1

which, although correct from the computer's point of view, is definitely not the answer the user desired. A more appropriate set of instructions would be

    L   1,6380
    SL   1,1
    A   1,5124

The meaning of the instructions is:

1. *Load* fixed-point register 1 with the contents of memory location 6380. Fixed-point register 1 now contains.

$$\boxed{000153} \quad \text{Fixed-Point Register 1}$$
$$\wedge$$

2. *Shift left* fixed-point register 1 by 1 place. Fixed-point register 1 now contains:

$$\boxed{001530} \quad \text{Fixed-Point Register 1}$$
$$\wedge$$

3. *Add* to fixed-point register 1 the contents of memory location 5124. Fixed-point register 1 now contains:

$$\boxed{001771} \quad \text{Fixed-Point Register 1}$$
$$\wedge$$

which is a more appropriate result.

All computers have instructions for shifting left and right for use in cases such as this. Fixed-point subtraction would be performed in an analogous manner.

Fixed-point multiplication and division use double registers because multiplication produces a double product and division produces a smaller quotient. Consider the following values:

Memory Address	Value
3638	$\boxed{078312}$
	$\wedge$ Implied decimal point
7150	$\boxed{000641}$
	$\wedge$ Implied decimal point

A set of instructions to multiply the two numbers is given as follows:

```
L   2,3638
M   1,7150
```

The meaning of the instructions is:

1. *Load* fixed-point register 2 with the contents of memory location 3638, giving

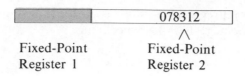

078312

∧

Fixed-Point   Fixed-Point
Register 1   Register 2

2. *Multiply* the contents of fixed-point register 2 by the contents of memory location 7150 producing a double product in the combined registers 1 and 2, that is,

000050	197992

∧

Fixed-Point Fixed-Point
Register 1   Register 2

(Note the location of the implied decimal point.) The product can be stored as two words or be used in subsequent calculations. In most cases, however, the product is small enough to be contained in fixed-point register 2 and it can be used accordingly.

Fixed-point division is the inverse of multiplication. Consider the following values:

Memory Address	Value
5550	001298
9874	000036
2000	000000

A set of instructions to divide the contents of 5550 by the contents of 9874 is given as follows:

```
L    1,2000
L    2,5550
D    1,9874
```

The quotient is found in register 2 and the remainder is placed in register 1. The meaning of the instructions is:

1. *Load* fixed-point register 1 with the contents of memory location 2000. In this case, fixed-point register 1 is set to zero since the dividend is not a double word.

2. *Load* fixed-point register 2 with the contents of memory location 5550. This is the dividend, so that the registers contain:

000000	001298

Fixed-Point   Fixed-Point
Register 1   Register 2

3. *Divide* the contents of fixed-point registers 1 and 2 combined by the contents of memory location 9874. The quotient is left in register 2 and the remainder in register 1, as follows:

000002	000036

Fixed-Point   Fixed-Point
Register 1   Register 2

As in previous fixed-point computations, the programmer must take care of decimal point alignment by using the shift instructions in conjunction with the conventional rules of arithmetic.

Floating-Point Operations

Floating-point arithmetic operations use a single floating-point "accumulator-type" register. The computer is constructed to interpret the exponent and fraction fields separately, and after radix points have been aligned, addition and subtraction operations are essentially reduced to fixed-point operations.

As an example, consider the addition of the numbers 64 and 8 in scientific notation and in floating-point format:

Scientific Notation	*Floating-Point Format* (Exponent bias = 50)
0.64×10^2	+ | 52 | 640000
0.8×10^1	+ | 51 | 800000

To align the exponents, the smallest number is shifted right until the exponents agree:

Scientific Notation	*Floating-Point Format* (Exponent bias = 50)
0.64×10^2	+ | 52 | 640000
0.08×10^2	+ | 52 | 080000

Then, disregarding the exponents, the fractions can be added as in fixed-point arithmetic to produce the following results:

Scientific Notation	Floating-Point Format
	(Exponent bias = 50)
0.72×10^2	$\boxed{+\ \boxed{52}\ \boxed{720000}}$

After the arithmetic operation is complete, the fraction is normalized by shifting it left or right until the first nonzero digit appears immediately to the right of the implied decimal point; the exponent is updated accordingly. As another example, consider the subtraction operation: $0.103 \times 10^3 - 0.97 \times 10^2$. The subtraction operation would be executed as follows:

1. Equalize exponents
   $$0.103 \times 10^3 - 0.097 \times 10^3$$
2. Subtract
   $$0.103 \times 10^3 - 0.097 \times 10^3 = 0.006 \times 10^3$$
3. Normalize
   $$0.006 \times 10^3 = 0.6 \times 10^1$$

Floating-point instructions to the computer are executed in a similar manner to the way fixed-point operations are executed. Consider the following instructions:

```
LE    2,5380
SE    2,7000
STE   2,4164
```

The symbolic LE instruction tells the computer to load floating-point register with the contents of memory location 5380. The datum in location 5380 is assumed to be a floating-point value. The symbolic SE instruction instructs the computer to subtract the contents of memory location 7000 from the contents of floating-point register 2. The difference is left in floating-point register 2. The symbolic STE instruction causes the contents of floating-point register 2 to be stored in memory location 4164.

Conceptually, floating-point multiplication and division are less complex than addition and subtraction, since the exponents do not need to be compared. Consider floating-point numbers of the form $N_i = n_i \times b^{e_i}$. The multiplication of two floating-point numbers N_1 and N_2

requires a multiplication of fractions and an addition of exponents, as follows:

$$(n_1 \times b^{e_1}) \times (n_2 \times b^{e_2}) = (n_1 \times n_2) \times b^{(e_1 + e_2)}$$

Similarly, the division of two floating-point numbers N_1 and N_2 requires a division of fractions and a subtraction of exponents, as follows:

$$(n_1 \times b^{e_1}) \div (n_2 \times b^{e_2}) = (n_1 \div n_2) \times b^{(e_1 - e_2)}$$

After either the multiplication or the division operation, normalization may be required, depending on the fraction of the result. For example, the multiplication of $(0.4 \times 10^2) \times (0.2 \times 10^1)$ would involve the following steps:

1. Add exponents and multiply fractions
   $$(0.4 \times 10^2) \times (0.2 \times 10^1) = 0.08 \times 10^3$$
2. Normalize result
   $$0.08 \times 10^3 = 0.8 \times 10^2$$

Similarly, the division of (0.63×10^2) by (0.9×10^1) proceeds as follows:

1. Subtract exponents and divide fractions,
   $$(0.63 \times 10^2) \div (0.9 \times 10^1) = 0.7 \times 10^1$$
2. No normalization is required.

The primary advantage of floating-point data is that the programmer need not be concerned with the location of the radix point and the management of double-length products and dividends. The use of floating-point data, however, does raise questions of the range and precision of computed results and of the rounding of floating-point numbers. These topics are considered in Chapter 14.

Another consideration involves the use of memory addresses to reference data in main storage. Normally, data values are referred to by name, since a name can be selected in a meaningful and useful manner. For example, a memory location containing an interest rate might be given the name RATE. Names, assigned by the programmer, are translated into memory addresses when a computer program is prepared for execution.

5.3 VARIABLES, OPERATORS, AND EXPRESSIONS

In mathematics, the name given to an unknown quantitiy is a *variable*. For example, one might say, "Let *x* equal the ... ." In actual practice, the concept is more general and enables principles to be developed independently of a particular problem. The term *variable*, in contrast to the word *constant*, implies that the entity can assume any one of a set of values, or, in other words, that the value of a variable is not constant but is subject to change. A variable is also used as a symbolic name in everyday discourse. Thus, variables such as X or Y are frequently used to represent an unknown quantity or to help in explaining a complex idea for which ordinary language is inadequate.

Variables and Identifiers

In computing, a *variable* is the name given to a location in main storage. In the computer instructions

    L   1,HOURS
    M   1,RATE
    ST   1,PAY

for example, the names HOURS, RATE, and PAY are variables. The implicit understanding here is that during the course of computation, PAY is to be computed for several cases as HOURS and RATE assume different sets of values. The symbolic names L, M, and ST identify the computer instructions "load," "multiply," and "store." In its most general sense, a symbolic name is known as an *identifier*. Thus, a variable is an identifier that names a data item.

In a computer programming language, a variable also names a location in main storage. In the expression

    A + B

for example, A and B are variables and the expression means, "add the contents of B to the contents of A." (The example is abbreviated, since the expression A + B is taken out of context.) When using a programming language, most people think of variables as quantities that can be manipulated as in ordinary mathematics. This is certainly a good idea and is one of the primary reasons that programming languages are used. It is important to note, however, that every data item must be stored somewhere and if one really presses the subject, a variable actually names a memory location.

The term *identifier* is used very generally in computer science to refer to any symbolic name. Some identifiers are used to name units of the computer system or constituents of a programming language. In the statement

READ A,B

for example, the identifier READ is used to identify a particular kind of statement in a programming language. The name READ serves two purposes: (1) It identifies a particular kind of statement; and (2) it denotes the specific function the statement is intended to perform. The name of a statement is selected so that it is meaningful to the user and is usually referred to as a *mnemonic name*.

Operators and Expressions

A computer can perform a variety of operational functions, known as computing or computation. Some of these functions are: (1) arithmetic and logical operations; (2) data movement; (3) sequence and control functions; and (4) input and output. Normally, these functions are available to the user through computer instructions or statements in a programming language; when the user desires to specify a particular type of operation, he uses the most appropriate instruction or statement for that purpose.

Assume it were desired to add the contents of A to the contents of B and store the result in C. We know that the computer must execute a series of instructions, such as

```
L    1,A
A    1,B
ST   1,C
```

In computer programming languages, the user is permitted to write

C = A + B

The equals sign and the plus sign are known as *operators*. The equals sign denotes replacement and the plus sign denotes addition. Thus, the statement means, "add A to B and replace C with the sum." C, A, and B are known as *operands*—in other words, they are the "things" on which the operators "operate." Operands can also be constants, as in the following statement:

TEMP = X + 1.738

An operator, such as addition, subtraction, multiplication, division, or replacement, that uses two operands is known as a *binary operator*. An operator that uses one operand is known as a *unary operator*. A common unary operator is negation, as used in the following example

$E = -D$

Negation is used to change the sign of a quantity, so that $-x$ is equivalent to $0 - x$.

As in mathematics, operators and operands can be combined to form an *expression* denoting that a sequence of operations is to be performed. For example, the expression

$A + B*C$

means that the product of B and C is to be added to A. When two or more operators are contained in an expression, the operators must obviously be executed in some prescribed sequence. Each operator has a priority and that priority determines the order in which the operations are executed. A simple priority scheme is

Operator Symbol*	Priority
* or /	Highest
+ or −	↓
=	Lowest

Thus, * is executed before +, and so forth. The expression, $2 + 3*4$, for example, has the value 14. As in ordinary mathematics, parentheses can be used to denote grouping and to depart from the established priority among operators, so that $(2+3)*4$ has the value 20. This convention is further demonstrated in the following examples:

Ordinary Mathematics	Computer Programming Language
$ax + by + z$	$A*X + B*Y + Z$
$\dfrac{a + b}{a + c}$	$(A+B)/(A+C)$

There are other kinds of data in computing, and other operators. A quick review of a variety of programming languages, for example, would

---

* The meanings of the operator symbols are: * for multiplication, / for division, + for addition, − for subtraction or negation, and = for replacement.

uncover at least the following varieties: complex data, logical data, label data, pointer data, mode data, event data, character data, and file data. Although all data types are meaningful from the viewpoint of computer science, the manner in which a particular data type is used is frequently related to a given programming language and its operational environment. One type of data that is indispensable in computer operation is logical data, covered in the next section.

5.4 LOGICAL DATA

A logical datum is one that can assume the truth values "true" or "false." There is no standard means of representing logical data and logical procedures are frequently "built-in" to a computer program. For example, a zero fixed- or floating-point value is used to denote "false" and a nonzero value is used to denote "true." In binary computers, a 1 bit is commonly used to represent "true" and a 0 bit is used to represent "false"; this convention is used in this section.

Basic Logical Operations

Three fundamental operations are defined on logical data: *and, or,* and *not.* (Logicians recognize and use other operations, which are not in widespread use in computing.) The operator symbols for the binary *and* and *or* operations are $\wedge$ and $\vee$, respectively. The operator symbol for the unary *not* operation is $\sim$. The logical operations are defined by the following tables:

And				*Or*				*Not*		
$\wedge$	0	1		$\vee$	0	1		$\sim$	0	1
0	0	0		0	0	1			1	0
1	0	1		1	1	1				

Thus, the expression $P \wedge Q$ is true if both P and Q are true; the expression $P \vee Q$ is true if either P or Q is true or both are true; and $\sim P$ is true if P is false, and $\sim P$ is false if P is true. As with arithmetic operators, logical operators and operands can be used in programming languages to construct logical expressions. Thus, the following logical expression:

$$\sim((P \wedge Q) \vee (R \wedge T))$$

has the value true for the following cases:

    P, Q, R, and T are all false.
    P and R or P and T are false.
    Q and R or Q and T are false.

and has the value false for the following cases:

    P, Q, R, and T are all true.
    P and Q are true.
    R and T are true.

Logical Operations in Computers

Most binary computers include logical instructions that treat the bits of a binary computer word as true or false values. Consider the following values:

Symbolic Name	Value
DLTA	11000001 11010010
MSK13	00000000 11111111

The computer instructions

    L   1,DLTA
    N   1,MSK13

where N is the symbolic operation code for an "and" instruction, serve to produce the following value in register 1:

    0000000011010010

In this case, the "and" operation processes the operands on a bit-by-bit basis, as follows:

```
    1100000111010010
 ∧  0000000011111111
    0000000011010010
```

This is an example of masking—a procedure used to "mask off" (or eliminate) a prescribed set of bits of the word. A bit-by-bit "or" instruction operates in a similar manner, except that the logical "or" is taken instead of the logical "and." Given the following values:

Symbolic Name	Value
CH1	1100000100000000
CH2	0000000011010010

The instructions

```
L   1,CH1
O   1,CH2
```

where O is the symbolic operation code for an "or" instruction, serve to produce the following value in register 1:

1100000111010010

The "or" operation processes the operands on a bit-by-bit basis, as follows:

```
   1100000100000000
∨ 0000000011010010
   1100000111010010
```

This is an example of using the "or" operation to combine two fields to form a single word.

The logical "not" operation, or bit-by-bit complementation, simply changes each 1 bit to a 0 bit and each 0 bit to a 1 bit. Given the following values:

Symbolic Name	Value
FIVE	0000000000000101
ONE	0000000000000001

The following instructions compute the two's complement of FIVE:

```
L    1,FIVE
CM   1
A    1,ONE
```

where the symbolic instruction CM is used to take the one's complement of the contents of register 1. The instructions produce data values, as follows:

$$
\begin{array}{ll}
0000000000000101 & \\
1111111111111010 & \text{One's complement} \\
+\,0000000000000001 & \\
\hline
1111111111111011 & \text{Two's complement}
\end{array}
$$

Bit-by-bit logical operations are frequently referred to as "masking instructions" or "Boolean instructions." Since most computer programming is done in a programming language, most users simply deal with logical values and variables that can assume a true or false value. Boolean instructions are normally used in "machine-level" programming.

Comparison Operations

Logical values can arise in any of three ways:

1. They can be read into the computer with an input operation.
2. A logical value can be assigned to a logical variable.
3. They can result from a comparison operation.

A *comparison operation* compares the value of two data items and involves the recognition of the following conditions:

Less than
Less than or equal to
Equal to
Not equal to
Greater than or equal to
Greater than

Comparison operations are used in two principal ways. In the first method, two values are compared and a condition indicator is set to indicate which condition exists, as demonstrated in the following set of instructions that compares the values of variables A and B:

L   1,A
C   1,B

Here, the symbolic instruction C (for "compare") compares the contents of register 1 with the value of the variable B and sets a condition indicator that is built into the computer hardware. The indicator can be used in subsequent "conditional" branch instructions.

In the second method, a value is placed in a computer register and is used in a subsequent branch instruction that includes a conditional test, as demonstrated in the following example:

```
L       1,A
BPLUS   1,HERE
```

The load instruction places the value of variable A in register 1. The BPLUS instruction is a conditional branch instruction that causes program control to be directed to location HERE if the contents of register 1 are "plus."

When using a programming language, the user is allowed to use a condition explicitly, as in the following IF statement:

IF A$>$B THEN GO TO HERE

This statement instructs the computer to operate as follows: "If the value of A is greater than the value of B, branch to symbolic location HERE." The statement would be roughly equivalent to the following computer instructions:

```
L       1,A        (load)
S       1,B        (subtract)
BPLUS   1,HERE     (branch on plus)
```

As demonstrated in the preceding example, programming languages permit a specific condition to be tested, with either a true or false value provided, depending upon whether the condition is true or false. Table 5.1 summarizes the comparison operators.

5.5   DATA ORGANIZATION

One of the essential characteristics of computing is that all data must be stored somewhere and the manner in which they are stored determines to a large extent how they can be used. Thus far, data have been primarily characterized as being numeric or nonnumeric. This section goes into more detail on how numeric and nonnumeric data can be organized.

Table 5.1
Comparison Operators

Operation	Operator Symbol	Form	Definition (R = result)	Example (↔ denotes equivalence)
Less than	<	A < B	R is true if A is less than B and is false otherwise	3 < 2 ↔ false
Less than or equal to	≤	A ≤ B	R is true if A is less than or equal to B and is false otherwise	3 ≤ 3 ↔ true
Equal to	=	A = B	R is true if A is equal to B and is false otherwise	3 = 2 ↔ false
Not equal to	≠	A ≠ B	R is true if A is not equal to B and is false otherwise	3 ≠ 2 ↔ true
Greater than or equal to	≥	A ≥ B	R is true if A is greater than or equal to B and is false otherwise	2 ≥ 3 ↔ false
Greater than	>	A > B	R is true if A is greater than B and is false otherwise	3 > 2 ↔ true

Fields, Numbers, and Scalars

A *field* is a unit of storage that would lose its meaning if it were broken down further. For example, several consecutive columns on a punched card might represent a person's name; these columns are called a field. A character in that field is simply a character of the alphabet. Collectively, the characters of a field have a definite meaning. The concept is similar to that of a number discussed earlier; in fact, a number is usually stored as a field. In the computer, a field is stored as a series of bits, characters, or words—depending upon the design of the computer. Normally, we disregard the form in which a data item is stored and refer to it as an entity in its own right.

A single item of data is known as a *scalar*. Thus, a value such as a person's age, the name of a part, or the result of a comparison operation is considered to be a scalar value—regardless of its data type and the amount of storage it occupies. In programming, a scalar can be expressed as a constant or a variable. For example, in the statement

```
JOB=I+1
```

the variables JOB and I are scalar variables and the value 1 is a scalar constant.

Arrays

A set of related data items is known as an *array*. When dealing with an array, it is desirable to give the entire array a name rather than naming each individual element. As an example of a simple case where an array might be used, consider the problem of data recording and analysis of an organization designated to certify the miles per gallon achieved by a given set of automobiles. A test driver might come up with the following list:*

Automobile Number	*Name*	*Miles per Gallon*
1	Datsun	25
2	Pinto	20
3	Toyota	22
4	Vega	20
5	Volkswagen	26

Clearly, each test value for a given automobile is a scalar value. However, the set of scalar values comprises a family of related data items known as a *vector*. Each value has an index given by the automobile number, and that index can be used to select a value of the vector. For example, the miles per gallon achieved by automobile 3 is 22. The value 22 is said to be the third component (or element) of the vector.

The concept is easily extended. If the road tests were made under different driving conditions, then the following values might result:

Automobile Number	*Driving Condition* 1	2	3	4
1	21	23	25	22
2	15	24	21	18
3	18	20	22	21
4	16	24	21	17
5	20	22	26	23

* All data are hypothetical.

where the miles per gallon of automobile 4 for driving condition 3 is the value 21. The value 21 is selected by two indexes: the row index and the column index. A two-dimensional collection of values is known as a *matrix*.

Vectors and matrices are specific cases of arrays, which can be extended to as many dimensions as necessary. In the preceding examples, a three-dimensional array might be obtained if more than one test driver were involved, as follows:

Driver Driving Condition

	1	1	2	3	4
	1	21	23	25	22
Automobile	2	15	24	21	18
Number	3	18	20	22	21
	4	16	24	21	17
	5	20	22	26	23

Driver Driving Condition

	2	1	2	3	4
	1	20	23	26	21
Automobile	2	17	23	22	20
Number	3	15	21	24	23
	4	16	22	24	21
	5	21	24	28	26

The value corresponding to indexes (2,5,1), denoting driver 2, automobile number 5, and driving condition 1, is 21.

In programming, the process of retrieving an element of an array is termed *selection* and uses the name of the array and the relative position of the element in the array, as demonstrated above. The indexes used to select an element from an array are termed a subscript and can be expressed as constants, variables, or expressions. For obvious reasons, it is necessary to reduce an index to an integer before selection takes place. If the above three-dimensional array were named MPG, for example, a reference to MPG (2,5,1) would select the value 21. When expressing an array variable in a programming language, the indexes are separated by commas and enclosed in parentheses following the array name since subscripts or superscripts, in the usual sense, are cumbersome to enter into the computer.

Properties of Arrays

An array can be characterized in a variety of ways. The first characteristic of an array is that each of its elements must have the same properties. This property is referred to as *homogeneity*. Another characteristic is the number of dimensions. Consider, for example, the array *A*, defined as follows:

$$A = \begin{pmatrix} a_{1,-2} & a_{1,-1} & a_{1,0} & a_{1,1} & a_{1,2} \\ a_{2,-2} & a_{2,-1} & a_{2,0} & a_{2,1} & a_{2,2} \\ a_{3,-2} & a_{3,-1} & a_{3,0} & a_{3,1} & a_{3,2} \\ a_{4,-2} & a_{4,-1} & a_{4,0} & a_{4,1} & a_{4,2} \end{pmatrix}$$

The array *A* has two dimensions. Each dimension is further characterized by a bounds and an extent. The *bounds* of a dimension are the beginning and ending index for that dimension and determine the manner in which the elements are selected. *A* has row bounds of 1 and 4 and column bounds of -2 and 2. The *extent* is the number of elements in a dimension—regardless of how they are referenced. *A* has a row extent of 4 and a column extent of 5. The final characteristic of an array is how it is stored. Arrays are almost always placed in contiguous locations in main storage. Two conventions are in widespread use: row order and column order. Both methods are demonstrated in Figure 5.1. *Row order* (also known as index order or lexicographic order) denotes that the elements of an array are stored in successive locations in main storage in a rowwise fashion. *Column order* denotes that the elements are stored in a columnwise fashion.

Indexing Into an Array

When a computer program is executed, the subscripts may vary during the course of execution when variables are used for indexes. Although the location of the entire array is known, the location of the element needed has to be computed.

Simple formulas for indexing into a two-dimensional array are given and the concepts can easily be extended to arrays of higher dimension.

Given an array A with M rows and N columns, suppose that the element desired is A(I,J). When the array is stored in row order, the location of A(I,J) can be computed with the following formula:*

$$location[A(I,J)] = location[A(1)] + (I-1)*N + J - 1$$

Thus, if A has 3 rows and 4 columns, then the location of A(2,3) is computed as

$$location[A(2,3)] = location[A(1,1)] + (1)*4 + 3 - 1 = location[A(1,1)] + 6$$

---

* The lower bound for each dimension is assumed to be 1.

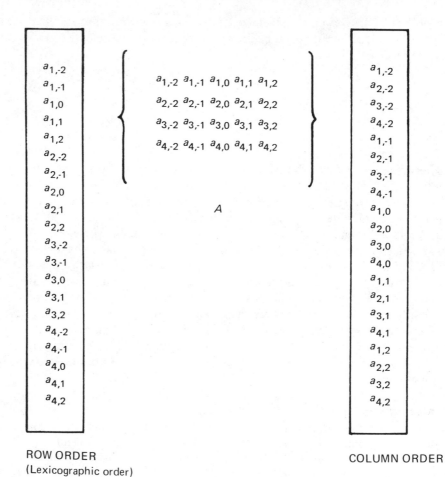

ROW ORDER
(Lexicographic order)

COLUMN ORDER

Figure 5.1   Two methods of placing an array in main storage.

When the array is stored in column order, the location of A(I,J) can be computed with the formula

$$location[A(I,J)] = location[A(1,1)] + (J-1)*M + I - 1$$

Thus, if A has 3 rows and 4 columns, then the location of A(2,3) is computed as

$$location[A(2,3)] = location[A(1,1)] + (2)*3 + 2 - 1 = location[A(1,1)] + 7$$

The process of locating A(2,3) is visualized as follows:

Location of $A(1,1) \rightarrow$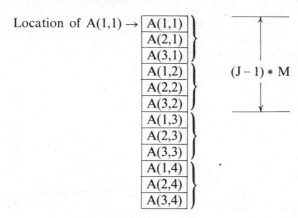

The method is easily understood if one realizes that the formula is derived from simply skipping over previous rows or columns, as demonstrated above.

There are other types of data structures that are used in computer science and computational procedures that use these structures. A more extensive background is needed, however, and this topic is explored further in a later chapter.

QUESTION SET

1. Convert the following floating-point numbers to decimal (the exponent is binary and the bias is 10000):

   | 1 | 11010 | 0000000101 |

   | 1 | 01100 | 1010000000 |

   | 0 | 10101 | 1100000000 |

2. Convert the following floating-point numbers to decimal (the exponent is hexadecimal and the bias is 1000000):

   | 0 | 1000001 | 0001 0000 0000 0000 0000 0000 |

   | 1 | 1000011 | 1101 0011 1001 1000 0000 0000 |

   | 0 | 0111111 | 0011 0000 0000 0000 0000 0000 |

3. Memory location 1430 contains a fixed-point value less than 100 and

location 1684 contains a fixed-point value less than 10. In a computer with accumulator registers 1 and 2, write a short program segment to multiply the two values and place the result in location 6000.

4. Given the following fixed-point values:

Memory Location	Value
6834	$\boxed{000297}$
	$\wedge$ Implicit decimal point
4730	$\boxed{001637}$
	$\wedge$ Implicit decimal point

Write a short program segment to add the two values and leave the result in the accumulator.

5. Perform the following floating-point calculations and normalize the result, if necessary:

   (a) $(297 \times 10^2) + (0.1637 \times 10^0)$
   (b) $(0.297 \times 10^2) - (0.216 \times 10^2)$
   (c) $(0.85 \times 10^1) \times (0.12 \times 10^2)$
   (d) $(180 \times 10^3) \div (0.15 \times 10^1)$

6. Evaluate the following expressions when $A = 10$, $B = 20$, and $C = 3$:

$A + 2*B$	$-B$
$(A + B - 6)/8$	$-B*C$
$A + B + 17.3$	$2*(A - B)$
$2*A - 4$	$-(B + 4/C)$

7. Evaluate the following logical expressions for $Q = true$, $R = false$, $S = true$, and $T = false$:

   $(Q \wedge R)$
   $(((R) \wedge S) \vee T)$
   $Q \wedge R \wedge S \wedge T$
   $Q \vee R \vee S \vee T$

8. Evaluate the following:

10110100	10110100	11100010
$\vee$ 11001011	$\wedge$ 11100110	$\wedge$ 01001111

9. Give values for the following expressions when $A = 5$, $B = 10$, $C = 20$, $P = true$, and $Q = false$:

$A < B$
$(B \neq C) \wedge P$
$P \wedge ((B < C) \vee Q)$
$((2 * A + B) > C) \wedge (P \vee Q)$

10. Complete the following tables for the given comparison operators:

		B			
A<B	-10	-5	0	5	10
-10					
-5					
A 0					
5					
10					

		B			
A≥B	-10	-5	0	5	10
-10					
-5					
A 0					
5					
10					

11. Given the array:

$$B = \begin{pmatrix} -7 & 3 & 9 & 6 \\ 5 & 1 & 4 & 3 \\ 2 & 8 & 1 & 7 \end{pmatrix}$$

and the values $I = 2$ and $J = 3$. Give values for the following expressions:

(a) $B(2,3)$
(b) $B(I, J-1)$
(c) $B(1,2) + 16$
(d) $B(3,3) + B(2,4) - B(1,1)$

12. Develop a formula for indexing into a one-dimensional array C that contains N elements.
13. Given a two-dimensional array D that contains 5 rows and 6 columns stored in row order, compute the locations of D(1,2), D(4,3), and D(2,6).
14. A triangular matrix is a matrix that is symmetrical about the main diagonal, as shown in the following example:

$$\begin{pmatrix} 6 & 3 & 2 & 7 \\ 3 & 9 & 4 & 6 \\ 2 & 4 & 1 & 5 \\ 7 & 6 & 5 & 8 \end{pmatrix}$$

Can you develop a method of storing this matrix and also of selecting elements without storing duplicate values?

SELECTED READINGS

Awad, E. M., *Business Data Processing*, chap. 9, Prentice-Hall, Englewood Cliffs, N.J., 1971.

Korfhage, R. R., *Logic and Algorithms: With Applications to the Computer and Information Sciences*, chap. 4, Wiley, New York, 1966.

Maurer, W. D., *Programming: An Introduction to Computer Techniques*, chap. 1, Holden-Day, San Francisco, 1972.

Price, W. T., and M. Miller, *Elements of Data Processing Mathematics*, chap. 2, Rinehart, San Francisco, 1970.

PART
II

COMPUTER
SYSTEMS

6

INTRODUCTION TO COMPUTER HARDWARE

6.1 INTRODUCTORY REMARKS

Although computer components are normally designed according to established engineering principles, there is no one principle that determines how the components must be put together. This fact is typical of engineering design work and accounts for the differences between products, as well as between computers. Behind every engineering design is a design objective based on economic, technical, or even marketing factors.

In the computer field, there are large computers, medium-sized computers, minicomputers, and even small business computers. (Computers are *generally* classed by speed, storage capacity, functional capabilities, and input/output systems. However, these are not definitive criteria.) Moreover, computers in each of these classes differ in basic "architecture"—a term referring to the functional characteristics of the computer system as it appears to the user. In spite of this diversity, it is still possible to identify a set of characteristics that can be used to distinguish between computers and at the same time provide an introduction to computer hardware.

More specifically, computers differ in obvious and subtle ways. Obvious differences between computers involve the major components that comprise a computer system and how they are utilized. Subtle differences involve the manner in which data is represented and is used internally by the components of the computer system. Another difference between computers is the "software" available for using the computer. *Computer software* is collectively defined as the programs required to use a computer; a familiar example is the compiler, mentioned previously, for translating a program written in a programming language into machine language. Computer software is discussed in Part III.

This chapter presents a collection of topics related to computer hardware; the objective is to provide the reader with a feeling for the internal structure and operation of a computer. The concepts are extended in the next chapter to include basic computer architecture, and in a subsequent chapter to cover computer instructions, assembler language, and macros. The final chapter in this part of the book covers input and output devices and concepts.

6.2 DATA REPRESENTATION

Like the human brain, the computer is a symbol processor. What does this mean? The most obvious answer goes somewhat as follows: When we think about a house or a train, we don't have a house or train in our brain. We have a mental image of a house or a train stored in our brain, and our thinking process uses that mental image. One might say, therefore, that a mental image is a symbolic representation of an object. (Obviously, the human brain goes further and we frequently deal in abstract concepts.)

The computer operates in a similar manner and is designed to process symbols. However, a computer is not a natural phenomenon; it is a man-made physical machine and the symbols processed must be something physical that a computer designer can work with. Modern computers use binary symbols, representing "on" and "off" conditions, for two reasons:

1. Binary symbols can easily be represented physically, as depicted in Figure 6.1.
2. Binary symbols are an efficient means of recording a given amount of information.

Each binary device must be in either of the two states. It is convenient to ignore the type of device and to represent the two states by the symbols 1 and 0. (Note that any two other symbols, such as + or −, would be equally useful.*) The symbols 1 and 0, used in this manner, are not to be regarded as numerals but as marks representing the two states of a binary system.

---

* Morse code is another example of a binary system. A short electrical signal (represented by . and pronounced "dit") and a long electrical signal (represented by - and pronounced "dah") are used to represent characters of an alphabet. For example, the distress signal SOS is represented by: ... --- ... .

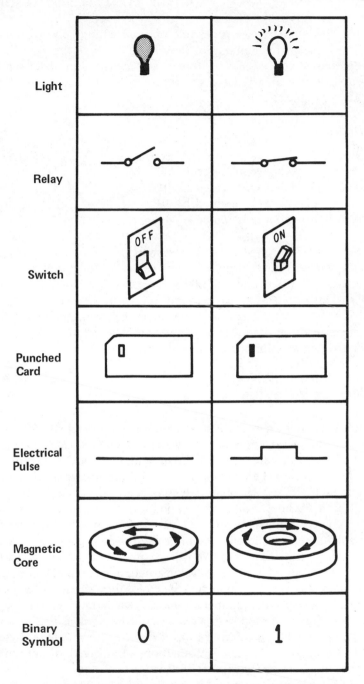

Figure 6.1   Representation of binary symbols.

A single binary device is capable of representing only two symbols and is insufficient for building or describing a computer. Thus, binary devices are used in combination to represent a larger number of symbols. For example, two binary devices can be used to represent four distinct symbols, as follows:

Device

1	2

0 0   Symbol represented by 00
0 1   Symbol represented by 01
1 0   Symbol represented by 10
1 1   Symbol represented by 11

A single 1 or 0 is referred to as a *bit*, so we can say that two bits can be used to represent four symbols. Similarly, three bits can be used to represent eight symbols, that is, 000, 001, 010, 011, 100, 101, 110, 111. It follows that n bits can be used to represent 2^n symbols, that is, $2 \times 2 \times 2 \dots \times 2$, where 2 appears as a factor n times. One of the major differences between computers is the manner in which bits are combined for the storage of information.

6.3 WORDS VS. BYTES

Recall that in Chapter 2 it was mentioned that main storage consists of "locations" used to hold information and that each location is identified by and referenced with an address, usually taken to be numeric in nature. The question is, "How much information should a location hold?" Two basic philosophies, or schools of thought, are widely used. The first school says that a location should be capable of storing a relatively large number of bits, say, 36. A computer that employs this philosophy is referred to as a *word-oriented computer* and each group of 36 bits is referred to as a *word*. We will see in the next section that a word can represent a number, a computer instruction, or several characters of information. The second school says that a location should be capable of storing a relatively small number of bits, say, 8. A computer that employs this philosophy is referred to as a *character* or *byte-oriented computer* and each group of 8 bits is referred to as a *character* or a *byte*. A byte can represent a single character of information; successive bytes are used to represent numbers and computer instructions.

It is important to note that in a word-oriented computer, a word in main storage is directly addressable, and in a byte-oriented computer, a byte in main storage is directly addressable.

6.4 CHARACTERS AND NUMBERS

Information in the computer is stored and interpreted according to conventions established by computer designers and users. In other words, a series of bits, such as 010001, has an agreed upon meaning.* It is important to note, however, that a series of bits may have a different meaning, depending upon how they are used. Thus, more than one convention exists, depending upon how the information is used. Table 6.1 gives commonly used 6-bit and 8-bit character representations. Using the 6-bit representations, the characters UNITED STATES OF AMERICA would be stored in a word-oriented computer, with 36-bit words, as depicted in Figure 6.2. Using the 8-bit representation, the characters OMAR KHAYYAM would be stored in a byte-oriented computer, with 8-bit bytes, as depicted in Figure 6.3. There are advantages to both the

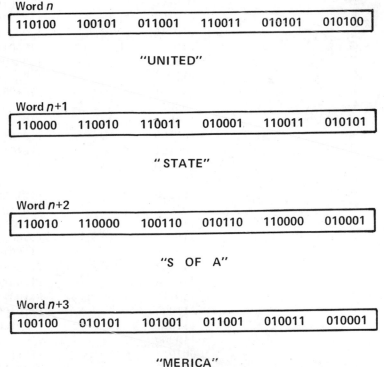

Word *n*

| 110100 | 100101 | 011001 | 110011 | 010101 | 010100 |

"UNITED"

Word *n*+1

| 110000 | 110010 | 110011 | 010001 | 110011 | 010101 |

" STATE"

Word *n*+2

| 110010 | 110000 | 100110 | 010110 | 110000 | 010001 |

"S OF A"

Word *n*+3

| 100100 | 010101 | 101001 | 011001 | 010011 | 010001 |

"MERICA"

Figure 6.2   Storage of the characters UNITED STATES OF AMERICA using 6-bit representation with 36-bit computer words.

* In 6-bit character code, 010001 is a representation for the letter A.

Table 6.1
Representative 6-bit and 8-bit codes

Character	6-bit code	8-bit code
0	000000	11110000
1	000001	11110001
2	000010	11110010
3	000011	11110011
4	000100	11110100
5	000101	11110101
6	000110	11110110
7	000111	11110111
8	001000	11111000
9	001001	11111001
A	010001	11000001
B	010010	11000010
C	010011	11000011
D	010100	11000100
E	010101	11000101
F	010110	11000110
G	010111	11000111
H	011000	11001000
I	011001	11001001
J	100001	11010001
K	100010	11010010
L	100011	11010011
M	100100	11010100
N	100101	11010101
O	100110	11010110
P	100111	11010111
Q	101000	11011000
R	101001	11011001
S	110010	11100010
T	110011	11100011
U	110100	11100100
V	110101	11100101
W	110110	11100110
X	110111	11100111
Y	111000	11101000
Z	111001	11101001
blank character	110000	01000000
=	001011	01111110
+	010000	01001110
−	100000	01100000

Character	6-bit code	8-bit code
*	101100	01011100
/	110001	01100001
(	111100	01001101
)	011100	01011101
, (comma)	111011	01101011
. (period or dec. pt.)	011011	01001011
$	101011	01011011
' (quote)	001100	01111101

word- and byte-oriented methods that are discussed after the representation of numbers is presented.

Numbers are stored as computer words using the binary number system, as presented in the preceding chapter. The 1 bits in a binary number correspond to "on" conditions of a binary device and the 0 bits in a binary number correspond to an "off" condition. In a word-oriented computer, the bits of the word correspond to the bits in a binary number. For example, the binary word

| 0 | 00000 000000 000000 000000 000101 010001 |

represents the number*

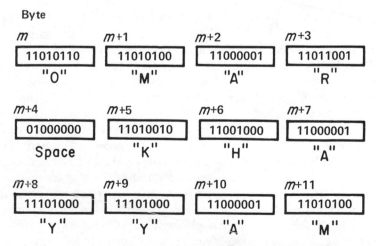

Figure 6.3   Storage of the characters OMAR KHAYYAM using 8-bit representation in a byte-oriented computer with 8-bit bytes.

*The first bit gives the sign: 0 for plus and 1 for minus.

$$0 \times 2^{34} + \cdots + 0 \times 2^{11} + 0 \times 2^{10} + 0 \times 2^9 + 1 \times 2^8 + 0 \times 2^7 + 1 \times 2^6$$
$$+ 0 \times 2^5 + 1 \times 2^4 + 0 \times 2^3 + 0 \times 2^2 + 0 \times 2^1 + 1 \times 2^0$$

which is evaluated as

$$0 + \cdots + 0 + 0 + 0 + 256 + 0 + 64 + 0 + 16 + 0 + 0 + 0 + 1$$
$$= 337$$

It is also important to note that the same word can represent the characters "00005A" using the 6-bit codes in Table 6.1.

In a byte-oriented computer, words are comprised of two or more bytes, depending upon the precision desired by a particular computer application. Standard word sizes are established by the computer manufacturer. For example, one well-known computer allows 2-byte, 4-byte, and 8-byte words. For example, the 2-byte word

$$\boxed{0} \boxed{1001101} \boxed{11000010}$$

represents the number*

$$1 \times 2^{14} + 0 \times 2^{13} + 0 \times 2^{12} + 1 \times 2^{11} + 1 \times 2^{10} + 0 \times 2^9 + 1 \times 2^8$$
$$+ 1 \times 2^7 + 1 \times 2^6 + 0 \times 2^5 + 0 \times 2^4 + 0 \times 2^3 + 0 \times 2^2 + 1 \times 2^1$$
$$+ 0 \times 2^0$$

which is evaluated as $16384 + 0 + 0 + 2048 + 1024 + 0 + 256 + 128 + 64 + 0 + 0 + 0 + 0 + 2 = 19906$. The same two bytes can also represent the characters "(B" using the 8-bit codes in Table 6.1.

In both of the above examples, the information stored as words or bytes could be interpreted as character data or as numeric data. The precise meaning is dependent upon the instructions that process the data. If an instruction designed for character data references the data, then it is interpreted as character data. Similarly, if an instruction designed for numeric data references the data, then it is interpreted as numeric data. The computer is a precise instrument that does not allow any ambiguity.

The relative merits of 6-bit characters and 8-bit bytes are discussed later. As far as this section is concerned, it is important to note that a 6-bit character allows 2^6 (or 64) possible different characters and an 8-bit byte allows 2^8 (or 256) possible different characters; 8-bit bytes are characteristic of some modern computers and one of the reasons they were adopted is that a range of 64 different characters is insufficient for some applications.

* Again, the first bit represents the sign: 0 for plus and 1 for minus.

6.5 COMPUTER INSTRUCTIONS

The basic parts of a computer instruction are the operation code, the modifier, and the instruction operands. In a word-oriented computer, the length of a computer instruction is usually fixed in length and takes the following general form:

Operation Code	Modifiers	Operand Address

Each of the three fields exists as a series of bits that represents a specific computer instruction. It is composed of an operation code that specifies the operation to be performed, a modifier that augments the instruction in some fashion, and an operand address. The operand address is the address of the location in main storage of data to be used in the instruction. The bits comprising the address field are interpreted as a positive number that denotes the relative location of the data word used as an operand. Thus, the number of bits in the operand field implicitly specifies the number of locations there can be in main storage. As a trivial example, if the operand address field comprised 4 bits, then main storage could contain 2^4 (or 16) locations, numbered 0000, 0001, 0010, 0011, 0100, 0101, 0110, 0111, 1000, 1001, 1010, 1011, 1100, 1101, 1110, and 1111. If the operand address field contained 15 bits, then main storage could have 2^{15} (or 32,768) locations. Similarly, if the operation code field contained 5 bits, then 2^5 (or 32) different computer instructions could be possible.

In a byte-oriented computer, different sized instructions are permitted. Thus, some instructions can utilize registers only, as in the following 2-byte instruction:[*]

```
←————— 2 bytes —————→
```

Operation Code	Register No.	Register No.

```
←8 bits→←4 bits→←4 bits→
```

A sample instruction might be: Add the contents of register 1 to the contents of register 2. A typical 4-byte instruction, including a modifier, might be:

```
←——————— 4 bytes ———————→
```

Operation Code	Register No.	Modifier	Operand Address

```
←8 bits→←4 bits→←4 bits→←16 bits→
```

---

[*] The instructions given are hypothetical but representative of several modern computers.

A sample instruction might be: Subtract the contents of the specified main storage location from the contents of the specified register. A typical 6-byte instruction would be:

← —————————— 6 bytes —————————— →			
Operation Code	Modifier	Operand Address-1	Operand Address-2

←8 bits→←8 bits→←16 bits→←16 bits→

A sample instruction might be: Move the bytes starting at operand address 2 to byte locations beginning in operand address 1; the length of the move is specified in the modifier field. In all cases, the *length in bytes of the instruction* is implied in the operation code.

Although this discussion of computer instructions has indeed been simplified, it demonstrates two important points:

1. The format of the instructions for a particular computer determines the range of main storage addresses that can be addressed and the number of different operation codes that can be used.
2. The word- vs. byte-oriented storage question does make a difference in the types of instructions (e.g., one operand vs. two operands) that can be used.

Clearly, the difference between word- and byte-oriented computers does not matter for some computer applications, such as those that deal primarily with numerical calculations. When a substantial amount of character handling is involved, however, then there seems to be some advantage to a byte-oriented computer over a word-oriented computer. Basic computer design, however, can be misleading, since most users do not deal with the computer, per se. They use "computer software" to interface with the computer, so that the effectiveness of the computer system is ultimately related to the software and is not completely dependent upon hardware. Good software can compensate for poor hardware, and vice versa. The current trend is to integrate the design of the hardware and the software.

Another difference between computers was briefly discussed in Chapter 2: the number of arithmetic registers (or accumulators). Recall here that an arithmetic register is synthesized from high-speed circuitry, so that retrieving an operand from a register is much faster than retrieving an operand from main storage. The key point is that registers are expensive. Consider the calculation of the statement

$$A = B*C + D*E$$

which means: multiply B by C; multiply D by E; add the results of the two multiplications; and replace the value of A with the result of the addition. In a computer with one accumulator, the computations might exist as follows:*

Operation	Operand
L	B
M	C
ST	TEMP1
L	D
M	E
ST	TEMP2
L	TEMP1
A	TEMP2
ST	A

In a computer with two registers, numbered 1 and 2, the calculations might be:

Operation	Operand
L	1,B
M	1,C
L	2,D
M	2,E
A	1,2
ST	1,A

The number of instructions is reduced by 33 percent, which may be significant depending upon the calculations being performed.

6.6 BASIC COMPUTER OPERATIONS

There are only a few basic operations that can be performed on binary symbols. The instruction-processing circuitry of the computer is built up from these basic operations. The operation tables for these operations are given in Figure 6.4. The AND gate takes two input wires and a pulse is generated from the output wire only if a pulse is present on

---

* The mnemonic symbols L, M, A, and ST represent the operations load, multiply, add, and store.

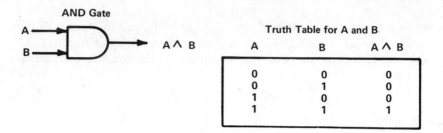

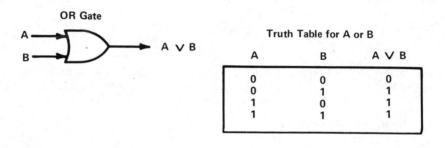

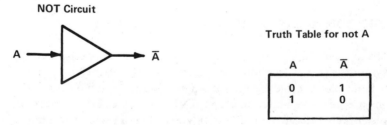

Figure 6.4 Basic computer operations and their corresponding truth tables.

both input wires. The OR gate takes two input wires and generates an output pulse if a pulse is present on either or both of the input wires. In the NOT circuit, the output is simply the opposite of the input.

As an example of how computer instructions are synthesized from basic computer operations (or computer logic, as it is frequently called), consider the problem of binary addition. Most of us remember that binary addition is similar to decimal addition, except that only two digits are involved:

$$0 + 0 = 0$$
$$0 + 1 = 1$$
$$1 + 0 = 1$$
$$1 + 1 = 0 \quad \text{with a carry of 1}$$

so that the addition of 1100 and 0101 proceeds as follows:

```
    1110
  +0101
```
1	Carry
10011	Sum

The problem is to develop a circuit of ANDs, ORs, and NOTs that performs the operation of addition on binary numbers the size of a computer word. The problem is depicted as Figure 6.5.

First, it is important to note that two kinds of addition are involved. When A_0 is added to B_0, the addition takes two inputs, A_0 and B_0. When A_1 is added to B_1, the addition takes three inputs, A_1, B_1, and C_0, where C_0 is the carry from the high-order bit addition. An adder circuit that takes two inputs is referred to as a *half adder*, depicted as follows:

(Input) $A_i \rightarrow$	Half	$\rightarrow S_i$	(Sum)
(Input) $B_i \rightarrow$	Adder	$\rightarrow C_i$	(Carry)

The logic of a half adder is given in Figure 6.6. An adder circuit that takes three inputs is referred to as a *full adder*, depicted as follows:

(Input)	$A_i \rightarrow$	Full	S_i	(Sum)
(Input)	$B_i \rightarrow$	Adder	C_i	(Carry)
(Input from rightmost carry)	$C_{i-1} \rightarrow$			

A full adder can be constructed from two half adders and an OR gate, as depicted in Figure 6.7.

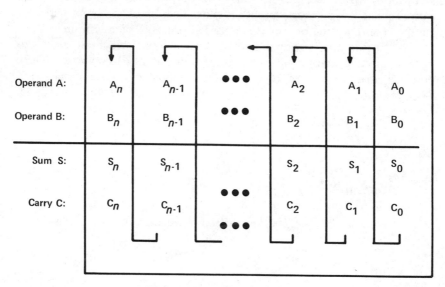

Figure 6.5 Binary addition.

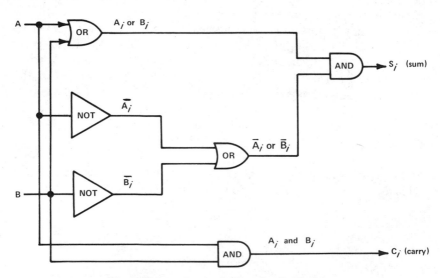

Figure 6.6 Logic design of a half adder.

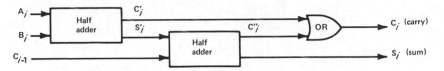

Figure 6.7   A full adder constructed from two half adders and an OR gate.

As far as the complete addition is concerned, the circuitry for the add instruction is constructed from $n - 1$ full adders and one half adder—that is, when the word to be added contains n bits. Computer designers synthesize computer circuits, such as the one just described, from electronic components such as transistors or vacuum tubes.

Most of the other arithmetic operations use the addition circuitry. For example, the subtraction operation is implemented by taking the negative (or two's complement) of the subtrahend and adding it to the minuend; that is, the subtraction operation $A - B$ is computed as $A + (- B)$. In a somewhat analogous fashion, multiplication is performed as repeated additions and division is performed as repeated subtractions.

There are obviously other operations in the instruction repertoire of a computer; for example, all computers include load, store, shift, branch, and input/output instructions. The circuitry for these instructions, as well as the instruction-decoding circuitry, the control circuitry, and the circuitry for referencing main storage, would be synthesized from basic computer operations, just as the add operation was synthesized above. The key point, however, has been made: the computer is a complex device "built up" from a collection of relatively simple components.

6.7 MAIN STORAGE

Main storage is one of the critical components in a computer system because large amounts of it are costly. Two technologies for implementing main storage are generally used: passive and active. *Passive* memory devices possess two states and energy (i.e., electricity) is not needed to maintain a given state. Energy is only needed to change the state. Passive devices are also nonvolatile in the sense that the information is not destroyed when the power is turned off. *Active* memory devices require energy to maintain the state of the device.

The most frequently used main storage technology uses ferromagnetic cores, a passive device, referred to as core storage. A magnetic core is an "iron doughnut" about 1/16 of an inch in diameter with wires

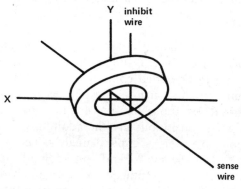

(A) Magnetic core

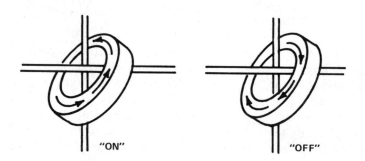

(B) Two states of a magnetic core

Figure 6.8   Magnetic core storage.

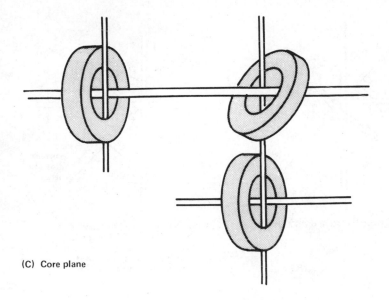

(C) Core plane

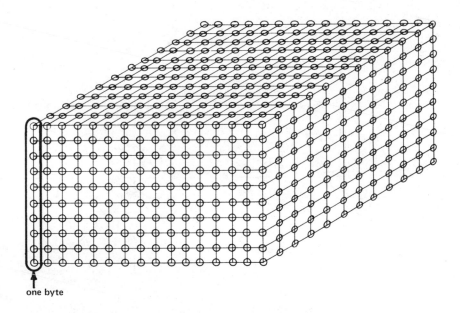

one byte

(D) Core Stack

Figure 6.8 (continued)

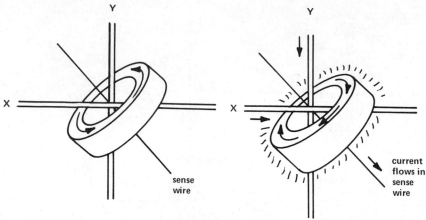

(A) Representation of "1" bit

(B) Current is applied to X and Y to "select" the core. The core is flipped (magnetism is reversed) causing current to flow in sense wire denoting presence of bit.

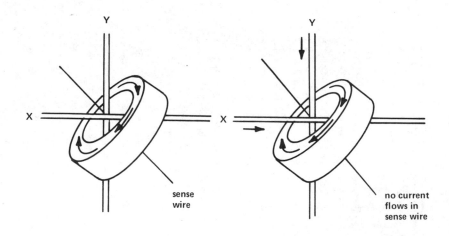

(C) Representation of "0" bit

(D) Current is applied to X and Y to "select" the core. The core is not flipped and no current flows in the sense wire.

Figure 6.9   Operation of core storage.

144

strung through it, as depicted in Figure 6.8(A). The presence of a bit (i.e., a 0 or a 1) is represented by the fact that a core can be magnetized in either of two directions, as shown in Figure 6.8(B). Cores are organized into planes and into stacks, as shown in Figures 6.8(C) and 6.8(D), to represent bytes or words.

A core is selected for reading by sending half the current necessary for "sensing it" through the X and Y wires, as depicted in Figure 6.9. Note that only the core at the intersection of the two wires receives the full current; other cores receive only half the current. The presence of a 1 bit is detected by the fact that the presence of current in the X and Y wires causes the state of the core to "flip" so that current flows in the sense wire. This process is referred to as "destructive read-out," since a 1 bit is cleared to a 0 bit. The core must be reset by sending current through the X and Y wires in the opposite direction. This is where the *inhibit wire* is used (see Figure 6.8); current is sent through the inhibit wire to prevent the core from being reset if it was originally 0. The process of writing a magnetic core is essentially the same as the procedure for resetting a core after a destructive read-out. The primary advantage of core storage is that it is relatively inexpensive to manufacture. One of the main disadvantages of core storage is that as the size of main storage is increased, its physical size becomes a limiting factor on its speed, remembering that modern computers operate at speeds measured in billionths of seconds.

One means of implementing main storage with very high speeds is to use electronic components, such as transistors. Figure 6.10 depicts a schematic of a basic storage cell that utilizes two transistors to collectively represent the on and off states. The storage cell, referred to as a "flip-flop," is read by raising the word-line voltage, causing the flip-flop current to transfer to one of the bit lines and be detected by a current-sensing amplifier. Writing is accomplished by varying the voltage on the bit lines and thereby forcing the flip-flop into the specified state. This is an example of an "active" memory device. The primary advantage of using circuitry for main storage is that many memory circuits can be etched into chips, frequently made of silicon, so that physical size becomes less of a limiting factor. (In the IBM System/370 Model 145, for example, a silicon chip approximately 1/8 inch square has 1434 circuit elements etched in it. These circuit elements form 128 bits of main storage.) Also, the cost of circuitry of this type has been reduced by modern manufacturing methods.

Clearly, the design of high-speed main storage is in the domain of the electrical engineer and it is only fair to mention that other methods of storing information exist. The average user of computers need not be concerned with how main storage is constructed. All he has to do is use it with the techniques given previously. In fact, many computer programmers and systems analysts actually know very little about the computer hardware. Although at first this seems to be a bit unusual, one quickly realizes that the same philosophy also applies to a wide variety of other modern machines.

6.8 SUMMARY

The next step is to put the pieces together to form a computer system. This topic is covered in the next chapter, "Computer Systems Architecture." The following list summarizes what we already know about computers and their operation:

1. The computer is constructed from electronic components that are synthesized in a logical fashion.
2. The computer operates under control of instructions that perform well-defined operations; the instructions along with data are held in main storage.
3. The central processing unit controls the operation of the computer.
4. Before a computer can be used, a computer program must be written.
5. Computer languages and other descriptive techniques are used in program preparation.
6. Computer programs, called language processors, are used to translate programs written in a computer language into internal machine language.

QUESTION SET

1. Describe five devices (other than those given in Figure 6.1) that are binary in nature.
2. Decipher the following quotation using the 6-bit codes in Table 6.1:

```
010001  110000  100011  100110  010001  010110  110000  100110
010110  110000  010010  101001  010101  010001  010100  110011
110000  010001  110000  100001  110100  010111  110000  100110
010110  110000  110110  011001  100101  010101  111011  110000
010001  100101  010100  110000  110011  011000  100110  110100
110000  010010  010101  110010  011001  010100  010101  110000
100100  010101  110000  011001  100101  110000  110011  011000
010101  110000  110110  011001  100011  010100  010101  101001
100101  010101  110010  110010  011011
```

3. Convert the following numbers from the binary positional number system to the decimal positional number system:

10	1	1000000	1010
110	10101	1000	10100
10111	1111	100	11110

4. Given a computer with the following instruction format:

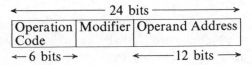

Compute the maximum size of main storage and the total number of operation codes permitted.

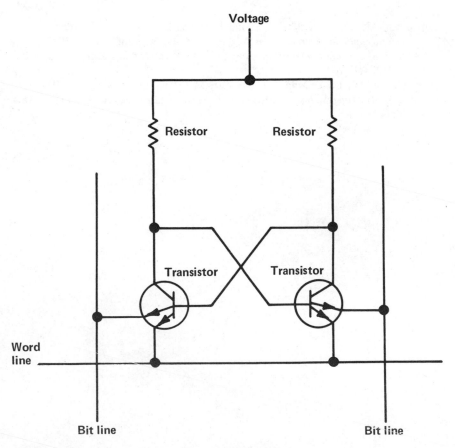

Figure 6.10 Schematic of a basic memory cell using electronic components.

5. Try to develop a rationale for determining how many arithmetic registers a computer should have.
6. Draw logic circuits for the following expressions:

$$S = (A \wedge B) \vee C$$
$$S = (\sim A \wedge \sim B \wedge C) \vee (\sim A \wedge B \wedge \sim C) \vee (A \wedge \sim B \wedge \sim C)$$
$$\vee (A \wedge B \wedge C)$$

7. The chapter mentions that many machines (or devices) exist in our everyday lives about which the user actually knows very little. Other than the automobile and the kitchen can opener, try to name 12 others.

SELECTED READINGS

Abrams, M. D., and P. G. Stein, *Computer Hardware and Software: An Interdisciplinary Introduction*, Addison-Wesley, Reading, Mass., 1973.

Awad, E. M., *Business Data Processing* (3d ed.), Prentice-Hall, Englewood Cliffs, N.J., 1971.

Crowley, T. H., *Understanding Computers*, McGraw-Hill, New York, 1967.

Davis, G. B., *Introduction to Electronic Computers* (2d ed.), McGraw-Hill, New York, 1971.

7

COMPUTER SYSTEMS ARCHITECTURE

7.1 INTRODUCTION

A *system* is commonly regarded as a set of components with a relationship between the components. The relationship can be a physical connection, a logical similarity, a causal rule, or any one of a large number of related entities. Moreover, all systems possess a structure, and operational rules govern how the system responds to input conditions.

A computer is a system that is controlled by a program. The operation of a computer system is deterministic in the sense that the dynamic behavior of the system in response to input conditions can be predicted, and each component of the system performs a well-defined function. The components of a computer system communicate through the transfer of control information and data.

A schematic of a computer system is given in Figure 7.1. The following components (or units, as they are usually called) are shown:

Main storage
Central processing unit
Data channels
Input/output control units and devices

Main storage and the central processing unit have been mentioned previously; they are covered in more detail in this chapter.

The *central processing unit* is composed of a control unit and an arithmetic/logic unit. The *control unit* maintains the current program address,* fetches instructions from main storage, decodes the instruc-

---

* The current program address is the location in main storage of the next instruction; normally, the program address is stored in a current address register.

149

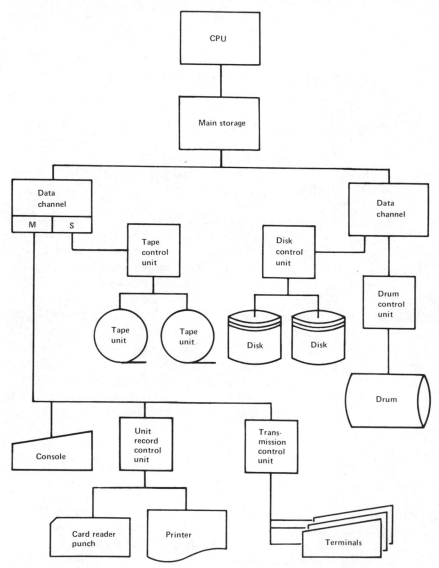

Figure 7.1   Schematic of a typical computer system.

tions, and sends control signals to the arithmetic/logic unit to have the instructions executed. The *arithmetic/logic unit* contains the arithmetic registers and electronic circuitry for executing computer instructions. The central processing unit provides a variety of other control functions that are covered later.

Modern computers use the stored program concept, which means that both computer instructions and data are available to the central processing unit at electronic speeds from a component referred to as *main storage*, as mentioned in previous chapters. Main storage is not used for the permanent storage of programs and data, and a program is placed in main storage only when it is being executed. Usually, computer instructions and constant data values are placed in main storage by a loader program. Program data are read into main storage with input instructions; data are recorded on a storage medium, such as magnetic tape or punched cards, with output instructions. Main storage is organized and used in a variety of ways, as discussed later in this chapter.

The schematic of a typical computer system given in Figure 7.1 is a static representation of the structure of a computer. Figure 7.2 gives a description of a computer system that is more functionally oriented. It is referred to in subsequent paragraphs.

The central processing unit and main storage are electronic devices. Input and output devices are both electronic and mechanical, and since electronic devices are inherently faster than mechanical devices, the central processing unit is faster than input and output devices. For example, it takes approximately 100 milliseconds for a card reader to read one punched card. In that time, an average computer can execute approximately 50,000 instructions. Therefore, the central processing unit, which is an expensive component, should not be kept waiting for input and output. This is where the data channel comes in. A *data channel* is essentially a small, hard-wired computer connected to main storage; it receives control from the central processing unit. The central processing unit, under control of a computer program, tells a data channel to transfer data between main storage and an external device (and also gives the amount and location of the data). Then while the central processing unit continues to operate, the data channel signals to the input/output device and manages the data-transfer operation concurrently. A read operation is taken as an example. The data channel accepts information from an input device (perhaps a card reader) one character at a time at a relatively low speed. The characters are put into

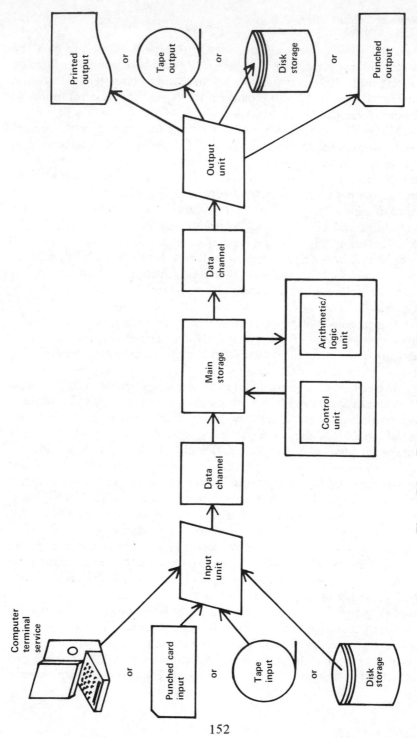

Figure 7.2 Functional representation of a computer system.

152

a buffer.* When enough characters are accumulated, the operation of the central processing unit is interrupted and the information is placed in main storage by the data channel. The central processing unit and data channels are designed to operate concurrently and this fact contributes to the input/output and computer overlap that exists with most computer systems. The effective use of data channels is directly related to computer system efficiency. This topic is also covered later in this chapter.

An input/output *control unit* monitors and controls the operation of one or more input/output devices. The input/output control unit manages the data flow to and from an input/output device and performs other non-data-transfer operations such as a tape rewind or a disk seek (covered later).

An *input/output device* serves to transfer data between the computer and the external world. Input/output devices can be grouped into four classes: (1) unit record devices, (2) serial devices, (3) direct-access devices, and (4) miscellaneous devices. *Unit record devices* include the card reader, the line printer, and the card punch; a "block" of information transmitted between main storage and the device normally corresponds to a physical unit, such as a card or a line. *Serial devices* include magnetic tape and paper tape; these devices are characterized by the fact that information is stored serially and that access to the ith block requires that the unit pass over the $(i - 1)$st block. *Direct-access devices* include disk storage and drum storage; these devices, frequently referred to as rotating devices, are characterized by the fact that a block of information can be located directly, on the medium, prior to an input or output operation. *Miscellaneous devices* include data terminals, cathode-ray-tube (CRT) devices, audio-response units, and so on. Each device has characteristics of its own. The *terminal device* is frequently used in programming and has the general characteristics of a unit record device. More specifically, a terminal is a keyboard-driven unit used to transmit information between a computer and the terminal unit via telecommunications facilities. Input and output devices and their respective storage media are considered in the next chapter.

In a given installation, two or more computers can be used collectively to increase performance, reliability, and work throughput. The computers may be connected physically (which includes electronic connections) or may exchange information via input/output storage media. Operational environments that contain more than one computer are referred to as *multiple computer systems*.

* A *buffer* is a storage area or register used to compensate for the difference in the speed of two devices.

7.2 CENTRAL PROCESSING UNIT

The central processing unit controls the operation of the entire computer system by fetching instructions from main storage, decoding them, and setting up control signals to have the instructions executed. The central processing unit processes *all* instructions and initiates all input and output operations. This section covers the functional organization that permits the central processing unit to control the operation of the computer system in a complex operating environment. The material presented here is representative of the many computers in existence today. Computer organization is an area of study in its own right; this section provides an introduction to the topic.

Registers and Addressing

The most obvious differences between the central processing units of various computer systems are the arithmetic registers and the instruction repertoires. As far as registers are concerned, two design philosophies are generally used: (1) a single accumulator and an extension to it along with special registers called *index registers*, for use during addressing; and (2) several floating-point and fixed-point registers, of which the fixed-point registers can be used for addressing and for fixed-point arithmetic. Obviously, many variations to these techniques exist. Another method does not involve the use of addressable registers and requires that all computer operations operate from storage to storage. Since most arithmetic/logic operations require two operands, two main storage fetches and one store are required for each instruction executed. Moreover, each instruction must contain at least two address fields. This method is generally classed as being inefficient, except when "variable length" data items are concerned, and is not discussed further in this chapter.

When a single accumulator and index register are included in the design of the central processing unit, then the accumulator is used for both fixed-point and floating-point arithmetic operations. The computer instruction format includes fields for an operation code, an address field, and an index register specification, depicted as follows:*

Operation Code	Index Register	Address Field

---

* The index register in the given format serves as the modifier field of an instruction, as discussed earlier.

The number of index registers in specific computers usually varies between 1 and 16, although computers with as many as 99 index registers have existed in the computer marketplace.

Index registers are used to "effectively modify" the address field without actually changing it. The following LOAD instruction is used as an example of how the method operates:

| LOAD | 2 | 5678 |

(Remember, a single accumulator is used and all loads, stores, and arithmetic/logic operations use it.) The instruction is fetched and decoded by the control unit of the central processing unit. The instruction involves a reference to main storage. The contents of index register 2 are added to the address field of the instruction to form what is called an effective address. The location in main storage specified by the effective address is the location that is referenced. As an example of how an index register would be used, assume a one-dimensional array A placed in main storage beginning with location 4000 (in decimal for simplicity). Suppose that it were desired to reference the ith element of A, where I is located at main storage address 6371. Computer instructions to load $A(I)$ into the accumulator might exist as follows:*

Assembler Language (Symbolic operands)		Assembler Language (Numeric operands)	
LDX	2,I	LDX	2,6371
L	A-1,2	L	3999,2

Thus, if I contained the value one, then A(1) located at address 4000 would be referenced; if I contained the value 2, then A(2) located at address 4001 would be referenced; and so forth. The process of effective addressing, using index registers and a single accumulator is depicted in Figure 7.3. Computer instructions that allow the contents of the index registers to be manipulated are included in the instruction repertoire of computers that use index registers.

Computers with multiple fixed- and floating-point registers use base/index/displacement addressing of main storage that is organized on a byte basis. The range of addresses is high in computers of this type and a lengthy address field would ordinarily be required. Therefore, a base register is used that effectively points to a segment of a program, so

* The LDX instruction is used to load the specified index register, and the L instruction is the conventional load instruction.

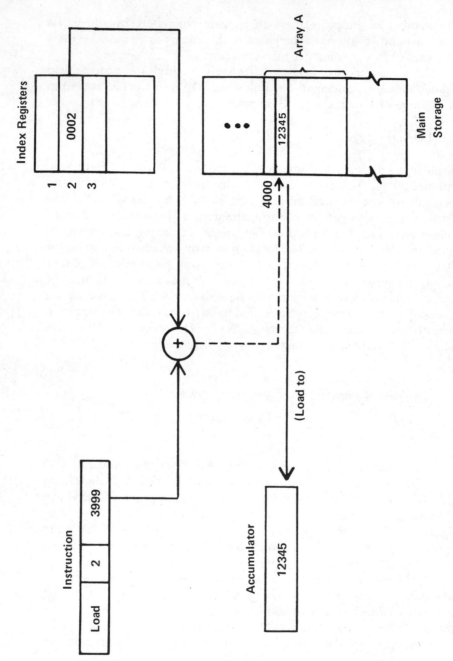

Figure 7.3 Effective addressing using a single accumulator and index registers.

that only a displacement is needed in the computer instruction. A typical instruction format for an operating environment such as this is given as follows:

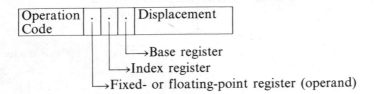

An effective address is computed by adding the contents of the base and index registers and the displacement field, as depicted in Figure 7.4. One of the advantages of base/index/displacement addressing is that the size of main storage is not limited by the length of the displacement field.

Operating Control

In previous chapters, it was mentioned that the location in main storage of the next instruction to be executed is contained in a current address register and when the control unit of the central processing unit is ready for the next instruction, it uses the current address register to determine its location. (The current address register usually is not addressed directly by a computer program.) This is only part of the story. There are other indicators besides the current program address that determine the current state of the computer system. Some of the most frequently encountered state indicators are a storage key used for referencing main storage (covered later), mask bits that determine the kinds of events that can take place in the system, and a condition code that is set as the result of a comparison operation. Collectively, these state indicators, along with the current address, are contained in a word termed the *status word*. At any point, the state of the computer system is reflected in the status word and changing the contents of the status word is tantamount to altering the state of the computer.

Supervisor and Problem States

When introducing the data channel earlier in this chapter, the difference in the relative speeds of the central processing unit and input/output devices was mentioned. Although the use of a data channel alleviated the situation somewhat, delays of the central processing unit are inevitable. Modern computer systems are designed to accommodate several programs, for an equal number of users, in main storage at one time. When one program experiences an unavoidable delay, control of

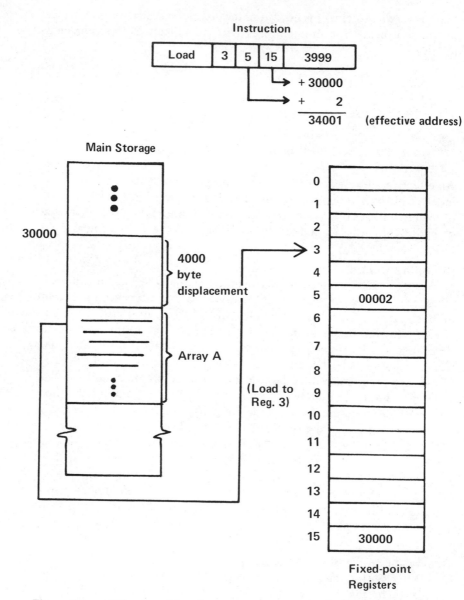

Figure 7.4   Effective addressing using the base/index/displacement method.

the central processing unit is given to another program. The technique is referred to as *multiprogramming* and is intended to keep the costly central processing unit busy. A set of programs that manages the resources of the computer system is referred to as an *operating system*.

Because several programs can share main storage and mass storage media, it is necessary that the various users be protected from each other by limiting the functions they can perform. Two states of the central processing unit are defined in most modern computer systems: the supervisor state and the problem state. A program operating in the *supervisor state* has access to all of the facilities of the computer system, including the ability to reference all of main storage, to change the status word, and to perform input and output operations. Operating system programs normally operate in the supervisor state. A program operating in the *problem state* is limited in the sense that it can execute only instructions that cannot affect other programs. Instructions that can be executed in the problem state (and also in the supervisor state) are referred to as "nonprivileged instructions." Typical nonprivileged instructions are the arithmetic/logic instructions, the branching and control instructions, and shifting, comparison, and character manipulation instructions. Instructions that can be executed only in the supervisor state are referred to as "privileged instructions." Instructions that perform input and output functions, modify the status word, and deal with storage protection (covered later) are classed as privileged instructions.

It would seem that a program being executed is dependent upon the operating system for critical operations, such as input and output. This is true. When a program executing in the problem state needs to have an input or output operation performed, it makes an appropriate request to the operating system to have that function performed. Thus, the operating system is able to manage critical resources on a system-wide basis. The operating system, which performs other functions such as job-to-job scheduling and storage allocation, is a topic in its own right and is covered in Part III of the book.

In an operating system environment, user programs, such as a payroll program or a program that performs some mathematical calculations, operate in the problem state. The central processing unit enters the problem state when an appropriate bit is set in the status word. That bit can be set only when the central processing unit is in the supervisor state. When an operating system program executing in the supervisor state decides to give control of the computer to a user program, it loads a new status word with the problem-state bit set and the current instruction address field, also in the status word, set to the address in main storage of the user program. The new status word immediately changes the state of the central processing unit to the problem state and execution continues with the specified address in the user program. There are, of course, other methods of implementing operational control in a computer system, and the above technique is a typical representation. Other terms that are frequently associated with operational control are "monitor mode" and "master and slave modes."

External Events

The use of a data channel to permit the overlap of processing and input/output activity was mentioned earlier. The central processing unit sends information to the data channel on what input or output it needs to have performed and then continues with normal processing. The data channel subsequently performs the requested input or output operation simultaneously. The situation is analogous to a supervisor instructing one of his workers to perform a certain task. After the instructions are received, both employees go about their respective duties. When the worker is finished with his task, he interrupts his supervisor for further instructions. The data channel operates in a similar manner. When an input or an output operation is complete, it interrupts the execution of the central processing unit. In a computer system, an independent event that interrupts normal computer processing is called an *interruption*. An interruption can occur for one of many reasons, such as: (1) The computer detects an erroneous condition in an executing program; (2) a component external to the computer (such as a data channel) requires attention or signals completion; (3) the error correction circuitry of the computer detects a hardware error; and (4) a program executing in the problem state requires services that can be performed only in the supervisor state and executes an instruction that causes an interruption to be initiated.

Computers are designed and built to recognize a fixed number of different kinds of interruptions. The actual number varies depending upon the primary market for the computer and ranges from as low as five to as high as 99. One method of handling interruptions is described here. Associated with each type of interruption are two fixed locations in main storage. Each of these locations is designed to hold a replica of the status word. One of the fixed locations is referred to as the "old status word" and the other is referred to as the "new status word." When an interruption occurs, the "current status word," maintained in the central processing unit on a dynamic basis as a program is executed, is stored in the old status word location and the status word located at the new status word location replaces the current status word in the central processing unit. The process of swapping status words is depicted in Figure 7.5. The current address field of the new status word contains the address of the first instruction in a routine designed to process that type of interruption and the supervisor-state bit is usually set. Interruptions are normally processed in the supervisor state and the central processing unit continues processing in the interruption handling routine. The old status word reflects the state of the central processing unit when the interruption occurred, so that execution of that program can be resumed when the interruption processing has been completed.

Computer Instructions

Another major difference between computers lies in the instruction repertoire, or, put in a slightly different manner, the basic operations the computer is designed to execute. The instruction repertoire of large general-purpose computers is extensive and can be justified by the fact that the computer is used for a wide range of applications. Small and medium-sized computers have more restricted instruction repertoires and many operations performed with one instruction in a large computer require two or three instructions in a smaller computer. Computer instructions can be grouped into five convenient classes that seem to be invariant among computers. They are described in the following list:

1. *Arithmetic instructions* include the fixed-point and floating-point operations used for performing arithmetic on a digital computer.

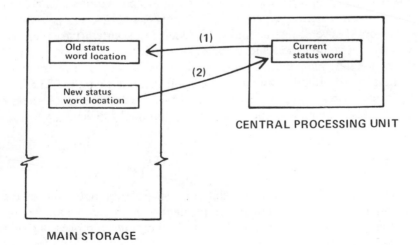

Figure 7.5   The swapping of status words after an interruption.

Also included in this category are instructions for making arithmetic comparisons and for converting values from one number base to another.

2. *Logical instructions* perform operations on bytes and bits that include data movement, logical comparisons, testing, and data editing.

3. *Branching instructions* provide the capability for altering the sequential flow of program execution on either a conditional or an unconditional basis. Branching instructions frequently operate in conjunction with index or general-purpose registers so that each time a branch is made, a counter is incremented or decremented until a specified condition is reached.

4. *Input and output instructions* initiate input or output operations by passing appropriate commands to data channels and allow the status of specific devices to be tested. Input and output instructions are normally implemented as privileged instructions.

5. *Status switching instructions* permit the status word and storage keys (see next section on "storage") to be loaded and stored under program control. Instructions in this category are also privileged and effectively change the status of the computer system.

Most general-purpose computers have a basic set of instructions that allow most computational processes to be programmed. Since most programs are written in a higher-level language, the instruction repertoire is usually not of concern to most users of the computer. An area in which the instruction repertoire is of concern, however, is that of efficiency. If several instructions are needed to execute a basic computational operation, then the actual execution time of a program is proportionately high. On the other hand, an extensive set of instructions requires more circuitry and is more sophisticated to build. The end result, of course, is that the choice of a particular computer is a trade-off of cost, basic computing speed, and computational efficiency.

7.3 MAIN STORAGE

Although the central processing unit controls the operation of the computer, the organization and implementation of main storage implicitly determines the manner in which the central processing unit functions.

When discussing main storage, two characteristics are of prime importance:

1. The physical technique (or device) used to implement main storage
2. The physical arrangement of the storage elements that constitute main storage

These characteristics determine how main storage is organized and addressed, and how it can be accessed. The objective of main storage must again be stated. It should be directly addressable by and must operate at speeds approaching that of the central processing unit.

Organization, Addressing, and Access Width

The manner in which main storage is organized determines how it is accessed. The process of accessing main storage by the central processing unit* is performed as follows:

1. Place the address of the desired data item in a *memory address register*.
2. Initiate a "fetch" operation.
3. Main storage is accessed and the desired data item is placed in a *memory data register* for reference by the central processing unit.

How much data are placed in the memory data register? With a word-oriented computer, the addressed word from main storage is placed in the memory data register. With byte-oriented computers, the concept of an "access width" is used. *Access width* refers to the amount of data that is transferred between main storage and the central processing unit with each access. In small byte-oriented computers, the access width can be as small as one or two bytes, while in large byte-oriented computers, the access width can be as high as 16 bytes. Access width is significant for the following reason. Suppose an instruction using 8-byte operands is executed. Execution of the instruction on a large computer would require one storage reference, whereas on a small computer, execution of the instruction might require as many as four references. Therefore, even if the basic speeds of the central processing units are the same, main storage determines how quickly the instruction can be executed.

The significance of access width is also related to whether main storage is implemented by using circuitry or whether a physical medium such as magnetic cores is used. There are a variety of physical processes available for implementing main storage, such as magnetic cores, thin film, or plated wire. Magnetic cores are assumed in the following

---

* Actually, any component that accesses main storage would perform the same steps.

section; in fact, main storage is frequently referred to as *core storage*. Any good book on computer design covers the various recording media.

Access Time

When magnetic cores are used as the storage technology, access time is determined by the storage cycle time that involves a read-out and a write-back, as discussed in Chapter 5. The write-back is required to reset the cores because of the read-out process, which sets the cores to zero. The process of read-out and write-back is depicted in Figure 7.6. At time t_i, the central processing unit sends a signal to the main storage unit to initiate a storage cycle. At time t_{i+1}, the information is available to the central processing unit and processing may continue as outlined below. The time from t_i to t_{i+1} is referred to as *access time*. The write-back half cycle extends from t_{i+i} to t_{i+2}; during that time, the main storage unit is busy and another access cannot be made.

When main storage is implemented using electronic circuitry, then the read-out and write-back half cycles do not apply and a full storage cycle consists only of access time. Obviously, electronic circuitry is the preferred method of implementing main storage from a performance point of view. Although modern manufacturing methods permit the

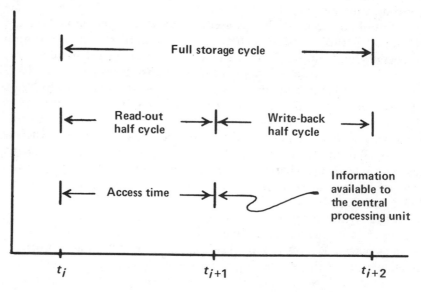

Figure 7.6   Main storage access time.

fabrication of solid state chips that contain several circuits, electronic circuitry is more expensive than magnetic core technology. As a result, computer designers use other techniques to reduce the effective cost of main storage.

All computers operate in cycles determined by an electronic clock that emits electronic pulses at a very high rate. When the central processing unit and main storage operate in tandem with each other in real time, the system is operating in the *synchronous mode*. In this mode, the central processing unit does not continue execution until a storage cycle is complete, so that each storage cycle is synchronized with a central processing unit execution cycle and the entire system operates at the speed of the slowest unit. When one unit requires more than one cycle (e.g., when the access width is smaller than the operand size), then the other unit is forced to wait. In the *asynchronous mode* of operation, the central processing unit and main storage are uncoupled so that each may operate independently of the other. This technique allows the operation of the central processing unit and main storage to overlap so that instruction execution may proceed as soon as the required data is received and so that instructions and data may be prefetched from main storage.

Main Storage Interleaving

One of the methods used to reduce the effective storage cycle time is to employ a technique called "interleaving." The storage cycle time comprised of read-out and write-back half cycles applies to a single storage unit; when multiple storage units are designed into a computer system, they can be accessed in parallel.

Assume that main storage is designed as two independent units —called two-way interleaving. Suppose further that odd-numbered addresses are in the first unit and even-numbered addresses are in the second unit. If sequential main storage locations are accessed, then read-out half cycles can be overlapped with write-back half cycles, as depicted in Figure 7.7. This technique effectively eliminates the write-back half cycle, so that the effective cycle time for main storage that is two-way interleaved approaches half its value if storage we~e not interleaved. Ultra-high-speed computers employ as high as 16-way interleaving with access widths of up to 128 bytes.

Large Capacity Storage

A method used to balance the cost and performance of main storage is to employ a form of bulk storage known as *large capacity storage*, which is also called *large core storage* because magnetic cores are used;

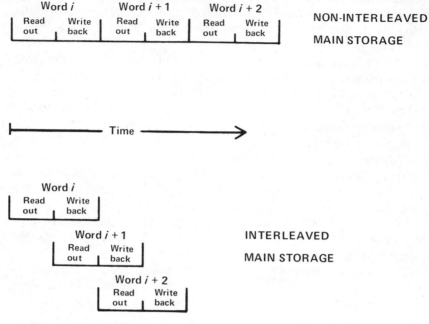

Figure 7.7   Access to noninterleaved and interleaved main storage.

the acronym for both is LCS. LCS is less expensive than main storage and has a slower cycle time. Thus, main storage and LCS form a storage hierarchy in which frequently referenced instructions and data items are placed in main storage and infrequently used information is placed in LCS. Large capacity storage can be used regardless of the technology used for implementing main storage.

Large capacity storage may be a directly addressable extension to main storage or it may be implemented through a specially designed set of instructions that transfer a specified quantity of data between the two units. In the former case, instructions can be executed directly from LCS and data can be accessed from it by an executing program. It is evident that when executing instructions out of LCS or using data that is stored there, the central processing unit is operating in a degraded state as compared to the case where the same information is held in main storage. In some cases, it is efficient to transfer information from LCS to main storage before it is used. In other cases, the overhead involved is not justified and storage references are made to LCS directly.

7.4 DATA CHANNELS

The data channel, which is essentially a small, hard-wired computer, is used to compensate for the difference in speeds between electro-mechanical input and output devices and the purely electronic operation of the central processing unit and main storage. In addition, modern operating techniques, such as multiprogramming and time sharing, require asynchronous input and output operations and device independence. These facilities are provided through the use of a data channel.

As far as the functioning of the entire computer system is concerned, the input and output facility is a critical resource in the sense that input and output are needed to justify the use of a computer* and because a single program can monopolize the entire input/output system if it is not constructed properly. Moreover, incorrectly written input/output procedures can affect the execution of other programs in multiprogramming and time-sharing environments. In modern computers, therefore, input and output instructions are permitted as privileged instructions that can be executed only in the supervisor state. When a program executing in the problem state needs to have an input or output operation performed, it requests that service from an input/output control system that manages *all* input and output on a system-wide basis. In addition to assuring the integrity of individual programs, one of the primary functions of the input/output control system is to schedule input and output operations so as to keep as many units busy at one time as possible.

Channel Operation and Organization

In order to satisfy the above needs, a data channel must be designed to operate independently of other data channels and the central processing unit. It uses a channel program, composed of channel commands, placed in main storage in the same manner that the central processing unit uses a computer program composed of instructions. Typical channel commands are read, write, control, sense, and transfer in channel. These commands are covered later.

An input/output operation is initiated in the central processing unit by a privileged instruction that specifies the channel and device

---

* In other words, a computer is of very little value without provisions for entering information into the system and retrieving information and computed results, when needed, from the system.

addresses on which the operation is to take place. The address in main storage of the channel program is also provided to the channel at this time. If the channel and device are free, then the central processing unit continues with the next instruction and the data channel takes charge of the input/output operation. This is how the frequently mentioned compute and input/output overlap is achieved in the computer.

The format of a typical channel command is given in Figure 7.8. The *command code* field specifies the input/output operation to be performed. The *data address* field specifies the beginning address in main storage of data to be written out or in the case of a read operation, the beginning address of where the data are to be placed. The *count* field specifies how many bytes (or words) are to be transferred between main storage and the input/output medium during the operation. The *flags* field specifies a variety of things, such as: (1) whether the channel program is continued; (2) whether an interruption should be generated when the operation is complete; (3) whether the data should be skipped (i.e., read from the input/output medium but not placed in main storage); and (4) whether a data record should be "split" between two or more areas in main storage.

The data channel operates like a "data manager"; it decodes channel commands and sends orders to input/output control units and devices. For a *read operation*, the data channel accepts data from the control unit and accumulates them in a buffer within the channel. When the buffer is full, the central processing unit is interrupted and the accumulated data is placed in main storage. For a *write operation*, the data channel fetches a "buffer's worth" of data from main storage and feeds it to the control unit on a byte (or character) basis. Data channel organization is conceptualized in Figure 7.9, in which two concepts are depicted: the standard input/output interface and the access width. The *standard input/output interface* refers to the amount of data that can pass at any point in time between a data channel and a device attached to it. Usually all devices attached to the computer system adhere to the standard input/output interface, permitting a wide range of different devices to be utilized. Most modern computer systems use a standard input/output interface of one byte (or character). The *access width*,

Command code	Data address	Flags	Count

Figure 7.8   Typical channel command format.

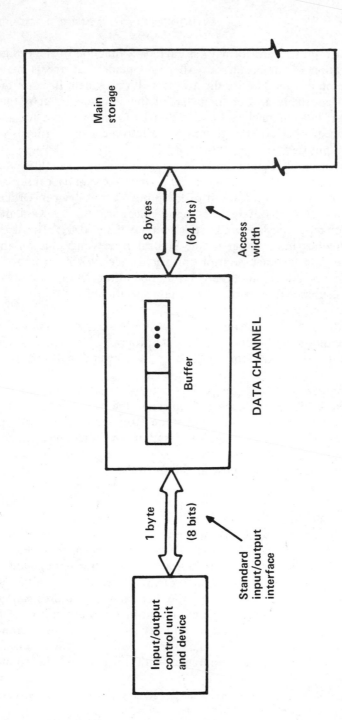

Figure 7.9   Data channel organization. (Access width typically varies from 2 to 128 bytes and is dependent upon the design and organization of main storage.)

169

covered earlier with regard to main storage, is a function of the design and organization of main storage. All components that access main storage must be designed to use the access width provided. Because the access width is usually greater than that of the standard input/output interface, the data channel includes a buffer to compensate for the electronic speeds of main storage and the electromechanical speeds of input and output devices.

Two other input/output operations are typically available in a computer system: control and sense. The *control operation* causes an order to be sent to the control unit of the input/output devices. Orders mean different things to different devices. Typical orders are rewind and backspace for magnetic tape and "seek" for magnetic disk.* The *sense operation* provides information to the central processing unit on the status of the data channel, control unit, or device. When an unusual condition occurs during an input/output operation, the central processing unit can issue a sense order to obtain specific information on the cause of the condition.

The final channel command is *transfer in channel*, which is used to cause an unconditional branch in a channel program; it is analogous to the unconditional branch (or GOTO) in a conventional computer program.

It is obvious from the preceding discussion that a data channel actually operates like a small computer through the process of decoding and executing channel commands. In some large-scale scientific computer systems (i.e., number crunchers, as they are sometimes called), small programmable computers—termed satellite computers—have been used to achieve the same purpose as the data channel.

Channel Design

Normally, several data channels and the central processing unit compete for access to main storage. Therefore, when a data channel gains access to main storage, it is desirable to transfer enough information to make the effort worthwhile. (This fact relates to the access width mentioned earlier.) As a result, the data channel requires storage facilities for each input/output operation that includes a count, a main storage address, the main storage address of the current channel command, control and status data, and a buffer for incoming or outgoing data. This storage combined with logical and functional

---

* A "seek" for magnetic disk storage refers to the process of moving the access arms to the desired position prior to reading or writing a data record.

facilities constitutes a data channel and is a substantial investment in physical equipment.

The speed* of input/output devices varies from 10 bytes per second (BPS), in the case of a low-speed data communications terminal, to 3 million BPS, in the case of a high-speed disk storage device. In order to justify the cost of a data channel economically, it is necessary to share data channel facilities for low-speed devices. The reason is obvious. For high-speed devices, the logical and functional facilities are fully utilized, whereas with low-speed devices, the same facilities are idle for a good portion of time.

The data channel facilities that are necessary to sustain an input/output operation are referred to as a *subchannel*. Logical circuitry of the data channel is shared among the subchannels; storage areas are used to record the state of an input/output operation and are not shared. The manner in which subchannels are implemented is used to distinguish between three types of data channels: the selector channel, the byte-multiplexer channel, and the block-multiplexer channel.

The *selector channel* is used with high-speed input/output devices, such as magnetic disk or drum, that provide high data-transfer rates that exceed 300,000 bytes per second.† The selector channel includes one subchannel and can manage only one data-transfer operation at a time. Once a logical connection is made between an input/output device and the selector channel, the channel is regarded as being "busy" until the input/output operation is complete.

The *byte-multiplexer channel* is used for controlling several low-speed devices that do not justify the exclusive use of a data channel because of the low speeds involved. (The key point is that a data channel can sustain a given data rate from one fast device or several slow devices.) A byte-multiplexer channel contains several subchannels and can sustain an input/output operation on each of its subchannels concurrently. A device remains connected to a subchannel for the duration of an input/output operation but uses only the logical and functional facilities of the data channel during the transfer of a single byte of information. In reality, therefore, the data channel services one subchannel, then another subchannel, on a "multiplexed" basis.

The *block-multiplexer channel* combines the concepts of the selector and byte-multiplexer channels. Here, a block refers to a complete data record. The block-multiplexer channel is shared by several high-speed devices in the same manner that a byte-multiplexer channel is shared by

---

* The term *data rate* also would be appropriate here.
† The data rates given here are nominal values intended to serve as examples.

several low-speed devices—except that blocks are multiplexed rather than bytes. The logical and functional facilities of a block-multiplexer channel are freed during non-data-transfer operations, such as a disk seek, for use by another subchannel.

Input/Output Completion and Interruption

The central processing unit and data channels operate asynchronously; the central processing unit initiates an input/output operation in the data channel, and from then on the units function independently of each other. The central processing unit is in control—much like the traditional supervisor-employee relationship. In fact, the central processing unit can halt an input/output operation in most computers through an instruction designed for that purpose.

Normally, however, the data channel operates until it has completed an input/output operation and then "informs" the central processing unit that it is finished. The central processing unit is informed of the completion of an input/output operation through an input/output interruption, one of the types mentioned earlier.

An input/output interruption can result from a variety of conditions that might arise in the input/output system. Therefore, a *channel status word* is stored when an input/output interruption occurs. (The exact details of how and where the channel status word is stored are dependent upon a particular computer.) A partial list of the information that is normally found in the stored channel status word is as follows:

1. Storage protection key of the areas of main storage that are involved in the data transfer operation
2. The address of the last channel command
3. Status bits
4. A residual count from the input/output operation

The status bits are of prime importance because they indicate the condition that initiated the interruption that caused the channel status word to be stored. The set of possible conditions varies among computers but usually includes error conditions, busy indicators, exceptional conditions, and channel and device end conditions. The completion of a data-transfer operation is indicated by two conditions: channel end and device end. The *channel end* condition denotes that the data-transfer portion of the operation is complete and data channel facilities are no longer required. The *device end* condition indicates that the operation has been completed at the input/output device. A control operation (such as a tape rewind) that does not require the use of an input/output channel causes the data channel to signal channel end as soon as the order is sent to the device; later, when the control operation is complete, a device end condition is generated.

Comment

In most (if not all) computer systems, the data channel is a logical extension to the central processing unit and main storage and is independent of input and output devices attached to the system. In large-scale computing systems, data channels are designed as separate components. In many small-scale systems, the data channels are integrated into the central processing unit.

7.5 MULTIPLE COMPUTER SYSTEMS

The manner in which a computer system is organized and used determines to a large extent how effective the computer system is as a computing resource. The situation is more a matter of functional organization than it is of physical structure. If a task is assigned to a high-cost (and in most cases, a high-performance) component that could be performed equally well by a lower-cost component, then the effectiveness of the system could be improved by functional reorganization within realistic limits. The concept could be viewed as the "systems approach" to computer utilization because the objective is to maximize the performance of the entire system.

One method of increasing computer performance is to add another computer to the total system configuration. The additional computer is usually a small computer to which routine tasks are assigned. In other types of multiple-computer systems, only a central processing unit is added and main storage is shared between the computers involved.

Peripheral Computers

A *peripheral computer*, in its traditional form, is used to replace low-speed input/output devices, such as a card reader and line printer, with a higher-speed device, such as magnetic tape. The peripheral computer is a relatively small system used to read input cards and place them on magnetic tape and also to read print lines placed on magnetic tape and print them on its line printer. Thus, input to the main computer is magnetic tape and printed output is also placed on magnetic tape for subsequent printing.

This method is justified because a nominal figure for the input rate of punched cards is between 300 and 1200 80-column cards per minute, which amounts to 1600 characters per second or less. Printed output ranges from 1000 to 2400 120-character lines per minute, which amounts to 4800 characters per second or less. An average figure for magnetic tape input and output is in the neighborhood of 100,000 characters per second.

Peripheral computers are still used but the technique of input and output buffering with the data channel has decreased their need in recent years.

Satellite Computers

A *satellite computer* is a small programmable computer attached to the main computer. Each satellite computer is used to manage input/output operations and perform data editing for a given set of devices. Normally, several satellite computers are employed when this technique is used.

Satellite computers are similar in concept to the data channel; they normally include features for interrupting the main computer and for sharing portions of main storage. In fact, satellite computers substitute for data channels in some computer systems.

Attached Support Processors

An *attached support processor* (see Figure 7.10) is a computer system that is attached to the main computer via a channel-to-channel adapter or with shared main storage. Usually, when the channel-to-channel adapter is used, the attached computer performs input/output and editing for the main computer. The low-speed input and output devices of the main computer are replaced by the adapter connection, so that data can be transferred between the systems at electronic speeds. The attached support computer performs low-speed input and stacks the information on a direct-access storage device, in anticipation of a request from the main computer for input data. Similarly, output lines received by the attached support computer from the main computer are stacked up on a direct-access device for subsequent printing or punching. The attached support computer serves as a buffering system for the main computer and is not normally used for the processing of user programs.

Multiprocessing Systems

A computer system that includes more than one central processing unit is referred to as a *multiprocessing system*. The concept of multiprocessing is employed to increase either the reliability or the performance of the system. As depicted in Figure 7.11, the central processing units in a multiprocessing system share main storage and so they can service the same set of jobs.

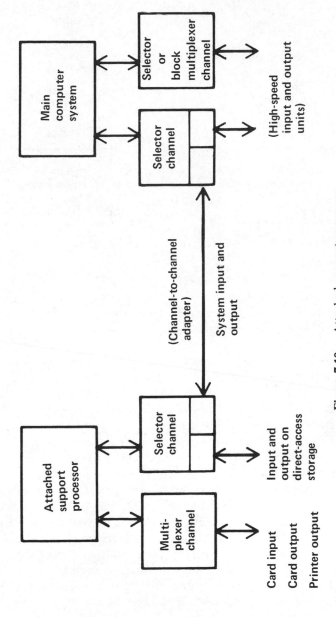

Figure 7.10 Attached support processor.

175

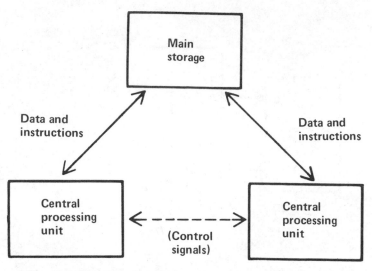

Figure 7.11   Conceptual view of a multiprocessing system.

When multiprocessing is used to improve system performance, the central processing units operate asynchronously and effectively share the work load. In many operating environments, such as an airline reservation system, response is critical. In fact, the success or failure of an enterprise may be dependent upon a computer. In cases such as this, an extra central processing unit is available to take over in the event of malfunction in the primary central processing unit. Thus, both central processing units must have access to the same information (main storage, direct-access storage, magnetic tape units, etc.) and must be able to exchange control signals when one central processing unit fails.

Modern computer systems contain circuitry for error checking and correction. When the hardware detects an instruction error or a parity error (when transferring information from one part of the computer to another), it attempts to correct the error condition through sophisticated logical procedures. When an error condition cannot be corrected, a malfunction is signaled. Sometimes, an error occurs in a bank of main storage or in an input/output or mass storage device. If possible in these cases, the failing component is logically disconnected from the system, under program control, and operation continues in a degraded state. The key point, obviously, is that in many applications, it is preferable to operate in a degraded state than to fail completely.

QUESTION SET

1. Describe the relationship between the supervisor state, the data channel, and the interruption.
2. Draw a flow diagram of the processes involved in performing an input/output operation.
3. Describe how interleaving and access width contribute to access time.
4. In what way do access width and the standard interface contribute to the need for a data channel?
5. Give the similarities and differences between the block-multiplexer channel and the byte-multiplexer channel.
6. Describe techniques that are used for minimizing the input/output bottleneck.

SELECTED READINGS

Gear, C. W., *Computer Organization and Programming*, McGraw-Hill, New York, 1969.

Katzan, H., *Computer Organization and the System/370*, Van Nostrand-Reinhold, New York, 1971.

Stone, H. S., *Introduction to Computer Organization and Data Structures*, McGraw-Hill, New York, 1972.

8

INPUT AND OUTPUT

8.1 INTRODUCTION

Almost anyone who has registered at a college, paid a telephone bill, or made a purchase at a large department store has dealt with computer media of some kind. The problem, of course, involves entering recorded information into the computer, and that is where input devices come into the picture. Output devices reverse the process. Because main storage is limited in size, data are also placed on mass storage devices when not being used. Magnetic tape and direct-access storage (such as magnetic disk) are used for this purpose. In general, the process of reading data into main storage is referred to as input, regardless of whether it is from a mass storage device or it involves manual preparation. Similarly, the process of writing data from main storage to an external device is referred to as output, again regardless of whether the device is for mass storage or for human use.

It is important to distinguish between the medium and the device used to read or write it. For example, a punched card is a medium for recording information; a card reader or a card punch is a device.

Four media and associated devices are presented in detail: punched cards, magnetic tape, magnetic disk, and the line printer. A variety of other devices are covered briefly to acquaint the reader with current thinking with regard to input and output devices. Telecommunications facilities are widely used these days and much of the concern over large data banks is related to the manner in which they can be accessed via ordinary telephone lines and a terminal device. Telecommunications and terminal devices are also covered in this chapter.

8.2 INPUT AND OUTPUT ORGANIZATION

Figure 8.1 depicts a simplified input/output subsystem, including input/output control units and devices. An input/output control unit is designed to control the operation of one or more devices of a given class. Typical input/output control units are magnetic tape control units, disk control units, and unit record control units. Normally, input/output devices share control units, since all devices are not being used at a particular point in time.

An input/output device operates as a "slave" to its control unit; the control unit sends an order to the device to perform an elementary operation, such as read, write, rewind, or seek, and the device routinely performs the requested operation. If a device happens to be busy when an order is received, it returns a busy indication (i.e., a flag) to the control unit. The control unit can then save the requested operation for subsequent execution or it can return a busy signal to the data channel. An input/output control unit is frequently integrated into the device itself; in addition, an input/output control unit and a set of devices are sometimes housed in the same cabinet and one often hears of a "disk system" or a "tape system." In general, however, the concept of control units and devices holds true, regardless of the engineering design employed.

Classification of External Storage Media

External storage media and devices are classified by whether they use unit records or volumes. When the external storage medium takes the form of a punched card or a printed line, it is referred to as a *unit record* and is used with a *unit record device*. As examples, line printers produce printed lines and card reader/punches read and punch punched cards.

When the external storage medium can store several sets of records, such as a magnetic tape, it is referred to as a *volume*. As an example, a familiar storage volume is a reel of magnetic tape that is read and written by a magnetic-tape unit. An important consideration is whether a storage volume is removable. Although the number of input/output devices in any computer system is limited by the available equipment, the number of storage volumes is not limited as long as a given storage volume can be removed from its associated device.

Code Conversion

One of the major functions performed by an input/output control unit is code conversion. In most cases, information is not recorded on a storage medium in exactly the same form that it exists in main storage.

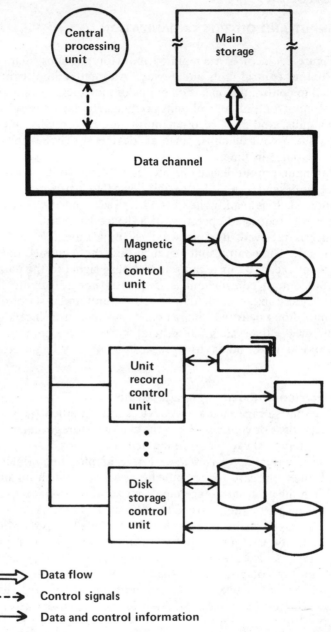

Figure 8.1   Simplified input/output subsystem. The viewpoint is conceptual, since unit record and disk devices usually do not utilize the same channel.

The punched card is an ideal example. In main storage a character exists in a 6-bit or an 8-bit coded form; in a punched card, a character is recorded as a column of 12 bits. A unit record control unit makes the necessary code conversions.

The preceding discussion implies great flexibility in the kinds of devices that can be connected to a computer. All that is needed to make a device compatible with a given computer system is to have an input/output control unit that can perform the necessary code conversions.

The process of attaching foreign devices to a computer system is further simplified by the standard input/output interface mentioned in Chapter 7.

8.3 PUNCHED CARDS

The punched card as we know it today was invented by Herman Hollerith in the 1880s for work on the U.S. Census. In fact, card code is frequently referred to as Hollerith code in honor of its inventor. The standard punched card, frequently referred to as the IBM card, measures 7 3/8 by 3 1/4 inches and is 0.007 inch thick. A punched card costs about 1/10 of a cent. The corners may be rounded or square and one corner is usually cut to detect when a card is upside down. A card is organized into 80 columns, numbered 1 through 80, with 12 punching positions in each column, numbered 12, 11, and 0 through 9. Information is recorded by punching rectangular holes in the card; one column represents one character. Thus, in a single column, there are 12 positions that can be punched. By established convention, combinations of the various punches represent the characters of the computer alphabet. Figure 8.2 depicts the various card code combinations. For example, the letter B is represented by punches in the 12 row and the 2 row. Similarly, the character 7 is represented by a punch in the 7 row, and the character * is represented by punches in the 11 row, 8 row, and the 4 row.

The primary use of punched cards is as an input media for data prepared through human participation. Figure 8.3 shows a typical keypunch machine, which contains a keyboard like an ordinary type-writer. Blank cards are entered into the keypunch machine and appropriate holes are punched when a given key is depressed. Figure 8.4 gives a typical input card. It contains three fields: name, social security number, and hours. (A *field* is a group of columns that represents one data item.) Punched cards are convenient for human use because individual cards can easily be added, deleted, replaced, and sorted.

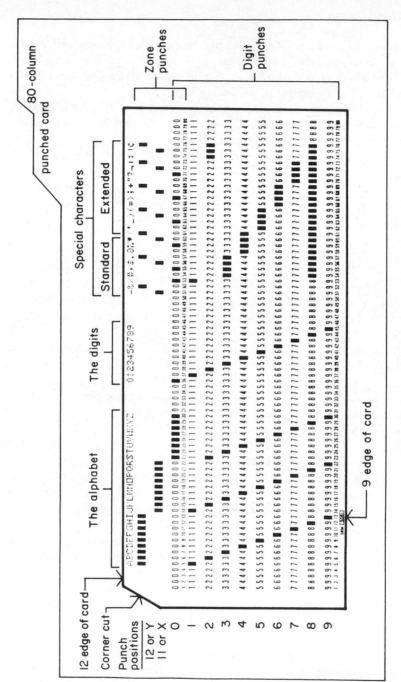

Figure 8.2 Hollerith card code.

182

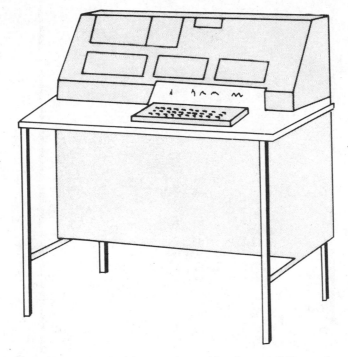

Figure 8.3   Typical keypunch machine for punching cards.

Most computer systems include a combined card reader and card punch, depicted as Figure 8.5. The objective of the card reader is to detect (i.e., recognize) the contents of a card and place the corresponding information in main storage. Figure 8.6 shows the internal workings of an automatic card reader/punch. Holes in the card are sensed by brushes that protrude through the card and make an electrical connection, or by photo-electric cells. Reading is performed on the right side of the unit. Cards to be read are placed in the read hopper; a card is read when a read signal is received from the computer, via the data channel and control unit. The card passes through two read stations and is finally deposited in an output stacker. Each card is read twice so that the results can be compared as a means of error checking. Punching is performed on the left side of the unit. Blank cards are placed in the punch hopper; a card is punched when a punch signal is received from the computer, again via the data channel and control unit. The card is punched at one station and read at another to verify that the card was punched correctly. The punched card is also deposited in an output stacker. The cards may

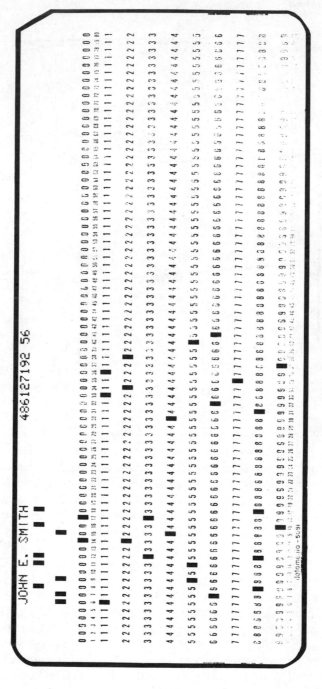

Figure 8.4 Typical input card.

184

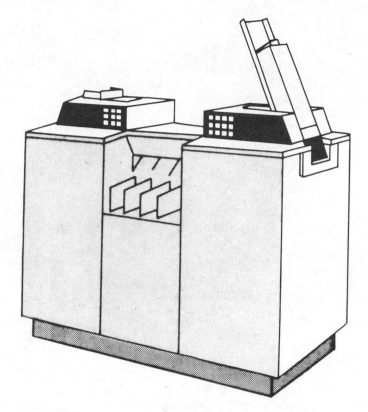

Figure 8.5   Combined card reader/punch unit.

be routed to alternate stackers (i.e., pockets) under computer control.

Figure 8.7 depicts the process of reading a card, which is initially read by the card reader and the information on it sent to the control unit. The input/output control unit performs a code conversion from 12-bit card columns to 8-bit bytes. Each byte is sent individually to the data channel, which deposits it in a buffer. When the number of bytes corresponding to the access width is received, the central processing unit is interrupted and the characters are placed in main storage. (In this example, the read operation instructs the computer to place columns 1 to 4 of the card into locations 1000 to 1003 of main storage.) As far as data transfer is concerned, all input/output control units and devices appear essentially the same to the data channel. The process of reading is reversed for punching.

Punched cards are used as an input medium, a storage medium, and

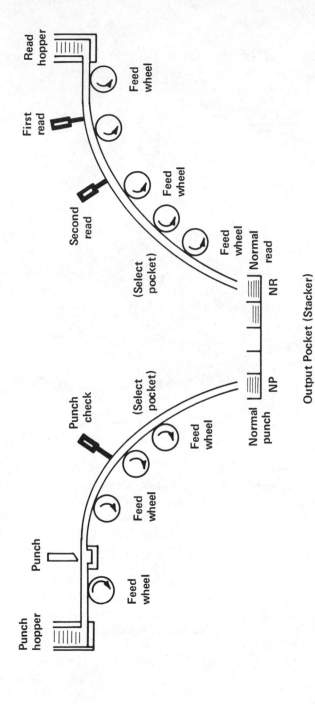

Figure 8.6 Internal mechanism of the card reader/punch.

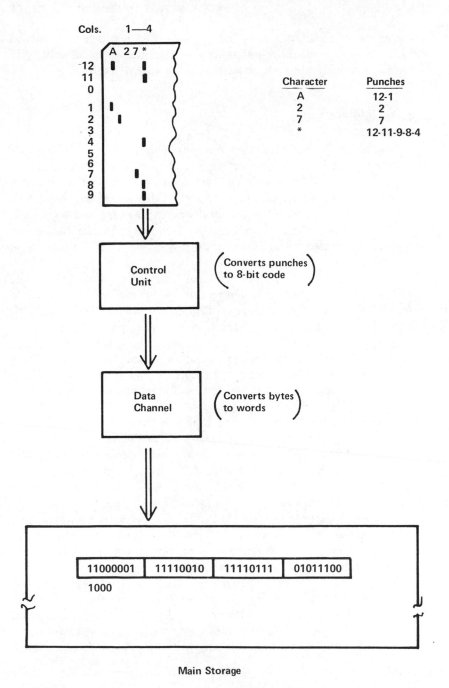

Figure 8.7 The code conversion process in reading a punched card.

187

occasionally as an output medium. A major disadvantage of punched cards as a storage medium is that they are cumbersome to handle and occupy a relatively large space when a large volume is involved.

8.4 MAGNETIC TAPE

Magnetic tape is a recording medium similar to that used with an ordinary tape recorder. Computer magnetic tape is 1/2 inch wide and consists of a plastic base with an iron oxide coating. The length of a magnetic tape varies up to approximately 2400 feet. One character's worth of information is recorded laterally across the tape and a group of characters (called a block) is recorded in one write operation. Successive blocks are separated by approximately 3/4 of an inch of blank tape, called an interblock gap.

Figure 8.8 gives a set of 7-bit magnetic tape codes. Iron oxide particles are magnetized in one direction or the opposite direction to represent the presence or absence of a bit. Longitudinal rows are labeled CBA8421 for identification and the C row denotes parity.* The tape is always written with even (or odd) parity, using the C bit for codes that are odd (or even). When the tape is subsequently read, an error condition is raised for all characters without the correct parity.

Magnetic tape is read and written by a magnetic tape unit, such as the one depicted in Figure 8.9. One reel serves as the supply reel and the other serves as the take-up reel. The tape is written or read as it passes over a magnetic read-write head, as depicted in Figure 8.10.

The process of reading a magnetic tape is similar in concept to that of reading a punched card (see Figure 8.7). The control unit performs a code conversion from 6-bit code (7 bits including the parity) to 8-bit bytes.† Magnetic tape is a sequential device, in the sense that the tape unit must pass over the $(i - 1)$st data item before the ith data item can be accessed. In the example of Figure 8.11, the "next" information on tape (A27* in this case) is read into locations 1000 to 1003. Again, the conversion process is reversed for writing.

Magnetic tape is characterized by the width of the tape, the recording density, and the tape speed. As mentioned above, magnetic tape with a width of 1/2 inch is the most widely used. However, tape up to 1 inch has been used to increase the data transfer rate. *Density* refers to the number of bytes that is recorded per inch. Typical values range

---

* *Parity* refers to whether the number of bits that is set in a lateral row across the tape is odd or even.
† Nine-track tape, which does not require a code conversion, is also in widespread use.

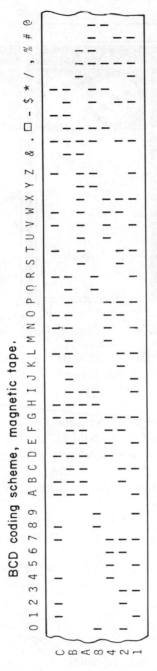

Figure 8.8 Magnetic tape codes.

189

Figure 8.9   Magnetic tape units.

from 200 bytes per inch (BPI) to 3200 BPI. Tape speed varies from 37.5 inches per second to 200 inches per second. Overall, the data rate of magnetic tape varies from 7500 bytes per second to 320,000 bytes per second.

The primary advantages of magnetic tape are that it is inexpensive (the average 2400-foot reel costs about $12) and that it can store a large amount of information for its size. A tape reel ranges from 8 to 12 inches in diameter and can hold from 1 to 20 million bytes. Magnetic tape, unlike punched cards, is reusable by simply writing over previously stored information.

Magnetic tape is useful for storing large amounts of data that can be accessed sequentially. Typical applications that lend themselves to the use of magnetic tape involve the processing of large data files, such as those that might be found in payroll, personnel management, customer billing, and inventory control.

8.5 MAGNETIC DISK

Although magnetic tape provides reasonably high data transfer rates and is a relatively inexpensive storage medium, it is ineffective

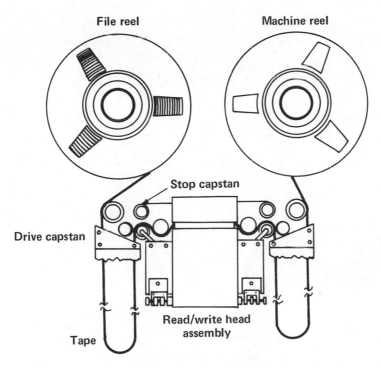

Figure 8.10   Internal mechanism of a magnetic tape unit.

when data must be accessed directly. Recall that with magnetic tape, the computer (or more precisely, the magnetic tape unit) must pass over the $(i - 1)$st data item to be able to access the ith data item, unless perhaps, the tape unit was initially positioned at the $(i - 1)$st item. Many applications, such as information storage and retrieval, require that data be accessed directly. A reasonably good example is an insurance company that uses a computer to store policy data. When a policy holder inquires about his policy, his records are retrieved directly. Implied in this case is the fact that the policy files of most insurance companies are usually large.

One of the most widely used devices for direct access is magnetic disk. The recording medium is a set of metal disks coated with magnetic material, such as ferrous oxide. The disks are mounted on a rotating spindle, as depicted in Figure 8.12. Data are recorded on tracks on the disk surfaces and are read or written as the disks rotate. The concept of disk storage is similar to that of a phonograph record, except that the tracks are concentric instead of spiral. The stack of disks is referred to as

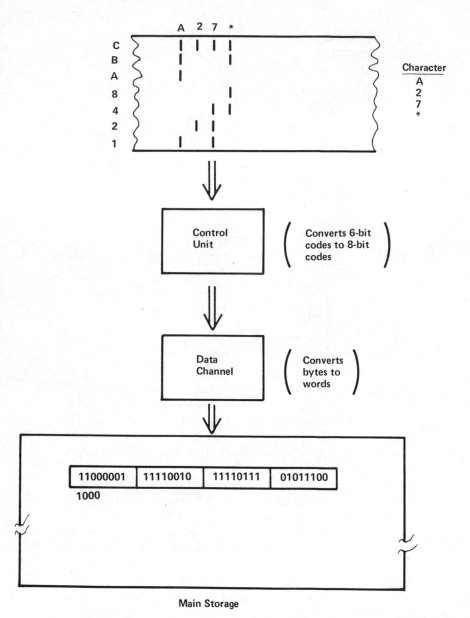

Figure 8.11 The code conversion process in reading a magnetic tape.

192

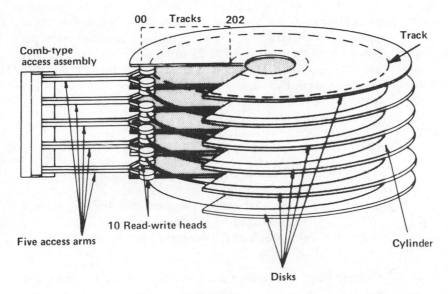

Figure 8.12   Disk storage mechanism.

a *disk volume*, and if the volume is removable, it is referred to as a *disk pack*.

Data are recorded on both surfaces of a disk (except perhaps the top and bottom surfaces of a volume, which are used for protection) and a single access arm controls two read/write heads, one for the upper surface and one for the lower surface. The access arms form a comb-type assembly that moves in and out together. A single read/write head is used to access a single surface.

Each track can store the same number of bits and is identified by a track address. Typically, track addresses range from 000–199. Each surface is also identified by a head address (i.e., the read/write head used to read the surface); the implication is that the heads are switched electronically when a given surface is to be read. Thus, a particular track is identified by (and located by) a track number and a head number. A magnetic disk is read or written by first moving the access arms to the proper track address prior to the input or output operation and by then switching on the desired read/write head. The process of moving the read/write head to the proper place is referred to as the *disk seek*. The time necessary to retrieve information from disk storage is therefore a function of three variables: seek time, the time necessary for the disk to rotate to the desired position on a track, and data-transfer time. Rotation speed is about 2400 revolutions per minute and recording density varies from 3500 to 15,000 bytes per track. As a result, the data-transfer rate of disk storage varies from 300,000 bytes per second to 1.5 million bytes per second. Average seek time varies from 25 to 60 milliseconds.

A disk storage module has three major components: the disk volume, the access arms and read/write heads, and the disk mechanism that causes the recording surfaces to rotate and works in conjunction with the access arms and read/write heads to record and retrieve data. A disk storage unit is usually classed by several factors:

1. The number of disk storage modules per unit
2. The number of recording surfaces per module
3. The capacity of each track and the number of tracks per surface
4. Seek time and rotation speed
5. Whether the disk volume is removable or not

Figure 8.13 depicts two disk storage units, one that contains a single disk module and the other that contains eight disk modules. Both utilize removable disk packs, such as the one shown in the same figure. The major advantage of removable disk packs is that they can be removed from the disk storage unit, so that the total disk capacity of a computer system is not limited by the number of disk units. Disk packs range in capacity from approximately 7 million bytes to approximately 100 million bytes. Therefore, a single storage facility, such as the eight-disk module of Figure 8.13, can hold as many as 800 million bytes. Not all disk volumes are removable. Nonremovable disk volumes generally provide faster access but have a smaller capacity.

Data that are stored on magnetic disk can be stored and retrieved sequentially or directly, depending upon the needs of a particular application. However, the cost of magnetic disk is approximately 20 times that of magnetic tape, all factors considered. (For example, the cost of a small disk pack with 10 recording surfaces that can hold about 7 million characters ranges from $350 to $500. The average 2400-foot magnetic tape reel also holds about 7 million characters. These figures obviously depend upon how the respective media are used.) For computer applications that require direct-access capability, there is no alternative. For applications that require only sequential access, the choice between magnetic tape and magnetic disk is a matter of input/output time and cost.

Magnetic disk is used primarily as a storage medium, for storing information on either a temporary or a permanent basis.

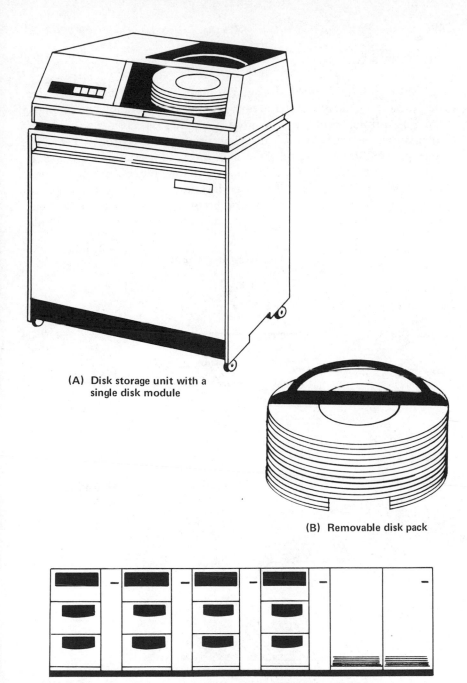

(A) Disk storage unit with a single disk module

(B) Removable disk pack

(C) Disk storage facility with 8 disk modules

Figure 8.13 Disk storage.

195

8.6 LINE PRINTER

From a human point of view, the most widely used output device that produces readable material is the line printer. As the name implies, the line printer prints a line at a time and is normally used for high-volume output. The speed of line printers varies from 60 to 5000 lines per minute. To sustain these high rates, continuous form paper is used. A *continuous form* (see Figure 8.14) is a long piece of paper with pin feed holes on the edges and with perforations to provide the required form size. Continuous forms can be preprinted to provide reports of various kinds. Common examples of preprinted forms are student grade

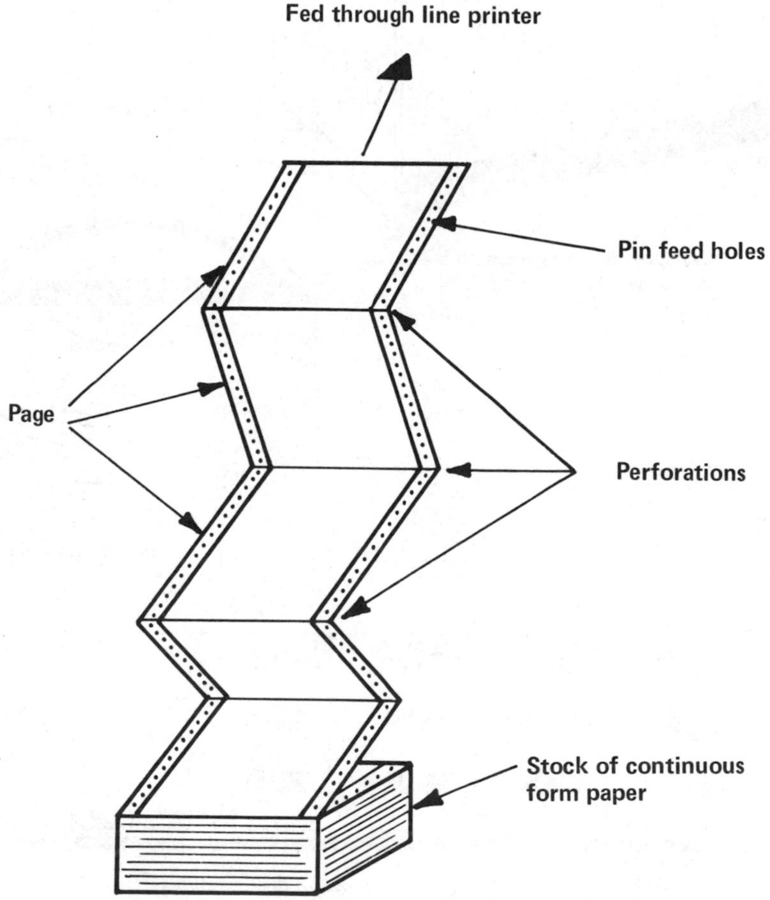

Fed through line printer

Pin feed holes

Page

Perforations

Stock of continuous
form paper

Figure 8.14   Continuous form paper.

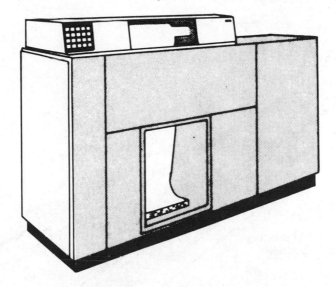

Figure 8.15   Line printer.

reports and everyday paychecks. A typical line printer is depicted in Figure 8.15.

A line printer prints a line of information (usually 120 or 132 characters) at one time by one of two methods:

1. Impact printing
2. Chemical or photographic techniques

The impact technique is more widely used because it generally produces better quality printing at a lower line speed. Impact printing uses a print chain, a print wheel, or a print drum and involves impacting the paper (and the ribbon) with the printing mechanism, or vice versa. Figure 8.16 shows a print chain that contains several sets of print characters mounted on a chain that moves horizontally in front of the paper. An electromechanically controlled hammer behind the paper forces the paper against the type face as the character to be printed passes in front of the proper position on the paper. The speed of impact line printers usually varies between 500 and 3500 lines per minute. Line speed less than 500 lines per minute are used for small computers or special purposes.

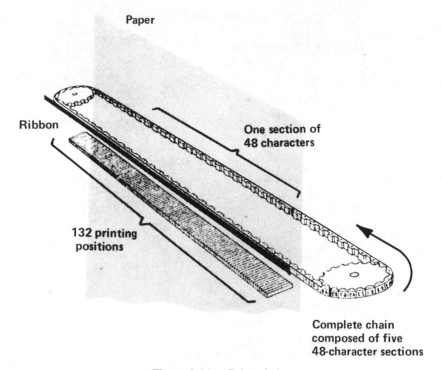

Figure 8.16   Print chain.

Chemical or photographic techniques generally are used in printers with ultra-high speed in the range of 3000 to 5000 lines per minute. Nonimpact techniques usually result in lower printing quality; however, this comment is more of an observation on the past, and it is expected that the use of nonimpact printers may surpass the use of impact printers as the quality of the former improves.

Figure 8.17 depicts the process of printing a line. As in previous cases, data is sent from main storage to the data channel and then on to the control unit through the standard interface on a byte basis. Information is collected in a buffer in the control unit until a complete line is formed; then, the print mechanism is activated to print the line.

The line printer is the primary output device for printed material because of the fact that there usually is a large amount of printing to be done. Typewriter-like devices that print on a character-by-character basis are frequently used for low-volume output. The printed page is also

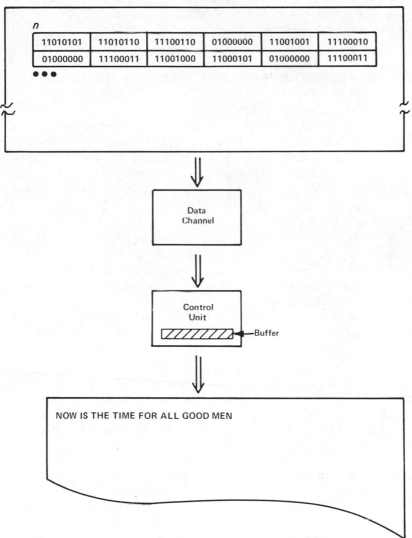

Figure 8.17   The code conversion process in printing a line on a line printer.

a storage medium, of a sort, but it is difficult to read the information back into the computer without rekeypunching the information. Optical readers, which are presented in the next section, are occasionally used for this purpose.

8.7 MISCELLANEOUS INPUT AND OUTPUT DEVICES

Because of the standard interface mentioned earlier in the previous chapter, a wide variety of devices have been developed that provide input, storage, and output facilities. The market for peripheral devices of this type is large and engineers have been known to develop input and output devices in their basement prior to embarking on a new business venture. This section summarizes a variety of well-known devices.

Keytape and Keydisk

Punched cards are the primary means of entering original data into the computer; however, card reading is relatively slow. An alternative approach to data entry is to use a *keytape device*, wherein the data is placed directly on magnetic tape. The data is entered via a keyboard and placed into a small memory by the keytape unit. The data is also displayed on a CRT* screen so that the operator can inspect the input data for accuracy. When the operator has finished typing a line, it is entered directly on magnetic tape. A variation to the keytape approach is to use a *keydisk system*, wherein the data is placed directly on magnetic disk. A limiting factor with keydisk systems is that disk storage units are expensive and it is difficult to justify stand-alone units for the data entry operation. A recent technique is to connect several keydisk entry stations to a minicomputer that writes the entered data on a few disk units. Thus, the disk units are shared among many keydisk stations.

Optical and Magnetic Character Readers

An *optical reader* is a device that reads letters, numbers, and special characters from printed, typed, or handwritten documents. The optical reader scans the document, compares the result with prestored images, and enters appropriate data into the computer. Documents with invalid characters are rejected.

A *magnetic ink character reader* reads characters printed with ink containing metallic materials. The most common example of magnetic

---

* CRT is an acronym for cathode-ray tube, which is a display device similar in concept to a common television tube.

ink characters are found at the bottom of bank checks. These characters can be read visually and by a magnetic ink character reader. Special magnetic ink character readers have been developed for the banking industry.

Paper Tape

A medium that is used for input, storage, and output is punched *paper tape*. Punched paper tape is similar to magnetic tape, in concept, except that data are recorded by actually punching holes in the tape. The advantage of paper tape to cards is that paper tape does not have an 80-character limit on data records. The major disadvantages of paper tape are that errors are difficult to correct and readers and punches are relatively slow, operating at approximately 500 and 300 characters per minute, respectively. Some types of computer terminals permit punched paper tapes to be prepared "off-line" prior to entry to the computer, minimizing errors when the user is connected to the computer.

Magnetic Drum

Magnetic drum is a mass storage device that uses a metal cylinder coated with a magnetizable material as a storage medium. Data are stored in circular tracks, referred to as *bands*, that are generally analogous to a track on disk. The magnetic drum is housed in an upright cabinet and frequently contains its own control unit. Data-transfer rates are generally faster than disk storage and range from 300,000 to 1.5 million bytes per second. Access time is somewhat faster than disk, as is storage capacity. The drum, per se, is not removable and a drum storage unit is generally more expensive than disk storage. Magnetic drum storage is usually used to store programs and tables.

Magnetic Strip and Card Devices

Magnetic strip and *magnetic card* devices are high-capacity electro-mechanical devices. A magnetic strip consists of a plastic strip coated with iron oxide, similar to magnetic tape. A magnetic card consists of a card coated with iron oxide. Both devices consist of several storage media (i.e., strips or cards) mounted in a removable cartridge holder. When an instruction from the computer is received, a strip or card drops from the holder and is moved under a read/write head. Each strip or card can be addressed directly. The cost of magnetic strip and magnetic card storage is less than disk storage. Because of the mechanical access mechanism, access times are high. Devices of this type are used for applications that require immediate access to high-volume data.

Graphic Devices

Two types of graphic display units are graph plotters and drafting machines. Units of this type are either on-line or off-line. On-line devices are connected directly to the computer. Off-line devices use a magnetic tape as input; the magnetic tape is written by a computer program as a separate operation.

Graphic devices operate under control of instructions, such as "move the pen to point (10,5)." By synthesizing sequences of such instructions, the device can be made to prepare a desired figure. *Graph plotters* usually operate by drawing straight lines from point to point. *Drafting machines* allow a variety of plane curves to be drawn.

One of the advantages of using graphic display units is that a figure can be redrawn as many times as necessary by simply rerunning the program, whereas a skilled artist or draftsman would invariably include differences between two copies of the same figure.

Microfilm

Printed output from the computer can be voluminous, and a means of solving the volume problem is to write the output directly on microfilm. The process is referred to as "computer output microfilm" and is abbreviated as COM. Computer output microfilm operates as follows:

1. The data is converted to a form that can be displayed on a CRT screen.
2. The pictures appear on a CRT.
3. The face of the CRT is photographed.
4. The film is processed and developed.

Steps 2 to 4 are performed by a COM device, available as an ordinary peripheral device. COM output can be produced in one of the well-known forms of microfilm technology, that is 16, 35, 70, or 105 mm film, microfiche, or aperture cards (punched cards with microfilm windows).

COM devices operate at very high speeds, up to 1000 lines per second, which is approximately 50 times faster than the average line printer. One of the primary advantages of COM output is that printed and graphic output can be conveniently incorporated on the same report.

Other Devices

Several other well-known devices exist, ranging from CRT devices to audio response units. Devices, such as these, that are normally used with data communications facilities are covered in the next section. It should be emphasized that not all input and output devices have been covered, but only the devices that the reader is most likely to encounter. The reader is directed to the references given at the end of the chapter for additional information on input and output devices.

8.8   DATA COMMUNICATIONS FACILITIES

Data communications refers to the use of teleprocessing facilities, such as ordinary telephone lines, for the transmission of data between remote locations. Technologically, data communications is not new and has been used with military/defense systems since the early 1950s. With the widespread use of computers in nonmilitary organizations, the use of data communications facilities is a natural technical extension. Data communications has given rise to a "popular" set of computer applications, such as time sharing, computer networks, message transmission and switching, and information-based systems, such as airline reservations and brokerage reservation systems. Data communications is cumbersome because interfacing two different types of equipment invariably leads to problems and because many of the privacy and security issues relate to data communications. As a problem, privacy and security would exist without data communications (or even computers, as a matter of fact); however, the widespread use of data communications simply makes the problem worse. In short, the benefits to be derived from the use of data communications greatly outweigh the difficulties, and this means of communication is here to stay.

Data communications facilities are used for three major reasons:

1. To provide computational facilities to a user at a remote location
2. To permit information to be entered or retrieved from a data management system on a dynamic basis from a remote location
3. To transfer data between locations at a high rate of speed

On the surface, the three areas appear to be diverse, but from a technical point of view, they are essentially the same and can be generally categorized as "communications systems."

A *communications system* has five components:

1. A message source
2. An encoder
3. A signal channel
4. A decoder
5. A message destination

A conceptual model of a communications system is given as Figure 8.18. In a computer communications system, the source or the destination is a computer system and the channel is either telegraph or ordinary telephone. Telegraph and telephone facilities usually are designed as open wires, coaxial cable circuits, and microwave systems.

As depicted in Figure 8.19, data is represented as a train of bits for data transmission. Successive bits represent a character, as covered previously with respect to computer codes. Data can be transmitted in one of three modes: asynchronous start-stop, synchronous, and parallel. When *asynchronous transmission* is used, one character is transmitted between source and destination at a time and extra bits called start and stop bits are used to achieve calibration between transmitter and receiver. Asynchronous transmission is almost always used when a human is involved in the communications process. When *synchronous transmission* is used, an entire block of characters is transmitted between source and destination without employing start and stop bits. The block is accumulated in a buffer prior to transmission and the synchronization of transmitter and receiver is precisely controlled by oscillators. Obviously, synchronous transmission is more efficient, since there are no start and stop bits and no pauses as a result of human response time. Synchronous transmission is frequently used when human intervention is not used in the transmission process. *Parallel transmission* uses several communications channels to transmit a character—usually, one channel exists for each bit in the code.

Data communications lines (i.e., the communications channel) are classified as to the data rate, or speed of transmission, they can sustain. Three classes are usually identified: subvoice grade, voice grade, and wide band. *Subvoice lines*, customarily used for teletype service, transmit at rates from 45 to 180 bits per second. *Voice-grade lines*, used for ordinary telephone, transmit at rates from 600 to 1200 bits per second. *Wide-band lines* are used for high-volume data and transmit at rates of 19,200 to 50,000 bits per second. The most significant characteristic of data communications lines is whether they are switched or private. *Switched lines* go through public exchanges and are located practically

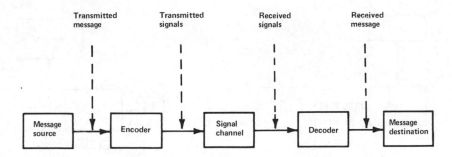

Figure 8.18   Conceptual model of a communications system.

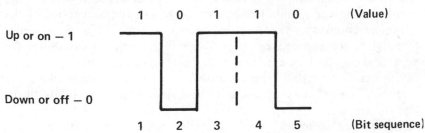

Figure 8.19   Data can be represented as train of bits for data transmission.

everywhere. Telegraph and public telephone lines fall into this category. *Private* (or leased) *lines* avoid the public switching network and are frequently used for high-volume traffic. Private lines are normally available in the three grades given previously. Many companies lease lines when many calls are made between remote offices.

Data can be transmitted over conventional telephone lines. A key problem, however, is that computers operate digitally (i.e., by pulses) and communications lines use analog transmission (i.e., by waves). Therefore, data must be converted from digital to analog form prior to transmission and back to digital form when the data is received. The process is depicted in Figure 8.20.

The process of converting digital signals to analog signals is called *modulation*; the process of converting analog signals to digital signals is called *demodulation*. A hardware device that performs modulation/demodulation is called a *modem*; it must be attached to both ends of the communications line. Two types of modem are widely used: a dataset

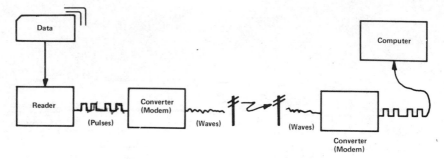

Figure 8.20   Data transmission.

and an acoustical coupler. A *dataset* is a fixed connection between the telephone line and a unit of computer equipment and is supplied by the telephone company. An *acoustical coupler* is attached to a computer terminal device and converts digital signals to audible tones. Since the acoustical coupler is not attached to a communications line, the terminal device can be portable. The acoustical coupler mechanism allows the receiver of an ordinary telephone to be clamped into it to establish the line connection.

Use of an acoustical coupler has great advantages. A salesman can have a battery-powered computer terminal with an acoustical coupler in his car. All he need do to access the computer is to stop at a telephone booth, dial the number of the computer, clamp the receiver into his acoustical coupler, and he is ready to use the computer.

Data communications systems can take several forms: computer to computer, input/output device to computer, terminal device to computer, and so on. From the computer's point of view, a data communications terminal is essentially treated as an ordinary input/output device, such as a card reader or printer.

There is a variety of terminal devices, ranging from keyboard/typewriter devices to audio response units. Figure 8.21 shows five major devices: a keyboard/typewriter unit, a CRT device, an audio response unit, a data collection station, and an intelligent terminal.

A *keyboard/typewriter terminal device* resembles an ordinary typewriter in all respects, except that the terminal device is connected to the computer via data communications lines. The unit serves for both input and output. For input, the user types the information he wants sent to the computer. As each character is typed, it is printed at the terminal and sent to the computer. When the line is complete, the user presses RETURN to return the carriage and to send a special code to the

CRT Device

Data Collection Terminal

Audio Response Unit

Intellegent Terminal

Keyboard/Printer

Figure 8.21 A variety of terminal devices.

computer indicating "end of line." Output is under control of a computer program. As each character is sent to the terminal device, it is handled immediately. Printable characters are typed. Control characters tell the terminal to "carriage return," "double space," and so on.

A *CRT terminal device* contains a display device that resembles a portable television set and a keyboard. The display device essentially replaces the carriage and paper of the previous device. As each character is typed for input, it is displayed on the screen. As above, pressing RETURN completes the line and returns a position indicator to the beginning of the next line. As lines are displayed, preceding lines are successively "rolled up" until the top line disappears at the top of the screen. The output lines are displayed in a similar manner. CRT-type devices are more costly than keyboard/typewriter devices and provide no "hard copy"; however, CRT-type devices allow faster display speeds.

An *audio response unit* is used to provide convenient low-volume output. A device of this type consists of a small magnetic drum and an audio speaker unit. The drum contains a small number of prerecorded syllables, words, or phrases. To generate a particular message, the computer sends an appropriate sequence of codes to the audio response unit, which selects the corresponding sounds from the drum and outputs them through the speaker unit. Audio response units are commonly used with stock quotation or credit verification systems.

A *data collection station* is an input device located in a remote location, such as an assembly plant or a medical ward in a hospital. Normally, data is entered through keys, dials, or switches. The data is stored at the computer on a recording medium such as tape or disk for subsequent processing.

An *intelligent terminal* is a terminal device that can be programmed to perform relatively minor data verification and editing functions. The use of an intelligent terminal, when appropriate, provides better service to the user and reduces the work load on the main computer. Intelligent terminals are commonly used in data entry systems to verify input data. Another interesting use of intelligent terminals is for computer consoles designed for use by executives. The terminal is programmed to dial the computer automatically when the executive turns the device on for use.

The above devices are only a few of the devices that can and have been used with data communications facilities. Remote tape units, card readers, and line printers are also in widespread use.

One of the more exotic uses of data communications facilities involves computer-to-computer communications without human intervention. Systems of this type are referred to as computer networks. (Again, computer programs are necessary for instructing the computer when and what to do.) One computer is simply programmed to dial the telephone number of the other computer to establish a data communications link. Once the link is established, appropriate programs are designed to make requests for information or respond to requests for information, as the case may be.

QUESTION SET

1. The chapter emphasized the difference between a device and a medium. Give as many analogous "combinations" as you can that exist in the noncomputer world. Example: pencil and paper. What about pen, ink, and paper?
2. Interpreting a punched card is the process of determining the recorded information. Interpret the card on page 210.
3. Suppose columns 10–17 of the card on page 211 were read into computer storage, byte locations 5320–5327:
   Give the contents in binary form of those byte locations.
4. The contents of byte location 5320–5327, of question 3, are written on magnetic tape. Give a picture of that segment of tape showing the recorded information.
5. Given a magnetic tape unit that records at 800 BPI and moves at 75 inches per second, compute the data rate of that unit.
6. Data is recorded on magnetic tape in blocks of 80 characters with 3/4-inch gaps between blocks. The recording density is 800 BPI. What percentage of the tape is blank (i.e., contains gaps) and what percentage contains recorded information?
7. What is the storage capacity of the following disk pack?

Recording surfaces:	10
Tracks per surface:	200
Bytes per track:	3620

8. Why is continuous form paper used?
9. Prepare a short but in-depth report on one of the following devices:

   Keytape or keydisk device
   Optical or magnetic character reader
   Paper tape (including codes)
   Magnetic drum
   Magnetic strip or card device
   Graph plotter device
   COM

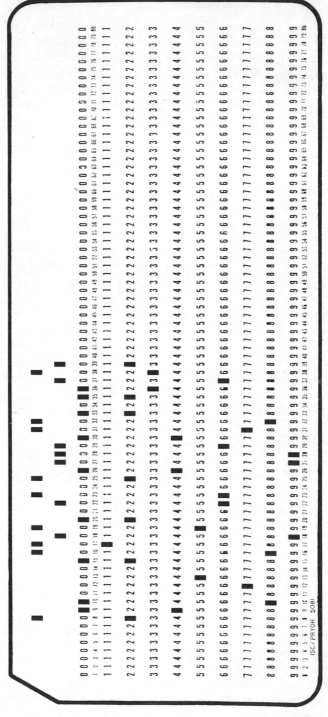

(question 2)

210

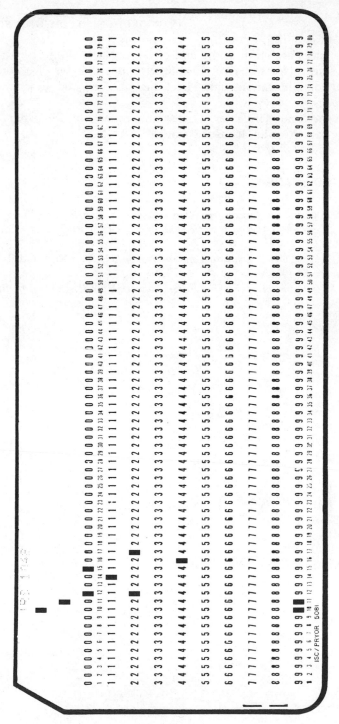

211

(question 3)

References are given at the end of the book.

10. Your instructor will give you the telephone number of a computer data communications line. Dial the number and describe what happens.

11. Visit the computer center or a terminal room. Prepare a short report on a dataset or an acoustical coupler.

SELECTED READING

Bohl, M., *Information Processing*, Science Research Associates, Chicago, 1971.

Flores, I., *Data Structure and Management*, Prentice-Hall, Englewood Cliffs, N.J., 1970.

Katzan, H., *Computer Organization and the System/370*, Van Nostrand-Reinhold, New York, 1971.

Martin, J., *Introduction to Teleprocessing*, Prentice-Hall, Englewood Cliffs, N.J., 1972.

PART
III

COMPUTER SOFTWARE

9

ASSEMBLER, MACRO,
AND PROGRAMMING LANGUAGES

9.1 INTRODUCTION

The need for a language to facilitate the programming process was emphasized in preceding chapters through a variety of examples. Although several concepts were covered, the coverage was not exhaustive and should be supplemented. The objective of this chapter, therefore, is to complete the subject matter, within the scope of the book, and to tie together the concepts presented earlier and the languages themselves to form a reasonably sound structure.

Languages for computer programming vary in both scope and complexity. At one end of the spectrum is assembler language, which resembles the instruction format of the computer. At the other end are complex programming languages that can be used to describe computational procedures in an unambiguous fashion. This chapter covers assembler language, macros, and programming languages.

9.2 ASSEMBLER LANGUAGE

Assembler language is designed to allow programs to be written in the machine language of the computer without having to deal with internal codes and machine addresses. There are several reasons why a user might write a program in assembler language rather than in a programming language:

1. A higher-level programming language is not available for the computer.

2. The user requires a functional capability or option that is outside of the scope of a programming language.
3. Using special features of a particular computer, an experienced programmer can produce a more efficient program in assembler language than he can in a programming language.

Assembler language is used primarily for systems programs for a given computer, such as language processors, operating systems, and data communications and graphics packages. Most applications programs are written in a language such as COBOL or FORTRAN because it is more economical* to write programs in these languages and because a program can be transferred to another machine with a minimum of effort. Thus, programs written in a standard programming language are said to be more "portable" than programs written in assembler language.

Program Structure

A program in assembler language is a series of statements that describe the procedure that the computer should follow at each stage of a computation. In an assembler language program, all entities in the program must be described, including constants, storage areas, and indicators. (It is important to note that this requirement is not a characteristic of most programming languages, since the compiler takes care of generating temporary storage areas, constants, etc.).

A program written by a user in assembler language is translated to an equivalent program in machine language by a program called an "assembler program," or simply an "assembler." The assembler is a language processor, as defined in an earlier chapter. Another characteristic of a program written in assembler language is that it does not have to make sense to the assembler, which makes a straightforward translation of a program to machine language. A compiler, on the other hand, does perform an analysis of the structure of a program.

Two final remarks are necessary. For the most part, each statement in an assembler language program causes one machine instruction to be generated by the assembler. There are some minor exceptions because some statements provide information to the assembler and do not correspond to computer instructions. Lastly, assembler language is largely dependent upon the computer, and assembler language operation codes normally correspond to actual computer instructions.

---

* The economics of the situation include lead time, personnel requirements, program verification, etc.—all of which can be translated into economic variables.

Statement Format

A statement in assembler language is designed to supply the following information to the assembler:

1. The relative location of an instruction or data item; this entry allows the statement to be referenced in the program and normally does not reflect where the program is to be loaded in main storage.
2. The operation code of a machine instruction or a statement providing information to the assembler.
3. The operands required by the operation code.

Entries in an assembler language program can be made symbolically, whenever appropriate, which is one of the primary advantages of using assembler language.

Statements are read by the assembler on a line-by-line basis. In addition to the statement itself, a line of input may optionally contain comments and a sequence number. Some assemblers inspect the sequence numbers to verify that lines are in the correct sequence and that a line is not inadvertently left out.

Entries in the statement portion of a line are usually formatted in one of two ways:

1. By placing the entries in columns, as in the following example:

Location	Operation	Operands
HERE	READ	ABLE
	READ	B
	LOAD	ABLE
	MULT	B
	ADD	CHARLY
	STORE	DOG
	BR	HERE
	.	
	.	
	.	

2. By using a set of rules that allows a statement to be essentially "mapped" into a columnar representation. A typical set of rules is: (a) The location field always starts in column one of a line; (b) Fields must be separated by at least one blank character; (c) If

no entry exists in the location field, the operation field must not begin before column two. This is a *free form*, as depicted in the following representation of the above program:

```
HERE READ ABLE
     READ B
     LOAD   ABLE
        MULT B
     ADD CHARLY
             STORE   DOG
     BR   HERE

           .
           .
           .
```

Clearly, the columnar form is a special case of the free form.

Types of Instructions

Assembler language normally incorporates three types of instructions: machine instructions, assembler instructions, and macro instruction. *Machine instructions* correspond to actual computer instructions. Typical examples are LOAD, ADD, MULT, and STORE. Machine instructions tell the computer "what to do." *Assembler instructions* are designed to provide information to the assembler on how the program should be assembled. Assembler instructions tell the assembler "what to do." *Macro instructions* allow a predefined set of statements to be used in an assembler language program. This topic is covered in a separate section.

Absolute and Relocatable Programs

Programming conventions and requirements vary between different computer systems and between different applications. For some applications, a program must be written so that it can be placed in a specific area of main storage. On-board computers in ships, planes, and space vehicles might fall into this category. For the majority of computer applications, a program can be placed in any appropriate area of main storage, as long as instructions that reference specific locations are adjusted accordingly.

An assembler language program that is developed for a specific area of main storage is referred to as an *absolute program*, and all symbolic names correspond to fixed addresses in main storage. Thus, in the example:

```
        ORG    100
   A    EQU    6320
   LP   LOAD   A
        ADD    B
         .
         .
         .
```

the assembler instruction ORG (for origin) tells the assembler to assemble the program so that it can be placed in main storage locations beginning with 100. Similarly, the assembler instruction EQU (for equivalence) tells the assembler to equate the symbol A to the machine address 6320. As a result, the LOAD instruction would be assembled for location 100, and the ADD instruction would be assembled for location 101, assuming that a word-oriented computer is involved. Note here that symbols name addresses and not values, so that when the LOAD instruction is generated by the assembler, its operand field contains the address 6320.

An assembler language program that is written to be loaded into an area of main storage that is not fixed is referred to as a *relocatable program*. Symbols in a relocatable program refer to addresses that are relative to the beginning of the program rather than to specific locations in main storage.

When an assembler assembles a program, it essentially substitutes numeric operation codes for symbolic operation codes and numeric operands (i.e., machine addresses) for symbolic operands. Machine instructions are synthesized in this manner and they are written along with control information on an output medium, such as cards, tape, or disk, for subsequent loading into the computer. The control information and the loader program collectively determine how a program is loaded into main storage for execution, so that the attribute of being absolute or relocatable is primarily an operating convention.

Assembler Instructions

Assembler instructions, frequently referred to as pseudo-operations, do not always cause machine code to be generated by the assembler. As mentioned above, assembler instructions provide information to the assembler and can be grouped into four classes:

1. Program control instructions
2. Symbol defining instructions
3. Data defining instructions
4. Listing control instructions

Program control instructions are used to specify to the assembler the precise manner in which the program should be assembled. Two frequently used program control instructions are ORG and END. The ORG instruction, as mentioned above, specifies the origin (or beginning location) of a program. The END instruction is used to denote the end of the program.

Symbol defining instructions permit a symbol to be assigned a specific address or be made equivalent to the address of another symbol. Two frequently used symbol defining instructions are EQU and SYN. The EQU instruction (for equate or equivalence) is used to assign an address to a symbol. The SYN instruction (for synonym or synonymous) is used to assign the address of one symbol to another symbol.

Data defining instructions are used to introduce data into an assembler language program or to define storage areas for later use. Data can be specified in any of a wide variety of forms. For example, all of the following forms assign the fixed-point value 5 to the symbol FIVE:

Location	Operation	Operand
FIVE	CONST	5
FIVE	DEC	5
FIVE	DC	F'5'
FIVE	DC	B'101'

Here, DC denotes "define constant," B denotes "binary," and F denotes "fixed point." Similarly, the following instruction establishes a storage area composed of 100 fixed-point locations:

Location	Operation	Operand
APR1	DS	100F

Here, DS denotes "define storage."

Listing control instructions are used in preparing the printout of the program and provide the following types of facilities:

1. Supply a "title" for each page of the program listing
2. Command the assembler to skip a line in the program listing
3. Command the assembler to eject the page on the line printer so that the next line printed begins on a new page

Typical listing control instructions would be TITLE, SPACE, and EJECT.

As an example of the assembler instructions covered here, several parts of an assembler language program are given. The statements are numbered for reference.

Location	Operation	Operand	
	TITLE	'SAMPLE PROGRAM'	(1)
	ORG	2500	(2)
CRIT	EQU	7531	(3)
	LOAD	VAL	(4)
	SUB	CRIT	(5)
	ADD	S23	(6)
	.		
	.		
	.		
	EJECT		(20)
*	THIS SEGMENT PREPARED BY A.B. JONES		(21)
IMPT	SYN	CRIT	(22)
DELTA	EQU	8000	(23)
	LOAD	ALPHA	(24)
	SUB	IMPT	(25)
	.		
	.		
	.		
	SPACE	2	(70)
*	TEST PROCEDURE BEGINS HERE		(71)
	ORG	4000	(72)
	LOAD	SUPPL + 4	(73)
	.		
	.		
	.		
VAL	DC	F'67.34'	(121)
S23	DC	F'0'	(122)
ALPHA	DS	F	(123)
SUPPL	DS	50F	(124)
	END		(125)

It is obvious that the program is hypothetical and is not complete. However, the general structure of an assembler language program and most assembler instructions are shown. The TITLE instruction in statement (1) specifies a title that is printed at the top of each page of the listing. The ORG instruction in statement (2) tells the assembler to assign addresses to the program beginning with 2500. The EQU instruction in statement (3) assigns the address 7531 to the symbol CRIT. When CRIT is used as an operand in a symbolic instruction, the assembler uses 7531 in the address field of the corresponding machine instruction. In the computer listing of the program, the EJECT instruction in statement (20) would cause subsequent printing to begin on the top of the next page. The SYN instruction in statement (22) specifies that the symbol IMPT should be assigned the same address as CRIT, that is, 7531. Statements (121) and (122) specify fixed-point constants. Statement (123) reserves one storage location and assigns it the name ALPHA. Statement (124) reserves 50 locations and assigns the symbolic name SUPPL to the beginning address. The END instruction in statement (125) denotes the end of the program.

Address Arithmetic and Other Concepts

Statement (73) in the preceding program gives the instruction:

LOAD SUPPL + 4

The statement specifies that something should be loaded into the accumulator. Remember that we are dealing with addresses in assembler language and the objective is to generate machine language instructions. Thus, the operand SUPPL + 4 means that the address of SUPPL plus the value 4 is generated as the address in the corresponding machine instruction. (Note that in a programming language, SUPPL + 4 would cause a compiler to generate two instructions: LOAD SUPPL followed by ADD 4.)

Most versions of assembler language also permit *absolute addresses* to be used. This means that a programmer can use an actual machine address as an operand in an instruction, such as

LOAD 6385

which means "load the contents of location 6385." Values that are to be used literally must then be denoted with a special character, such as an equals sign, as in

LOAD = F'25'

which is equivalent to

```
        LOAD   V1
          .
          .
          .
   V1      DC   F'25'
```

where V1 is an arbitrary name.

The preceding program includes statements with an asterisk (*) in the first column of the line. These are comment lines that are ignored by the assembler; a comment line is normally used by a programmer to include descriptive information.

Final Remarks

The preceding information represents a general overview of assembler language. Most people who use computers do not need to know an assembler language for any computer, and it should be added that most people who use computers are not computer scientists. Because computer scientists design computers, systems, languages, and language processors and must know the processes of computation, every computer scientist will know and should have used at least one assembler language.

9.3 MACROS

Most versions of assembler languages include a macro facility whereby predefined sets of instructions can be inserted in a program. A macro is invoked by using its name along with arguments, if any, in a program. The macro instruction processor replaces macro parameters with the arguments and inserts the required instructions into the program.

The use of macros is not restricted to assembler language and some programming languages include macro facilities. The concepts differ in scope and complexity, but the basic objective is the same: To facilitate programming by giving frequently used sequences of statements a name so that they can be retrieved and used in a program without writing down each statement separately.

In assembler language, the macro facility is usually provided through the assembler; that is, macros are expanded during the assembly process. Macros could be expanded prior to assembly by a preprocessor program. In fact, this technique is the method by which a macro facility has been incorporated into at least one programming language.

Reasons for Using Macros

A macro is normally used for one of three reasons: convenience, efficiency, and standardization. A macro is used for *convenience* when the same sequence of statements is used in several places in a program. A macro is used for *efficiency* when a complicated sequence of statements is involved, and it would be inefficient for each programmer to develop his own statements. A macro is used for *standardization* when several programmers are working cooperatively on a project and it is desirable to have everyone involved use the same programming conventions.

Characteristics of a Macro

An important defining characteristic of a macro facility is that it causes statements to be generated in the language with which it is used. Thus, in assembler language, for example, a macro is defined in assembler language and the macro processor generates assembler language statements that are translated to machine language by the assembler.

Macro Definition

A macro must be defined before it can be used, and this involves the specification of the following information to the macro processor:

1. The macro instruction code (i.e., the name of the macro) and the parameters of the macro
2. The statements that comprise the macro

Consider the following macro definition:

Location	Operation	Operand	
	MACRO		(1)
	BIOP	&A,&B,&C	(2)
	LOAD	&A	(3)
	MULT	&B	(4)
	ADD	&C	(5)
	STORE	&A	(6)
	MEND		(7)

Statement (1) is referred to as the *macro definition header* statement; it specifies that a macro definition follows. Statement (2) is called the *macro instruction prototype statement*; it gives the form in which a macroinstruction should be written and the parameters of the macro.

Statements (3) through (6) are referred to as *model statements*; these statements comprise the body of the macro and determine the statements that are generated. Statement (7) is the *macro trailer statement*; it specifies the end of the macro. Parameters are signified by a special character such as the ampersand.

Any constituent in a model statement (i.e., symbolic location, operation, or operand) may contain a macro parameter, as demonstrated in the following example:

Location	Operation	Operand
	MACRO	
&LOC	ATMAC	&OP,&VAL,&FINI
&LOC	LOAD	BIGV
	&OP	A
	ADD	&VAL
	B	&FINI
	MEND	

The macro processor simply performs a replacement of parameter with argument so that the statements generated must be meaningful to the assembler and to the user as far as the validity of the program is concerned.

Macros are defined in one of two ways:

1. The user includes a macro definition as part of his program.
2. Predefined macros are stored in a macro library that is maintained as part of the operating system. Macros in this category are normally referred to as *system macros* and are defined to help the programmer use the computer and the operating system.

When a macro is used for convenience, the macro definition usually accompanies the program in which it is used. When a macro is used for efficiency or standardization, several users are normally involved and the macro definition is placed in a macro library.

Generation

A macro is "invoked" in an assembler language program by using its name as an operation code along with the necessary arguments. A particular invocation of a macro is referred to as a *macro instruction*. In an assembler language listing of a program, a macro instruction is followed by the generated instructions, as in the following expansion of the BIOP macro defined earlier:

Location	Operation	Operand
	BIOP	PIL,JON,ABLE
+	LOAD	PIL
+	MULT	JON
+	ADD	ABLE
+	STORE	PIL

The plus signs identify generated instructions. Instructions generated by the macro processor are treated as though they were actually written in the program; thus, in this case, the variable names PIL, JON, and ABLE would have to be defined somewhere in the program. A macro may be invoked any number of times in a program.

The ATMAC macro defined earlier would be expanded in a similar manner as follows:

Location	Operation	Operand
FILK	ATMAC	MULT,FIVE,BLOCK
+ FILK	LOAD	BIGV
+	MULT	A
+	ADD	FIVE
+	B	BLOCK

In this example, it should be noted that entries from the location, operation, and operand fields serve as macro parameters.

Conditional and Other Facilities

Most macro systems allow instructions that command the macro processor in the same way that assembler instructions command the assembler and machine instructions command the computer. Instructions that command the macro processor permit the selection and reordering of statements of the macro definition.

The macro processor scans a macro on a statement-by-statement basis. Statements containing machine instructions are inserted (i.e., generated) into the program on a sequential basis. Instructions to the macro processor may involve a limited amount of data manipulation and may cause model statements to be scanned repeatedly on a conditional basis.

These concepts are illustrated in the next macro definition and expansion. The macro uses the concept of a "list," which is a collection of variables separated by commas and enclosed in parentheses. The function performed by the macro is to generate instructions to add the variables constituting the list and store the result in a specified location. In other words, the macro instruction that takes the form

ADDLST   (A,B,C),D

for example, adds A, B, and C and stores the result in D. The macro should apply to cases where the list contains a variable number of items.
Consider the macro definition given as:

Location	Operation	Operand	
	MACRO		(1)
	ADDLST	&LIST,&RES	(2)
	LCLA	&COUNT	(3)
&COUNT	SETA	2	(4)
	AIF	(N'&LIST GT 0 AND N'&RES LE 1).GOOD	(5)
	MNOTE	ERROR IN ADDLST MACRO	(6)
	MEXIT		(7)
.GOOD	LOAD	&LIST(1)	(8)
.CONT	AIF	(&COUNT GT N'&LIST).FINI	(9)
	ADD	&LIST(&COUNT)	(10)
&COUNT	SETA	&COUNT+1	(11)
	AGO	.CONT	(12)
.FINI	AIF	(N'&RES EQ 0).LAST	(13)
	STORE	&RES	(14)
.LAST	MEND		(15)

Prior to explaining the macro, two sample expansions are given:

Location	Operation	Operand
	ADDLST	(X1,Y2,Z3),FLOP
+	LOAD	X1
+	ADD	Y2
+	ADD	Z3
+	STORE	FLOP
	ADDLST	TOM,JERRY
+	LOAD	TOM
+	STORE	JERRY

The manner in which the ADDLST macro is defined and expanded is given in the following list (the numbers correspond to statement numbers):

1. The MACRO statement specifies the beginning of a macro definition.
2. The ADDLST instruction is the macro prototype. ADDLST is the name of the macro; &LIST and &RES are parameters. The ampersands denote "macro variables" as compared to "program variables."
3. LCLA is an instruction to the macro processor that establishes the temporary arithmetic macro variable &COUNT that is to be used during the macro expansion.
4. SETA is an instruction to the macro processor; it sets an arithmetic variable to a specified value. In this case &COUNT is set to 2.
5. AIF is a conditional instruction to the macro processor. If the truth value of the expression in parentheses is true, then control of the macro expansion passes to statement with location .GOOD. The period preceding GOOD denotes a "macro location" as compared to a "program location." The expression

   N'&LIST

   gives the "number" of items in &LIST. Similarly, the expression N'&RES gives the number of items in &RES. To sum up, this statement says, "If the number of items in &LIST is greater than zero and the number of items in &RES is less than or equal to 1, then transfer macro control to .GOOD."
6. MNOTE is an instruction to the macro processor that causes a comment line to be inserted into the program listing.
7. MEXIT is an instruction to the macro processor that causes the expansion of the macro to be terminated.
8. LOAD is a machine instruction. When the macro processor encounters a machine or assembler instruction, that instruction is generated after parameters are replaced. In this case, &LIST(1) specifies that the first item in &LIST should be used as an operand.
9. AIF causes macro control to pass to .FINI if the value of macro variable &COUNT is greater than the number of items in &LIST. The location .CONT is a macro location used in an AIF or AGO statement for macro control purposes.

10. ADD is a machine instruction. The *i*th item in &LIST is generated as an operand, where *i* is stored in &COUNT.
11. The SETA instruction (see note 4) adds 1 to &COUNT and replaces &COUNT with the result.
12. AGO is an instruction to the macro processor that causes macro control to be passed to statement labeled .CONT.
13. AIF causes macro control to pass to .LAST if the number of items in parameter &RES is zero, that is, the argument for parameter &RES is not supplied. This would be the case, for example, in the following expansion:

```
  ADDLST    (UP,DOWN,OUT)
+ LOAD      UP
+ ADD       DOWN
+ ADD       OUT
```

14. STORE is a machine instruction. The argument for parameter &RES is generated as an operand.
15. MEND specifies the end of the macro and causes macro processing to be terminated.

It should be recognized that a macro is "programmed" in a similar manner to the way that the computer is programmed.

9.4 THE NATURE OF PROGRAMMING LANGUAGES

The advantages of using programming languages have been implied earlier: The use of a suitable language subordinates the details of programming to a language processor and a program can be developed independently of a particular computer. Both advantages can be related to economic or technical considerations.

Programming languages differ in scope and complexity, and the objective of this section is to point out the differences between languages and between the technical facilities of the languages. Examples are given frequently from the various programming languages. In these cases, the objective is not to "teach" the languages but rather to augment the presentation of the topic being discussed.

Alphabet

A programming language is similar to most natural languages in the sense that the main objective is to "communicate." With a programming language, the parties involved are a human being and a computer, and statements in the language are written through the use of an alphabet established for that purpose. Alphabets for computer languages are fairly similar, with characters being grouped into the following classes:

1. *Alphabetic characters*, such as A, B, and C and X, Y, and Z
2. *Digits*, such as 0, 1, . . ., 9
3. *Special characters*, such as +, −, =, and $, in addition to punctuation characters, such as the period, comma, colon, and semicolon

The major differences between alphabets of different languages tend to be in the area of special characters.

The alphabet of a programming language is also related in some sense to the equipment for recording information. The PL/I language, for example, utilizes the greater-than symbol ($>$). This character is used in the full 60-character PL/I alphabet. In addition, a 48-character set is defined for PL/I for cases where the recording units, such as the keypunch machine, do not allow all 60 characters. In the 48-character set of PL/I, the greater-than symbol is represented by GT. This is a notational facility that is built into the language.

Most characters in the alphabet of a programming language have a meaning determined by the context in which they are used. The letter A, for example, could be used in a variable name, such as ALPHA, or in the name of a statement, such as READ. A few characters or sequences of characters have a special meaning in the language and are referred to as *symbols of the language*. Some common examples are:

+	for the addition operator
**	for the exponentiation operator
GT	for the greater than operator (in PL/1 48-character set)
.GT.	for the greater than operator (in FORTRAN)
$>$ =	for the greater than or equal to operator (in PL/I 60-character set)

All programming languages have conventions of this kind that give the language a distinctive "flavor." However, it should be remembered that the alphabet and symbols of a language are simply an implicit agreement between the parties involved and that the functional capabilities of the language are of prime importance.

Identifiers

A series of characters that names a constituent of a programming language is called an *identifier*. As mentioned in Chapter 4, a variable is a common example of an identifier. One disadvantage of the term *variable* is that it is ordinarily associated with computational entities,* as in mathematics; moreover, the use of the term does not imply what kind of information is being named. In many programming languages, the concept applies to several kinds of information and so more specific terms are needed. In general, therefore, an identifier normally begins with a letter and is optionally followed by one or more letters or digits. Sample identifiers are:

B3	READ
Z	DIMENSION
DO	TRUE

Identifiers are used in the following ways in modern programming languages:

1. Data names
2. Data file names
3. Statement labels
4. Entry point names (i.e., program or subprogram names or points at which routines can be entered)
5. Keywords

Items 1 through 4 vary among the different languages. In the BASIC language, for example, data names are restricted to a single letter or a letter followed by a digit, whereas in FORTRAN, a data name may consist of up to six characters. In the BASIC and FORTRAN languages, statement numbers are used to label statements, while in the PL/I language, an identifier is used as a statement label.

A *keyword* is an identifier that has special meaning in a programming language, depending upon how it is used. A typical keyword is GOTO in the following FORTRAN or BASIC statement:

GOTO 100

In some programming languages, keywords are *reserved*, which means that they may not be used as names or labels. In most programming languages, however, keywords are not reserved and meaning is determined by context. For example, the following valid statement in the FORTRAN language has a completely different meaning from the one given above:

GOTO = 100

---

* This comment refers only to common usage and is not a definitive statement.

It means replace data name GOTO with the value 100, whereas the GOTO 100 statement means transfer program control to the statement numbered 100. Keywords can be conveniently grouped into three classes: statement identifiers, auxiliary words, and built-in function names. Each class of keyword is described in the following paragraphs and sample statements are given. The keyword being discussed is set in italics.

A *statement identifier* names a type of statement and normally indicates the function it performs. The keyword is placed at the beginning of the statement, as demonstrated in the following examples:

READ A,B1,C2   (BASIC language)
DO I = 1 TO 10;   (PL/I language)
INTEGER CNT,FIL   (FORTRAN language)

An *auxiliary word* is used as an attribute, separator word, the name of an option, or a condition. An auxiliary word can be placed anywhere in a statement, as demonstrated in the following examples:

DECLARE I *DECIMAL*;   (PL/I language)
IF A>B *THEN* 600   (BASIC language)
PUT EDIT(TITLE)(A) *PAGE*;   (PL/I language)
ON *ENDFILE*(MFILE) GOTO CLOSEUP;   (PL/I language)

A *built-in function* name represents a computational subprogram; the name is recognized by the language processor and an appropriate subprogram is invoked. A function can be used as a term in an expression and usually, but not necessarily, requires an argument, as demonstrated in the following examples:

ROOT = (- B + *SQRT*(B**2 - 4.*A*C))/(2.*A)   (FORTRAN language)
A = *SIN*(2*C + 1)   (BASIC language)

A programming language in which the meaning of an identifier is dependent upon how it is used (that is, its context) is referred to as a *context-sensitive language*. In some cases, substantial analysis is required by the language processor to distinguish one statement from another. As an example, consider two FORTRAN statements:

DO10I = 1,10
DO10I = 1

Blanks are ignored in FORTRAN. The first statement is a DO statement and the second is an assignment statement. Blank characters are not ignored in PL/I, so that the following statements:

IF IF<THEN THEN   THEN = ELSE;ELSE GOTO GOTO;
DO DO = TO TO BY BY END;

pose more difficulty to the reader than the PL/I language processor.

Because variable names are simplified in the BASIC language, there is no confusion between keywords and variables. The only widely used language to use reserved words is the data processing language COBOL. This means that if a word such as READ is used as a keyword, it cannot be used as a programmer-defined name. A frequently used technique is to spell every programmer-defined name wrong to circumvent the problem of inadvertently using a reserved word as a name. But even this method has its problems, since many poor spellers have been known to misspell a name "right" and cause a compiler diagnostic message.

Data

Data are important in programming languages because the manner in which they are stored and organized determines to a large extent the applications for which a language can be used and how efficiently the programs will execute on the computer.

A fundamental distinction is whether the data are stored in computational form or in a noncomputational form. A datum stored in computational form can be used in an arithmetic or logical operation without requiring a conversion step. This naturally relates to the manner in which information is stored in the computer.

In computer applications that involve a significant amount of mathematical computation,* and relatively little input and output, it is useful to store data in a computational form, usually binary, so that a data conversion is not required each time a datum is accessed. As depicted in Figure 9.1, data are converted between external and internal forms during input and output operations. This technique allows computational procedures to be performed more efficiently, but input and output operations must carry the overhead of data conversion. In computer applications with a significant amount of input and output, such as data processing, data are read directly into main storage without going through a data conversion procedure. Then, as depicted in Figure 9.2, data conversion is made between external and computation forms before and after mathematical computations.

---

* Frequently referred to as scientific computation.

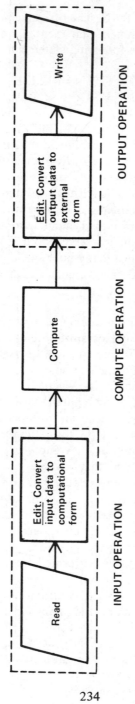

Figure 9.1 The general flow of input, computation, and output in scientific processing.

234

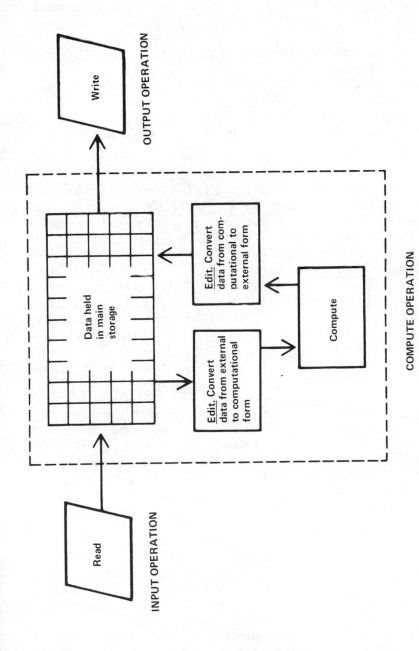

Figure 9.2 The general flow of input, computation, and output in data processing.

The manner in which arithmetic data are stored can be described with four properties:

1. *Base*—either external form (e.g., decimal)* or an internal form (e.g., binary)
2. *Scale*—using either fixed-point notation or floating-point notation
3. *Mode*—as a real number or a complex number
4. *Precision*—the number of digits of precision that is stored with the number

The four properties were developed for the PL/I language, which allows all combinations of the options. In the FORTRAN language, numeric data are stored using a binary base in either a real or complex mode. Real data can assume a floating-point scale (called REAL data) or an integer fixed-point scale (called INTEGER data). Complex data can only be stored using a floating-point scale. In all cases with FORTRAN, precision is determined by the word-size of the computer. In the use of the BASIC language, no consideration need be given by the user to the manner in which data are stored. The precise forms are implementation-dependent; in most cases, however, numeric data are stored in binary floating-point form and complex numbers are not defined. As mentioned above, all combinations of the above properties are available to users of the PL/I language.

Character data is stored in a binary-coded-decimal (i.e., external) form in all programming languages. No character data type is available in the FORTRAN language but facilities are available for reading and writing character data (called Hollerith data in FORTRAN). Once character data is stored as integer or real variables, a limited capability for data manipulation is available through the normal computational facilities for replacement and comparison. In the BASIC language, a variable of type character is permitted; its name is composed of a letter followed by a dollar sign—e.g., A$. Data manipulation facilities for character data are limited, as in FORTRAN, but the user is permitted to use read and print statements involving character data and can perform replacement and comparison operations. A character data type is permitted in PL/I and most operations defined on character data, such as concatenation, substring, and so on, are allowed. In BASIC and

---

*Decimal implies some form of binary-coded-decimal requiring a conversion to a precise computational form before it can be used in mathematical operations. Decimal form may vary greatly depending upon the programming language and computer.

FORTRAN languages, character data is included in the language definition to serve descriptive purposes, such as page and column titles. Character manipulation facilities are more extensive in the PL/1 language, so that it can be used for a wide variety of word processing applications.

There is more to data than how they are stored. The process of assigning a data type to scalar and array variables is referred to as "specification"; also included under specification is the process of declaring the bounds and extent* of an array and assigning of initial values. This topic is covered later in the chapter.

Statements

Programs are composed of statements and statements are composed of language elements, such as identifiers, constants, operators, and punctuation characters. A meaningful program is synthesized by selecting statements from the language that perform the functions required by the respective steps in the algorithm being programmed. Each statement adheres to a well-defined format.

Statements are normally punched on cards or typed in at a computer terminal. Different statements must be separated (or delimited) in some way, and a convenient means of doing that is to start each statement on a new card (or a new line). Using this method, the end of a card (or line) denotes the end of a statement, unless a continuation is specified by some lexical feature, so that a program is composed of a collection of data records (i.e., cards or lines). In other programming languages (namely PL/I), a program unit is a string of characters formed by concatenating the data records that comprise the program unit. Each statement is terminated by a semicolon. Using the second method, a given data record may contain one or more statements or parts of statements.

Program Structure

The term *program unit* was mentioned in the preceding section. A *program unit* is a main program or an external subprogram, so that a *program* is composed of a main program and zero or more external subprograms. A program may contain only one main program and when the program is loaded for execution, the main program is given control of the central processing unit.

Each program unit is compiled separately and consists of optional

* See Chapter 4.

specification statements, at least one executable statement, and a trailer statement (such as END) that denotes the physical end of the program unit. A program unit may contain both closed and open subprograms. An open subprogram normally corresponds to a mathematical function defined to be part of the programming language and sometimes called an *intrinsic function*. The absolute value function (ABS) is a common example of an intrinsic function. In some languages, a closed sub-program can be defined internally to a program unit and is referred to as an *internal subprogram*, as in the following PL/I example:

```
BIG:PROCEDURE; ───────────────────────────────┐
      ────                                      │
      ────                                      │   External
      ────                                      │   Subprogram
      CALL LITTLE;                              │
      ────                                      │
      ────                                      │
      ────                                      │
      LITTLE: PROCEDURE; ─────┐                 │
            ────              │  Internal        │
            ────              │  Subprogram      │
            ────              │                 │
            END LITTLE; ──────┘                 │
      ────                                      │
      ────                                      │
      ────                                      │
      END BIG; ───────────────────────────────┘
```

An internal subprogram is known only to its own program unit. A closed subprogram that is compiled separately is known as an *external subprogram*; it is accessible to all program units in a program, which means that it can be "called," or used, by other program units.

An external subprogram, which may be a function or a subroutine as defined earlier, can be supplied by the user or be loaded from a program library when the complete program is loaded into main storage for execution. In fact, some operating environments permit main programs to reside in a program library. Program units are stored in libraries in machine language form. When supplied by the user, program units can be in source language (assembler language or a programming language) or in machine language form.

The process of structuring a program into a main program and subprogram is significant for several reasons. First, the use of a well-defined subprogram facilitates programming and eliminates duplicate machine code. Second, it gives a "scope" for variable names; a name is known only to program units in which it is used. Thus, a name may be used elsewhere without conflict. In fact, once a program is compiled, a symbolic name ordinarily loses its significance. Third, program units can be developed in several languages and combined at "load time" to form an executable program. This facility allows a FORTRAN program to use assembler language subprograms and other elements. Lastly, program libraries can be developed so that each time a program is needed, a programmer does not have to "reinvent the wheel."

The remaining paragraphs in this section of the chapter survey the various kinds of statements that can be used to synthesize a program; the following categories are covered: specification statements, data manipulation statements, program control statements, input and output statements, and subprogram statements.

Specification Statements

Specification statements provide information to the language processor on how a program should be processed, on how data should be stored, and on what a programmer-defined name or condition is supposed to mean.

A common use of specification statements is to specify the type of a variable or an array, that is, floating-point, fixed-point, integer, character, and so forth. For example, the following specification statements from the FORTRAN language:

```
INTEGER COUNT,LIST(150),BVAL/6/
REAL PROB,INVAR,T(5,10),PI/3.14159/
```

specify the following information: COUNT and BVAL are integer variables; BVAL has an initial value of 6; LIST is a one-dimensional integer array that contains 150 elements; PROB, INVAR, and PI are real variables, which means in FORTRAN that they are stored and used in the floating-point mode; PI has an initial value of 3.14159; T is a two-dimensional real array with 5 rows and 10 columns, the lower bound for each dimension is 1 and the upper bounds are 5 and 10, respectively. In the statements given, the parentheses denote array declarations and the slashes delimit initial values. A similar technique is used with the BASIC language for declaring arrays; for example,

```
DIM A(10),B(16,2)
```

Note that in FORTRAN, the base is not specified because it is known implicitly to be binary; however, the scale is given—integer for fixed point and real for floating point. In the BASIC language, neither the base nor the scale is necessary. In fact, some implementations of the BASIC language incorporate implicit array declarations of 10 elements for one-dimensional arrays and 10 rows and 10 columns for two-dimensional arrays. If the user desires other array extents, then a DIM statement must be used.

Because a variety of data attributes are permitted in the PL/I language, a more general DECLARE statement is used, as follows:

DECLARE COUNT FIXED BINARY, LIST(100)
    FIXED BINARY, BVAL FIXED DECIMAL INITIAL (6),
    PROB FLOAT BINARY, INVAR FLOAT DECIMAL,
    T(5,100) FLOAT BINARY, PI FLOAT BINARY(3.14159),
    NAME CHARACTER(25);

In this example, COUNT, LIST, BVAL, PROB, INVAR, T, PI, and NAME are data names; in each case, the attributes of a data item follow its name. The declarations are essentially the same as those given in the FORTRAN example, except for NAME, which is a character string with a length of 25 characters.

One of the features introduced with the FORTRAN language is referred to as "implicit typing." With *implicit typing*, variable names in FORTRAN that begin with the letters I, J, K, L, M, or N are integer variables. Explicit type declarations (i.e., the REAL or INTEGER statements) naturally override implicit typing. The advantage of implicit typing is that it reduces the amount of information necessary to describe a program. The PL/I language also incorporates implicit typing; data names beginning with the letters I, J, K, L, M, or N are assigned the attribute FIXED BINARY, and data names beginning with the other alphabetic characters are assigned the attribute FLOAT DECIMAL.*

A *constant* also possesses the data attributes from the language in which it is used. In FORTRAN, for example, a numeric constant written with a decimal point or an exponent, such as 2.17E3 (meaning 2.17×10^3), is regarded as a real constant, and a numeric value written without a decimal point or an exponent is an integer constant. The topic

---

* In the IBM implementation of PL/I, the DECIMAL attribute refers to an internal decimal format and not a form of binary-coded-decimal. However, floating-point-decimal arithmetic is not available, so that values must be converted to binary prior to floating-point calculations.

does not arise in the BASIC language, and in PL/I a constant can even be written in the binary base, as demonstrated in the following examples:

PL/I Constant	Attributes
25	FIXED, DECIMAL
– 1011B	FIXED, BINARY
– 1.23	FIXED, DECIMAL
10.101B	FIXED, BINARY
123E – 2	FLOAT, DECIMAL
7.89E3B	FLOAT, BINARY
'TEA FOR TWO'	CHARACTER

Specification in programming languages is considerably more sophisticated than this brief introduction, which is intended to serve as an overview of the concepts involved. Other facilities that are normally available to the user of a programming language include: data sharing among program units, storage equivalence within a program unit, other data types,* and the detection of special conditions.

Data Manipulation Statements

The statement used for data manipulation is the *assignment statement*,† written as

$$v = e$$

where v is a variable and e is an expression. The assignment statement is interpreted to mean: "Replace the value of v with the value of e that is evaluated at the point of reference using the current values of the operands of which the expression is composed." During assignment, only the value of the variable to the left of the equals sign is changed and variables used in the expression retain their original values. Thus, in the following sets of statements:

A = 10	A = 10
B = A**2	B = A**2
C = B/4	A = 0
	C = B/4

---

* Other data types include complex, logical, and double precision data in FORTRAN and "bit" string and a variety of program control data types in PL/I.
† The assignment statement is also referred to as the *replacement statement*.

identical values are computed for C. The assignment statement can be used for simple data movement, such as

TO = FROM

which means replace the value of TO with the value of FROM, or it can be used to perform machine computation, as demonstrated above.

Because every variable and every constant has a data type, the fundamental question of mixed data types frequently arises. For example, the FORTRAN statements

INTEGER I,J	(1)
REAL A,B	(2)
B = A + 1	(3)
J = I*2.1	(4)
A = I + 1	(5)
I = B/2.4	(6)

exhibit a variety of combinations. Statements (3) and (4) contain mixed-mode expressions that are illegal in standard FORTRAN. Statements (5) and (6) contain valid expressions but the data type of the variable to the left of the equals sign is different from the data type of the expression. This is permitted in FORTRAN; the value of the expression is converted to the data type of the replacement variable just prior to the assignment operation. Thus, the following statement:

C = 5

where C is a real variable, is interpreted to mean: (1) Take the integer constant 5 and convert it to a floating-point value; and (2) replace the value of C with the result. Similarly, the statement

K = 23.4

where K is an integer variable, is interpreted to mean: (1) Take the real constant 23.4, stored as a floating-point value, and convert it to an integer fixed-point value; and (2) replace the value of K with the result.

The set of values upon which an operator (including assignment) operates is defined as its *domain*, and the result of an operator is termed its *range*. If an operand is not in the domain of an operator, an attempt is made to convert it to a value that is in the domain, and a conversion of this type is referred to as a *type conversion*. Conversion during assignment is a simple case of type conversion.

Type conversion does not arise in the BASIC language except with regard to character-string variables, which cannot be combined in any way with arithmetic variables.

Complete flexibility is provided in the PL/I language, wherein an attempt is made to convert any operand to the data type required by an operator. Thus, a user could write

A = B + '1.23';

and it would make sense in the PL/I language; obviously, an absolutely inappropriate operand, such as

A = B + 'TEA FOR TWO';

would cause an error condition to be generated.

The PL/I language and some versions of the FORTRAN language allow mixed-mode arithmetic expressions, and as a result, operands may differ in at least one of the following properties: base, scale, or mode. When this occurs, *arithmetic conversion* is performed as follows:

1. *Base conversion.* Computations must be performed in computational form for the computer involved. If binary is the only form, then decimal operands must be converted to binary. Otherwise, if operands differ, then the operand with the decimal base must be converted to binary.
2. *Scale conversion.* Except for the exponentiation operation, fixed-point (or integer) operands must be converted to floating point.
3. *Mode conversion.* If the modes differ, the real operand must be converted to a complex value with a zero imaginary part.

Type and arithmetic conversions are normally handled by the compiler, in the sense that the need for conversion is recognized at compile time and the machine code necessary to perform the conversion is generated by the compiler.

The concept of an expression is not covered here, since the use of an expression is not restricted to data manipulation statements. Expressions are covered in Chapter 4. One use of an expression is important here. A subscript is used to select an element of an array and must contain a subscript expression for each dimension of the array.* Subscript expressions are separated by a comma when more than one is needed in

---

* This statement is not exactly true, since some programming languages permit entire arrays and complete rows or columns to be used as operands.

an array reference. In standard FORTRAN, a subscript expression is limited to one of the following forms:

$$c*v$$
$$c*v+k$$
$$c*v-k$$
$$v+k$$
$$v-k$$
$$v$$
$$k$$

where c and k are integer constants and v is a scalar integer variable. Most modern versions of FORTRAN permit generalized subscripts consisting of conventional arithmetic expressions that are evaluated at the point of reference and truncated to an integer before selection is performed. Given the declarations

INTEGER ALL(9,7)
REAL FILLET(100)

and the integer values $J=3$ and $N=4$, for example, then ALL(2*J + 1,5) selects the integer value located in the seventh row and the fifth column of two-dimensional array ALL, and FILLET(11*N) selects the real value located as the 44th element of one-dimensional array FILLET.

The BASIC and PL/I languages allow conventional arithmetic expressions as subscripts.

Program Control Statements

Program control statements provide a means of departing from the sequential execution of statements. Statements in this category are grouped into three general classes: unconditional branch statements, conditional statements, and looping statements.

An *unconditional branch statement* terminates the normal sequential execution of statements and indicates the statement to be executed next. This function is served by the GO TO statement that takes the form:*

GO TO <statement-number>

in the BASIC and FORTRAN languages, and

---

* The angular brackets are used to indicate the name of something; this topic is covered in the next chapter.

GO TO <statement label>;

in the PL/I language. Sample statements are

GO TO 975

for BASIC and FORTRAN, and

GO TO LOOP1;

for PL/I. A "multiple-path" branching facility is provided in three different ways in BASIC, FORTRAN, and PL/I. In BASIC, the ON statement is used; it takes the form

ON e GO TO $s_1, s_2, ..., s_n$

where e is an arithmetic expression and the s_i are statement numbers. The arithmetic expression is evaluated at the point of reference and its value determines the statement number to which program control is directed. If the value of e is 1, then control passes to statement numbered s_1; if the value of e is 2, then control passes to statement numbered s_2; and so on. Thus, if T contains the value 5, then the statement

ON T-2 GO TO 150,375,615,931

passes program control to statement numbered 615. In FORTRAN, a computed GO TO statement is used; it takes the form

GO TO$(s_1, s_2, ..., s_n), i$

where the s_i are statement numbers and i is an integer variable. Program control is directed to statement numbered s_i. Thus, if LP contains the value 4, then the statement

GO TO(150,375,615,931,10,1287),LP

passes program control to statement numbered 931. In PL/I a "label" variable is used, so that a GO TO statement of the form

GO TO <statement label variable>;

can be used. Thus, in the PL/I statements

DECLARE SWITCH LABEL;

   .

   .

   .

SWITCH = HERE;

   .

   .

SWITCH = THERE;

   .

   .

GO TO SWITCH;

   .

   .

HERE: _____

       _____

       _____

THERE: _____

       _____

       _____

program control would be directed to statement labeled HERE or statement labeled THERE, depending upon the current "label" value of variable SWITCH.

A *conditional statement* permits the sequence of execution to be altered or allows a statement (or group of statements) to be executed on a conditional basis. This function is normally provided with the IF statement, which can be used for iterative procedures, for testing exceptional cases, and for making basic decisions during the course of ordinary program execution. In FORTRAN, the IF statement can be based on an arithmetic or a comparison expression. The arithmetic IF statement takes the form

IF $(e)s_1,s_2,s_3$

where e is an arithmetic expression and the s_i are statement numbers. Program control is passed to s_1, s_2, or s_3 if the computed value of e is less than zero, equal to zero, or greater than zero, respectively. An example is

IF $(A**2 - B + 1.5)210,210,70$

The logical IF statement in FORTRAN takes the form

IF (*b*) *statement*

where *b* is a logical expression and *statement* is an executable statement. If the computed value of *b* is true, then the given statement is executed. Several examples follow:

IF (A.LT.0) A = 0
IF (A**2 − B + 1.5 .GT. DELTA) GO TO 1573
IF (Q .AND. R)STOP

In the BASIC language, the conditional statement takes the form

IF *c* THEN *s*

where *c* is a comparison expression and *s* is a statement number. If the value of *c* is true, computed at the point of reference, then execution of the program continues with statement numbered *s*. The following example depicts the use of an IF statement in the BASIC language:

IF (R1 + R2)/W > 16.38 THEN 700

A conditional option is provided in the PL/I language that is not available with BASIC or FORTRAN. The IF statement in PL/I takes the form

IF <expression> THEN <group> ELSE <group>

where *expression* is a logical expression or an arithmetic expression. If the expression is an arithmetic expression (i.e., it has a numerical result), then it is converted to a string of bits and is regarded as being true if any of the bits are 1. The structure of the IF statement is shown in Figure 9.3. The THEN clause is required and is executed if the specified expression is true. The ELSE clause is optional and is executed only when the specified expression is false. After the IF statement is executed, sequential execution continues with the following expression. An example of a simple IF statement is

IF A < 0 THEN A = 0; ELSE A = B + 1;

Consider the procedure given in Figure 9.4 that depicts a situation in

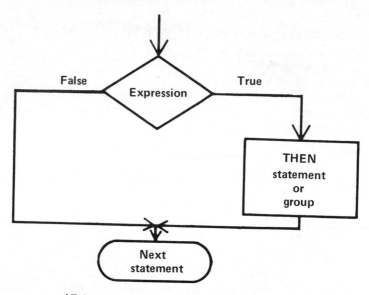

IF Statement with THEN Clause

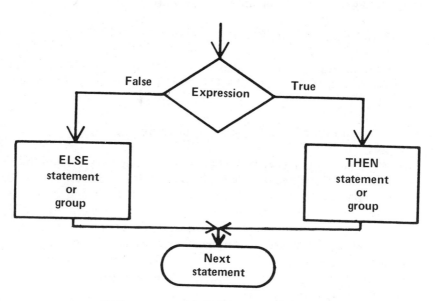

IF Statement with THEN and ELSE Clauses

Figure 9.3   Structure of the IF statement in the PL/I programming language.

248

which more than one statement must be executed for both true and false conditions. The PL/I language includes a facility, called a *DO group*, in which a series of statements can be treated as a single statement by enclosing them in the keywords DO and END. This option is used in the following PL/I program segment, which represents the algorithm of Figure 9.4:

IF A<B THEN DO;C=D+1; E=F+1; END
         ELSE DO;G=H+1; I=J+1; END
K=L+1;

In this case, DO and END are used to denote a group and serve as *statement parentheses*.

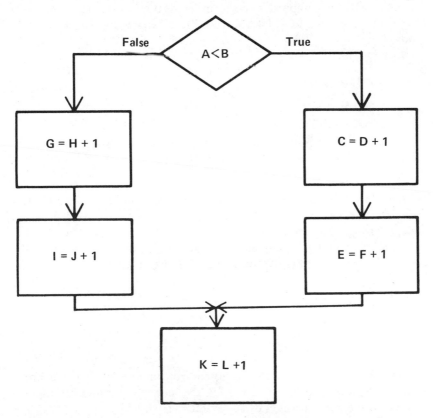

Figure 9.4   Algorithm to demonstrate the use of a DO group in PL/I.

Looping statements facilitate the preparation of program loops. A series of statements that is executed repetitively is a loop and a single pass through the loop is referred to as an iteration. A program loop has three major constituents: a control variable, a set of statements, and a condition that controls the number of iterations. For example, consider the following FOR loop in the BASIC language:

```
100     FOR I = 1 TO N
110        S = S + X(I)
120        P = P*X(I)
130     NEXT I
```

Statement 100 specifies I as the control variable and indicates that the loop should be repeated as I takes on the values from 1 to N in steps of 1. Statements 110 and 120 comprise the body of the loop. The NEXT statement tells the computer to perform the next iteration. The same loop programmed in the FORTRAN and PL/1 languages would exist as follows:

```
     FORTRAN                  PL/I

     DO 50 I = 1,N            DO I = 1 TO N;
     SUM = SUM + X(I)            SUM = SUM + X(I);
  50 PROD = PROD*X(I)            PROD = PROD*X(I);
                             END;
```

In the above loops the quantities 1 and N are known as control parameters and effectively determine the number of passes the program makes through the loop. The following statements from the BASIC, FORTRAN, and PL/1 languages initiate program loops in which the control variable K ranges from 2 to L in steps of 3:

```
     FOR K = 2 TO L STEP 3    (BASIC)
     DO 75 K = 2, L,3         (FORTRAN)
     DO K = 2 TO L BY 3;      (PL/I)
```

In the BASIC and PL/I languages, control parameters may be arithmetic expressions, while in FORTRAN, control parameters are restricted to integer constants or scalar integer variables.

Input and Output Statements

Input and output statements can be categorized by whether editing or conversion is performed during data transmission. This is a lengthy and complex topic* and the treatment given here is intended to present the various concepts by selecting topics from the BASIC, FORTRAN, and PL/I languages.

A technique used in the BASIC language is to "build" the data into the program with a DATA statement that is used to build an internal data set. Data are retrieved from the internal data set with a READ statement. For printed output, a PRINT statement that includes a list of data items is used. If the data items are separated by commas, then the output is printed in columns. If the data items are separated by semicolons, then the output is "run together," as demonstrated in the following example:

```
100 READ B,H
110 PRINT B,H
120 LET T = SQR (B↑2 + H↑2)
130 PRINT "HYPOTENUSE = ";T
140 GO TO 100
150 DATA 5,12,3,4,7,24
160 END
RUN


  5     12
HYPOTENUSE = 13
  3     4
HYPOTENUSE = 5
  7     24
HYPOTENUSE = 25
OUT OF DATA IN 100
```

The FORTRAN language incorporates two modes of input and output: formatted and unformatted. *Formatted* input and output uses a FORMAT statement that describes the data on the external medium. The FORMAT statement contains field descriptors that correspond to variables in the input and output statement. The following READ and FORMAT statements amplify the above concept:

---

* For additional information on the subject of input and output, the reader should consult a standard book on programming languages, such as Katzan, H., *Introduction to Programming Languages*, Petrocelli/Charter, New York, 1973.

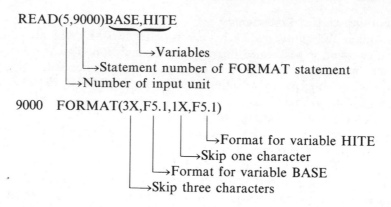

A FORTRAN version of the preceding BASIC program is given as follows:

```
       REAL  BASE,HITE,HYP
   50  READ(5,9000)BASE,HITE
 9000  FORMAT(3X,F5.1,1X,F5,1)
       HYP = SQRT(BASE**2 + HITE**2)
       WRITE(6,9001)BASE,HITE,HYP
 9001  FORMAT(1X,F5.1,2X,F5.1/1X,12HHYPOTENUSE = F7.2)
       GO TO 50
       END
```

Input:*   7.0   24.0
          3.0   4.0
          5.0   12.0

Output:
          5.0   12.0
          HYPOTENUSE = 13.00
          3.0   4.0
          HYPOTENUSE =   5.00
          7.0   24.0
          HYPOTENUSE = 25.00
          END OF INPUT REACHED – PROGRAM TERMI-
          NATED

The FORTRAN language also includes facilities for unformatted input or output that uses statements of the form

    WRITE(*unit*)*list*
    READ(*unit*)*list*

---

* Input and output characters may not be formatted precisely.

where *unit* is the number of an external data file and *list* is a list of variables. With unformatted input and output, data is transmitted in an internal form. (It should be noted here that data recorded on an external medium in an internal form is not, in general, in a form for human absorption.)

In the PL/I language, input and output can take two forms:

1. *Stream input/output*, in which the external medium is regarded as a continuous stream of characters
2. *Record input/output*, in which the external medium exists in the form of physically separate words

With stream input/output, input and output operations involve a conversion operation, as demonstrated in the following PUT statement that is used for output:*

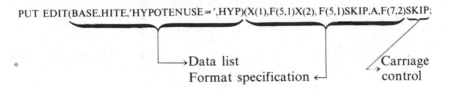

PUT EDIT(BASE,HITE,'HYPOTENUSE = ',HYP)(X(1),F(5,1)X(2), F(5,1)SKIP,A,F(7,2)SKIP;

　　　　　　　　　　　　　　└──→Data list
　　　　　　　　　　　　　　　　Format specification ←──┘　　Carriage
　　　　　　　　　　　　　　　　　　　　　　　　　　　　　　control

With record input/output, input and output operations do not involve a conversion operation and records are read into and written directly from main storage. When records are defined, data fields that make up the record are described and identified. Thus, the necessary conversions can be made when the various data items are accessed during computation. A typical record input/output statement is the following READ statement, used for input:†

READ FILE(MASTER) INTO(PAYREC);

　　　　　　　　　　　　　　└→Record area

　　　　└→File name

Another topic that is closely related to input and output is the manner in which data is organized and accessed. This topic, referred to as data management, is covered in Chapter 11, "Operating Systems."

---

* GET and PUT statements are used for stream input and output, respectively.
† READ and WRITE statements are used for record input and output, respectively.

Subprogram Statements

Subprogram statements permit functions and subroutines to be defined through operational statements and a variety of operating conventions of a programming language. Subprogram facilities fall into three classes: single-line user functions, function subprograms, and subroutines.

A single-line user function is referred to as a *statement function* in FORTRAN; a function definition consists of a single expression that must be placed at the beginning of the program unit. A statement function is known only to the program unit in which it is defined. A sample statement function is

$$ROOT(A,B,C) = (- B + SQRT(B**2 - 4.0*A*C))/(2.0*A)$$

The ROOT function would be used in an expression somewhat as follows:

$$ARM = ROOT(1, - 2, - 15) + 1.0$$

so that ARM would be replaced with the value 6. In the BASIC language, the same "root" function is defined as

$$DEF\ FNR(A,B,C) = (- B + SQR(B\uparrow 2 - 4*A*C))/(2*A)$$

and serves exactly the same purpose as in FORTRAN. Single-line functions are useful for evaluating equations, such as

$$f(x) = ax^2 + bx + c$$

or to compute quantities, such as

$$\log_b x = \log (x)/\log (b)$$
$$\text{sind}\ (a) = \sin (a\pi/180)$$

Function subprograms are used for functional procedures that require more than one line. In the BASIC language, a function subprogram is internal to the program in which it is defined and the value of variables that are known to the calling program are also known to the function. The following defined function in the BASIC language computes the factorial function:

```
100  DEF FNF(K)
110  FNF = 1
120  IF K< = 1 THEN 160
130  FOR I = 2 TO K
140     FNF = FNF*I
150  NEXT I
160  FNEND
```

In the FORTRAN language, a function subprogram is compiled separately, so that the value of variables in the calling program are in general not known to the function. The following defined function in the FORTRAN language also computes the factorial function:

```
     FUNCTION IFACT(K)
     IFACT = 1
     IF(K .LE. 1) GO TO 70
     DO 50 I = 2,K
50   IFACT = IFACT*I
70   RETURN
     END
```

In the PL/I language, defined functions can be internal to the calling program or can be compiled separately. The following PL/I procedure computes the factorial function:

```
FACT:  PROCEDURE(K) RETURNS(FIXED,BINARY);
       DECLARE P INITIAL(1) FIXED BINARY;
       DO I = 1 TO K; P = P*I;END;
       RETURN(P);
       END FACT;
```

The structure of the three functions is similar:

BASIC	*FORTRAN*	*PL/I*
DEF FNF(K)	FUNCTION IFACT(K)	FACT: PROCE-DURE(K) ...
.	.	.
.	.	.
.	.	.
	RETURN	RETURN(...)
FNEND	END	END FACT;

The first statement in a function definition is known as the *function header statement*; it denotes the beginning of a function definition and specifies the name of the function and its parameters. The RETURN statement causes program control to be returned to the calling program and the trailer statement, that is, FNEND or END, denotes the physical end of the subprogram. Otherwise, the same statements can be used in subprograms as are used in ordinary programming.

A *subroutine* is a subprogram that does not return an explicit result, so that it cannot be used in an expression. The BASIC language does not include facilities for "stand-alone" subroutines, and procedures are executed with GOSUB/RETURN statements, as follows:

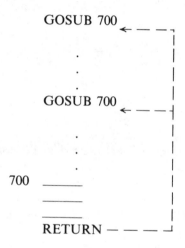

The GOSUB statement operates as a GOTO statement, except that a return path to the next sequential statement is established. The RETURN statement returns program control to the statement following the last active GOSUB statement.

In the FORTRAN and PL/I languages, subroutines are given a name and are invoked with the CALL statement. The following subroutines in the FORTRAN and PL/I languages print a page title and a page number each time they are called:

FORTRAN

```
SUBROUTINE PGNUM(I)
WRITE(6,9000)I
```

```
9000   FORMAT(1H1,30X,10HABC REPORT,45X,4HPAGE,I5)
       RETURN
       END
```

PL/I

```
PGNUM:PROCEDURE(I);
       PUT EDIT('ABC REPORT','PAGE',I)(X(30),A,X(45)A,I(5))PAGE;
       RETURN;
       END PGNUM;
```

Both subroutines are called with a statement of the form

CALL PGNUM(I)

Where I is the running count of the current page number, and their structure is similar to that of function subprograms. In FORTRAN, a subroutine must be compiled separately; in PL/I, a subroutine may be internal or can be compiled separately.

Other Facilities in Programming Languages

It was mentioned earlier that the area of programming languages is practically a field of study in its own right. It should be obvious now why the statement is true. Many features have not been covered, including: data initialization, storage management, special conditions, local and global variables, block structure, list processing, asynchronous procedures, passing arguments to subprograms, format codes, array operations, and so forth. Moreover, popular languages such as COBOL, SNOBOL, LISP, and ALGOL have not been introduced. These topics are the subject of other computer science courses and this chapter serves only as an introduction. The reader is encouraged to review the Selected Readings at the end of this chapter and explore the questions, which attempt to expand upon the topics covered here.

QUESTION SET

1. Give three computer applications for which the use of assembler language would be appropriate. Characterize these applications. Can you draw any conclusions?
2. What does assembler language format have to do with machine level programming? Why aren't several instructions normally placed on a single line?

3. Select a computer of your choice. Investigate assembler language instructions used for linkage and attempt to explain them.

4. Develop assembler language statements that perform the following computation:

$$A = \frac{\dfrac{B+C+D}{E/F-G}}{H+1}$$

Use a computer with one accumulator and a computer with two arithmetic registers. Compare the instructions used.

5. How does a macro differ from an open subprogram?

6. Why is a special character used with a macro parameter?

7. Develop a macro to perform the linkage function. Use the macro names SAVE and RETURN. (Your instructor will help with the precise formats.)

8. List two advantages of using reserved words in programming languages.

9. How does a compiler distinguish a function reference from an array name?

10. In the FORTRAN statements

$$DO \ 10I = 1,10$$
$$DO10I = 1$$

give precise procedures for recognizing the DO statement.

11. What advantages exist for ignoring blanks, as in FORTRAN?

12. Develop hypothetical operations for use on character operands.

13. What operations could be performed on entire arrays?

14. Describe and compare the following PL/I calculations:

DECLARE A FLOAT DECIMAL, B FIXED BINARY,
    C FLOAT BINARY, D FIXED DECIMAL;
$B = B + 25;$
$D = B + 101B;$
$C = A + 123E - 3;$

15. Consider the storage of one-dimensional complex array A. The following methods have been used:

A(1) real
A(1) imaginary
A(2) real
A(2) imaginary
A(3) real
A(3) imaginary
.
.
.
A(n) real
A(n) imaginary

A(1) real
A(2) real
A(3) real
.
.
.
A(n) real
A(1) imaginary
A(2) imaginary
A(3) imaginary
.
.
.
A(n) imaginary

Compare the advantages of either method. (This is a good question for class discussion.)

16. An interesting exercise is to divide the class into groups of three or four. Prepare verbal reports on the following topics:

Local vs. global variables
Call by value vs. call by name
Block structure
Format codes
Operators in the APL language
Input and output facilities in PL/I
Introduction to the SNOBOL language
Program structure in COBOL
Storage management in FORTRAN
Matrix operations in BASIC
Table handling in COBOL
Asynchronous processing in PL/I
Basic concepts of the LISP system
Survey of different kinds of programming languages
Structures in PL/I and COBOL

SELECTED READINGS

Elson, M., *Concepts of Programming Languages*, Science Research Associates, Chicago 1973.

Forte, A., *SNOBOL3 Primer*, MIT Press, Cambridge, Mass., 1967.

Galler, B. A., and A. J. Perlis, *A View of Programming Languages*, Addison-Wesley, Reading, Mass., 1970.

Higman, B., *A Comparative Study of Programming Languages*, American Elsevier, New York, 1967.

Katzan, H., *Advanced Programming: Programming and Operating Systems*, Van Nostrand-Reinhold, New York, 1970.

Katzan, H., *A (PL/1 Approach to Programming Languages,* Petrocelli/Charter, New York, 1972

Katzan, H., *APL User's Guide*, Van Nostrand-Reinhold, New York, 1971.

Katzan, H., *Introduction to Programming Languages,* Petrocelli/Charter, New York, 1973.

Sammet, J. E., *Programming Languages: History and Fundamentals*, Prentice-Hall, Englewood Cliffs, N.J., 1969.

Wegner, P., *Programming Languages, Information Structures, and Machine Organization*, McGraw-Hill, New York, 1968.

Weissman, C., *LISP1.5 Primer*, Dickenson, Belmont, Calif., 1967.

10

LANGUAGE PROCESSOR METHODOLOGY

10.1 INTRODUCTION

One of the most important factors contributing to the widespread use of assembler language and of programming languages is that much of the detail of programming is subordinated to another computer program, known as a "language processor." More specifically, a *language processor* is a program that accepts another program as input; the output of a language processor is either a translated version of the input program or a set of computed results. The concept is an important one. A computer system is a complicated device and preparing a program that can control it in an effective and useful manner is a complex task. The use of an appropriate language facilitates the programming process and allows computational facilities to be available to more people. The fact that a computer can help to prepare its own program—via the language processor—is a notion worthy of considerable thought, especially when one considers the fact that the concept can be extended to several levels of program preparation.

This chapter presents a collection of methods, techniques, and ideas that are useful for understanding language processors. The methodology is general in nature and applies to a variety of languages.

Terminology

A program as expressed in assembler language or in a programming language is referred to as a *source program*; it is read by a language processor from cards, tape, a direct-access storage device, or a terminal device via telecommunications facilities. Language processors are grouped into three categories: assemblers, compilers, and interpreters. An assembler or compiler is regarded as a *language translator*, because it produces an output program, called an *object program*, that is a translated version of the source program. Assembler language programs are translated into an equivalent form in machine language. Programs written in a programming language are translated into equivalent machine language or assembler language programs. Most compilers produce machine language programs. Occasionally, compilers are designed to produce assembler language output, which must then be run through the assembler. A program listing normally accompanies an assembly or a compilation; it is used for program checking and debugging and frequently provides the machine language produced by the translation process. The object program is recorded on cards, tape, or a direct-access storage device for subsequent input to the computer for execution. The terminology of the translation process is depicted in Figure 10.1.

An *object program* is composed of three types of entities:

1. Machine instructions
2. Control information denoting the instructions in which the address field must be relocated when the program is loaded into main storage for execution

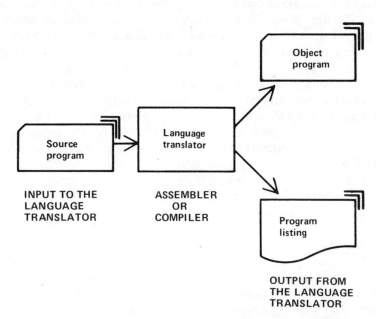

INPUT TO THE   ASSEMBLER
LANGUAGE   OR
TRANSLATOR   COMPILER

OUTPUT FROM
THE LANGUAGE
TRANSLATOR

Figure 10.1   The programming translator accepts a source program as input and produces an object program and a program listing as output.

3. An external symbol dictionary that gives the name and address of all external symbols defined or referenced in the program.

Item 3 refers to cases in which an object program references other object programs, such as in the statements

RES = SQRT(DELTA − 3.4)

or

CALL PGNUM(I)

which require that the subprograms SQRT and PGNUM be loaded into main storage and combined with the object program containing these statements. The loading and linking of object programs is covered in the next chapter, "Operating Systems."

The following paragraphs describe the three principal language processors: assemblers, compilers, and interpreters.

Assembler Programs

An *assembler program* (usually referred to as an *assembler*) converts a program written in assembler language to an equivalent program in machine language. The translation process is usually referred to as *assembly* or the *assembly process*. Assembly is usually performed in two passes over a source program. In the first pass, relative addresses are assigned to symbols in the location field. In the second pass over the source program, symbolic operation codes are replaced by internal machine codes and symbolic operands are replaced by corresponding addresses that were determined during pass one. The object program and the program listing are also produced during pass two. Various forms of error checking and analysis are performed during both passes.

Compiler Programs

A *compiler program* (usually referred to simply as a *compiler*) converts a program written in programming language either to machine language or to assembler language. In the second case, the resulting assembler language program must then be processed by the assembler. Figure 10.2 depicts sample assembler language statements that would be generated by a single statement in a programming language. In contradistinction to assembly, where one machine instruction is usually generated for each assembler language source statement, the compiler usually generates several machine instructions for each source statement

Higher-Level Language	Assembler Language
I=J*K+L	L 6,J (Load reg. 6 with J)
	M 5,K (Mult. regs. 5-6 by K)
	A 6,L (Add L to reg. 6)
	ST 6,I (Store reg. 6 in I)

Figure 10.2   Sample assembler language statements that would be generated for a single statement in a higher-level language.

in a programming language. Compilation is generally considered to be more complicated than assembly, since programming language structure tends to be more complex than assembler language structure. Although a compiler is necessarily dependent on the language being compiled, the following steps are usually involved:

1. The compiler reads the source program on a statement-by-statement basis and performs the following processing for each statement:
    (a) Lexical analysis to identify keywords, names, constants, punctuation characters, and so on, is performed.
    (b) Syntactical analysis to identify the type of statement and determine that its structure is admissible is performed.
    (c) The constituents of that statement are placed in lists and tables to facilitate the generation of machine code and to allow a global analysis of the program.
2. A flow analysis of the program is performed to check for interstatement errors and to provide information on how machine registers should be assigned.
3. Program optimization is performed and machine instructions are generated.
4. An object program and a program listing are produced.

A compiler and an assembler have one important feature in common: Each has the complete source program at its disposal, so that the various steps in the assembly and compilation processes can be executed at the discretion of the person designing the assembler or the compiler. Only after a source program has been completely analyzed by an assembler or compiler and an object program is produced is that object program actually executed.

Interpreter Programs

One type of language processor that allows program modification during execution is the interpreter. The *interpreter* is a language processor that executes a source program without producing an object program. An interpreter operates as follows:

1. The interpreter reads the source program on a statement-by-statement basis and performs the following processing for each statement:
    (a) The statement is scanned, identified, analyzed, and interpreted to determine the operations that should be performed.
    (b) The required operations are executed by the interpreter and the intermediate results are retained.
2. The next statement that is interpreted depends on the results of the statement just executed (such as in the case of a GOTO statement).

Although different interpreters vary in internal design,* the key point is that an object program is not produced and that all statements are not necessarily processed by the interpreter. The interpretive technique is frequently used with simple, easy-to-use language (such as a desk calculator language) or in an operational environment (such as time sharing) where programs are not likely to be rerun many times.

General Comments

In most cases, a language translator and the program it produces run on the same computer, and the normal sequence of operations is:

1. Translate source program to object program
2. Load object programs into main storage
3. Execute the programs loaded in step 2.

The translation process, however, is not restricted to the computer on which the object program is to be executed. In some cases, a program is assembled or compiled on one computer and executed on another. The only restriction is that the format of the object program and the computer on which it is executed must correspond. An example of a case

---

* Some interpreters convert a source program into an intermediate function language and then interpretively execute the statements in the intermediate form. One of the principal disadvantages of the interpretive technique is "slowness."

where translation and execution take place on different computers occurs with some small military computers that do not contain the necessary capability to support the translation process. In these cases, an assembler program designed to produce object programs for the small computer is programmed to run on a general-purpose system with sufficient capability.

The remainder of this chapter includes a presentation of the assembly process, compiler methods, and the syntax of programming languages. Assembly is a straightforward process that can be covered in sufficient detail to acquaint the reader with the actual operations performed. Compilation is a more sophisticated process that has become an area of study in its own right. This presentation is restricted to introductory methodology that is frequently used with compilers. Syntactical methods are used to describe a programming language, so that the compiler writer and the user of the language are talking about the same thing.

10.2 THE ASSEMBLY PROCESS

In the assembly process, the instructions written by the programmer determine the precise functions that the assembler must perform to generate an appropriate object program from a source program. These instructions serve as "input" to the assembler and are grouped into three classes:

1. Machine instructions
2. Assembler instructions
3. Macro instructions

These classes were introduced in the preceding chapter. Macro definitions are treated as a "special case" during the assembly process.

In subsequent paragraphs of this section, the basic functions performed during assembly are presented and demonstrated through the use of a hypothetical computer and assembler language. The assembly process utilizes symbol tables for programmer-defined symbols, operation codes, and macro names. Symbol table methodology is covered in Chapter 13.

Basic Functions Performed During Assembly

The basic functions performed during assembly are essentially the same, regardless of the computer involved and the specific characteristics of the assembler language. The overall logic of the assembler is designed around the basic functions that must be performed

Objective of Assembly. The objective of the assembly process is to generate machine instructions in which symbolic operation codes are replaced by numeric codes and symbolic operands are replaced by their address values. (Recall that the *value* of a symbol in assembler language is an address* and not the data item stored at that address.) A basic rule of assembler language is that the value of a symbol must be known before the assembler can construct a machine instruction that uses the symbol as an operand. If the statements in an assembler language program are translated in a linear fashion, a symbol is frequently used before it is defined. (A symbol is defined when it is used in the location field of an assembler language statement. The same symbol may not be used in the location field of more than one statement. If the same symbol is used more than once, it is referred to as a *duplicately defined symbol* and the assembly process cannot be completed because the assembler ordinarily does not know which address to use.) Therefore, the generation of machine instructions is postponed until all symbols and their corresponding addresses are placed in a table. This takes one complete pass over the program. In the second pass, instructions are generated.

Syntax Analysis. A program written in assembler language must adhere to established rules for writing statements. The rules ensure that the correct format is used so that the assembler program can recognize the meaning of a statement. The mechanical process of inspecting a source statement to ensure that the rules have been observed and of determining symbolic locations, operations, and operands is referred to as *syntax analysis*. The process of syntax analysis involves scanning a statement on a character-by-character basis to determine the contents of the various fields; the pertinent information from a statement is usually put into an internal form (such as a table), so that the statement need not be scanned again when the statement is referenced. The symbol table is built during the syntax analysis process.

Macro Definitions. As mentioned earlier, macro definitions can be supplied with the program or can reside in a macro library that can be accessed by the assembler. Macro definitions are usually placed at the beginning of an assembler language program. When a macro definition is encountered during the initial pass through the program, the macro

---

* Usually, it is an address relative to the origin of the program.

definition is placed intact in a temporary macro library, which exists only for the duration of the current assembly.

Macro Instructions. During syntax analysis, each operation code is looked up in a table of valid operation codes to determine if it is a machine or an assembler instruction. If it is neither, then the assemption is made that the operation code is a macro instruction. The temporary and system macro libraries are searched to determine if the operation code is the name of a macro.* If it is, then the model statements are retrieved from the library and expanded, as outlined in Chapter 9, by replacing parameters with arguments, and so forth. The statements generated during macro expansion are inserted into the assembler language program at the point of reference. If, on the other hand, the operation code is neither a machine instruction, an assembler instruction, nor a macro instruction, then it is flagged as an illegal operation code.

Location Counter. During assembly, each program has an origin that indicates the relative address of the location in which the program is to be placed. The origin is usually zero unless specified otherwise by the programmer. The value of the origin initially is stored during the first pass of assembly as a variable called the *location counter.* As the assembler steps through a program during syntax analysis, the location counter is modified accordingly. When a symbol is encountered in the location field during the scan of a statement, it is placed in the symbol table along with the current value of the location counter. This is the manner in which numeric addresses are assigned to symbols. It is important to realize, however, that all instructions do not physically occupy storage space in the object program; instead, they provide information to the assembler program. Instructions that physically occupy storage space in an object program are known as *generative instructions.* Machine instructions and data-defining assembler instructions fall into this category. Instructions that provide information to the assembler program on how the source program is to be assembled are referred to as *nongenerative instructions.* Program control, symbol defining, and listing control assembler instructions fall into this category.

Generation. The machine instructions and control information that make up an object program are generated during a second pass over the

---

* In some assemblers, the macro libraries are searched first. The subject is a matter of design philosophy, and both techniques have their advantages and disadvantages.

program. A machine instruction is synthesized by replacing symbolic operation codes by numeric operation codes from a table of operations. Similarly, symbolic operands are replaced by addresses from the symbolic table constructed during the first pass over the program. Constants and storage areas are formed in an analogous fashion. The generated instruction or constant is placed in an output buffer along with control information. When the buffer is full, its contents are written to an external storage medium for subsequent loading into the computer for execution.

Hypothetical Computer and Assembler Language

A hypothetical one-address word computer with multiple accumulators numbered 0 through 9 is used to demonstrate the assembly process. Each instruction word consists of a two-digit operation code, a one-digit register designator, and a four-digit address field, depicted as follows:

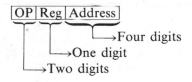

(The hypothetical computer is purposefully simplified to avoid being interpreted as a real machine!)

Each source statement is permitted three major fields:

1. Location field
2. Operation field
3. Operand field

An asterisk in column one denotes a comment line.

Instructions are divided into three categories: machine instructions, assembler instructions, and macro definition instructions. Macro instructions may be defined by the user.

Machine instructions have the following format:

Location	*Operation*	*Operands*
(Optional)	Symbolic Operation Code	One or two operands separated by a comma

Table 10.1

Machine instructions in the hypothetical computer used for demonstration of the assembly process

Symbolic Operation Code	Internal Operation Code	Operands	Description
LOAD	01	R, MS	R ← MS
STORE	02	R, MS	MS ← R
ADD	03	R, MS	R ← R + MS
SUB	04	R, MS	R ← R − MS
MULT	05	R, MS	R ← R * MS
DIV	06	R, MS	R ← R/MS
BR	07	MS	Branch to location MS
BZERO	08	R, MS	Branch to location M if contents of R ⩽ 0
READ	09	MS	MS ← □
PRINT	10	MS	□ ← MS

Key: R-register designator   MS-symbolic location in main storage

The operand field consists of a register indicator if one of the accumulator registers participates in the operation. Otherwise, the statement uses a single symbolic or numeric operand, and the corresponding field of the machine instruction is zero. The machine instructions in the hypothetical computer are given in Table 10.1.

Assembler and macro definition instructions in the hypothetical assembler language are given in Table 10.2. The instructions form a basic set demonstrating each of the categories of assembler language instructions given in the previous chapter.

Overview of the Assembly Process Using a Sample Program

Input to the assembly process is a program composed of statements; output from the process is a program listing and an object program. Figure 10.3 gives a sample source program as it normally would be punched on cards for input to the assembler. Figure 10.4 lists the same program with nongenerative instructions removed* and macros expanded, similar to the manner in which it would be handled during the first pass over the program during assembly. The relationship of the

---

* That is, except ORG and EQU that affect the location counter and symbol table, respectively.

Table 10.2

Assembler and macro definition instructions in the hypothetical assembler language used for demonstration of the assembly process

	Location	Symbolic Operation Code	Operand	Definition
Symbol Definition	Symbol	EQU	Number	Make symbol equivalent to given address
	Symbol1	SYN	Symbol2	Make symbol1 equivalent to symbol2
Data Definition	Symbol	DCONST	Number (constant)	Form constant and give symbolic name
	Symbol	DSTOR	Number	Reserve designated amount of storage
Program Control		ORG	Number	Set location counter to given address
		END		Indicates end of assembler program
Listing Control		TITLE	Title	Causes a title on each page of listing to be printed
		SPACE	Number	Skip designated number of spaces in program listing
		EJECT		Ejects page in program listing
Macro Definition		MACRO		Specifies beginning of macro definition
		MEND		Specifies end of macro defintion

location counter to the program and the resultant symbol table are also included in the same figure. The complete program listing is given in Figure 10.5. The listing includes macro instructions, and macro expansions, and gives the location and object code for generative instructions. Some assemblers also provide an edited form of the symbol table, called a *cross reference listing*, for use in program analysis and debugging.

Location	Operation	Operand
	TITLE	ABC CORPORATION – ORCHARD PROJECT
	MACRO	
	MUSUB	&RN,&OP1,&OP2,&OP3,&OP4
	LOAD	&RN,&OP1
	MULT	&RN,&OP2
	SUB	&RN,&OP3
	STORE	&RN,&OP4
	MEND	
	ORD	350
AC	EQU	8
DELTA	EQU	1296
FINI	EQU	5374
	READ	CLOK
	READ	WIBI
	LOAD	2,WIBI
	BZERO	2,OUTSIDE
	LOAD	AC,CLOK
	ADD	AC,MACY
	BZERO	AC,NOTOK
	SPACE	2
	MUSUB	4,WIBI,CLOK,TIL,DELTA
EXIT	LOAD	9,FLAG
	BR	FINI
NOTOK	LOAD	8,FATTY
	STORE	8,DELTA
	BR	EXIT
OUTSIDE	MUSUB	AC,WIBI,NAT,TIL,DELTA
	BR	EXIT
CLOK	DSTOR	1
WIBI	DSTOR	1
MACY	DCONST	131
TIL	DCONST	57
FLAG	DCONST	1
FATTY	DCONST	6000
NAT	DCONST	4
	END	

Figure 10.3 Listing of source program (sample) prior to the assembly process. (See Figure 10.4.)

	Location	Operation	Operand	Location Counter
		ORG	350	350
	AC	EQU	8	
	DELTA	EQU	1296	
	FINI	EQU	5374	
		READ	CLOK	350
		READ	WIBI	351
		LOAD	2,WIBI	352
		BZERO	2,OUTSIDE	352
		LOAD	AC,CLOK	354
		ADD	AC,MACY	355
		BZERO	AC,NOTOK	366
		MUSUB	4,WIBI,CLOK, TIL,DELTA	
+		LOAD	4,WIBI	357
+		MULT	4,CLOK	358
+		SUB	4,TIL	359
+		STORE	4,DELTA	360
	EXIT	LOAD	9,FLAG	361
		BR	FINI	362
	NOTOK	LOAD	8,FATTY	363
		STORE	8,DELTA	364
		BR	EXIT	365
	OUTSIDE		AC,WIBI,NAT, TIL,DELTA	
+	OUTSIDE	LOAD	AC,WIBI	366
+		MULT	AC,NAT	367
+		SUB	AC,TIL	368
+		STORE	AC,DELTA	369
		BR	EXIT	370
	CLOK	DSTOR	1	371
	WIBI	DSTOR	1	372
	MACY	DCONST	131	373
	TIL	DCONST	57	374
	FLAG	DCONST	1	375
	FATTY	DCONST	6000	376
	NAT	DCONST	4	377
		END		

Symbol Table

Symbol	Address
AC	8
DELTA	1296
FINI	5374
EXIT	361
NOTOK	363
OUTSIDE	366
CLOK	371
WIBI	372
MACY	373
TIL	374
FLAG	375
FATTY	376
NAT	377

Key: + denotes instructions generated during macro expansion.

Figure 10.4 Sample source program in assembler language with macros expanded and nongenerative instructions (except ORG and EQU) removed, showing relationship of statements, location counter, and symbol table.

273

LOC	OBJ CODE		SOURCE PROGRAM	
			TITLE	ABC CORPORATION – ORCHARD PROJECT
			MACRO	
			MUSUB	&RN,&OP1,&OP2,&OP3,&OP4
			LOAD	&RN,&OP1
			MULT	&RN,&OP2
			SUB	&RN,&OP3
			STORE	&RN,&OP4
			MEND	
350			ORG	350
8		AC	EQU	8
1296		DELTA	EQU	1296
5374		FINI	EQU	5374
350	0900371		READ	CLOK
351	0900372		READ	WIBI
352	0120372		LOAD	2,WIBI
353	0820366		BZERO	2,OUTSIDE
354	0180371		LOAD	AC,CLOK
355	0380373		ADD	AC,MACY
356	0880363		BZERO	AC,NOTOK
			SPACE	2
			MUSUB	4,WIBI,CLOK,TIL,DELTA
357	0140372 +		LOAD	4,WIBI
358	0540371 +		MULT	4,CLOK
359	0440374 +		SUB	4,TIL
360	0241296 +		STORE	4,DELTA
361	0190375	EXIT	LOAD	9,FLAG
362	0705374		BR	FINI
363	0180375	NOTOK	LOAD	8,FATTY
364	0281296		STORE	8,DELTA
365	0700361		BR	EXIT
		OUTSIDE	MUSUB	AC,WIBI,NAT,TIL,DELTA
366	0180372 + OUTSIDE		LOAD	AC,WIBI

Figure 10.5 Program listing for the sample source program in assembler language, showing the locations, object code, and the source program.

ABC CORPORATION – ORCHARD PROJECT

LOC	OBJ CODE	SOURCE PROGRAM		
367	0580377 +	MULT	AC,NAT	
368	0480374 +	SUB	AC,TIL	
369	0281296 +	STORE	AC,DELTA	
370	0700361	BR	EXIT	
371		CLOK	DSTOR	1
372		WIBI	DSTOR	1
373	0000131	MACY	DCONST	131
374	0000057	TIL	DCONST	57
375	0000001	FLAG	DCONST	1
376	0006000	FATTY	DCONST	6000
377	0000004	NAT	DCONST	4
			END	

Figure 10.5 (continued)

Operation of the Assembler Program—Pass One

Most assemblers use two passes over the source program to translate it into a machine language form. Occasionally, more than two passes are designed into the assembly process; however, the concepts are easily introduced in two passes.

For this presentation that uses the hypothetical computer and assembler language given earlier, assembler language statements are classified into six types for convenience and to facilitate presentation of the assembly process:

Type I	*Type II*	*Type III*	*Type IV*	*Type V*
LOAD	DIV	DSTOR	TITLE	EQU	MACRO
STORE	BR	DCONST	SPACE	SYN	MEND
ADD	BZERO		EJECT	ORG	
SUB	READ			END	
MULT	PRINT				

The final class, type VI, is comprised solely of macro instructions.

The objective of the first pass of the assembler is to store macro definitions, expand macro instructions, maintain the location counter, build a symbol table for pass two, and prepare the source program for

pass two by copying it on an intermediate storage device or placing it in
a coded form in a table. The steps that make up the first pass of the
assembly procedure are given in Figure 10.6. While the procedure
reflects the hypothetical computer and sample assembler language given
earlier in this section, the methodology is representative of the techniques used in modern assemblers.

The outputs (or results) of the first pass of the assembler are the
symbol table and the source program, stored on an intermediate storage
device or in a table. These outputs are used as inputs to the second pass
of the assembler. In the design of the assembler, the obvious differentiation between pass one and pass two is used to break the assembler
program into phases. The first phase, corresponding to the first pass, is
read in to main storage and executed. The second phase, corresponding
to the second pass, executes independently of the first phase, so that it
can occupy the same area of main storage. Thus, the second phase is
read in "on top of" the first phase. The end result, of course, is that the
assembler is designed so that it requires a minimum amount of main
storage for execution.

Operation of the Assembler Program—Pass Two

The objective of the second pass of the assembler is to generate
actual machine code by looking up symbolic operation codes and
operands in appropriate tables and by converting numeric operands to
an internal form. The procedure involves retrieving the source program
from the intermediate storage device or table on a statement-by-
statement basis and determining whether a machine instruction or an
assembler instruction is to be processed. A machine instruction is
translated to internal machine code by making a simple replacement of
its symbolic constituents. An assembler instruction causes the assembler
program to perform a specific function, such as generating a constant
value or storage area, or skipping a line in the program listing.

Normally, the object program along with control information is
punched into 80-column cards or it is written on an intermediate storage
medium in an equivalent form. This operation is performed by placing
the translated machine code in a buffer as it is generated. When the
buffer is full, the information contained therein is released for the output
operation. The program listing, such as the example given in Figure 10.5,
is also produced during the second pass of the assembler.

A certain amount of error analysis is performed during the second
pass of the assembly process as a result of the fact that symbolic
operands are "looked up" in the symbol table developed in the first pass.

Step Number	Function
1	Initialize *location-counter* and *symbol-table.*
2	Set *error-location* (i.e., error field or variable) to all blanks.
3	Read a source statement
4	If there is an * in column one, go to step 12. (This denotes a comment line.)
5	MACRO statement? If so, go to step 13.
6	Type IV statement? If so, go to step 20.
7	Type III statement? If so, go to step 18.
8	Type I or II statement? If so, go to step 14.
9	Is operation code in the temporary or system macro library? If so, go to step 17.
10	Set *error-location* to "E."
11	Increase *location-counter* by 1.
12	Write *error-location* and source line on intermediate storage device or put in table. Go to step 2.
13	Store statements between MACRO and MEND in temporary macro library. Go to step 2.
14	If there is a symbol in the location field, attempt to enter symbol in the location field in the symbol table along with the current value of the *location-counter.*
15	If the symbol was duplicated—i.e., it was already in the symbol table—set the error field to "D," for duplicate.
16	Go to step 11.
17	Retrieve macro from macro library; expand macro replacing parameters with arguments; and replace macro instruction with generated statements. Go to step 4. (Generated statements are assembled as though they were in the source program.)
18	If instruction is TITLE, store title for pass two.
19	Go to step 12.
20	If instruction is ORG, go to step 24.
21	If instruction is EQU, go to step 26.
22	If instruction is SYN, go to step 31.
23	(Instruction must be END.) Write *error-location* and source line on intermediate storage device or put in table. Reposition intermediate storage device (containing source program) at beginning. Sort symbol table if desired. Go to pass 2. [Step 37 in Figure 10.7]

Figure 10.6   Steps in the assembly procedure—pass one.

Step Number	Function
24	If operand field is not numeric, set *error-location* to "E" and go to step 12.
25	Replace *location-counter* with operand (i.e., address) of ORG statement. Go to step 12.
26	If location field of source line is blank, set *error-location* to "E" and go to step 12.
27	If operand field of source line is not numeric, set *error-location* to "E" and go to step 12.
28	Attempt to enter symbol in location field of source line in the symbol table along with the operand field (i.e., an address).
29	If the symbol was duplicated (i.e., it was already in the symbol table) set the *error-location* to "D," for duplicate.
30	Go to step 12.
31	If location field of source line is blank and operand field of source line not symbolic, set *error-location* to "E" and go to step 12.
32	Attempt to look up symbol in operand field of source line in symbol table, and retrieve corresponding address.
33	If symbol (from operand field) was not defined, set *error-location* to "E" and go to step 12.
34	Attempt to enter symbol in location field of source line in the symbol table along with address retrieved in step 32.
35	If the symbol (from location field of source line) was duplicated, set *error-location* to "D."
36	Go to step 12.

Figure 10.6   (continued)

Statements containing undefined symbols are normally flagged accordingly.

The steps that make up the second pass of the assembly procedure are given in Figure 10.7.

Step Number	Function
37	Initialize *error-location, punch-buffer,* and *error-flag.*
38	Read a source line from intermediate storage device or retrieve next statement (in a coded form) from table. Note: error indicator and source line are both obtained in this operation.
39	Is *error-location* equal to "E"? If so, print diagnostic message, set *error-flag.* Go to step 64.
40	In this a comment line (i.e., * in column one)? If so, go to step 64.
41	Is *error-location* equal to "D"? If so, print diagnostic message and set *error-flag.* (Continue with step 42.)
42	Type I statement? If so, go to step 47.
43	Type II statement? If so, go to step 55.
44	Type III statement? If so, perform requested action (such as eject) and go to step 64.
45	Type IV statement? If so, go to step 58.
46	(Undefined instruction) Print diagnostic message; set *error-flag;* go to step 64.
47	(Prepare to synthesize machine instruction.) Initialize *build-code-location.*
48	Look up symbolic operation code in operation code table and insert numeric operation code in the *build-code-location.*
49	Is there a register designator in the statement? If none is given, set the register-designator field in the *build-code-location* to zero and go to step 52.
50	If the register designator is numeric, convert it to an internal form and insert it in the *build-code-location* and go to step 52. (Ordinarily, error checking would be performed here and in step 51 to ensure that the numeric value of the register designator is within prescribed limits.)
51	Look up symbolic register designator in the *symbol table.* If the symbol is defined, insert corresponding value as register designator in *build-code-location* and go to step 52 (i.e., next step). Otherwise, set the register designator in the *build-code-location* to zero, print diagnostic, set *error-flag,* and continue with the next step.

Figure 10.7   Steps in the assembly procedure—pass two.

279

Step Number	Function
52	Look up symbolic operand (i.e., the symbolic address location) in the symbolic table. If the symbol is not defined, go to step 54. Otherwise, insert corresponding value in the address field of the *build-code-location.*
53	Place machine instruction—or constant from the *build-code-location* in the *punch-buffer.* If the card is not full, go to step 63. If the card is full, write the *punch-buffer* to designated storage medium and go to step 63. (Symbol is not defined.) Set the address field in the *build-code-location* to zero, print diagnostic, set *error-flag,* and go to step 53.
55	If operation code is DSTOR, go to step 57.
56	(Operation code must be DCONST.) Initialize *build-code-location.* Convert operand to internal form. If constant is invalid, set *build-code-location* to zero; print diagnostic, set *error-flag,* and go to step 54. If constant is valid, insert it in *build-code-location.* Go to step 54.
57	Convert operand (to DSTOR instruction) to internal form. Place control information in object program to reserve the designated amount of storage. Go to step 64.
58	If operation code is ORG, convert operand to internal form, and punch (or write) special card (for the loader) specifying the new program origin. Go to step 64.
59	If operation code is SYN or EQU, go to step 64.
60	(Must be END operation code) Empty *punch-buffer.* Fill in "source line" part of print line of program listing with END statement and cause the line to be written out.
61	If *error-flag* is set, print diagnostic message stating that the program contains an error.
62	Terminate assembly process.
63	Fill in "machine code" part of the print line of the program listing from the *build-code-location.*
64	Fill in the "source line" part of the print line. Cause print line to be written out. Go to step 38.

Figure 10.7 (continued)

10.3 COMPILER TECHNIQUES

The process of developing a compiler primarily involves determining the machine language instructions that correspond to a given statement in the programming language under consideration.* Thus, even compilers for the same programming language differ, depending upon the object computer.

The greatest area of similarity and consistency among compilers involves the analysis and processing of expressions and the implementation of arithmetic and logical statements. Moreover, the handling of expressions is of particular significance because the expression is a constituent part of many other statement types.

The emphasis in this section concerns the processing of arithmetic expressions and arithmetic statements. However, the methodology can be extended in a systematic manner to apply to logical expressions and logical statements as well.

Mathematical Forms

Ordinary mathematical notation is referred to as *infix notation*,† which means that the operator symbol for operations requiring two operands separates the operands. Examples of infix notation are: $x + y$, which means "add the value of y to the value of x," and $-a$, which means "take the negative of a." When an expression includes more than one operation, then an operational convention is used to determine the order in which the operations are executed. The most widely used convention is to establish a hierarchy among operators, such as the following:

Operator Symbol	Hierarchy	Operational Meaning
**	High	Exponentiation
* or /	↓	Multiplication or division
+ or −	Low	Addition or subtraction

and then to execute operators by order of hierarchy. Thus, an expression such as

$$\frac{a}{x + y}$$

* Apparently, this is the origin of the term *compile*. Machine instructions that correspond to the statements of a source program are "compiled" to form an object program.

† A distinction is made between infix notation and an infix operator. An infix (or binary) operator requires two operands; a prefix (or unary) operator requires one operand.

requires the use of parentheses, that is,

A/(X + Y)

to specify the intended meaning.

A notation that does not require parentheses for expressions of this sort is called Polish notation, after the Polish mathematician J. Luka-sewicz, who used it for representing well-formed formulas in logic. In fact, Polish notation never requires parentheses and is known as a "parenthesis-free" notation. Polish notation comes in two varieties: *prefix notation*, which is also called simply Polish notation; and *postfix notation*, which is also called reverse Polish notation. In prefix notation, the operator always precedes its operands (reading from left to right), so that an expression such as A + B is denoted by +AB. More complex expressions are constructed by repeated application of the concept in a similar manner. Additional examples of mathematical expressions represented in prefix notation are given in Table 10.3.

Postfix notation is the most popular form of Polish notation and is characterized by the fact that the operands precede the operator (again reading from left to right), so that the infix expression A + B is represented by AB +. Additional examples of postfix notation are given in Table 10.3. The major advantages of postfix notation are inherent in the relative simplicity of the processes required to: (1) convert an expression from infix notation to postfix notation; and (2) execute the postfix notation interpretively or convert it to a set of equivalent machine language instructions. A description of the conversion process from infix notation to postfix notation is given in a subsequent paragraph.

Table 10.3

Examples of Polish Notation

Infix Notation	Prefix Notation	Postfix Notation
A∗B	∗AB	AB∗
A∗X−B	−∗AXB	AX∗B−
A∗ (X−B)	∗A−XB	AXB−∗
A+ (B/C−D)	+A−/BCD	ABC/D−+
A∗(B/ (C − D)+E)	∗A+/B−CDE	ABCD−/E+∗

Structure of Expressions

One means of showing the relationship between operators and operands in an expression and exhibiting the order in which operations should be executed is to use a *structural diagram*. In a diagram of this type, operators and operands are regarded as points (or nodes), and the relationship between them is denoted by lines, as shown in Figure 10.8. A structural diagram provides two important items of information about an expression: (1) its form, and (2) its structural meaning. In general, a structural diagram is independent of the syntactic structure of a programming language.

A structural diagram can be regarded as an upside-down tree. The topmost node is the "root" and operands are always terminal nodes or "leaves" of the tree. Another way to look at a structural diagram is to view it as a hierarchical collection of subtrees, where each operator is the root of a subtree and the operands (to that operator) are leaves of that subtree. Thus, an operator is always the root of a subtree. A binary operator has two subtrees, corresponding to each of its operands.* A unary operator has a single subtree, corresponding to its single operand. Figure 10.9 gives structural forms for binary and unary operators.

Trees (or structural diagrams) do not lend themselves to representation in the computer, for obvious reasons, and are stored as a linear sequence of symbols. The process of converting a tree to a linear sequence of symbols is accomplished by traversing (or walking through) the tree. Knuth defines three methods that are applied by systematically dividing a tree into subtrees.† The three methods (modified to meet our needs) are given as:

Preorder Traversal	*Postorder Traversal*
Visit the root	Traverse the left subtree
Traverse the left subtree	Visit the root
Traverse the right subtree	Traverse the right subtree
or	or
Visit the root	Visit the root
Traverse the single subtree	Traverse the single subtree

---

* A tree can also be viewed recursively as a collection of roots and descendents. A descendent may be a terminal node (i.e., operand) or the root of a subtree.

† A complete description of the methods is given in Knuth, D. E., *The Art of Computer Programming*, Vol. I, *Fundamental Algorithms*, Addison-Wesley, Reading, Mass., 1968, p. 315.

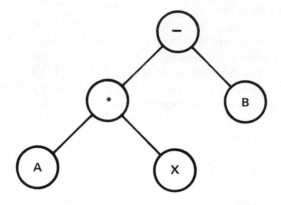

(A) Structure diagram for A ∗ X − B

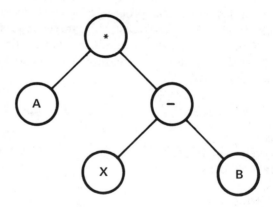

(B) Structure diagram for A ∗ (X − B)

Figure 10.8   Structure diagrams used to exhibit the relationship between operators and operands in an expression.

Endorder Traversal

Traverse the left subtree
Traverse the right subtree
Visit the root
or
Traverse the single subtree
Visit the root

The three forms of traversal are depicted in Figure 10.10. Figure 10.11 gives additional examples, of which the last includes unary operators.

An interesting relationship exists between the structural diagram (or tree form) of an expression and infix, prefix, and postfix notation. If the "tree of an expression" is denoted by TOE, then

Preorder (TOE) → prefix notation
endorder (TOE) → postfix notation
postorder (TOE) → infix notation without parentheses

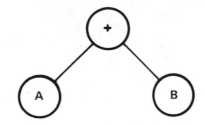

(A) Representation of a binary operator

(B) Representation of a unary operator

Figure 10.9   Structural forms for binary and unary operators.

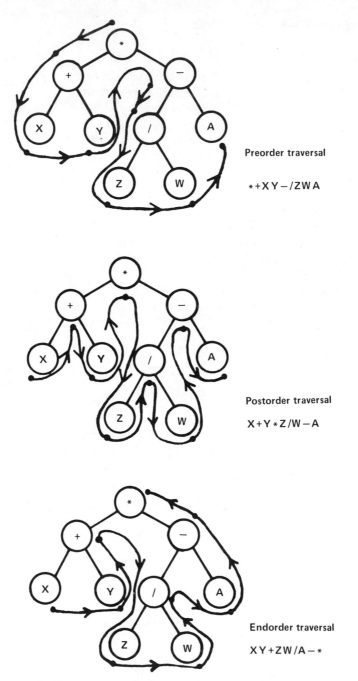

Figure 10.10 Preorder, postorder, and endorder traversal of the structural diagram of the expression $(X + Y)*(Z/W - A)$.

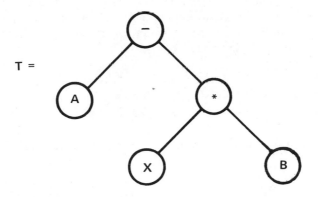

T =

preorder (T)→ − A * X B
postorder (T)→ A − X * B
endorder (T) ·›' A X B * −

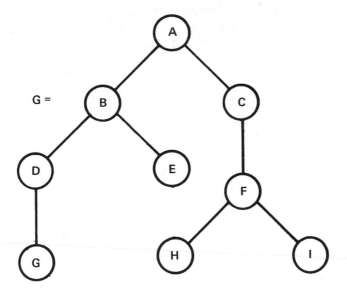

G =

preorder (G)→ABDGECFHI
postorder (G)→DGBEACHFI
endorder (G)→GDEBHIFCA

Figure 10.11 Examples of preorder, postorder, and endorder traversal.

In the last case, the relationship has validity only for expressions without parentheses, but is a useful conceptual tool. As an example of these concepts, consider the tree named Q in Figure 10.12. Application of the three forms of traversal gives

> *preorder* (Q) → = A + *BC/DE, which is prefix notation
> *postorder* (Q) → A = B*C + D/E, which is infix notation
> *endorder* (Q) → ABC*DE/ + =, which is postfix notation

This last example incorporates the replacement operation of the form

> $v = e$

where v is a variable and e is an expression. This can be regarded as a binary operation that takes the form $= ve$ in prefix notation and $ve =$ in postfix notation.

Conversion between Infix Notation and Postfix Notation

Postfix notation is used in many language processors as an intermediate form for representing expressions and logical and arith-

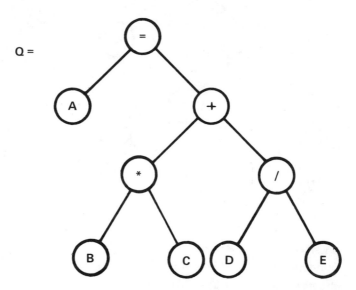

Q =

Figure 10.12   Structural diagram of the statement A = B*C + D/E. This example is used in the text to show the relationship between traversal and mathematical forms.

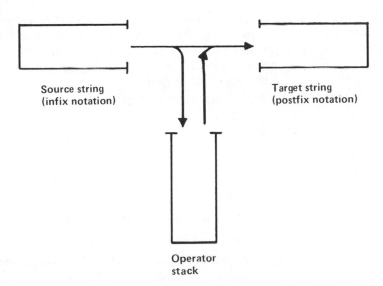

Figure 10.13 Basic diagram of the conversion process from infix and postfix notation.

metic statements. The conversion from infix notation to postfix notation is given here as a basic technique. The description of the method utilizes operands that are single letters and does not permit subscripted variables. These are topics that would be considered as extensions to the basic methods.* Methods for interpretively executing postfix notation are given later in the chapter. The conversion process from postfix notation to machine instructions is left as an exercise; however, this general topic is covered to some degree under the title "Bounded Context Translation," later in the chapter.

The conversion process requires the use of a *stack*, which is a table of values maintained on a last-in-first-out (LIFO) basis. All entries and deletions are made at the top, so that when an item is entered in a stack, all other items in the stack are pushed down. Similarly, when an item is removed from the stack, all remaining items are popped up. In a sense, a stack is analogous to a stack of plates in a cafeteria.

Conversion from infix notation to postfix notation uses a set of procedures and a hierarchy (or priority) among operators. The overall process is depicted in Figure 10.13. The terms *source string* and *target*

* Katzan gives a complete treatment of conversion from infix to postfix notation in *Advanced Programming*, Van Nostrand-Reinhold, New York, pp. 55–61.

string are particularly appropriate because the expression can be regarded as a string of characters. After conversion from infix to postfix notation, the order of operands (that is, variables) remains the same. During conversion, an *operator stack* is used to rearrange the operators so that they occur in the target string in the order in which they should be executed. The priority of operators is as follows:

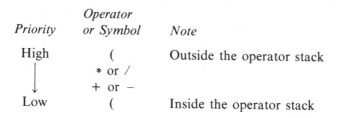

A small subset of operators, including parentheses, is selected to simplify the conversion process. Rules for manipulating the source and target strings and the operator stack can now be given:

1. The source string is scanned from left to right. Similarly, the target string is formed from left to right.
2. Operands (that is, variables) from the source string bypass the operator stack and are passed to the target string directly.
3. If the scan of the source string encounters an operator with a priority greater than the priority of the operator at the top of the operator stack, then the operator from the source string is entered into the operator stack. If the priority of the operator in the source string is not greater than the priority of the operator at the top of the operator stack, then the operator at the top of the operator stack is moved to the target string and this step is repeated. (Note: a left parenthesis always enters the operator stack.)
4. If a right parenthesis is encountered during the scan of the source string, then the operators in the operator stack are moved to the target string. This process continues until a left parenthesis is encountered in the operator stack; then the left and right parentheses are both discarded.
5. When the end of the source string is reached, all operators in the operator stack are moved directly to the target string.

Figure 10.14 gives a detailed "walk-through" of the conversion process using the above rules and operator priorities.

Source String	Operator Stack	Target String
↑A+(B*C–D)/E		
↑+(B*C–D)/E		A
↑(B*C–D)/E	+	A
↑B*C–D)/E	(+	A
↑*C–D)/E	(+	AB
↑C–D)/E	* (+	AB
↑–D)/E	* (+	ABC
↑D)/E	– (+	ABC*
↑)/E	– (+	ABC*D
↑/E	+	ABC*D–
↑E	/ +	ABC*D–
↑	/ +	ABC*D–E
(↑ Denotes scan pointer)		ABC*D–E/+

Figure 10.14 Conversion from infix notation to postfix notation.

291

Once an expression or assignment statement has been translated to postfix notation, retranslation is accomplished by scanning the postfix string from left to right until the first operator is encountered. The operator is then placed between the two preceding operands and the triad is enclosed in parentheses. The parenthetical group is then regarded as a single operand. The process is repeated, always beginning the scan from the left, until a fully parenthesized expression or statement in infix notation is formed. For example, the retranslation of the postfix string $AXY + ZW/B - * =$ would involve the following steps:

1. In the left-to-right scan, the first operator $+$ is placed between the two preceding operands and enclosed in parentheses, giving $A(\underline{X + Y})ZW/B - * =$ with the parenthesized expression regarded as a single operand.
2. The scan is repeated and the / slash is encountered and placed between the preceding operand giving $A \,(\underline{X + Y)}\,(\underline{Z/W})B - * =$
3. The operator $-$ is met next, giving $A(\underline{(X + Y))((Z/W)} - B)* =$
4. The operator $*$ is reached next, giving $A((\underline{(X + Y)*((Z/W)} - B)) =$
5. Lastly, the final operator $=$ is identified and the completely parenthesized statement in infix notation is

$$(A = ((X + Y)*((Z/W) - B)))$$

A fully parenthesized expression or statement explicitly specifies the order in which operations are to be executed. If fully parenthesized expressions or statements were used exclusively, then there would be no need to establish a hierarchy among operators.

Interpretive Execution of Postfix Notation

Interpretive execution of an expression in postfix notation involves a left-to-right scan and the use of an operand stack. If an operand is encountered during the scan, its value is placed in the operand stack.* If an operator is encountered during the scan, the required number of values (i.e., two operands for binary operators and one operand for unary operators) are taken from the operand stack.† The specified operation is performed on the operand(s) and the result is placed back in the stack. An example of interpretive execution is given in Figure 10.15.

---

*When a value is placed in a stack, the values already in the stack are pushed down.
†Values are taken from a stack on a LIFO basis; when the top value is removed, the remainder of values are moved up.

Postfix String	Operand Stack	Note
XY+ZW/A−*B+Y/	(empty)	Prior to scan of postfix string; stack empty
Y+ZW/A−*B+Y/	2	Value of X is pushed into stack
+ZW/A−*B+Y/	3 2	Value of Y is pushed into stack
ZW/A−*B+Y/	5	+ operator; two operands (3 and 2) are pulled from top of stack; operation is performed on them; result is pushed into stack
W/A−*B+Y/	12 5	Value of Z is pushed into stack
/A−*B+Y/	4 12 5	Value of W is pushed into stack
A−*B+Y/	3 5	/ operator; two operands (4 and 12) are pulled from top of stack; operation is performed on them; result is pushed into stack
−*B+Y/	1 3 5	Value of A is pushed into stack
*B+Y/	2 5	− operator; two operands (1 and 3) are pulled from top of stack; operation is performed on them; result is pushed into stack
B+Y/	10	* operator; two operands (2 and 5) are pulled from top of stack; operation is performed on them; result is pushed into stack
+Y/	5 10	Value of B is pushed into stack
Y/	15	+ operator; two operands (5 and 10) are pulled from top of stack; operation is performed on them; result is pushed into stack

Figure 10.15 Interpretive execution of the postfix expression $XY + ZW/A - *B + Y/$ that corresponds to the infix expression $((X + Y)*(Z/W - A) + B)/Y$.

Postfix String	Operand Stack	Note
/	3 15 5	Value of Y is pushed into stack

Value of Operands

Symbol	Value
X	2
Y	3
Z	12
W	4
A	1
B	5

/ operator; two operands (3 and 15) are pulled from top of stack; operation is performed on them; result is pushed into stack

	5	Execution of postfix string is complete; result is in the operand stack

Figure 10.15 (continued)

When the process is complete, the computed value of the expression is at the top of the operand stack.

Interpretive Execution of Prefix Notation

Interpretive execution of an expression in prefix notation involves a left-to-right scan and the use of two stacks: an operator stack and an operand stack. (It should be remembered that in this notation the operator precedes its operands.) When an operator is encountered during the left-to-right scan, it is placed into the operator stack along with a number indicating the number of operands the operator requires (i.e., two for binary operators and one for unary operators). When an operand is encountered during the left-to-right scan, it is placed in the operand stack and the number corresponding to the operands required by the topmost operator in the operator stack is decreased by one. Immediately after, the number of required operands of the topmost operator in the operator stack is tested. If the number is zero, then the required number of operands is taken from the operand stack, the indicated operation is executed, and the topmost operator in the operator stack is removed (i.e., "popped up") and discarded. The result of the operation is then placed in the operand stack and the number corresponding to the new topmost operator in the operator stack is decreased by one. This procedure is depicted in Figure 10.16. The process continues until the prefix string is exhausted; the computed value of the expression is at the top of the operand stack.

Prefix String	Operator Stack	Operand Stack	Note
/+*+XY−/ZWABY	(empty)	(empty)	Prior to scan of prefix string; stacks empty
+*+XY−/ZWABY	/ 2	(empty)	/operator and required number of operands are pushed into operator stack
*+XY−/ZWABY	+ 2 / 2	(empty)	+ operator and required number of operands are pushed into operator stack
+XY−/ZWABY	* 2 + 2 / 2	(empty)	*operator and required number of operands are pushed into operator stack
XY−/ZWABY	+ 2 * 2 + 2 / 2	(empty)	+ operator and required number of operands are pushed into operator stack
Y−/ZWABY	+ 1 * 2 + 2 / 2	2	Value of X is pushed into operand stack; number of topmost operator in operator stack is reduced by 1
−/ZWABY	+ 0 * 2 + 2 / 2	3 2	Value of Y is pushed into operand stack; number of topmost operator in operator stack is reduced by 1

Value of Operands

Symbol	Value
X	2
Y	3
Z	12
W	4
A	1
B	5

Figure 10.16 Interpretive execution of the prefix expression $/ + * + XY - /$ ZWABY that corresponds to the infix expression $((X+Y)*(Z/W-A)+B)/Y$.

295

Prefix String	Operator Stack		Operand Stack	Note
−/ZWABY	*	1	5	Number of topmost operator in operator stack is zero; two operands are pulled from operand stack; result is pushed into operand stack; top operator is removed from operator stack; number of *new* top operator in operator stack is reduced by 1
	+	2		
	/	2		
−/ZWABY	−	2	5	− operator and required number of operands are pushed into operator stack
	*	1		
	+	2		
	/	2		
ZWABY	/	2	5	/ operator is pushed into operator stack
	−	2		
	*	1		
	+	2		
	/	2		
WABY	/	1	12	Value of Z is pushed into operand stack; number of topmost operator in operator stack is decreased by 1
	−	2	5	
	*	1		
	+	2		
	/	2		
ABY	/	0	4	Value of W is pushed into operand stack; number of topmost operator in operator stack is decreased by 1
	−	2	12	
	*	1	5	
	+	2		
	/	2		

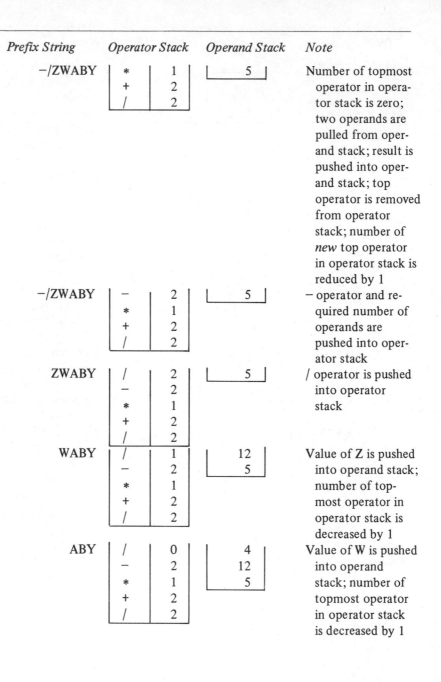

Figure 10.16 (continued)

296

Prefix String	Operator Stack		Operand Stack	Note
ABY	−	1	3	Number of topmost operator in operator stack is zero; two operands are pulled from operand stack; result is pushed into operand stack; top operator is removed from operator stack; number of *new* top operator in operator stack is decreased by 1
	*	1	5	
	+	2		
	/	2		
BY	−	0	1	Value of A is pushed into operand stack; number of topmost operator in operator stack is decreased by 1
	*	1	3	
	+	2	5	
	/	2		
BY	*	0	2	Topmost operator is executed and result is placed in operand stack; old operator is discarded and number of *new* operator is decreased by 1
	+	2	5	
	/	2		
BY	+	1	10	Topmost operator is executed and result is placed in operand stack; old operator is discarded and number of *new* operator is decreased by 1
	/	2		

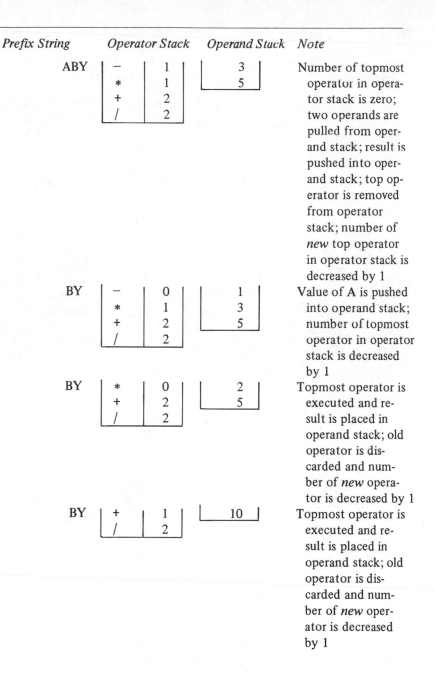

Figure 10.16 (continued)

297

Prefix String	Operator Stack	Operand Stack	Note
Y	+ 0 / 2	5 10	Value of B is pushed into operand stack; number of topmost operator in operator stack is decreased by 1
Y	/ 1	15	Topmost operator is executed and result is placed in operand stack; old operator is discarded and number of *new* operator is decreased by 1
	/ 0	3 15	Value of Y is pushed into operand stack; number of topmost operator in operator stack is decreased by 1
		5	Topmost operator is executed and result is placed in operand stack
		5	Execution of prefix string is complete ; result is in the operand stack

Figure 10.16   (continued)

Bounded Context Translation

Most language processor programs use an internal intermediate language to represent a program prior to generating actual machine code. A program is translated into the intermediate language, which is independent of the methods used to analyze the source statements and of the computer on which the program is executed. In fact, this technique is frequently employed in building compilers. Basic procedures are developed to translate a source program to intermediate form, and other procedures are developed to translate a program from intermediate form to machine code. When it is desired to produce a compiler for another computer, using the same programming language, only the second set of procedures needs be changed.

Prefix and postfix notation can be regarded as an intermediate language for arithmetic expressions. Prefix and postfix notation lends itself to interpretive execution, but it is a cumbersome form for the generation of machine code. A reasonably well-known intermediate language that lends itself to code generation is known as *matrix form*. Matrix form is related to the structural diagram of an expression and prefix notation, as demonstrated in Figure 10.17. The first column of the matrix is the operator, the second column is the left operand, and the third column is the right operand. The row index (1, 2, and so on) identifies the result of that row and specifies the order in which subexpressions are to be evaluated.

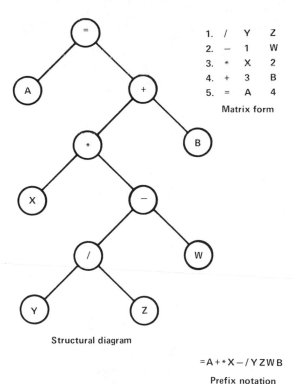

1.	/	Y	Z
2.	–	1	W
3.	*	X	2
4.	+	3	B
5.	=	A	4

Matrix form

Structural diagram

=A+*X−/YZWB

Prefix notation

Figure 10.17 Matrix form of the statement A = X*(Y/Z − W) + B and its relationship to the structural diagram and prefix notation.

The value of the matrix form lies in its close relationship to machine code, as demonstrated in Figure 10.18. For each operation that is recognized in the programming language, a sequence of machine instructions, such as

```
LOAD
Op
STORE
```

is defined; if the row of the table were + A B, for example, the following machine code would be generated:

```
LOAD    A
ADD     B
STORE   i
```

Matrix Form	First-Level Generated Code	Optimized Code
1. / Y Z	LOAD Y DIVIDE Z STORE T1	
2. − 1 W	LOAD T1 SUB W STORE T2	LOAD Y DIVIDE Z SUB W STORE T2
3. ∗ X 2	LOAD X MULT T2 STORE T3	LOAD X MULT T2 ADD B STORE A
4. + 3 B	LOAD T3 ADD B STORE T4	
5. = A 4	LOAD T4 STORE A	

Figure 10.18 Relationship of matrix form to the machine code generation process. (T1, T2, T3, and T4 refer to temporary locations.)

1. + B C	LOAD	B	LOAD	1,B
2. − D E	ADD	C	ADD	1,C
3. /1 2	STORE	T1	LOAD	2,D
4. = A 3	LOAD	D	SUB	2,E
	SUB	E	DIVIDE	1,2
Matrix Form	STORE	T2	STORE	1,A
	LOAD	T1		
	DIVIDE	T2	*Computer with*	
	STORE	A	*Multiple Accumulators*	

*Computer with One
Accumulator*

Figure 10.19 Code generation for a computer with one accumulator and for a computer with multiple accumulators, for the statement A = (B + C)/(D − E).

where i is the row index. Similarly, the row = P 7 would cause the following machine code to be generated:

```
LOAD    T7
STORE   P
```

In this example, T7 refers to a temporary location in which the result of row 7 of the matrix is stored.

A small amount of optimization can be performed during the code generation process. If a STORE operation is followed by a LOAD operation to the same temporary location, then neither operation is required and both can be discarded. Figure 10.18 also depicts code optimization of this form. When a computer with multiple accumulators is used, code generation would naturally involve the judicious use of registers. For example, the code generated for the statement A = (B + C)/(D − E) is shown in Figure 10.19 for a computer with one accumulator and for a computer with multiple accumulators. Register allocation is an advanced compiler technique.

The transformation of an expression has been studied by Graham* and is referred to as *bounded context translation*. The name is obvious

---

* This section is based on the work of Robert M. Graham, reported in a paper entitled "Bounded Context Translation," printed in Rosen, S. (ed.), *Programming Systems and Languages*, McGraw-Hill, New York, 1967, pp. 184–205.

from the methods employed. The concept of bounded context translation is introduced with a technique for transforming a completely parenthesized expression to matrix form and then by generalizing the method.

The following rules apply to the transformation of a completely parenthesized expression:*

1. The expression is scanned from left to right.
2. If the symbol (including single-letter variable names) is not a right parenthesis—that is—continue the scan.
3. If the symbol under scan is a right parenthesis, then the four symbols to the left of the right parenthesis should be of the form "$\alpha\theta\beta$" where α and β stand for variable names or row numbers (of the matrix form) and θ is any operator. Write $\theta\alpha\beta$ as the next row of the matrix and replace "$(\alpha\theta\beta)$" in the expression by the index of the row constructed. The scan is continued with step 2.

The method expects a properly formed expression. Figure 10.20 depicts a simple example of transforming a completely parenthesized expression to matrix form. In the figure, the caret denotes the point of scan; the corresponding row of the matrix is found at the right.

The extension of the preceding techniques to expressions that are not completely parenthesized uses a precedence table such as the one shown in Table 10.4.† The table is used to determine which of two sequential operators should be evaluated first, as in A∗B+C. The leftmost operator is used as a row index and the rightmost operator is used as a column index. The intersection of the row and column contains a "left" or a "right". The "left" indicator indicates that a matrix entry should be generated. The "right" indicator indicates that the scan should be continued to the right. The table is used in the transformation procedures that follow. Each expression is enclosed in the symbols "⊢" and "⊣" which serve as terminators. As with the fully parenthesized form, the scan is from left to right and the rules are applied to each symbol. The identification for operators and operands is

$\alpha\theta\beta\phi$
$\wedge$

where α and β are operands and θ and ϕ are operators. The caret points to the operator under scan. The following rules hold:

* The notion of a completely parenthesized expression is covered earlier in this chapter.
† The content of the precedence table is determined by the hierarchy of operators in the language.

(A=((X* ((Y/Z) −W)) +B))	1. / Y Z
(A=((X* (1 −W)) +B))	2. − 1 W
(A=((X* 2) +B))	3. * X 2
(A=(3 +B))	4. + 3 B
(A= 4)	5. = A 4
5	

Figure 10.20 Transformation of a completely parenthesized expression to matrix form.

1. If the symbol under scan is an operator, ϕ, and the left context is:
   a. $\vdash \alpha$, then continue the scan with the next symbol, applying rule 1 again.
   b. $(\alpha$, then continue the scan with the next symbol, applying rule 1 again.
   c. $\alpha\theta\beta$, then look up $\theta\phi$ in the precedence table. If the table entry corresponding to row θ and column ϕ is R, then continue the scan, applying rule 1 again. If the table entry is L, then write $\theta\alpha\beta$ as the next row of the matrix; replace $\alpha\theta\beta$ in the expression by the index of the row constructed; and apply rule 1 with the same symbol under scan.
2. If the symbol under scan is ")" and the left context is:
   a. $\alpha\theta\beta$, then write $\theta\alpha\beta$ as the next row of the matrix; replace $\alpha\theta\beta$ in the expression by the index of the row constructed; and apply rule 2 with the same symbol under scan.

Table 10.4
Precedence Table for Bounded Context Translation

		Right Operator			
		+	−	*	/
	+	L	L	R	R
	−	L	L	R	R
Left	*	L	L	L	L
Operator	/	L	L	L	L
	=	R	R	R	R

Key: L = left
R = right

b. (α, then replace (α) by α and continue the scan with the next symbol and apply rule 1 again. α is a variable or row index of the matrix.
3. If the symbol under scan is "$\dashv$" and the left context is:
    a. $\alpha\theta\beta$, then write $\theta\alpha\beta$ as the next row of the matrix; replace $\alpha\theta\beta$ in the expression by the index of the row constructed; and apply rule 3 with the same symbol under scan.
    b. $\vdash \alpha$, then the transformation of the expression to matrix form is complete.
4. Otherwise, continue the scan with the next symbol, applying rule 1 again.

These rules are applied to the expression $A = X*(Y/Z - W) + B$ in Figure 10.21; the resultant matrix form is the same as in Figure 10.20.

General Comments

The concepts presented in this section constitute a set of basic methods that apply to a wide range of applications. However, the implications are greater than the methods alone. The fact that compiler methods actually can be defined independently of a particular language emphasizes the fact that the processes of compilation and interpretation constitute a scientific discipline.

10.4   SYNTAX NOTATION

Most programmers recognize that the process of constructing a computer program is a creative act and that once a program is suitably encoded, it is as much a contribution to the world of knowledge as a poem, a mathematical formula, or an artist's sketch. In fact, computer programming is usually regarded as an art rather than a science. A computer program written in a programming language becomes a body of knowledge when a suitable description of that language is available that can be used to distinguish between a syntactically valid program and a syntactically invalid program and to determine the meaning of the program. A *metalanguage* is used for this purpose and most programming languages utilize a descriptive technique of this kind.

Backus-Naur Form

The first metalanguage to be used with any degree of regularity is *Backus-Naur Form* (BNF), developed for ALGOL 60. Essentially, BNF includes three metasymbols from which definitions are formed:

	Rule Applied	*Matrix Entry*
⊢A=X∗ (Y/Z–W) +B ⊣	Rule 4—continue scan	
⊢A=X∗ (Y/Z–W) +B ⊣	Rule 4—continue scan	
⊢A=X∗ (Y/Z–W) +B ⊣	Rule 1a—continue scan	
⊢A=X∗ (Y/Z–W) +B ⊣	Rule 4—continue scan	
⊢A=X∗ (Y/Z–W) +B ⊣	Rule 1c—continue scan	
⊢A=X∗ (Y/Z–W) +B ⊣	Rule 4—continue scan	
⊢A=X∗ (Y/Z–W) +B ⊣	Rule 4—continue scan	
⊢A=X∗ (Y/Z–W) +B ⊣	Rule 1b—continue scan	
⊢A=X∗ (Y/Z–W) +B ⊣	Rule 4—continue scan	
⊢A=X∗ (Y/Z–W) +B ⊣	Rule 1c—replace and apply rule 1 again	1. / Y Z
⊢A=X∗ (1 –W) +B ⊣	Rule 1b—continue scan	
⊢A=X∗ (1 –W) +B ⊣	Rule 4—continue scan	
⊢A=X∗ (1 –W) +B ⊣	Rule 2a—replace and apply rule 2 again	2. – 1 W
⊢A=X∗ (2) +B ⊣	Rule 2b—replace and continue scan	
⊢A=X∗ +B ⊣	Rule 1c—replace and apply rule 1 again	3. ∗ X 2
⊢A= 3 +B ⊣	Rule 1c—continue scan	
⊢A= 3 +B ⊣	Rule 4—continue scan	
⊢A= 3 +B ⊣	Rule 3a—replace and apply rule 3 again	4. + 3 B
⊢A 4 ⊣	Rule 3a—replace and apply rule 3 again	5. = A 4
⊢ 5 ⊣	Rule 3b—transformation complete	

Figure 10.21 Transformation of an expression that is not completely parenthesized to matrix form.

305

Symbol	Meaning
:: =	"Is defined to be"
|	To be read as "or"
< >	Angular brackets that denote a name of a constituent rather than the constituent named

It follows that the formal structure of a programming language can be systematically constructed from basic symbols with definitions such as the following, which are used to define a number:

<digit>:: = 0|1|2|3|4|5|6|7|8|9
<unsigned integer>:: = <digit>|<unsigned integer><digit>
<integer>:: = <unsigned integer>| + <unsigned integer>| –
                <unsigned integer>
<decimal fraction>:: =.<unsigned integer>
<exponent part>:: = 10$^{<integer>}$
<decimal   number>:: = <unsigned   integer>|<decimal fraction>
                      |<unsigned integer><decimal fraction>
<unsigned   number>:: = <decimal   number>|<decimal
                        number><exponent part>
<number>:: = <unsigned number>| + <unsigned number> –
                <unsigned number>

Note that two constructions written in sequence are considered to be juxtaposed.

Extended Backus Notation

The most frequent uses of a metalanguage are to describe a statement in a programming language in such a manner that the user can construct a valid instance of a particular statement and to give the compiler writer a syntactical model with which to work. In short, it is important that "we are all talking about the same thing." Thus, the metalanguage should utilize a notation outside of the programming language being described and should lend itself to use in the construction of valid statements by a user of the language described.

Through the years, Backus-Naur Form gradually evolved to a notation known as *Extended Backus Notation*, which is more convenient for "modern" programming languages, such as BASIC, COBOL, FORTRAN, and PL/1.

Extended Backus Notation employs eight rules and appropriate symbols, defined as follows:

1. A *notation variable* names a constituent of a programming language. It takes one of two forms: (1) Lower-case letters, digits, and hyphens—beginning with a letter; for example:

   constant
   arithmetic-variable
   array-dimension-specification

   or (2) two or more words separated by hyphens, where one word consists of lower-case letters and the others consist of upper-case letters; for example:

   DATA-statement
   MAT-READ-statement

   A notation variable represents information that must be supplied by the user and is defined formally or informally in preceding or adjacent text.
2. A *notation constant* stands for itself and is represented by capital letters or by special characters. A notation constant must be written as shown. For example, in the statements

   GOSUB statement-number
   NEXT arithmetic-variable

   the words GOSUB and NEXT are notation constants and must be written as indicated.
3. A *syntactical unit* is regarded as a notation variable, a notation constant, or a collection of notation variables, notation constants, and notation symbols enclosed in braces or brackets.
4. The *vertical bar* (|) is read "or" and indicates that a choice must be made between the item to the left of the bar and the item to the right of the bar. For example,

   character-reference|arithmetic-reference
   &PI|&E|&SQR2

5. A set of *braces* ({}) is used for grouping or to indicate that a choice is to be made among the syntactical units contained in the braces. For example,

   { + | − }
   {integer-constant|fixed-point-constant}

6. A set of *brackets* ([]) represents an option and the enclosed syntactical units can be omitted. For example,

[+|−]
alphabetic-character[numeric-character]

7. The relation *is defined to be* is denoted by the composite symbol :: = used in the following manner:

defined-type: : = definition

where "defined-type" is a notation variable and "definition" is a sequence of syntactical units. Any defined-type occurring as an element of a syntactical unit must also occur as the "defined-type" of some definition. For example,

digit:: = 0|1|2|3|4|5|6|7|8|9
fixed-constant:: = integer [.]|[integer].integer

8. The *ellipsis* (a series of three periods) indicates that the preceding syntactic unit may be repeated one or more times. For example,

DATA constant [,constant] . . .
REM [string character] . . .

It follows that in a syntactical specification of a programming language, every defined type must ultimately be constructible entirely out of terminal characters. However, one defined type in any syntactical specification will not appear in a definition; this is known as the *starting type*.

Extended Backus Notation is further described by giving some examples from the various languages. The *FOR statement* in the BASIC language is defined as

FOR-statement:: = FOR   arithmetic-variable =
arithmetic-expression TO arithmetic-expression
[STEP arithmetic-expression]

An example of the FOR-statement is

FOR I = 1 TO L/2 STEP J + 1

The *computed GO TO statement* in the FORTRAN language is defined as

computed-GOTO:: = GOTO(statement-number[,statement-number]
...), integer-scalar-variable

An example of the computed GO TO statement is

GO TO(6380,175,480,10),JILL

The *goto-statement, return-statement,* and *on-statement* in the PL/I
language are defined as

goto-statement:: = {GOTO|GO TO} reference;
return-statement:: = RETURN[(expression)];
on-statement:: = ON   condition   [SNAP]{unconditional-state-
   ment|SYSTEM;}

Examples of these statements are

GOTO LOOP;
RETURN (3*VOL – 1);
ON ENDFILE (MAST_FILE) GO TO CLOSEUP;

General Comments
The use of a suitable syntax notation is one means of studying the
structure of a programming language; it enables one to identify syntax
dependencies, ambiguities, and inconsistencies. A related area of study
concerns the "semantics" of a programming language. *Semantics*, which
is not covered here, refers to the operational meaning of a statement,
independently of its syntactic structure. Clearly, both areas of study are
important in computer science and provide a foundation for the theory
of programming languages.

QUESTION SET

1. Draw a HIPO diagram of the first and second passes of the
   assembler. (Use the information given in Figures 10.6 and 10.7.)
2. Develop flow diagrams of the first and second passes of the
   assembler. (Use the information given in Figures 10.6 and 10.7.)
3. (Class or term project) Implement the assembler program defined

here on your computer. Use the hypothetical assembler language, perhaps abbreviating the symbolic operation codes. Printed output from the assembly process should resemble the usual printed output from the assembler.

4. Convert the following expressions (given in infix notation) to prefix and postfix notation:

A – B*C
(A/B*C)/(D – E*F) – G
(A*(B + C) – D)*E
A + (B*(C + D) – E)*F – G
A*B/C
A + B – C

5. Draw structure diagrams for the expressions given in question 4.
6. Traverse the following tree:

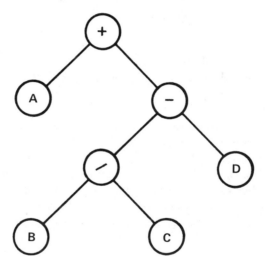

in *preorder, postorder,* and *endorder* form.

7. Develop a flow diagram of the conversion process from infix to postfix notation.

8. (Class or term project) Implement the conversion process from infix to postfix notation on your computer. Use single-letter operands, but ignore constants and the exponentiation operator. However, allow the use of parentheses and the following operator symbols: =,+,–,* and /.

9. Develop a flow diagram of the process of interpretively executing an expression in prefix notation, postfix notation, or both.
10. (Class or term project) Implement the process of interpretively executing an expression in prefix or postfix notation. Use symbolic operands and a symbol table to hold data values.
11. Give the bounded context matrix forms for the following statements:

$$A = B - C*D$$
$$A = (B/C + D)/(E - F*G) - H$$
$$A = (B*(C + D) - E)*F$$
$$A = B + (C*(D + E) - F)*G - H$$
$$A = B*C/D$$
$$A = B + C - D$$

12. (Class or term project) Implement the conversion process from infix notation to matrix form using bounded context translation.
13. (Class or term project) Choose a programming language, preferably an unsophisticated one such as BASIC or FORTRAN. Describe the language completely using either Backus-Naur Form or Extended Backus Notation.
14. (Class or term project) Write a small compiler that accepts a program containing the following statements:

READ
GOTO
END
Assignment statements

and generates assembler language statements, including appropriate constants and program control statements. You may assume single-letter variables but permit generalized arithmetic expressions. Also generate a compiler listing. Next, connect the assembler (question 3) to the compiler to form a complete "translation system."

SELECTED READINGS

Hopgood, F. R. A., *Compiling Techniques,* American Elsevier, New York, 1969.

Katzan, H., *Advanced Programming: Programming and Operating Systems*, Van Nostrand-Reinhold, New York, 1970.

Lee, J. A. N., *The Anatomy of a Compiler*, Van Nostrand-Reinhold, New York, 1967.

Pollack, B. W. (ed.), *Compiler Techniques,* Petrocelli/Charter, New York, 1972.

Rosen, S. (ed.), *Programming Systems and Languages*, McGraw-Hill, New York, 1967.

11

OPERATING SYSTEM TECHNOLOGY

11.1 BASIC CONCEPTS

An *operating system* is an organized collection of programs and data that is specifically designed to manage the resources of a computer system and to facilitate the creation of computer programs and control their execution on that system. The prime objective of an operating system is to effectively utilize the resources of a computer installation, which necessarily includes hardware resources, information resources, and human resources. *Hardware resources* pertain to the computer system; the objective is to keep the units with the highest cost/performance index as busy as possible so as to maximize overall system efficiency. *Information resources* pertain to programs and data that can be stored in the system for easy access and shared among different users. *Human resources* pertain to applications programmers, systems programmers, and computer operations personnel. One of the measures of a good operating environment is the degree to which it facilitates the programming and operating efforts.

The Need for an Operating System

Initially, the impetus for the development of operating systems programs came from the area of computer operations. Computers were originally used with a technique known as "basic programming support." *Basic programming support* requires manual intervention by the user during the processing of a job and involves the following steps:

1. The computer program to be compiled or assembled is punched on cards or tape.

2. The compiler or assembler program is loaded* into the computer.
3. The compiler or assembler program reads the program being compiled or assembled and produces a machine language program; it is punched into cards or tape.
4. The machine language program is loaded into the computer; it reads the users data and produces computed results, as programmed.

The basic programming environment is depicted in Figure 11.1. Between each of the steps, manual intervention by the user or a computer operator is required. If more than one source program needs to be compiled (or assembled), perhaps for a main program and a subprogram, then the compilation or assembly step is repeated as many times as necessary.

The disadvantages of basic programming support are obvious. The manual intervention between the various steps of a job (referred to as *setup time*) is extremely wasteful of computer time and involves loading the card reader, mounting tapes, setting switches, and readying programs for execution. The situation is depicted in Figure 11.2. For long-running jobs, as in data processing, the time spent in setup is significant; however, the situation is worsened for small jobs because the setup time and execution time are not proportional. The obvious solution of increasing the speed of the computer does reduce "total elapsed time" but makes the idle time proportionately higher, since jobs are processed in a shorter time but setup time remains the same. Another problem inherent in the use of basic programming support is that the scheduling of computer time is cumbersome.

The solution to the above problem is as obvious as the problem is. Have computer programs perform job scheduling and provide automatic job-to-job transition. Programs that schedule how the computer is used and allow the computer to pass between the various steps automatically without human intervention are known as "control programs." The end result is that the computer essentially runs itself; all we have to do is to get it started and tell it what we want done.

The Concept of a Job

Although it would be convenient to give instructions to the computer system with some means of verbal input, it is not feasible using today's technology, so that we must enter instructions through one of the

---

* In a primitive operating environment such as basic programming support, the process of loading a program into main storage for execution is performed by a small self-loading program that is designed to first load itself into the computer and then to load an accompanying program.

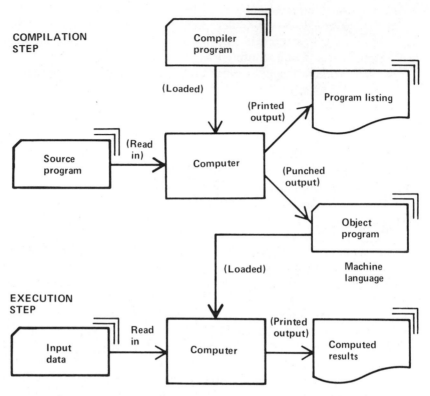

Figure 11.1   Basic programming environment.

input devices. Punched cards are used in this section for entering programs and instructions into the operating system.

The work performed by the computer for one user in one time span is referred to as a "job." Stated in another manner, a *job* is a single run on the computer. The operating system needs the following information to run a job:

1. The identity of the user
2. Control information
3. Program(s)
4. Data

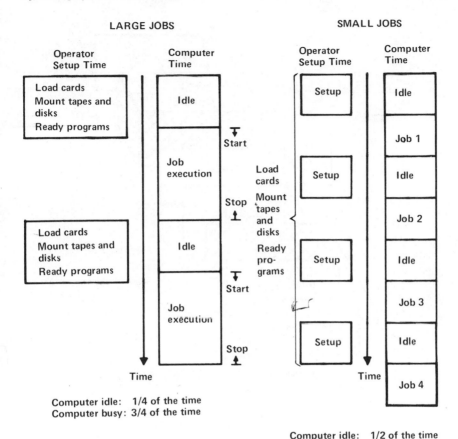

LARGE JOBS SMALL JOBS

Computer idle: 1/4 of the time
Computer busy: 3/4 of the time

Computer idle: 1/2 of the time
Computer busy: 1/2 of the time

Figure 11.2 Relationship between idle and busy time for large and small jobs.

Essentially, the control information tells the operating system what the user wants the computer to do. The operating system reads the control information and initiates the execution of programs that perform the required functions.

Figure 11.3 shows the deck setup for a hypothetical operating system. The $JOB card identifies the users and provides accounting information on whom to charge for the execution of the job. The $FORTRAN card tells the operating system to read in the FORTRAN

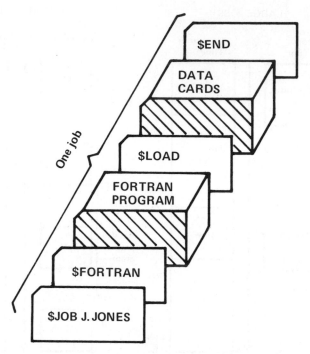

Figure 11.3   Sample deck setup showing representative control cards.

compiler from magnetic tape or disk. The statements of the FORTRAN program are read by the FORTRAN compiler, and the machine language program resulting from the compilation is placed on disk or magnetic tape for subsequent loading and execution. A printout of the program is produced as a by-product, so that the user has a record of his program. The printout is also used for debugging the program. Normally, a program such as the compiler passes control back to the operating system to read the next "control" card. In this case, the next card is the $LOAD card that causes the loader program to be read in. The loader program loads the machine language program, previously placed on magnetic tape or disk, into main storage and turns program control over to it for execution. Now the user program has control of the computer. It reads its own data and produces computed results, as mentioned previously. When the user program has completed its execution, it exits to the operating system for the next job, and the above process is repeated.

Each computer center has its own operational procedures and how a user actually submits a job differs widely. For example, in some computer centers, card decks are placed on a table outside the computer room. In others, the user submits his deck through a window established for that purpose. When the computer is in a remote location, a messenger is used to pick up jobs at a central station and transport them to the computer. Results are normally returned in the same manner.

In the computer room, a computer operator collects a set of jobs and enters them into the computer as a "batch of jobs," and the entire process is referred to as *batch processing*. In most modern computer installations, jobs are read in and placed on disk storage. When the operating system needs the next job, it goes to disk to get it.

The term *batch processing* has its origin in early operating systems and refers to the practice of collecting a batch of jobs and submitting them to the computer on an input tape. In a similar manner, output for the entire batch of jobs is placed on an output tape. As depicted in Figure 11.4, a peripheral computer is used for the card-to-tape operation and for the processing (i.e., printing or punching) of the output tape.

Early operating systems are also characterized by the fact that the steps (i.e., compile, assemble, load, execute, etc.) that constitute a job occupy the user area of main storage successively and that the jobs that constitute a batch are executed on a sequential basis. Main storage organization in systems of this type is depicted in Figure 11.5.

Input/Output Control Systems and Spooling

One of the most sophisticated aspects of programming is the management of input and output, especially when it is desired to perform the operations efficiently. An *input/output control system* (IOCS) is a collection of routines that allows the efficiency of input/output operations to be improved and also facilitates input/output programming. An input/output control system is comprised of two types of routines, collectively known as physical IOCS and logical IOCS. *Physical IOCS* (PIOCS) is part of the operating system control programs; it executes and manages input/output operations on a system-wide basis and eliminates the confusion and conflict that would normally result if each user program performed its own input and output. *Logical IOCS* (LIOCS) is part of a user program and links the program to the physical IOCS routines. Logical IOCS routines logically operate as subroutines. Logical IOCS is responsible for the blocking and deblocking of logical records and for performing input and output buffering. The latter concepts are covered under "Data Management" in this chapter. The use of an input/output control system is suggested in Figure 11.6.

One of the advantages of the "interruption philosophy," discussed

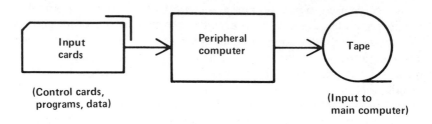

(Control cards,
programs, data)

(Input to
main computer)

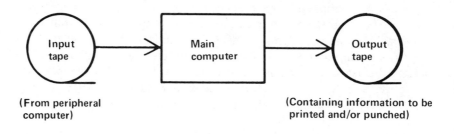

(From peripheral
computer)

(Containing information to be
printed and/or punched)

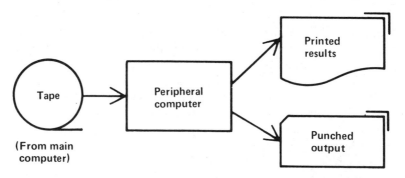

(From main
computer)

Figure 11.4 The use of a peripheral computer in an early batch processing system.

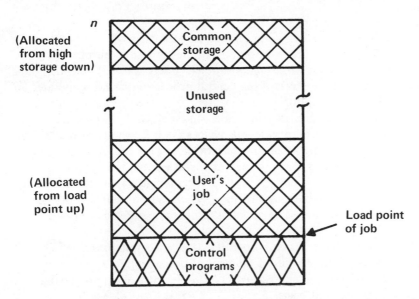

Figure 11.5 Main storage organization in a simple operating system in which jobs are executed sequentially. (Common storage is a FORTRAN concept and refers to storage that can be shared among program units.)

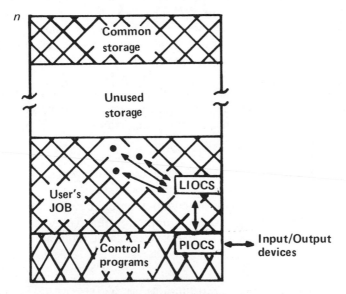

Figure 11.6 The logical organization of an operating system that utilizes an input/output control system.

319

earlier, is that it permits input/output activity and computation to overlap. The central processing unit initiates an input/output operation and then continues with computational operations. When the data channel needs the services of the central processing unit, it generates an input/output interruption.

Through the use of the data channel and the input/output interruption, low-speed peripheral devices (such as the card reader and line printer) operating at electromechanical speeds can be controlled by the central processing unit concurrently with normal job processing. The process, known as *spooling,** is used for placing input cards on disk storage and for printing and punching system output that was previously placed on disk storage. The spooling process operates as follows:

1. The spooling process operates at the highest priority. When it requires the services of the central processing unit, it signals with an interruption and receives control of the central processing unit on a demand basis.
2. A low-speed input/output operation is initiated by the spooling program. The entire process takes only a few machine cycles.
3. Control of the central processing unit is turned over to a user job that operates until an interruption occurs. (Compared with input/output initiation, job processing can operate for a relatively high number of machine cycles.)
4. An interruption is generated by a low-speed input/output operation, perhaps as the result of the completion of a single read or write. Control of the central processing unit is turned over to the spooling process.
5. The spooling program services the input/output request, taking a few machine cycles, and the execution of the interrupted user job is resumed from the point of interruption. The process is continued from step 4.

In modern operating systems, spooling essentially replaces the card-to-tape and the tape-to-print or punch operations and is frequently extended to control several low-speed input/output devices concurrently. In summary, the spooling process is normally transparent to user jobs and the use of several magnetic tape devices can be replaced by a single direct-access storage device.

---

* The term *spooling* was originally derived from the acronym SPOOL, which stands for Simultaneous Peripheral Output On-Line. The term has been extended through usage to apply to both simultaneous input and output.

Multiprogramming Concepts

In spite of automatic job-to-job transition and input/output control systems, normal delays in the processing of a job cause the central processing unit to "wait" for short periods of time on an intermittent basis. A typical delay might involve waiting for an input operation to be completed for needed data so that processing can continue. Delays of this type result in ineffective use of the central processing unit and of main storage.

Modern operating systems utilize a technique known as *multiprogramming* to allow several jobs to share the resources of the computer system and to allow card reading, printing, and punching to proceed concurrently with system operation. In a multiprogramming system, a scheduler routine is designed to give control of the central processing unit to another program when the executing program encounters a *natural wait*, such as waiting for an input operation. Thus, the more expensive units in the system are fully utilized. Input jobs are maintained in a queue on direct-access storage and output is maintained in a similar queue on the same or another device. When the operating system needs another job to process, it is selected from the input queue on either a sequential or a priority basis.

With the use of a multiprogramming system, several jobs coreside in main storage and overflow to an auxiliary storage device (such as disk or drum), when necessary. A system of this type is depicted conceptually in Figure 11.7, which also includes reader, writer, and job initiator programs. The *reader* and *writer* programs perform spooling and place jobs on direct-access storage and process printed and punched output, respectively. (It is interesting to note with multiprogramming, as in the batch processing systems mentioned previously, system input and output involves a high-speed input/output device.) The *job initiator* program is used to read the next job from the *input work queue* (i.e., the set of jobs placed on direct-access storage by the reader program) and prepare it for execution.

Remote Job Entry/Remote Job Output

By definition batch processing causes delays. First, a user's job must be transported to the central computer and entered into the system. Next, the job must wait in the input queue until its turn for processing. Lastly, the output queue must be printed or punched and the results sent back to the originator. A recent technique known as *remote job entry* allows a job to be transported from a remote location to the central computer over ordinary telephone lines. An analogous facility, known as *remote job output*, provides a means of sending results back to the

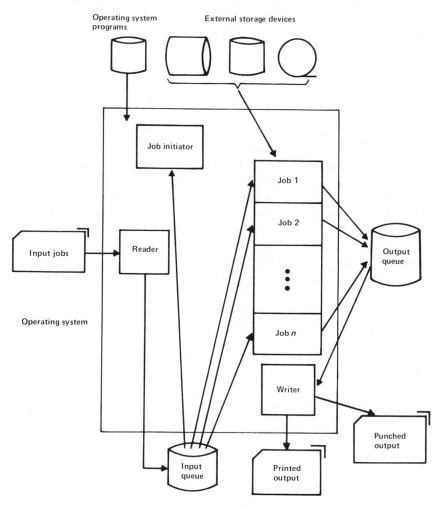

Figure 11.7   Conceptual view of an operating system that employs multi-programming to increase throughput and lower response time.

322

originator over telephone lines. The user (or originator) in this case must have an appropriate terminal device in his work area to send and receive information from the central computer.

When using remote job entry, a job enters the input queue directly and "people" delays are avoided. This technique is frequently employed when a centralized computer is used to provide service to offices in different locations.

Time Sharing

Although remote job entry/remote job output solves, in some cases, the problem of transporting programs and data to and from the central computer, the scheduling bottleneck at the computer still causes delays, especially when small, "one-shot" programs are involved. Another technique, known as *time sharing*, allows the user at a remote location to enter into a conversation with the computer (figuratively speaking), again using a terminal device and telephone lines. In a time-sharing system, however, computer time is scheduled differently. When time sharing, each user is given a short burst (called a *time slice*) of computer time on a periodic basis. The switching between programs, by the computer, is sufficiently fast that the user is given the illusion that he has the computer to himself, whereas, in reality, he is sharing it with many other users. Time sharing is most frequently used during program development, by problem solvers, such as analysts, scientists, or engineers, or to enter or retrieve information from the system on a demand basis. Time sharing is particularly useful in an academic environment. A student can sit at a terminal and, within a short period of time, solve an assigned problem using the computer. The greatest benefit of time sharing is that when an error is encountered, it can be corrected immediately and progress on the problem can continue. When using batch processing, an error is discovered only when a completed job is returned to the user. If an error does occur, at least one more run must be made to correct the error.

Figure 11.8 shows the terminal printout for a typical time-sharing session. Four major steps are involved:

1. *Sign-on*, where the user establishes a data connection to the computer and identifies himself to the system.
2. *Program initiation*, where the user specifies that he wants to use an old program or prepare a new one. The user also gives the name of the program so that it may be retrieved from or stored in a library (on direct-access storage) for easy access.

[User dials computer and makes line connection.]

HELLO
GOOD MORNING ON AT 9:13 MON.   11-18-74   Sign-on and user identi-
USER NUMBER?   08520   fication procedure
SYSTEM?   BASIC   User chooses BASIC
NEW   OR   OLD?   NEW   language and a new
NAME?   FACT   program named FACT
READY   Computer is ready to
                                                               accept program
```
100   PRINT "ENTER K"
110   INPUT K
120   LET F=1
130   FOR I=1 TO K
140        LET F=F*1
150   NEXT I
160   PRINT K; "FACTORIAL="; F
170   PRINT
180   GO  TO  110
190   END
RUN
```
                        Program to compute K
                        factorial, entered by
                        user

FACT   9:30   MON.   11-18-74
ENTER K   User enters data
?4
 4 FACTORIAL=24   Result

ENTER K
?6
 6 FACTORIAL=720

ENTER K
?0
 0 FACTORIAL=1

ENTER K   User terminates input
?STOP   loop

TIME 1 SEC.   Central processing unit
                                                        time

Figure 11.8   Sample terminal session for a time-sharing system. The program is
                        written using the BASIC language.

3. *Program preparation*, where the user enters a new program on a statement-by-statement basis, or enters modifications or corrections to an old program.
4. *Program execution*, where the program is actively executed by the computer.

In time sharing, a user may run one program or several programs—in other words, his needs may change depending upon the results he obtains. The concept of a job does not apply and the notion of a terminal session is used. A *terminal session* is the time between when a user first signs on to the computer and when he finally logs off. A terminal session may extend from minutes to hours. A key point is that the computer is not idly waiting while a user is thinking about what he wants to do next; it is doing work for other users. This is what is known as time sharing—people are sharing time on the computer.

On-Line and Information Systems

An *on-line system* allows a user in a remote location to access the computer via data communications facilities without necessarily resorting to the time-sharing mode of operation. A common example is a bank teller system used to assist in the making of banking transactions by banking personnel. Generally speaking, a bank teller program runs as a conventional job in an operating system environment; however, the job never terminates and is put into a dormant state when no transactions need to be processed. In fact, a single bank teller program has been known to service several hundred tellers. This is possible only because the volume of transactions is low, from the computer's point of view, and the computer processing involves straightforward record keeping.

An *information system* stores large amounts of information on a large-capacity storage medium for access by people through batch processing facilities or through an on-line data communications system. This area of computer utilization is commonly known as *information storage and retrieval* and relates to library services, literature and abstract search, market research, medical and academic record keeping, and a wide variety of other informational services.

Information systems are usually characterized by a large bank of data organized for fast retrieval and by a query language that enables a user to easily pose a question that can be answered by the information system. Most information systems are implemented as on-line systems wherein a single job can provide informational services to a large number of people on a dynamic basis.

An Important Note

A variety of systems concepts has been presented thus far in the chapter, ranging from simple batch processing to information systems. The objective of the remainder of the chapter is to introduce the methodology and techniques that are used to construct large-scale systems, such as these. It is important to note, however, that a given operating system is a collection of operating facilities constructed to satisfy the needs of a particular operating environment, and that a single system can satisfy several needs. For example, an operating system can be developed that permits multiprogramming and provides time-sharing and information system capabilities. In a general sense, this is the reason we study techniques and methodology rather than specific systems. The concepts introduced here include system structure and operation, linking and loading, data management, and storage management.

11.2 SYSTEM STRUCTURE AND OPERATION

A *system* is commonly regarded as a set of objects with relationships between the objects and between the properties of these objects. An *object* is a component of a system. In a computer system, typical components are the central processing unit, main storage, and a data channel. In an operating system or a time-sharing system, components are routines (or modules, as they are frequently called) that perform a specific function, such as to read a control card or field a hardware interruption. A *relationship* can be a physical connection, a logical similarity, a causal rule, and so forth. In computer-oriented systems, components communicate through the transfer of control information and data.

All systems possess a static and a dynamic structure. *Static structure* pertains to the physical arrangement of components and how they relate to each other. *Dynamic structure* concerns the manner in which the system responds to specific input conditions, or in other words, the manner in which the system operates. Both computer systems and "software" systems are deterministic in the sense that the behavior of the system in response to input conditions can be predicted. The latter assertion is no accident, since the operation of computer-oriented systems is governed by logical circuitry or a computer program.

General Structure of a Multiprogramming System

Even though multiprogramming systems* vary widely, the routines that make up such a system can be grouped by the functions they perform and by whether they require privileged facilities of the computer system. The routines fall into two broad categories: control programs and processing programs. *Control programs*, as introduced previously, are concerned with the operation of the computer and the execution of a job. *Processing programs* execute under the direction of control programs; the steps that constitute a user's job involve the execution of processing programs. The overall static structure of an operating system is given in Figure 11.9.

Control programs are the heart of an operating system, since they are concerned with the management of the resources of the system, necessarily including execution time of the central processing unit, main storage space, input/output device assignment and control, and space on direct-access storage media. Control program facilities are usually divided into three areas:

1. *System management* routines control the operation of the computer system and provide a logical interface between the hardware and the other routines of the operating system. System management routines monitor hardware functions, perform actual input/output operations, schedule jobs for execution, control peripheral input/output devices, allocate main storage, and handle abnormal conditions that arise during computation.

2. *Job management* routines provide a logical interface between a job (processing program) and the system management routines. Job management routines control and monitor the execution of a job, read control cards, and handle terminations.

3. *Data management* routines provide a software interface between processing programs and external storage. Data management routines control data-transfer operations, maintain catalogs and libraries, manage input/output device assignment, and allocate space on mass storage devices. Even though data management is generally concerned with input and output, it uses system management functions for that purpose so that all input and output is managed on a system-wide basis.

Processing programs perform computation on behalf of a user's job but are not concerned with the operation of the computer system.

---

* That is, operating systems that process jobs using a multiprogramming mode of operation.

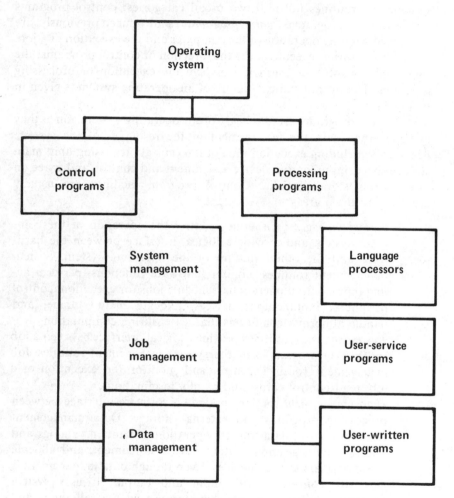

Figure 11.9   General structure of a multiprogramming system.

However, the facilities of certain processing programs are available through the use of an operating system and that is why processing programs, in general, are considered a part of an operating system. Processing programs are divided into three areas:

1. *Language processors* include the assemblers, compilers, generators, and editors normally provided with an operating system.
2. *User service* routines comprise utility programs, necessary for using a computer system, and service programs that facilitate the programming process. Utility programs include disk initialization, core dumps, card-to-tape, diagnostics, and the like. Service programs perform sort/merge, editing, loading, and many other similar functions.
3. *User-written programs* are object programs stored in a temporary or permanent program library managed through operating system facilities. Once an object program has been placed in a program library, it can be executed through conventional means, such as control cards or job control language.*

The primary objective of an operating system is to keep the computer going, through job-to-job transition, job control facilities, and input/output systems. This fact is taken for granted. An effective operating system also facilitates the programming process by performing functions that are difficult or cumbersome to develop. Data management capability is a good example of this type of operating system facility. Several related topics are covered later in this chapter.

Operation of a Multiprogramming System

A user's job becomes a unit of work to the operating system when its JOB control card is read from the input queue of jobs by a job management routine. An initial program structure is created for the job and input/output devices and main storage space are assigned to it. The object program for the first step of the job is loaded into the assigned storage space† and the job is ready for execution. A particular job is given control of the central processing unit by a scheduling routine that is part of the operating system. (Scheduling is generally regarded as a system management function.)

---

* It should be noted here that a source program is classed as "data" to a language processor; it is data because it is not in an executable form.
† This point (i.e., of what is actually loaded) is expanded upon in a subsequent section on linking and loading.

As each job is accepted as a unit of work by the operating system, it is assigned an internal priority that is computed as a function of external priority and arrival sequence. When system management control programs have completed their supervisory work, the central processing unit is assigned to the highest priority job that is in the "ready" state. The job executes until an interruption takes place, at which time control of the central processing unit is turned over to a system management routine to process the interruption.

An interruption can be caused by an executing program (such as a machine or program fault) or by an external event (such as the expiration of a timer or the completion of an input/output operation). Moreover, an interruption can take place anytime, that is, when either a processing program or a control program is executing. If an interruption occurs during the execution of a processing program, then the status of the program is saved, so that execution can be resumed from the point of interruption, and control of the central processing unit goes to a system management routine to process that type of interruption. If an interruption occurs during the execution of a control program, then a record of the interruption is "queued up" by the control program and the control program resumes execution from the point it was interrupted. This procedure allows operating system routines to process their work in an orderly manner.

The processing of an interruption may change the state of a processing program from "waiting" to "ready." Suppose, for example, that a processing program requests input that it must wait for. Control of the central processing unit goes to a lower priority processing program. When the input is complete, an interruption is generated. The processing of the input/output interruption by a system management routine includes placing the waiting program into the ready state. Thus, the next time the scheduler routine dispatches control of the central processing unit to a processing program, the highest priority program again is given control. An operating system that operates in this manner is said to be *interrupt driven*. Once a program or a routine is given control of the central processing unit, it continues to operate until an interruption occurs. Normally, interruptions occur when a processing program or an external device needs the services of one of the control programs.

To sum up, the objective of a multiprogramming system is to maximize the use of the resources of the computer system. Toward that end, jobs and interruptions are processed on a priority basis. The central processing unit is given to the highest priority job that is ready to execute. When a job must wait for some reason, the next-highest-priority job is given control of the computer. Interruptions are processed when they occur so as to minimize delays. Interruptions that take place when another interruption is being processed by a system management routine are queued up and processed on a priority basis. When there are no more interruptions to be processed, then control of the computer is turned over to the highest priority job that is ready, as described above. Thus, scheduling and priority take care of themselves. A high-priority job that loses control of the central processing unit because of an interruption eventually regains it when the processing of the interruption is completed. If as the result of an interruption a higher-priority job becomes ready, then it is given control of the central processing unit the next time around.

Structure and Operation of a Time-Sharing System

A time-sharing system is similar in concept to the operating system mentioned earlier in this chapter. System management routines manage the resources of the computer system and determine which user programs use the central processing unit and when they use it. Job management routines read and interpret control information supplied by people from terminals. Data management routines manage input and output operations and maintain libraries of programs on direct-access storage. When a person desires to use one of his programs, all he need do is supply its name and data management routines can make the program available for use, However, the basic objective is different. In a multiprogramming system, the objective is to keep the computer busy and to get as much work done (by the computer) as possible. When time sharing, the objective is to keep the user busy and the time-sharing system is designed to provide that service. A time-sharing system is definitely more people-oriented, but this service is costly because computer resources are used to switch between users.

There are normally many users of a time-sharing system. A distinction must be made, however, between the users who *can* use the system and between the users who *are* using the system at any point in time. The time-sharing system contains a list (or table) of the identification codes of people who can use the system. The number of identification codes may be as large as 2000. At any point in time, however, only a small subset of these people can be actively using the computer. Large time-sharing systems allow as many as 200 active users. A small time-sharing system may limit the number of active users to between five and ten.

For purposes of demonstration, assume a time-sharing system with 100 active users. (The number 50 would work just as well.) Obviously, the programs of 100 users could not possibly occupy main storage at one time. What this means is that system management routines must manage main storage on a dynamic basis, and programs and data must be moved back and forth between main storage and a backup direct-access storage device. This process is referred to as *swapping*. When a person requests the services of the computer, his programs and data must be "swapped in." When main storage space is needed for another user, programs and data must be "swapped out." Swapping takes computer time and requires space on direct-access storage media.

Another function that must be performed by system management routines is that of scheduling. Active users can be placed into three groups:

1. *Active*—this user's program is currently being executed
2. *Ready*—programs for these users are waiting to use the computer
3. *Waiting*—these programs are "inactive" in the sense that the computer is waiting for the user to respond

Obviously, active and ready programs can use the central processing unit. Normally, a program is placed in the waiting group when the computer issues a "read" instruction to a user's terminal. In the time it takes a user to read and react to a message from the computer, several programs can be serviced. There are several methods of scheduling in time-sharing systems. A straightforward method is given here. Ready programs are given control of the central processing unit on a round-robin basis. The technique operates as follows: A small value, such as 100 milliseconds, is put into a computer timer. Then the central processing unit is turned over to a program. The program executes and the timer counts down. When the timer reaches zero or the program needs input data, the program's time slice is over and the central processing unit is given to the next program on the ready list. As depicted in Figure 11.10, several activities are taking place at any point in time in a time-sharing system:

1. A program that has finished its time slice is being swapped out.
2. A program is currently going through a time slice.
3. A program is being swapped in for its next time slice.

Normally, the computer goes through the above procedure so rapidly that there is no appreciable delay in response time, that is, the time it takes the computer to respond to a person's input. There is a saturation point, however, and when the number of users passes the saturation point, response time increases rapidly. A typical response-time curve of a time-sharing system is shown in Figure 11.11.

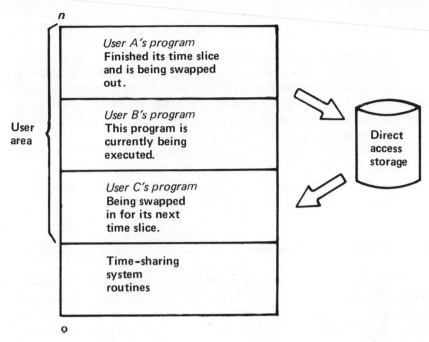

Figure 11.10 Simplified diagram of main storage in a time-sharing system.

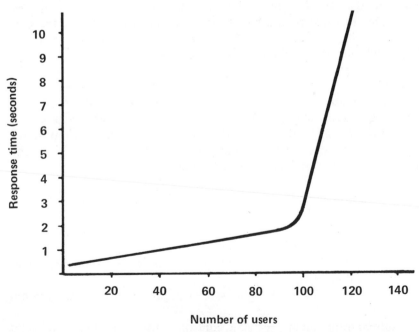

Figure 11.11 Response-time curve for a typical time-sharing system.

333

Time-sharing systems are classed as closed or open. A *closed* system provides computer service exclusively through one or two programming languages. An *open* system allows the user at a remote terminal to utilize all facilities of the computer system, including assembler language, a variety of input/output devices, and data management capabilities. Most time-sharing facilities provide closed service, since the intended audience is the problem solver, such as the engineer, analyst, or student mentioned previously. An open system is more powerful and can be used for system development and debugging by professional programmers and for a wide range of problem-solving activities.

11.3 LINKING AND LOADING

The structure and use of subprograms have been introduced previously. The manner in which a main program and one or more subprograms are combined to form an executable program is one of the many "messy" topics in computer technology. The techniques are largely machine-dependent, so that the entire process is unfortunately regarded as a mystery more frequently than it should be. The methods for linkage given in this section utilize a computer with 16 general-purpose fixed-point registers (numbered 0-15) and four floating-point registers (numbered 0, 2, 4, and 6). The concepts presented can easily be "mapped" onto the characteristics of most digital computers.

Linkage

The machine instructions involved in the process of invoking a subprogram and subsequently returning to the calling program are referred to as *linkage instructions*; the process of "calling and returning" is known as *linkage*. Prior to branching to a subprogram, the calling program must perform the following functions:

1. Establish the address (at execution time in main storage) of the subprogram being called
2. Establish a save area so that the subprogram being called can store the contents of the calling program's registers
3. Establish a return address where the subprogram should return in the calling program
4. Establish a list of the addresses of arguments to the subprogram

The subprogram, upon receiving control, must save the contents of machine registers in the designated save area and set up arguments that are passed to it by the calling program. After the subprogram has completed its execution, it must restore the contents of machine registers and return to the calling program. A frequently used linkage convention utilizes the general-purpose registers as follows:

1. Register 15 is loaded with the address in main storage of the entry point to the subprogram.
2. Register 14 is loaded with the address in main storage of the return point to the calling program.
3. Register 13 is loaded with the address in main storage of the register save area.
4. Register 1 is loaded with the address in main storage of the argument address.

The above conventions are employed in the program segment given in Figure 11.12, which gives the machine instructions necessary to implement a CALL statement of the form

CALL   BIGSUB(A,B,C)

where BIGSUB is the name of the subprogram and A, B, and C are arguments. Statement (1) specifies that BIGSUB is an external symbol to be resolved at "load" time. Statements (2) and (3) load registers 13 and 1 with the addresses of the save area and argument list, respectively. Statement (4) loads register 15 with the address of the subroutine; note here that the address of the subroutine is filled in at "load" time. Statement (5) loads register 14 with the return address. Statement (6) branches to the main storage address in register 15. Statement (7) represents the location at which execution of the calling program is to resume. Statements (8) through (11) specify address constants; BIGSUB must be filled by the loader program because it is an external symbol. Symbols A, B, and C can be resolved at the assembly level. Statements (12) through (15) reserve storage for a 20-word save area and for variables A, B, and C.

A subroutine can return an implicit result through the argument list. Function subprograms normally return a fixed-point explicit result in general-purpose register 0 and a floating-point explicit result in floating point register 0.

The role played by the subprogram in the linkage procedure is partially dependent upon the computations performed by the subprogram. Minimally, the subprogram would initially store the registers in the designated save area, which is located via register 13. The arguments

Location	Operation	Operand	
	EXTRN	BIGSUB	(1)
	.		
	.		
	.		
	LA	13,SAVEAREA	(2)
	LA	1,ALIST	(3)
	L	15,SUBADDR	(4)
	LA	14,NEXTLOC	(5)
	BR	15	(6)
NEXTLOC	.		(7)
	.		
	.		
SUBADDR	DC	A (BIGSUB)	(8)
ALIST	DC	A (A)	(9)
	DC	A (B)	(10)
	DC	A (C)	(11)
SAVEAREA	DS	20F	(12)
A	DS	F	(13)
B	DS	F	(14)
C	DS	F	(15)
	.		
	.		
	.		

Figure 11.12 Sample linkage instructions for a call statement of the form
CALL   BIGSUB(A,B,C).

are located through register 1. The exit procedure from the subprogram involves a restoration of the registers and a branch to the main storage address contained in register 14.

The Basic Loading Process

One of the conveniences provided by an operating system is that programs or subprograms in a system library can be shared among users of the system without having to physically handle the programs as recorded on a storage medium. The basic idea is that a subprogram, such as the square-root routine, is stored in a library maintained by the operating system. The user need not include the square-root function in his program. When his program is loaded into main storage for execution, the fact that the square-root routine is referenced but not present is recognized by the loader program. The system library is searched for missing subprograms, which are retrieved and loaded into main storage for execution as though they were present in the user's deck setup. A block diagram of the loading process is depicted in Figure 11.13.

When loading an "absolute" object module, the loader program essentially places it in the main storage locations for which it was assembled. "Relocatable" loading, which is described here, requires that addresses be adjusted to correspond to the place in which the object program is loaded in main storage. The relocatable loading process is described in simplified form in the following procedures:

1. Each object has an origin specified at compile or assembly time. (Usually, source modules are compiled or assembled relative to 0.)
2. The relative location (to the beginning of the object module) of each address that must be adjusted is specified in a "relocation dictionary" that is part of the object module.
3. External symbols defined in the object program (DEFs) and external symbols referenced in the object program (REFs) are specified in an "external symbol dictionary."
4. As each object program is loaded, the address field of instructions is adjusted as follows:

$$a' = a + (l - o)$$

where

a' is the value of the adjusted address field
a is the value of the original address field
l is the load point of the object program
o is the origin to which the source program was assembled or compiled

5. Similarly, external REFs are resolved to correspond to the address of external DEFs in main storage.

An example of this procedure is given in Figure 11.14. As each object program is loaded into main storage, a table is built of subprograms needed (i.e., REFs) and subroutines present (i.e., DEFs). After the last object program, provided by the user, is loaded, the system library is searched for subprograms needed but not present.

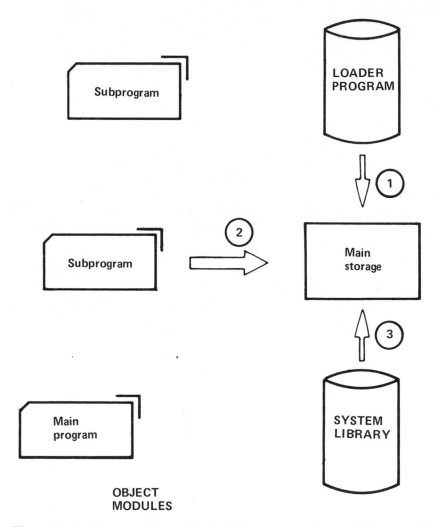

Figure 11.13 Conceptual view of the loading process. Object modules supplied by the user are loaded first. Missing subprograms are retrieved from the system library.

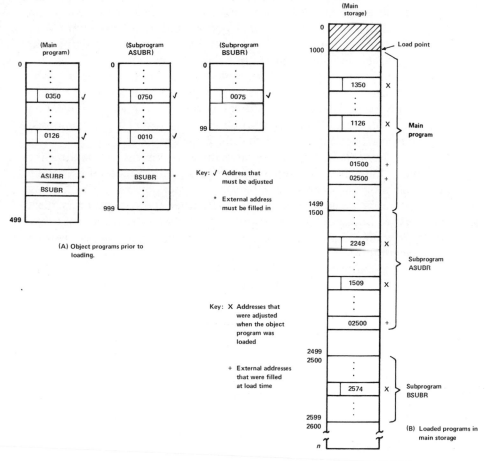

Figure 11.14 Relocation of object programs during the loading process.

Object Modules and Linkage Editing

The machine language program generated by a language translator is generated in the form of an object module that includes three major sections: an external symbol dictionary, a relocation dictionary, and the text of the program. (An object module is depicted conceptually in Figure 11.15.) The *external symbol dictionary* (ESD) contains an entry for each external symbol (such as the name of a subprogram) defined or referenced in the object program. The *relocation dictionary* (RLD) contains an entry for each relocatable address constant that must be adjusted after loading and before execution can commence. (An RLD entry specifies a relocatable address constant by giving its location relative to the origin of the object program.) The *text* (TXT) is composed of the instructions and data of the object program.

It is desirable in a multiprogramming environment to minimize the computer time spent in preparing a program for execution, especially when the program is expected to be used on a periodic basis. The loading process can be time-consuming, especially when the system library must be searched for needed subprograms. One method of reducing load time is to link object programs beforehand through a process known as linkage editing.

Linkage editing is defined as the process of linking object programs

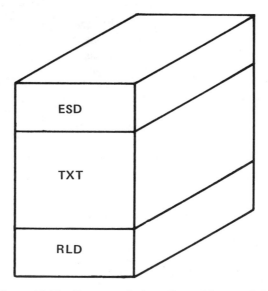

Figure 11.15 Conceptual view of an object module.

together prior to execution with a *linkage editor* program.* Output from the linkage editing process is a load module, in which all external references are resolved by matching referenced symbols to defined symbols. A *load module* is formed by combining the external symbol and relocation dictionaries and by assigning program text in consecutive relative addresses, as in the loading process. Linkage editing is depicted in Figure 11.16. In a load module, *all* external references are resolved so that the process of actually loading a link-edited program involves only the adjustment of address constants.

Input to the linkage editor program can include the following: (1) object modules; (2) a previously link-edited load module; and (3) control information specifying the operations the linkage editor should perform. Object modules can be prepared by the user or can be retrieved from the system library of subprograms.

Through the use of appropriate control statements, the linkage editor can be used to edit a load module by replacing an old version of an object program with an updated version. This process is depicted in Figure 11.17, in which the object program Y is replaced by Y'.

Execution

Load modules are placed by the linkage editor in a special kind of data set (i.e., a data file) known as a partitioned data set, and sometimes referred to as a *user library*. In fact, object modules are placed in the same kind of data set for subsequent input to a linkage editor or loader program. (The subject of partitioned data sets is covered in the next section.) When a job is selected for execution by a job management routine, the load module corresponding to the first step of the job is retrieved from the appropriate user library and loaded directly into main storage. This process is referred to as *program fetch*, and as mentioned previously, only addresses need be adjusted and execution can proceed. The use of a linkage editor and a loader are contrasted in Figure 11.18. Some operating systems utilize either the linkage editing concept, the loading concept, or both. As it turns out, program fetch as defined above is simply a special case of the loading process.

11.4 DATA MANAGEMENT

Data management facilities in an operating system are concerned with the nature of data itself and the manner in which it is organized and accessed. The topic of data management is particularly important for

---

* The linkage editor program is generally regarded as a language processor.

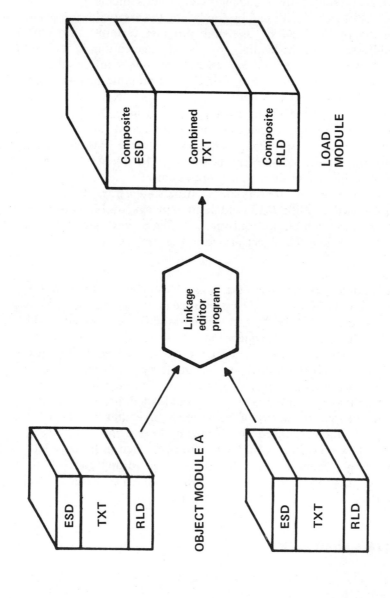

Figure 11.16 Linkage editing combines object modules to form a load module.

342

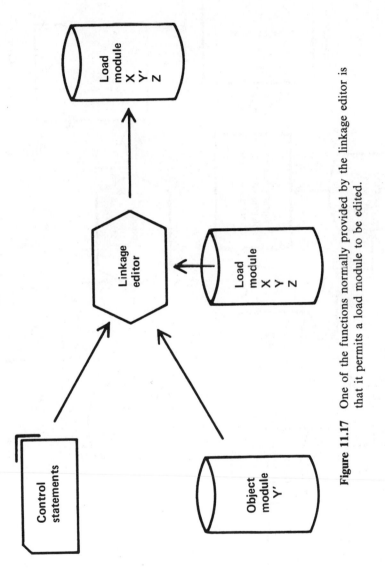

Figure 11.17 One of the functions normally provided by the linkage editor is that it permits a load module to be edited.

343

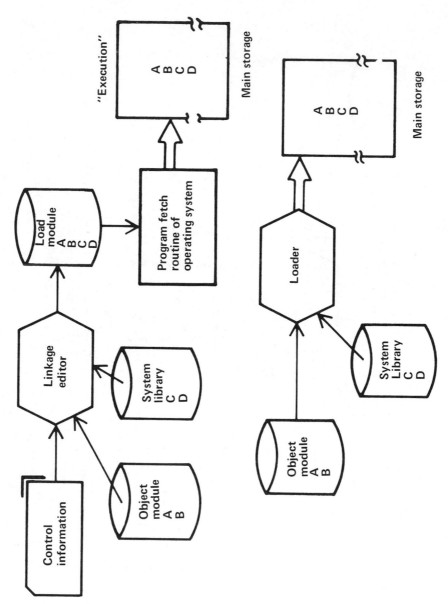

Figure 11.18 Contrasting functions of the linkage editor and the loader.

344

many computer applications because it strongly influences how efficiently information can be stored on external storage media and how efficiently it can be accessed during computer processing.

Data and Storage Structures

Because the various methods of storing data are well known, most readers rarely think about the subject and relevant terminology. The basic unit of storage is a *bit*, the commonly used acronym for binary digit. In main storage bits are grouped to form *bytes* or words. In a byte-oriented computer, bytes are grouped to form words; in a word-oriented computer, subdivisions of a word (such as 6 bits) are interpreted as characters, when necessary. On an external storage medium, information is stored as bits arranged in a characteristic manner. For example, bits are stored as lateral rows on tape, as columns on a card, or serially in tracks on a disk surface. In most cases, some sort of correspondence is made between a grouping of bits in main storage and a grouping of bits on the external media; for example, a byte or character in main storage usually corresponds to a column of a card or a lateral row in tape. A *block* is a unit of transfer between main storage and an external device. A block consists of several bytes or words, as specified in the count field of an input/output command controlling the data-transfer operation. The contents of a block are governed by a user's program and by the data management routines of the operating system. Frequently, the bits that make up a block are transformed by an algorithm implemented in hardware to achieve compatibility between the physical components involved. As an example, an 8-bit byte in main storage is transformed to a 12-bit card column by the control unit of the card punch.

A *field* is a unit of data that would lose its meaning if it were broken down further. Typical fields are a person's name or a number punched in a card. A character in either of these fields is simply part of the computer alphabet and has no meaning by itself.

In main storage, a group of consecutive fields that have some logical relationship to each other is termed a *data record*. Data records are frequently referred to as logical records. A simple data record might be an employee's record on a personnel file. A group of related records is termed a *file*; hence the familiar terms "payroll file" or "personnel file."

When performing data manipulation and input/output operations, the user deals in fields, records, and files. However, the computer and the input/output system deal in blocks, as mentioned previously. What happens is that the data management routines of the operating system group several records to form a block, prior to the output operation. This process is referred to as *blocking*. On input, the process is reversed and is termed *deblocking*. Thus, the user can visualize his file as a series of records. In reality, it is stored as a series of blocks, each of which can contain several data records.

The technique of using blocked records has two principal advantages: (1) It conserves space on the storage media; and (2) it contributes to efficient input/output operations.

Three record formats are generally used: fixed-length records, variable-length records, and undefined-length records, as depicted in Figure 11.19. The size of a *fixed-length record* is constant for all data records in a block; in addition, the size of the block is also constant in size. Fixed-length records may be blocked or unblocked. In the former case, several data records comprise a block; in the latter case, a block is composed of a single data record. With *variable-length records*, the size of each data record and of the block may be variable in length. Moreover, the record format includes length fields for use by the data management routines. *Undefined-length records* are established for cases in which the records to be processed do not meet the requirements of the preceding two types. When undefined-length records are used, it is the user's responsibility to perform blocking and deblocking, whereas with fixed-length and variable-length records, these functions are performed by data management routines.

The choice of a record format for a given application is a systems design problem and involves processing time and storage space. The characteristics of a data file are provided to the operating system with control cards or through facilities of a given programming language. Regardless of how the characteristics of a data file are specified, the blocking, deblocking, and housekeeping operations are normally transparent to the user through the use of a programming language.

Storage Organization

Data can be organized in storage using four basic methods: consecutive organization, linked organization, keyed organization, and regional organization. *Consecutive organization* requires that an allocation of storage occupies contiguous storage positions. As depicted in Figure 11.20, blocks placed on magnetic tape is a common example of a storage structure that is organized consecutively. Storage structures can also be organized consecutively on direct-access media by assigning contiguous tracks or cylinders.

Linked organization permits distinct data blocks to occupy discontiguous storage space; a block includes pointers to preceding and/or succeeding data blocks to facilitate storage access. This type of

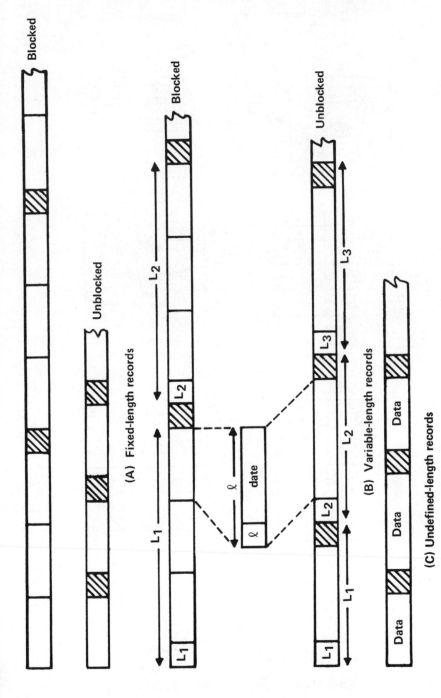

Figure 11.19 Conceptual view of data record formats.

(A) Fixed-length records

(B) Variable-length records

(C) Undefined-length records

Blocked

Unblocked

Blocked

Unblocked

L_1

L_2

L_3

ℓ

date

Data

347

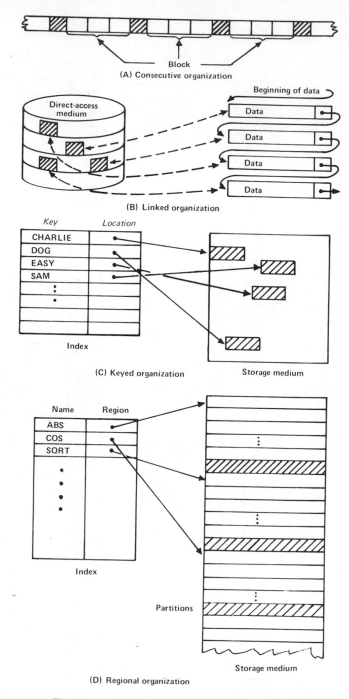

Figure 11.20 Types of storage organization.

348

organization is used with direct-access storage, where the pointers exist as cylinder/head addresses of other blocks. Linked organization is also depicted in Figure 11.20.

Keyed organization is a method of storage organization in which data is located by means of a data key that is a part of the information being stored (for example, part of a data record) or is maintained as a separate data area distinct from the data record. In keyed organization, data is retrieved by key value, either by direct search or with the aid of a table of keys that points to associated data. Keyed organization is most frequently used with direct-access storage devices, in which tables of keys effectively point to the various locations of data on the storage media. Keyed organization is suggested by Figure 11.20.

With *regional organization*, a region of storage is located by name, index, or key. After a region is identified and located, data are accessed as though that region were organized consecutively. In many cases, regional organization is used to partition a storage space that is allocated consecutively, such as a "library" of programs in object module format. The library is organized by program name; once a program is located in that library, it is accessed sequentially. Regional organization is also depicted in Figure 11.20.

Storage Access

The modern theory of data structure and organization emphasizes the distinction between storage organization and storage access. Two methods of storage access are usually identified: sequential and direct. *Sequential access* denotes that data blocks are referenced in an order dependent on the order in which the data blocks are physically stored. Card decks and tape files are usually accessed sequentially. However, a keyed data file can also be accessed sequentially by following the pointers or by referencing the keys in order.

Direct access denotes that a data block is referenced without having to reference preceding information. Direct access can be implemented in several ways:

1. The cylinder/head number of a data block on direct-access storage is known and that physical address can be used to reference the item desired.
2. A key is matched against a table that provides the physical location of the data block.
3. One or more mathematical operations are performed on the key, giving the relative location of the desired data block on a direct-access storage medium.

The main point to be emphasized here is that the manner in which data is accessed is independent of its format and how it is organized. The flexibility inherent in the different methods of format, organization, and access permit data management operations to be adapted to the needs of a particular application.

Data Management Facilities

A variety of data management facilities is available from most operating systems. First, the concept of a data file is generalized to what is known as a *data set*, which is defined as a named data file. The idea behind a data set name is that an ordinary collection of related data items* can be accessed by name alone. Data set names are held in a tree-oriented *catalog* held in direct-access storage. In order to use a data set, the user specifies its name and a routine of the operating set retrieves the number of the device media from the catalog as well as the characteristics of the data set. Another management problem involves the allocation of space on direct-access storage, which can be quite a "hassle" when performed manually. Collectively, normal data management facilities are inherent in the structure of the data management routines of the operating system, described as follows:

1. *Direct-access space management routines* control the allocation of storage space on direct-access devices.
2. *Catalog management routines* provide information on data sets and catalog and uncatalog data sets on a demand basis.
3. *Input/output routines* initiate and control input and output operations and perform buffering, blocking/deblocking, and error-recovery capabilities.

Another significant feature provided by data management facilities of an operating system is device-independence. Within reasonable limits, a program can be written to utilize any type of input/output medium, such as cards, tape, or disk. The assignment of device to data set is made at run-time through control cards and the device characteristics are absorbed by the input/output routines of the data management system.

11.5   STORAGE MANAGEMENT

One of the fundamental operating system requirements implied by the multiprogramming and time-sharing modes of operation is that several user jobs must reside in main storage at the same time. The

---

* Such as a file, source program, object program, table, or collection of subroutines.

allocation of main storage to jobs is regarded as a system management function in operating system technology and the techniques are generally known as *storage management*. In the introduction to time sharing earlier in the chapter, reference was made to the concept of swapping, which is an example of one means of managing main storage.

Three methods are covered in this section: partition allocation, region allocation, and virtual storage. The presentation is not exhaustive in the sense that other methods have and will be developed. However, the methods covered here are the most widely used and are necessary for an understanding of operating systems.

Environment for Storage Management

Before multiprogramming and time-sharing concepts were established, jobs were executed serially by the operating system. Normal delays in the execution of a job simply caused the central processing unit to wait. Main storage organization in a serially operating environment is depicted in Figure 11.21. It should also be noted that main storage is not fully utilized, so that serial operation results in the inefficient use of the two most costly components of a computer system: the central processing unit and main storage. The problem, as we already know, is alleviated through multiprogramming.

With multiprogramming, the upper limit on the number of active jobs is usually determined by the design of the computer and/or the operating system.* Although some multiprogramming systems permit the movement of programs on a dynamic basis between main storage and an external storage medium in a manner similar to swapping, programs are resident in most systems for the duration of execution. Thus, the level of multiprogramming is partially determined by the size of main storage and the size of individual programs.

With time sharing, the main objective is to service many users and the size of main storage does not in general determine the number of active users the system can sustain. However, the size of main storage *does* determine the efficiency and response time of the system. In time sharing, therefore, programs are expected to be moved between main storage and an external storage medium on a dynamic basis.

Of the three methods covered here, partition allocation and region allocation are used in a "static" multiprogramming environment. The third method, virtual storage, is used for both multiprogramming and time-sharing.

---

* IBM's most widely used operating system, OS/MVT (also known as OS/VS1 and OS/VS2), for example, limits the number of active jobs to 15.

Partition Allocation

With the *partition method* of storage management, main storage is partitioned into fixed-sized areas; the size of each partition is established by the computer operator when the computer is started through operator commands to the system. A typical partitioned storage organization is depicted in Figure 11.22.

The user must specify the amount of main storage required (usually with the JOB card) when a job is submitted. Using this information, job management routines of the operating system can assign the job to the smallest partition in which the programs of the job can be placed. (The concept is similar to the placement of different sized books in a bookcase with different sized shelves. Books are placed on shelves so as to obtain

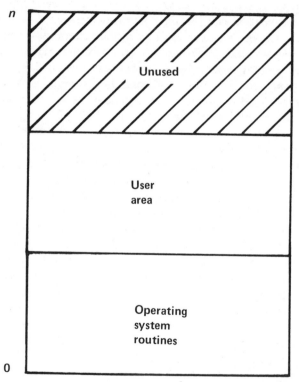

Figure 11.21 Main storage organization in an operating environment in which jobs are executed serially, causing the central processing unit to wait when normal delays in program execution occur. Also, main storage is not fully utilized.

the best utilization of the bookcase.*) Once a job is assigned to a partition, it is required to execute in that partition until the job is completed.

The major advantage of partition allocation is that the assignment of a job to a partition is straightforward and efficient. The disadvantages are almost obvious. First, the number of active jobs is limited by the number of partitions, even if the jobs are small in size. Second, most jobs will not fit exactly in a partition and thus some main storage space is unused. Last, big jobs that fit only into the largest partition must be executed serially, even if there are no small jobs in the system.

One of the most frequent uses of partition allocation exists when one or more jobs must be resident for long periods of time, as in the case of an on-line information system. A partition is allocated to jobs of this type; the job is initiated, as any other job, and it stays resident by virtue of the fact that it does not terminate.

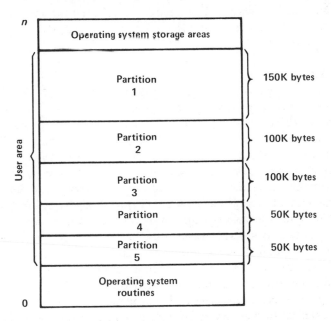

Figure 11.22 Partitioned storage organization. The size of partitions is established by the computer operator when the computer is started up using operating system facilities.

---

* Some parking lots have special areas for compact cars for similar reasons.

Region Allocation

The disadvantages of partition allocation listed above are partially eliminated by an alternate method known as *region allocation*. As in partition allocation, each job also specifies its main storage requirements in region allocation. When storage requirements are not stated, a default value is assigned. As suggested in Figure 11.23, as many jobs are loaded into the user area of main storage as possible; each job is given the requested amount of storage and is constrained to execute in that region. (In a logical sense, "fences" are established in the user area of main storage.) Jobs are selected for execution on the basis of internal priority; if insufficient "available" storage is available for that job, then it must wait. When a job completes execution, the main storage space assigned to it is freed for use by other jobs. Main storage does become fragmented after several jobs terminate and new jobs are initiated. However, region allocation is more efficient than in partition allocation because the case of a partially used partition never occurs.

The algorithm used for allocating storage using the region concept is worthy of further study. The reader is referred to Katzan* for a description of how this method is complemented in the OS/MVT operating system.

Virtual Storage

Virtual storage is a storage management technique that allows a large addressing capability that exceeds the physical main storage capacity of the computer—hence the name "virtual storage," which implies storage that does not exist. Virtual storage is "mapped" into a combination of real main storage and external storage, such as magnetic drum or disk. The basic idea behind a virtual storage system is that virtual storage, real main storage, and external storage are divided into fixed-size units of storage called *pages*. Typical page sizes are 2048 bytes and 4096 bytes. It follows that only needed pages of a program, including data and storage areas, must be in real main storage for the program to execute.† As a result, the amount of main storage can be "overcommitted"; when a particular page is needed, it can be retrieved from external storage on a demand basis. As a virtual storage system operates, pages are constantly being moved between main storage and the external storage device because new pages are constantly needed and old pages must be displaced to make room for new pages. The

---

* Katzan, H., *Operating Systems: A Pragmatic Approach*, Van Nostrand-Reinhold, New York, pp. 206–211.

† A *needed page* is defined as the page in which the program is actually executing or a page that contains an operand used by an instruction. Usually, several pages are needed to sustain execution, but this number is normally less than the complete program.

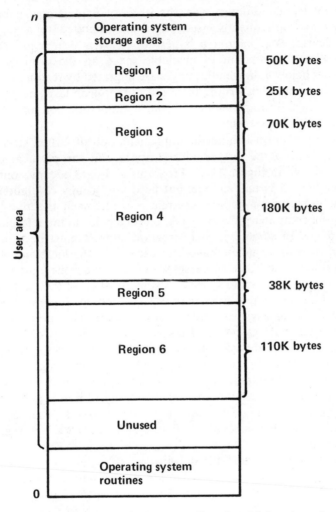

Figure 11.23 The region method of storage allocation. Main storage is assigned to jobs dynamically based on actual requirements.

355

process of moving pages in and out of main storage is referred to as *paging* and is depicted in Figure 11.24. The external device used to hold pages when they are not in use is referred to as the *paging device*. Under heavily loaded conditions, even the primary paging device becomes saturated and infrequently used pages are migrated to a secondary paging device. *Page migration* is performed by a system management routine when the amount of available space on the primary paging device goes below a threshhold; pages are migrated by reading them into main storage and then writing them out to the secondary paging device. Virtual storage is implemented through a combination of hardware facilities and software support.

The key concept behind the implementation of virtual storage is a mapping between the virtual address space and the physical address space, as shown in Figure 11.25. Programs and data occupy contiguous page locations in virtual storage, but need not occupy contiguous page locations in real main storage. The reason is that each effective address used during computer processing is translated prior to the referencing of main storage. In summary, each program address must be translated; however, because complete pages are used, only the locations of pages need be adjusted and byte addresses within a page are the same in virtual storage as they are in main storage. A simplification of the translation of virtual addresses to real addresses is suggested by Figure 11.26. The high-order bits of a virtual address are displacements in a page table containing the main storage addresses of pages. The low-order bits are unchanged because they denote storage addresses within a page. Thus, translation essentially consists of a table lookup. Page tables are constructed and maintained by software. In order to facilitate page table management and translation, the virtual storage address space is divided into segments, and segments are divided into pages. The segmented effective virtual address, shown in Figure 11.27, allows a hierarchical set of lookup tables.

The process of translating virtual addresses to main storage addresses is referred to as *dynamic address translation*, which uses the following hardware features and software concepts:

1. A *table register* that contains the address of the segment table
2. A *segment table* that contains the origin (i.e., addresses) of the page tables
3. A *page table* for each segment
4. An *associative memory* to speed up translation
5. A hardware feature known as the *DAT box* (for *d*ynamic *a*ddress *t*ranslation) that physically performs the address translation using the above tables

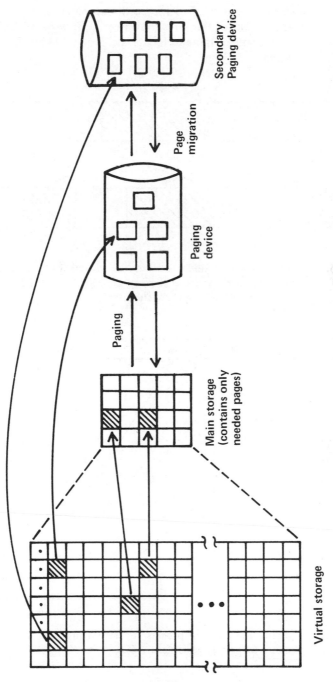

Figure 11.24 Conceptual view of the paging process.

Secondary
Paging device

Page
migration

Paging
device

Paging

Main storage
(contains only
needed pages)

Virtual storage

357

1. The table register is used to locate the segment table.
2. The segment field of the virtual storage address is added to the origin of the segment table to locate the page table for that virtual storage segment.

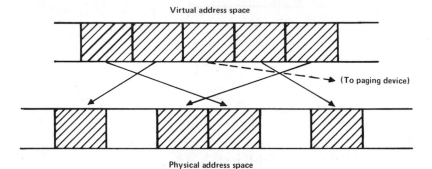

Figure 11.25   The mapping of address from the virtual address space to a physical address space is the key concept behind the implementation of a virtual storage system.

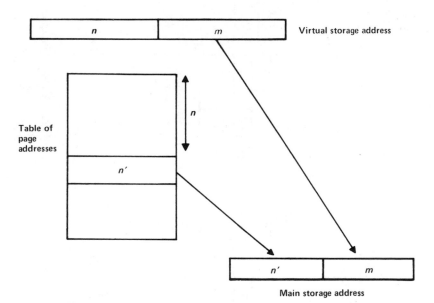

Figure 11.26   Simplification of the process of translating virtual storage addresses, using a page table.

3. The page field of the virtual storage address is added to the origin of the page table (step 2) to determine the real address of the page in main storage or to indicate that the page is not in main storage but resides on the paging device.
4. If the referenced page is in main storage, then the address in the page table becomes the high-order portion of the main storage address as indicated above. If the referenced page is not in main storage, then an interruption is generated so that the page can be "paged in" by the operating system.

Figure 11.28 gives a conceptual view of a page table entry. The control bits indicate if the main storage address found in the page table entry is valid. During dynamic address translation, the control bits are inspected by the DAT box so that an interruption can be generated if necessary.

When a paging interruption is received by the operating system, it locates the page through the external page address found in the appropriate page table entry. When the page is paged in, the high-order

The *dynamic address translation* procedure operates as follows:

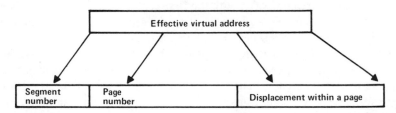

Figure 11.27   The virtual effective address is segmented to allow a hierarchical set of lookup tables.

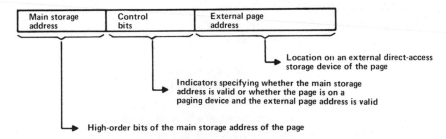

Figure 11.28   Conceptual view of a page table entry.

bits of the main storage location where the page was placed replace the main storage address field of the page table entry and the control bits are set to indicate that the page is in main storage. When a page is paged out because its space is needed in main storage, the process is reversed: (1) The page is written to the paging device; (2) The external location of the page replaces the external page address of the page table entry; and (3) The control bits are set to indicate that the page is not in main storage.

Dynamic address translation is performed automatically by the hardware using the DAT box for each reference to main storage. The segment and page tables are built and maintained by the operating system. Segment and page tables are held in main storage, so that each main storage reference by the executing program would effectively require three references: segment table, page table, and the actual reference itself. This is a high price to pay, from a performance point of view, for virtual storage capability. Most systems that employ virtual storage, therefore, augment the dynamic address translation process with a small associative memory that contains the virtual storage and main storage addresses of the most recent storage references. When a virtual storage address is to be translated, the segment and page fields of the virtual address are compared with the first part of *all* associative registers in parallel. If an equal match exists, then the second part of the matched associative register becomes the page address directly and the main storage accesses of segment and page tables required during dynamic address translation need not be made. Since the currently used instructions and data tend to cluster in a program, the use of an associative register speeds up the dynamic address process considerably. The process of dynamic address translation is shown in Figure 11.29, and an example of address translation is given in Figure 11.30.

Virtual storage is used in two primary ways in operating system technology. In multiprogramming systems, virtual storage is used to overcommit main storage that has been allocated as partitions or regions. This type of system is suggested by Figure 11.31. In systems of this type, a single virtual storage is used and one set of segment and page tables exists for the entire system. In time-sharing systems that utilize virtual storage, a complete virtual storage is assigned to each job, and each job has its own set of segment and page tables. Prior to giving control of the central processing unit to a job, its segment and page tables are brought into main storage by a system management routine and the table register is set to point to the segment table. A system that employs multiple virtual storage is depicted in Figure 11.32.

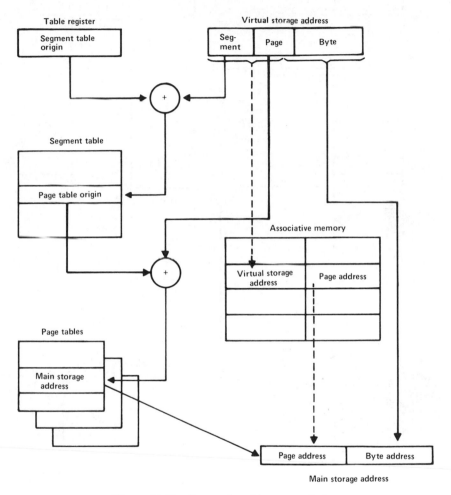

Figure 11.29 Dynamic address translation.

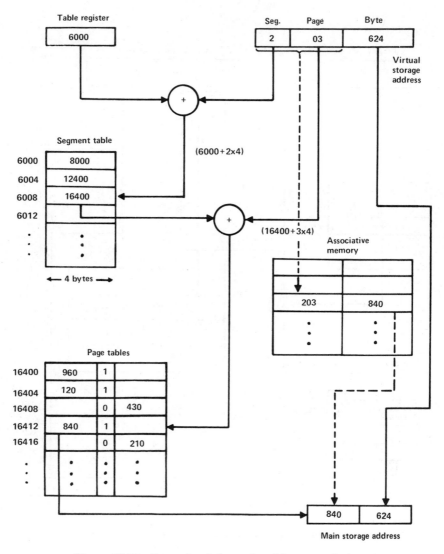

Figure 11.30 Example of dynamic address translation.

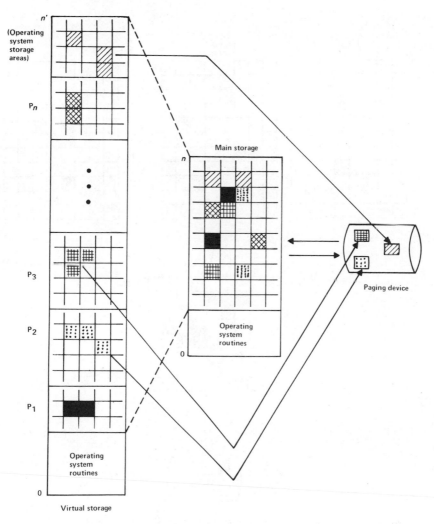

Figure 11.31 The use of virtual storage permits main storage to be over-committed in a multiprogramming system in which storage is allocated as partitions or regions.

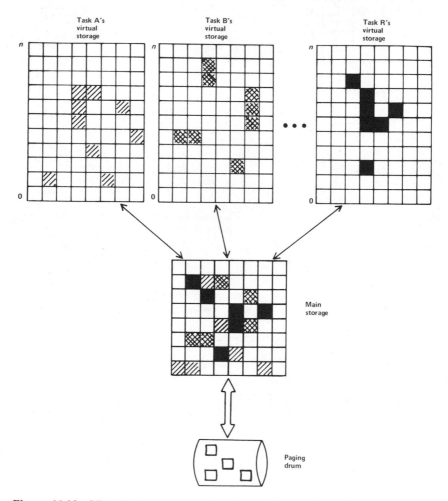

Figure 11.32 Virtual storage in a time-sharing system in which each task is assigned a complete virtual storage.

11.6 COMMENTS ON OPERATING SYSTEM TECHNOLOGY

The study of operating systems is an extensive topic in computer science, especially in light of the fact that the presentation given here can be considered to be an overview of the subject matter. Since an operating system is a collection of programs, each routine must be described in precise detail before a system can be constructed or analyzed. Moreover, control programs are exceedingly complex, and algorithms for performing the various functional capabilities of a system are frequently riddled with exceptions and special cases. For example, input/output routines that handle computer terminal devices must differentiate in many cases between the kind of device on the other end of the telephone line. It is important to emphasize, however, that every action performed by a computer system is controlled by an operating system program. As a result, every mundane operation, such as reading a control card, is important to the overall operation of the system.

There is a variety of topics that the interested reader will want to explore. The area of *job management* has been covered lightly. In this category one might expect to learn about job control language, job preparation, job accounting, device allocation, input readers, and output writers. In the area of *system management*, further study would necessarily include the following topics: interruption handling, scheduling, storage allocation, and error recovery and recording. In the area of *data management*, further study would include: access method routines, buffering techniques, catalog management, and methods for blocking and deblocking.

Performance analysis and measurement is a relatively new field that is concerned with how efficiently the computer system is utilized. Topics for further study in this area include: measurement techniques, mathematical modeling, and statistical analysis.

QUESTION SET

1. What is the advantage of using peripheral computers?
2. Give similarities and differences between batched input for data processing and batch processing with regard to operating systems.
3. Distinguish between physical IOCS and logical IOCS.
4. In what way is the use of peripheral computers and spooling related?
5. Explain the following assertion: The use of multiprogramming sells more main storage units and less CPUs.
6. What is natural about a "natural wait"?
7. Distinguish between a *job* and a *terminal session*.

8. Could a multiprogramming system use time slicing? When would it be desirable to do so?

9. (Class or term project) Develop a flow diagram of the manner in which an operating system operates. Five areas are of prime importance: (1) the manner in which the system responds to the input job stream; (2) the manner in which the system responds to interruptions; (3) the manner in which the CPU is scheduled; (4) the manner in which main storage is allocated; and (5) the manner in which input/output operations are controlled.

10. What factors determine the response time of a time-sharing system?

11. Develop a short flow diagram describing the process of loading an object program.

12. Why is an ESD used? An RLD?

13. Distinguish between storage organization and storage access.

14. Give the most efficient record format for each of the following:

> A deck of punched cards—contents unknown
> A source program
> A record from a personnel file

Since there is no "right" or "wrong" answer, state the reasons for the selections you made.

15. Develop a short flow diagram of the dynamic address translation process.

SELECTED READINGS

Chapin, N., *Computers: A Systems Approach,* Van Nostrand-Reinhold, New York, 1971.

Donovan, J. J., *Systems Programming,* McGraw-Hill, New York, 1972.

Flores, I., *Data Structure and Management,* Prentice-Hall, Englewood Cliffs, N.J., 1970.

Freiberger, W. (ed.), *Statistical Computer Performance Evaluation,* Academic Press, New York, 1972.

Hall, A. D., *A Methodology for Systems Engineering,* Van Nostrand-Reinhold, New York, 1962.

Katzan, H., *Operating Systems: A Pragmatic Approach,* Van Nostrand-Reinhold, New York, 1973.

Kindred, A. R., *Data Systems and Management,* Prentice-Hall, Englewood Cliffs, N.J., 1973.

Scherr, A. L., *An Analysis of Time-Shared Computer Systems,* MIT Press, Cambridge, Mass., 1967.

Wilkes, M. V., *Time-Sharing Computer Systems* (2d ed.), American Elsevier, New York, 1972.

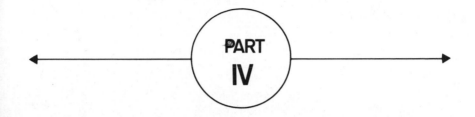

PART IV

TOPICS IN COMPUTER SCIENCE

12

STRUCTURED PROGRAMMING

12.1 INTRODUCTION

Structured programming is a method of computer programming that contributes to a program's reliability, maintainability, and readability. The technique exists as a set of mathematically based rules that apply to programming during each step of the process. Although structured programming is a distinct topic, it is related to top-down programming and the HIPO method, both of which were presented earlier in the book. For example, the concept of top-down programming lends itself to implementation using structured programming and to description using the HIPO technique.

Another advantage of structured programming is that it simplifies the control structures in a program, so that instead of using GOTO statements that effectively branch "all over the place," a program is composed of well-defined blocks of code, such as those achieved through the use of the conventional DO (or FOR) loop. With some programming languages, the use of structured programming facilitates object code optimization; however, optimization is not generally considered to be a significant reason for employing structured programming.

Structured programming requires a systematic and disciplined approach to programming. The objective and the result is that a more precise form of programming is achieved with structured programming than by using conventional programming practices.

12.2 THE STRUCTURE THEOREM

The concept of structured programming is based on the Structure Theorem, which states that a program with one entry and one exit (i.e., a

369

proper program) is functionally equivalent to a program constructed from the following logic structures:

1. A sequence of two or more functions
2. A conditional branch of the form

      If p THEN a ELSE c

3. Repeated execution of a function while a condition is true, that is, the DO WHILE statement

The basic idea behind structured programming is that a program can be represented as a function with one entry and one exit as shown in Figure 12.1, and that it can be constructed by systematically applying the three logic structures, listed previously. In actual practice, the logic structures are frequently supplemented by two additional logic structures that facilitate programming.

Sequence

The *sequence function*, shown in Figure 12.2, is equivalent to stating that two functions, each with one entry and one exit, can be regarded as a single function. Formally, the *sequence proposition* states that the **firstpart** followed by the **secondpart** does the sequence function.

Ifthenelse

The *ifthenelse function* (See Figure 12.3) provides a conditional facility that includes two subfunctions in its definition. Formally, the *ifthenelse proposition* states the following: Whenever the **iftest** is true, the **thenpart** does the ifthenelse function; and whenever the **iftest** is false, the **elsepart** does the ifthenelse function. Thus, the IFTHENELSE statement

entry ⟶ function ⟶ exit

Figure 12.1   A function is a program segment with one entry and one exit.

sequence = firstpart   secondpart

Figure 12.2   The sequence function.

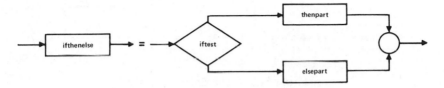

Figure 12.3   The ifthenelse function.

is equivalent to a function, as defined earlier. In this logic structure, **thenpart** and **elsepart** are functions.

Dowhile

The *dowhile function* (see Figure 12.4) provides a looping facility analogous to the DO or FOR loops in most programming languages. In its most elementary form, the dowhile function serves as a compound statement.* Formally, the *dowhile proposition* states the following: Whenever the **whiletest** is true, the **dopart** followed by the **dowhile** does the dowhile function; and whenever the **whiletest** is false, the identity does the dowhile function. In the latter case, the false result from the **whiletest** causes an exit from the function. In this logic structure, **dopart** is a function.

Dountil and Case

Structured programming is the repeated application of the sequence, ifthenelse, and dowhile functions to produce a program that exists as a function. The *dountil function* (Figure 12.5) and the *case function* (Figure

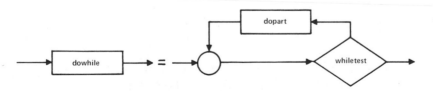

Figure 12.4   The dowhile function.

---

* A *compound statement* is a set of statements of the form **begin** S_1; S_2; ... S_n **end** that are treated as a single statement.

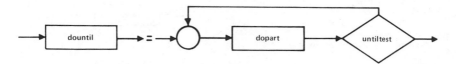

Figure 12.5   The dountil function.

12.6) are encountered sufficiently often that they warrant unique structures. The *dountil function* is an alternate form of looping in which the function is executed while the **untiltest** is true. The *case function* is a multibranch-multijoin structure that is equivalent to a set of nested ifthenelse functions.

Application of the Concepts

As an example of how the preceding concepts can be used to synthesize or analyze a structured program, consider the following program in text form:

        if p *then*
            a
            do while(q)
                    b
            end do
    else
            if r *then*
                    c
            else
                    do while(s)
                            d
                    end do
            end if
            e
    end if

The flow diagram form of the program is given as Figure 12.7. Analyzing the flow diagrams in Figure 12.7 from bottom-to-top, the diagrams become more easily understood because less detail is included. Synthesizing the program from top-to-bottom, detail is added in each successive step. The transition is made between the various flow diagrams by repeated application of the structure theorem.

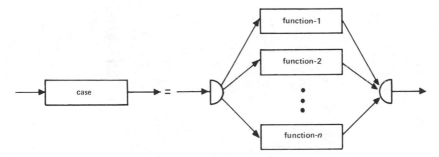

Figure 12.6 The case function.

12.3 IMPLEMENTATION OF STRUCTURED PROGRAMMING

One of the most significant characteristics of a structured program, which was exhibited in the preceding example, is that the program is highly readable. The text can be read from top-to-bottom without any "jumping around." There is a noted lack of GOTO statements, which are the major cause of the excessive branching found in many programs. Readable programs are useful during development, testing, and maintenance. In fact, different functions can be assigned to different programmers that are working cooperatively on a project.

Another factor that contributes to readability is the practice of indenting statements, so that the statements that correspond to a particular function can be easily identified. The fact that a pictorial representation of the logic is gained from the indentation is demonstrated in the PL/I programs given in Figure 12.8.

A coding practice that contributes to programs that are easily understood is to segment the code into reasonable amounts of logic. Effective segmentation is achieved through the use of library facilities, such as those accessed with the COPY statement in COBOL and the %INCLUDE macro facility in PL/I, or through the use of subprograms, such as those referenced with the CALL statement. A useful size for a segment to take is one page of program listing. Subsegments, in turn, are constructed of sub-subsegments, and so on, each of which is restricted to the one-page limit. The end result is that a reader can easily grasp the logic of a program, at any level of detail, by studying the segments that correspond to the functional structure of a program. Two straightforward examples of segmentation are given in Figure 12.9.

The use of structured programming and appropriate coding practices become a set of "project rules" when enforced by management

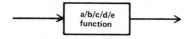

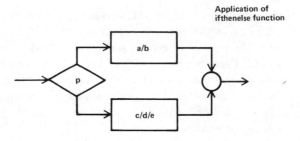

Application of
ifthenelse function

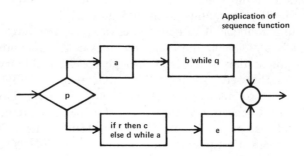

Application of
sequence function

Figure 12.7   Analysis or synthesis of a structured program.

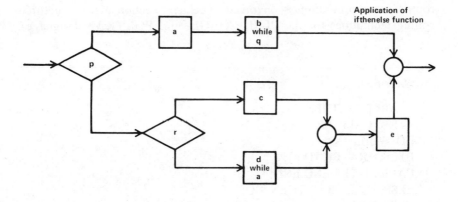

Application of
ifthenelse function

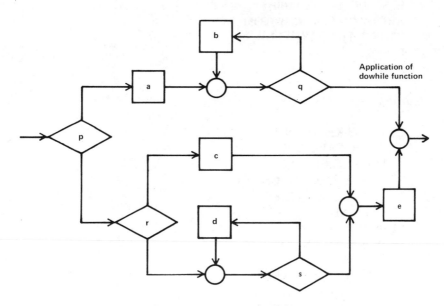

Application of
dowhile function

Figure 12.7 (continued)

control. Although most programming projects benefit from structured programming, large-scale software development projects are particularly amenable to the techniques because of the relatively large numbers of routines and programmers involved. The next section gives structured coding techniques for the PL/I, COBOL, and FORTRAN languages.

Not Indented

```
IF  AB<BKR THEN  DO;
A=B+C;CALL  BIG;
DO  WHILE(X>=Y);
BTL=Q+RATF(CHAL);
CALL LITTLE;END;END;
ELSE DO;IF  R=T THEN  DO;
COW=DOG+1;
CALL  DLMB;END;
ELSE DO I=1  TO  100;
ARRAY(I)=LIST  C(I)-TOM;
BFOX(I+1)=LFOX(I);END;
E=F+1;
END
```

Indented

```
IF  ABL<BKR THEN  DO;
    A=B+C;CALL  BIG;
    DO  WHILE(X>=Y);
        BTL=Q+RATF(CHAL);
        CALL LITTLE;
    END;END;
ELSE DO;
    IF  R=T THEN DO;
        COW=DOG+1;
        CALL  DLMB;END;
    ELSE DO I=1  TO  100;
        ARRAY(I)=LISTC(I)-TOM;
        BFOX(I+1)=LFOX(I);END;
    E=F+1;
    END;
```

Figure 12.8   A PL/I program demonstrating the advantages of the use of the practice of indentation.

IF ABL<BKR THEN	IF ABL<BKR
CALL SUB1	PERFORM SEG1-PAR
ELSE DO;	ELSE
CALL SUB2;	COPY SEG2-PAR.
%INCLUDE SEG1;END;	
PL/I Example	*COBOL Example*

Figure 12.9   The use of segmentation to reduce the size of a segment.

12.4 STRUCTURED PROGRAMMING TECHNIQUES IN FORTRAN, COBOL, AND PL/I

The concept of structured programming is not language-dependent and job control language, linkage editor, and assembler language procedures have been implemented to provide structured programming capability. A structured programming guide has been prepared by the Federal Systems Division of IBM and the coding conventions for the two main structured programming logic structures (excluding the sequence function), given in this section, are based on that report.* The conventions use the reference diagrams for the *ifthenelse* and *dowhile* functions given in Figure 12.10. The development of coding conventions for the dountil and case functions are left as exercises.

The use of structured programming eliminates the need for the GOTO statement. This does not mean that the GOTO statement is eliminated from structured programs, but only that it is not explicitly used as a control mechanism. Several of the coding conventions, especially in the FORTRAN language, employ the GOTO statement.

Structured Programming Coding Conventions in the PL/I Language

The coding convention for the ifthenelse function is defined in PL/I as

```
IF p THEN
    code for F₁
ELSE
    code for F₂
```

Alternately, the ELSE clause may be omitted.

---

* *Structured Programming Guide* (Form No. FSC72–5075), IBM, Federal Systems Division, Gaithersburg, Md.

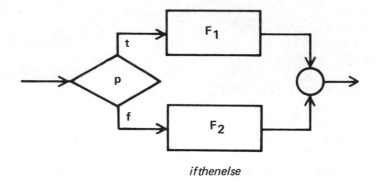

ifthenelse

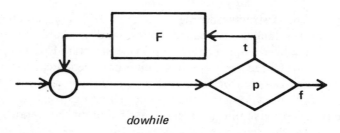

dowhile

Figure 12.10 Reference diagrams for the PL/I, COBOL, and FORTRAN coding conventions.

The coding convention for the dowhile function in PL/I has three options: (1) while clause only; (2) while clause with indexing; and (3) indexing alone. The three options are defined in the above order as follows:

```
DO WHILE(p);
    code for F
END;
```

```
DO  variable = expression_1  TO  expression_2  BY  expression_3
    WHILE(p); code for F
END;
```

```
DO variable = expression_1 TO expression_2 BY expression_3;
    code for F
END;
```

Compared with the FORTRAN and COBOL languages, the PL/I language is most amenable to structured programming because of its block structure and wide range of statement types.

Structured Programming Coding Conventions in the COBOL Language

The coding convention for the ifthenelse function is defined in COBOL as

```
IF p
     code for F₁
ELSE
     code for F₂
```

As with PL/I, the ELSE clause may be alternately omitted.

The coding convention for the dowhile function uses the PERFORM statement and includes the function F in a remote location in the Procedure Division. The function has two options: (1) while clause only; and (2) while clause with indexing. The PERFORM statement in COBOL contains an UNTIL option rather than a WHILE option, so that the coding convention uses a "not p" condition. The two options are defined in the above order as follows:

```
PERFORM paragraph-F UNTIL(NOT p).
```

```
PERFORM paragraph-F
     VARYING identifier-1 FROM identifier-2 BY identifier-3
     UNTIL(NOT p).
```

Because of the UNTIL option to the PERFORM statement in COBOL, the dountil function is relatively straightforward to implement.

Structured Programming Coding Conventions in the FORTRAN Language

The structured programming coding conventions for FORTRAN require more involved programming techniques, because FORTRAN is not a block-structured language and because of the operational limitations of many of the statements in the language. The lack of block structure means that additional statement numbers are required in a FORTRAN program; these statement numbers are denoted in the following statements by Greek letters.

The coding convention for the ifthenelse function is defined in FORTRAN as follows:

```
        IF (.NOT.(p)) GO TO α
            code for F₁
            GO TO β
    α   CONTINUE
            code for F₂
    β   CONTINUE
```

The .NOT.(p) condition is used in the above convention for compatibility with the case of the ifthenelse function where the ELSE clause is omitted, as follows:

```
        IF (.NOT.(p)) GO TO α
            code for F₁
    α   CONTINUE
```

The coding convention for the dowhile function is defined in FORTRAN as follows:

```
    α   CONTINUE
        IF (.NOT.(p)) GO TO β
            code for F
            GO TO α
    β   CONTINUE
```

A DO loop is *always* executed at least once in standard FORTRAN IV, and for that reason it is never used with the dowhile function. However, the DO loop can be used with the dountil function.

Remarks on Coding Conventions

Structured programming conventions for a programming language necessarily involve more than simply defining program segments that correspond to the structured programming functions. Formatting and indentation rules must be established for each statement in the language. In fact, formatting rules may be regarded as being closely akin to "documentation standards." It should be emphasized, however, that the coding conventions and formatting (and indentation) rules constitute a "structured programming package." Each component of that package contributes to effective programming in a unique way.

QUESTION SET

1. Develop a logic structure diagram for the dountil function using one or more of the following functions in combination: sequence, ifthenelse, and dowhile.

2. Develop a logic structure diagram for the case function using one or more of the following functions in combination: sequence, ifthenelse, and dowhile. If necessary, limit the number of cases to a small value, such as three.
3. Select PL/I, COBOL, or FORTRAN. Establish indentation and formatting rules for that language. The rules should cover the ifthenelse, dowhile, dountil, and case functions as well as other statements of the language. Two examples from FORTRAN follow:

ifthenelse clause*:

"Statements within the two clauses are indented two columns. The CONTINUE statements terminate each clause and are coded in line with the IF. There are two blanks between the IF and the condition, and two blanks between the condition and the GO TO clause or statement numbers."

COMMON statement†:

"The COMMON card will begin in column 8 with the identifier followed by a blank in column 14 and a '/' in column 15. The next six columns are reserved for the label which will be left justified in this field. Column 22 will contain another '/' and column 23 will contain a blank. If blank COMMON is desired, code the slashes but leave the label field blank."

4. Develop coding conventions for the ifthenelse function in FORTRAN using the arithmetic IF statement.
5. Select PL/I, COBOL, or FORTRAN. Develop coding conventions for the dountil and case functions.
6. Select a PL/I, COBOL, or FORTRAN program. (Your instructor may assign one of his choosing.) Rewrite the program using structured programming and the indentation and formatting rules developed in question 3.

SELECTED READINGS

Baker, F. T., "Chief programmer team management of production programming," *IBM Systems Journal* **11**, No. 1 (1972), 56–73.

Baker, F. T., and H. D. Mills, "Chief programmer teams," *Datamation* **19**, No. 12 (Dec. 1973), 58–61.

---

* *Structured Programming Guide*, p. 3–52.
† *Structured Programming Guide*, p. 3–54.

Baker, F. T., "System quality through structured programming," *Proceedings of the 1972 Fall Joint Computer Conference*, AFIPS Vol. 39, pp. 339–343.

Böhm, C., and G. Jacopini, "Flow diagrams, Turing machines, and languages with only two formation rules," *Comm. ACM* **9**, No. 5 (May 1966), 366–371.

Clark, R. L., "A linguistic contribution to GO TO-less programming," *Datamation* **19**, No. 12 (Dec. 1973), 62–63.

Dijkstra, E. W., "The humble programmer," *Comm. ACM* **15**, No. 10 (Oct. 1972), 859–866.

Donaldson, J. R., "Structured programming," *Datamation* **19**, No. 12 (Dec. 1973), 52–54.

IBM, *Structured Programming Guide* (Form FSC72–5075), IBM, Federal Systems Division, Gaithersburg, Md.

McCracken, D. D., "Revolution in programming," *Datamation* **19**, No. 12 (Dec. 1973), 50–52.

McHenry, R. C., *Management Concepts for Top Down Structured Programming*, IBM, Federal Systems Division, Gaithersburg, Md., Nov. 1972.

Miller, E. F., Jr., and G. E. Lindamood, "Structured programming: top-down approach," *Datamation* **19**, No. 12 (Dec. 1973), 55–57.

Mills, H. D., *How to Write Correct Programs and Know It* (Form No. FSC73–5008), *Mathematical Foundations for Structured Programming* (Form FSC72–6012), *On the Development of Large Reliable Programs* (no form number available), IBM, Federal Systems Division, Gaithersburg, Md.

Mills, H. D., "Syntax-directed documentation for PL360," *Comm. ACM* **13**, No. 4 (April, 1970), 216–222.

13

INTRODUCTION TO DATA STRUCTURES

13.1 INTRODUCTION

The subject of data arises repeatedly in computer science, primarily because the processing of data is the major objective of computer systems. Thus far, a variety of data-related topics have been presented, ranging from number systems to data management structures. The objective of this chapter is to tie the various topics together into a logical framework.

User Data Structures

The development of an algorithm requires a conceptualization of data sometimes referred to as a data structure. Usually, this conceptualization of data is intimately related to a programming language for constructing programs and may or may not be related to the manner in which data is actually stored. Conceptualizations of this sort are better referred to as *user data structures*. In earlier chapters, for example, a differentiation is made between numeric and character data and the manner in which it is organized, that is, as scalars, arrays, and so on. In the area of data management, data was similarly categorized into fields, data records, and files. The practice of allowing a user to conceptualize his data in this manner is an operational convenience, since most modern computer systems deal with more primitive forms of data. Therefore, the subject of *data structures*, as it is known in computer science, deals with methods for the computer representation of user data structures.

383

Units of Storage

In general, the methodology involved with the computer representation of data applies regardless of whether the storage medium is main storage or external storage, such as cards, tape, or disk. It is important initially, however, to establish the units of storage that are used. The *unit of main storage* is the byte or word. Essentially, this is the smallest addressable unit in a particular computer system. Although storage allocation schemes frequently manage larger units of storage, such as the page, these larger units are again regarded as an operational convenience. The *unit of external storage* depends on the medium used. Unit record storage is measured in columns and cards for punched card technology, and characters and lines for printer technology. For serial devices such as magnetic tape, the unit of storage is usually not given exactly and is frequently measured in terms of the number of feet used (of that medium) or the number of data records stored. For direct-access devices, the unit of storage is the number of tracks or cylinders used, recognizing that the storage capacity of a direct-access storage medium is relatively large.

The unit of storage has almost nothing to do with the data stored, except for storage capacity. A word in main storage, for example, can contain a number, a series of characters, or a main storage address. The important point is this: *A particular data structure is constructed by arranging units of storage in a characteristic manner.* The form of a given construction determines the kinds of data that can be stored in the structure and the manner in which they can be referenced.

Storage Class

One of the characteristics of a data structure is its *storage class*, which indicates how the storage for the data structure is allocated. Storage is allocated statically or dynamically by the operating system from the partition, region, or workspace assigned to a job or task. *Static storage* is allocated before the program that uses it begins execution. *Dynamic storage* is allocated during execution upon request.

In main storage, static storage for a program and its storage areas is allocated when the program is loaded by the operating system. Dynamic storage is normally allocated from residual space in a partition, region, or workspace. However, some operating systems manage a pool of free storage for dynamic storage allocation. Because main storage is a critical resource, it is usually allocated as a specific number of bytes or words.

The concept of storage class also applies to direct-access storage. Before a program can use disk storage, for example, space on a particular unit must be allocated to the program by data management routines of the operating system. Normally, direct-access storage is allocated both statically and dynamically. Before a program is executed, a user requests a primary allocation and a secondary allocation for a data set through the use of control cards. (An allocation is a number of tracks or cylinders.) The *primary allocation* is assigned to the program statically before execution commences. The *secondary allocation* is used when allocated storage is exhausted. Assume as an example that the primary allocation for a particular job is 50 tracks and the secondary allocation is 5 tracks. Fifty tracks are assigned to the job initially; every time the previously allocated storage is exhausted, five additional tracks are assigned dynamically. Primary and secondary allocation is a useful feature, since the user is protected against running out of space during a lengthy run and having his job terminated abnormally. If primary and secondary allocation did not exist, the user would have to plan for the worst case and thereby reduce the effective use of direct-access storage.

Storage is normally allocated as contiguous units of storage, that is, a contiguous group of bytes or words or a contiguous set of tracks or cylinders. However, successive allocations are not necessarily contiguous with previous allocations and, in most cases, are not. This fact entails a certain amount of record keeping, which is inherent in some of the data structures.

In main storage, a relatively large allocation of contiguous storage is called an *area*, and a small allocation of contiguous storage is referred to as a *node*. On direct-access storage, an allocation of contiguous storage units is known as an *extent*, so that a data set is a collection of extents.

Storage Organization

Storage organization is a structural characteristic of a data structure, and it applies to data structures in the same manner that it applied to data management in Chapter 11. Storage structures can be organized in four ways: consecutive, linked, keyed, and regional. *Consecutive organization* indicates that the data structure occupies contiguous storage units. Arrays in main storage and data files or magnetic tape are typical examples of data structures that are organized consecutively.

Linked organization indicates that the data structure does not occupy contiguous storage units and that areas, nodes, or extents are connected by pointers, which can take the form of main storage addresses or cylinder-head numbers.

Keyed organization indicates that the data elements of the data structure are located by means of a key field that may or may not be

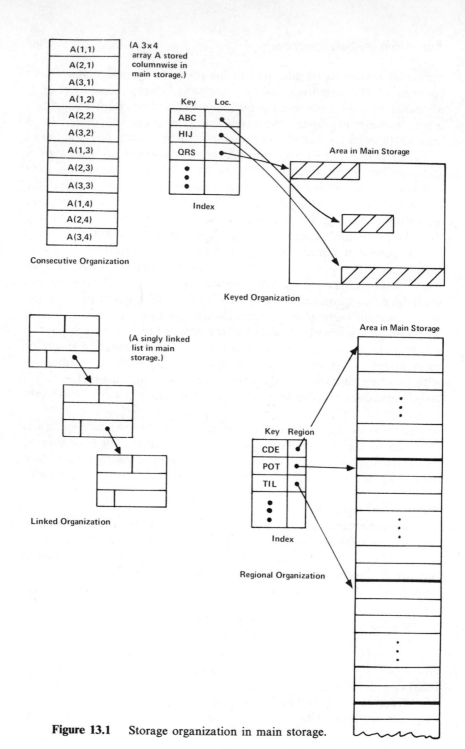

Figure 13.1 Storage organization in main storage.

386

embedded in the data itself. A data structure with keyed organization consists of two parts: an index of keys that gives the location of data elements in the second part, which is a set of areas in main storage or a set of extents on direct-access storage.

Regional organization indicates a data structure composed of an index of keys and one or more areas or extents that are organized consecutively. A particular region of the data structure is located through the index by using a given key.

Examples of storage organization for data management structures are included in Chapter 11. Examples of storage organization in main storage are given in Figure 13.1. A data structure is implemented using one or more of the four basic types of storage organization.

The remainder of this chapter is concerned with main storage data structures, such as strings, lists, and tables. As mentioned, data management structures using the methods discussed here are covered in Chapter 11.

Storage Access

Data structures are accessed (or referenced) in two ways: sequentially and directly. *Sequential access* indicates that the data elements of the data structure must be accessed in an order that is dependent upon the sequence in which the elements are physically stored. Data records on magnetic tape and punched card decks are familiar examples. However, simple lists or tables organized consecutively or linked in main storage also fall into this category. A data structure with keyed organization can be accessed sequentially by following the keys in order, and a data structure organized regionally can be accessed sequentially after the desired region is located.

Direct access indicates that a data structure is accessed without passing over preceding information. Direct-access can assume a variety of familiar forms:

1. Indexing into an array*
2. Matching a key in a table to locate a particular data element
3. Performing a mathematical operation on a key to give the relative location of a data element

Item 1 applies to main storage; items 2 and 3 apply to both main storage and direct-access storage.

* Methods for indexing into an array are given in Chapter 5.

13.2 STRINGS AND STRING MANIPULATION

A *string* is a sequence of characters that is normally regarded as a scalar value. Strings are used for symbol manipulation applications, such as symbolic mathematics or computational linguistics, or to store descriptive information. The basic characteristic of a string is its length.

Storage of Strings

The characters that make up a string are stored in consecutive locations in main storage. A set of strings is frequently stored using a form of keyed organization. In a main storage area, characters that make up the strings under consideration are represented in one of three ways:

1. One character per byte
2. One character per word
3. *n* characters per word

Regardless of the method used, the character positions can be ordered relative to the beginning of the storage area and accessed as the 1st position, 2nd position, and so on.

A specific string in the storage area can be located by giving its initial position and its length. Alternate methods are to specify the length implicitly by terminating each string with a special character, or by storing the length of a string with the characters. These methods are depicted in Figure 13.2.

Organization and Access

Because strings are usually accessed directly, keyed organization is the most frequently used storage technique. The exact form of the access table (i.e., the index) is dependent upon the manner in which the strings are used. If the strings are interpreted as elements of an array, then the starting positions of string elements can be stored as a linear array that serves as an access table. If the strings are interpreted as "values" of variables, then the variable names and starting positions are stored as elements of a symbol table. Both of the latter cases are demonstrated in Figure 13.3. (Clearly, the symbol table can be stored as a two-dimensional array or as two linear arrays.)

An alternate method of storing strings is depicted in Figure 13.4. The length of individual strings in the storage area is stored in the access or symbol table.

If it were desired to store strings consecutively and access them sequentially, then the only desirable methods would be the string-

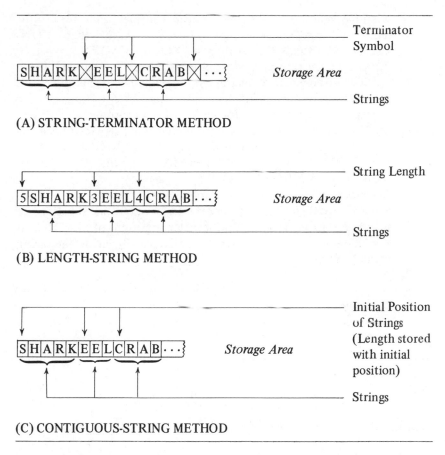

Figure 13.2   Methods of storing a string in main storage.

terminator method and the length-string method (see Figure 13.2). The contiguous-string method would be undesirable because the index is necessary to store the string lengths outside of the storage area.

String Operations

In any string manipulation application, the method used to store string values is dependent upon the operations to be performed on the strings and the algorithms used to implement the operations. Some typical string operations are as follows:

1. *Concatenation.* Strings are placed together so that individual strings lose their identity. The subroutine CONCAT(a,b,c), for

example, concatenates string *a* and *b* and places the result in *c*. Thus, if A = "VOLKS" and B = "WAGEN," then CON-CAT(A,B,C) yields the result: C = "VOLKSWAGEN."

2. *Pattern matching and replacement.* A string is scanned for a particular sequence of characters; the matched characters are replaced by another string. The subroutine MATCH(*a,b,c,d*), for example, searches string *a* for the leftmost occurrence of string *b*; the characters of *a* that have been matched are replaced by string *c* and the result is placed in *d*. Thus, if A = "A GOOD DAY," B = "GOOD," C = "GREAT," then MATCH(A,B,C,D) yields the result: D = "A GREAT DAY."

3. *Substring.* A substring is extracted from a given string. The function SUBSTR(*a,i,l*), for example, extracts the substring of length *l* starting at the *i*th character position of *a*. Thus, if A = "TEA FOR TWO," then SUBSTR(A,5,3) yields the string value "FOR."

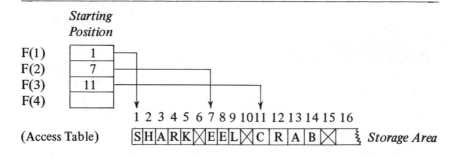

(A) Starting positions stored as elements of an array

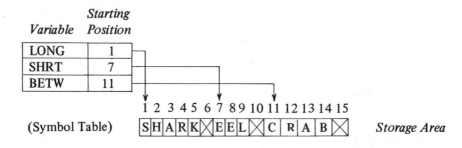

(B) Starting positions stored as values in an *n* × 2 symbol table

Figure 13.3   The use of keyed organization to store strings, where the length of individual strings is denoted by a terminator symbol.

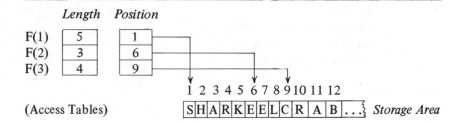

(A) Starting positions and lengths stored as elements of two linear arrays

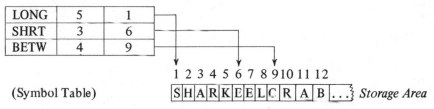

(B) Starting positions and lengths stored as elements of an $n \times 3$ symbol table

Figure 13.4   The use of keyed organization to store strings, where the length of individual strings is stored in access or symbol tables.

The reader is directed to the Selected Readings for additional string operations.

String operations are implemented in three ways:

1. As normal capabilities in a string manipulation language, such as SNOBOL
2. As built-in subprograms in a programming language with a "character" data type, such as PL/I
3. As ad hoc subprograms written for a programming language without a "character" data type, such as FORTRAN

13.3 LISTS AND LIST PROCESSING

A *list* is a linear data structure of data elements, E(1), E(2), . . ., E(n), where $n > 0$. The only essential properties of a list are the relative position of its elements, that is, E(i) precedes E($i + 1$) and is preceded by

---

DECLARE 1 TENTRY,
        2 NAME CHARACTER(8)
        2 VALUE FIXED DECIMAL,
        2 NENTRY POINTER;

(A) A structure describing a node of a linked list

DECLARE 1 SYMTAB(100),
        2 VARBLE CHARACTER(8),
        2 VALUE FIXED DECIMAL;

(B) A declaration of an array of structures

Figure 13.5   Examples of structure declarations in the PL/I language.

$E(i - 1)$ for $1 < i < n$, and the fact that each element has the same attributes. List elements are usually scalars or structures. The terminology used here is accurate but unfortunate. A *structure*, as known in programming languages such as COBOL or PL/I, is a data aggregate in which individual data items can have different attributes. Structures usually represent data records. Nodes in linked organized data structures include data items with different attributes, and the concept of a structure is appropriate there also. An array in which each element is a structure is known as an *array of structures*. (See Figure 13.5)

Consecutive Allocation

A list that is organized consecutively takes the form of an array, except that lists are normally accessed sequentially and arrays are accessed directly through a subscript computation and indexing. Figure 13.6 gives two examples of consecutively organized lists.

Because all list elements possess the same attributes, an element can easily be located through the following relationships:

$$location[E(i + 1)] = location[E(i)] + m$$
$$location[E(i)] = L_0 + (i - 1)*m$$

where L_0 is the origin of the list and m is the size in storage units of each element. Note here that accessing a list involves searching the list, adding an element at the beginning, adding an element at the end, and so on. The process of locating the ith element is a different matter.

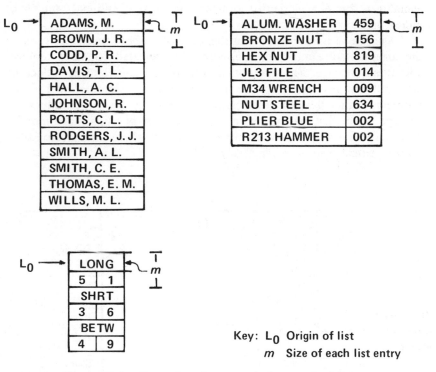

Key: L_0 Origin of list
m Size of each list entry

Figure 13.6 Examples of consecutively organized lists.

Consecutively allocated lists have advantages and disadvantages. Obvious advantages are that it is straightforward to locate the ith element to examine it or modify it, and it is relatively efficient to copy the list, sort the list, or search for the occurrence of a particular element. Obvious disadvantages are that additions, insertions, and deletions are inefficient and cumbersome, and that the space for the list is constrained by the storage area allocated to it.

The process of deleting an element of a consecutively allocated list is a good example of the difficulties. As shown in Figure 13.7, the deletion of a list element leaves an empty cell. In order to preserve the advantages of this type of list for sort, searching, and locating elements, several elements must be moved up. A similar disadvantage exists for adding and inserting elements, as shown in Figure 13.8.

One method of partially relieving the above disadvantage is to include an index of the next sequential element on the list, as depicted in

Figure 13.9. Deletion involves a change to a single index pointer, and addition and insertion operations involve the placement of the new element at the end of the list and the change to a minimal number of index pointers.

The use of index pointers, as demonstrated above, preserves some of the original advantages of consecutively allocated lists but requires additional storage. The major disadvantage of consecutively allocated lists still remains—space for the list is constrained. Another operational problem is that the user must plan for the worst case when allocating storage for his list and this is an inefficient way of using the computer, especially in a multiprogramming environment where the objective is to utilize critical resources effectively.

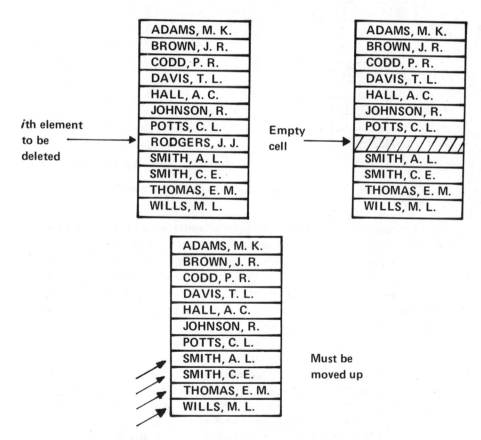

Figure 13.7   The deletion of an element of a consecutively allocated list leaves an empty cell. As a result, several elements must be moved to preserve the advantages of this type of list.

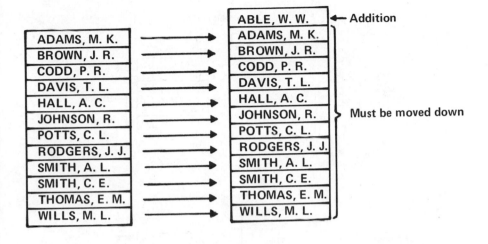

(A) ADDITION (at the beginning)

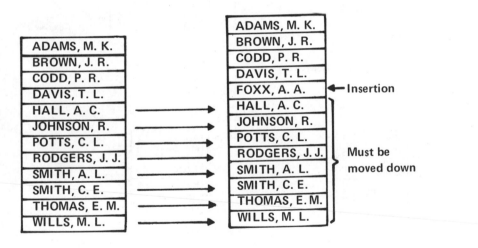

(B) INSERTION

Figure 13.8   The addition or insertion of a new element to a consecutively allocated list requires that elements be moved.

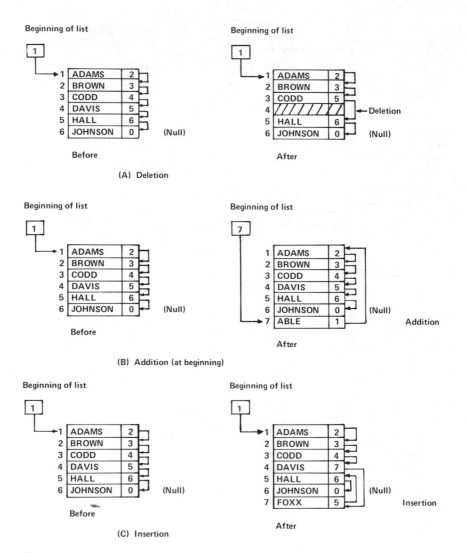

Beginning of list

1

1	ADAMS	2
2	BROWN	3
3	CODD	4
4	DAVIS	5
5	HALL	6
6	JOHNSON	0	(Null)

Before

Beginning of list

1

1	ADAMS	2
2	BROWN	3
3	CODD	5
4	/////////		← Deletion
5	HALL	6
6	JOHNSON	0	(Null)

After

(A) Deletion

Beginning of list

1

1	ADAMS	2
2	BROWN	3
3	CODD	4
4	DAVIS	5
5	HALL	6
6	JOHNSON	0	(Null)

Before

Beginning of list

7

1	ADAMS	2
2	BROWN	3
3	CODD	4
4	DAVIS	5
5	HALL	6
6	JOHNSON	0	(Null)
7	ABLE	1	Addition

After

(B) Addition (at beginning)

Beginning of list

1

1	ADAMS	2
2	BROWN	3
3	CODD	4
4	DAVIS	5
5	HALL	6
6	JOHNSON	0	(Null)

Before

Beginning of list

1

1	ADAMS	2
2	BROWN	3
3	CODD	4
4	DAVIS	7
5	HALL	6
6	JOHNSON	0	(Null)
7	FOXX	5	Insertion

After

(C) Insertion

Figure 13.9   Deletion, addition, and insertion of elements in a consecutively allocated list through the use of index pointers.

396

Linked Allocation

A *linked list* is a data structure with elements that do not necessarily occupy contiguous storage locations—in fact, the data elements are *not* contiguous in most cases. An element of a list is a structure, as defined earlier, so that at least one data item in the node can be used to point to other nodes. Normally, storage for nodes is allocated dynamically through facilities of the operating system or programming language.

A linked list employs linked organization, making the pointer values (i.e., addresses) that connect nodes necessary for tying the data structure together. However, the first element of a linked list must be anchored somewhere, and a variable serving that purpose is termed the *head of the list*. In applications where nodes are frequently added to the end of the linked list, a variable that points to the *tail of the list* is also used.

A linked list in which nodes are chained in one direction is shown in Figure 13.10; it is called a *singly linked list*. Nodes are connected through addresses, as in Figure 13.10, and the arrows serve only as a visual convenience. Normally, addresses are omitted when discussing linked lists in favor of arrows, which are more easily followed.

Figure 13.11 depicts the process of deleting a node from a singly linked list. Two items of information are required:

1. The address of the node to be deleted (α)
2. The address of the preceding node in the linked list (β)

The deletion process can be expressed symbolically as follows:

$$link(\beta) \leftarrow link(\alpha)$$

where *link* denotes the address portion of a node and α and β are defined as above.

The process of inserting a node into a linked list requires similar information:

1. The address of the node to be inserted (α)
2. The address of the node after which the new node should be added (β)

The insertion process is expressed symbolically as follows:

$$link(\alpha) \leftarrow link(\beta)$$
$$link(\beta) \leftarrow \alpha$$

Head of the list

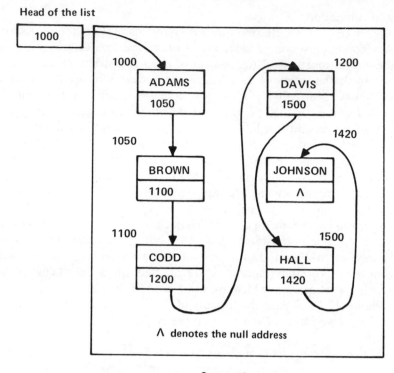

Storage Area

Figure 13.10   A singly linked list.

If variable HEAD is the head of the list (i.e., HEAD contains the address of the first node on the list) and α is the address of a node to be added to the beginning of a singly linked list, then the process of adding a node to the beginning of a singly linked list is expressed symbolically as follows:

$link(\alpha)\leftarrow$HEAD
HEAD$\leftarrow\alpha$

A node is constructed by requesting the required number of units of storage (bytes or words) from the operating system with an appropriate statement or macro instruction. The requested amount of storage is assigned and the address of that storage is returned to the requesting program. Normally, the data to be stored is placed in the node prior to addition or insertion.

Some applications of linked lists require that a list be searched in

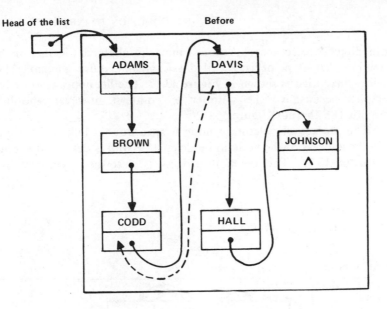

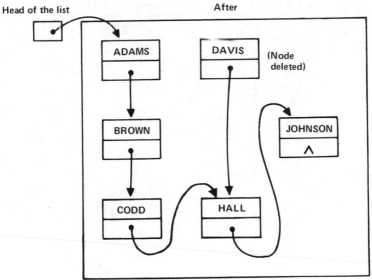

Key: – –> Pointer
movement. (The
pointer of DAVIS is
moved to the pointer
of CODD deleting
DAVIS from the chain)

Figure 13.11 The process of deleting a node from a singly linked list involves a
simpler pointer movement.

both directions, so that the nodes must be chained together in both directions. This type of list is called a *doubly linked list*; an example of a doubly linked list is shown in Figure 13.12. The list appears to be fairly complex because of the number of pointers; however, the list is simplified in the next figure.

The process of deleting a node from a doubly linked list requires only the address of the node to be deleted (α) and is described explicitly in Figure 13.13. The deletion process is described symbolically as follows:

$$flink(blink(\alpha)) \leftarrow flink(\alpha)$$
$$blink(flink(\alpha)) \leftarrow blink(\alpha)$$

Head of the list

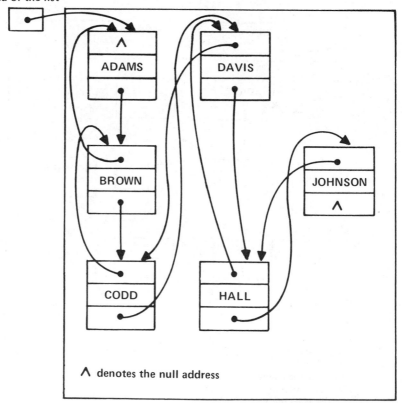

Storage Area

Figure 13.12   A doubly linked list.

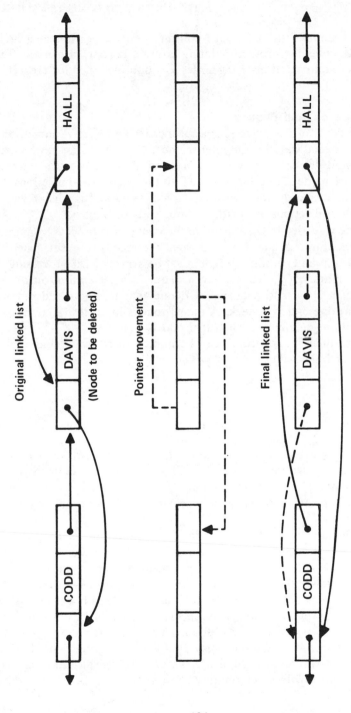

Figure 13.13 The process of deleting a node from a doubly linked list involves two simple pointer movements.

401

where *blink* denotes the backward-pointing address portion of a node and *flink* denotes the forward-pointing address portion of a node. The processes of adding and inserting nodes to a doubly linked list are left as exercises.

Stacks, Queues, and Deques

Three types of lists have special properties and special names, and are used in special ways in computer science. A *stack* is a list in which all insertions and deletions are made at one end. A *queue* is a list in which insertions are made at one end—the rear of the queue—and deletions are made at the other end—the front of the queue. A *deque** is a list in which insertions and deletions are made at both ends of the list.

A stack was used in Chapter 10 in the conversion process from infix to postfix notation. A queue is used when the record of events, such as interruptions in an operating system, must be arranged for processing in an orderly manner. The concept of a deque is a generalization of the concepts of a stack and a queue. A deque that is input- and output-restricted at one end is a stack. A deque that is input-restricted at one end and output-restricted at the other end is a queue.

Stacks, queues, and deques can be implemented using consecutive allocation or linked allocation.

13.4 TABLES

A *table* is a list of symbol-value pairs of the form $<s,v>$. The symbol field s is used for identification, insertion, and retrieval; the value portion v is used to store information and can correspond to one or more data fields. The entries in a table may be sorted on the symbol field or be left unsorted.

The objective of a table is to hold information, and as a result, two operations are required: posting and retrieval. The posting operation is dependent upon the application. In an inventory application, for example, posting is the process by which the quantity of a given part is updated, and it is desirable to find the identifying symbol in the table. With a symbol table for a language processor, on the other hand, posting is the operation by which a $<$symbol,value$>$ pair is entered into the symbol table, and it is desirable *not* to find the identifying symbol in the table. (Then it would be a duplicate symbol.) Retrieval is the same in either case and involves determining for a symbol s', the symbol table

---

* The term *deque* is pronounced "deck."

entry $<s_i,v_i>$, where $s' = s_i$. This process makes available the required value v_i.

This section covers symbol table methodology because of the emphasis on efficiency. The techniques can be easily extended to other applications.

Linear Accumulation and Search

Linear accumulation and search is a basic technique for maintaining a symbol table in which entries are posted in a linear fashion as they are encountered. Retrieval is performed by searching the table sequentially for a match on the symbol field. Linear accumulation and search can be implemented using either consecutive organization or linked organization, as depicted in Figure 13.14.

When consecutive organization is used as a means of implementing the linear accumulation and search technique, a fixed-size table is typically used. This was the method used with early assemblers, in which the source program was written on an intermediate tape during pass one in preparation for pass two. While the tape was being rewound for pass two, the symbol table was sorted. The number of symbols in an assembler language program was correlated with the length of the program, and as it turned out, both operations took approximately the same length of time. A sorted symbol table facilitates retrieval, since a search can be aborted when a table entry higher in collating sequence than the key is encountered.

The primary disadvantage of consecutive organization is that table size presents an operational limitation. Prior to the use of dynamic storage systems, this problem was circumvented in language processors by placing two symbol tables together, end-to-end, as suggested by Figure 13.15. Let the tables be denoted by the letters A and B. There is one storage area for both tables, perhaps as large as the combined sizes that tables A and B would ordinarily be if they were allocated independently. Table A is filled from the top of the combined storage area; table B is filled from the bottom of the combined storage area. This technique permits some flexibility in the sizes of the tables. If table A has a small number of entries, then table B can extend into A's space, and vice versa. The tables overflow only if the number of entries for both tables is large.

Next to capacity, efficiency is the most important consideration in symbol table methodology. One technique for improving the posting and retrieval operations of linear accumulation and search with linked organization is to link the nodes in a sorted order by the symbol field. This technique is feasible with a linked list because an insertion can be made with a simple pointer movement.

Symbol	Value
START	40
AGN	64
LOOP 3	128
TIME	4226
FINI	630

Table Entries

START	40
AGN	64
LOOP 3	128
TIME	4226
FINI	630
.	.
.	.
.	.

Consecutive Organization

Head of the list

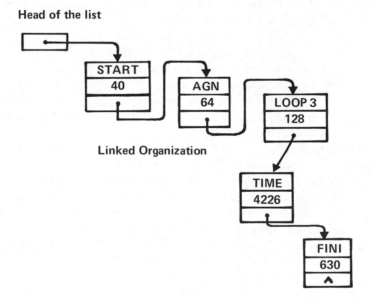

Linked Organization

Figure 13.14 Either consecutive or linked organization can be used to implement a symbol table for the linear accumulation and search method.

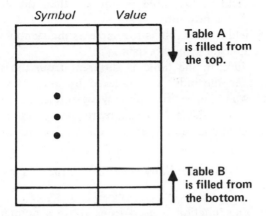

Figure 13.15   One method of adding flexibility to the capacity of symbol tables is to combine storage areas.

Hashing Techniques

Table searching for posting or retrieval is a time-consuming process and affects the overall efficiency of any program that uses symbol table methodology. A technique that is used to speed up posting and retrieval operations for symbol tables that utilize consecutive or linked organization is known as "hashing." *Hashing* utilizes the fact that the symbol field of a table entry exists as a series of consecutive bits, as a fixed-point number is stored. A function is performed on the bits of a symbol that partitions the universe of symbols into equivalence classes.* Two symbols are in the same equivalence class if they hash to the same value. One of the characteristics of a satisfactory hashing function is that it can be computed rapidly.

Linear hashing uses a hashing function with a consecutively organized symbol table and involves the following steps for the posting operation:

1. The hashing function is used to establish a pointer to a position i in the symbol table. (More specifically, the hashing function provides the index to a position in the symbol table.)

---

* A simple hashing function might be to take the bits corresponding to the symbol modulo 64. This function would partition the symbols into 64 classes. This is *not* a "good" hashing function but serves as an example. Another method is to multiply the [bits of the] symbol by itself and extract the middle n bits. Computer scientists have developed more complicated empirical functions that partition the symbols equally.

2. If the s_i field in the table is unused, then the $<s,v>$ pair is inserted at this position.
3. If the s_i field in the table is the same as the symbol being posted, then a duplicate symbol exists.
4. If the s_i field in the table is different from the symbol being posted, then the index is increased by one entry, and steps 2 through 4 are repeated. Table wraparound can occur. If it is determined that the table is full, by returning to the starting index value after wraparound, then a "table full" condition is returned.

The retrieval operation essentially reverses the process, as follows:

1. The hashing function is used to establish a pointer to an index position i in the symbol table.
2. If the s_i field in the table is unused, then the symbol is undefined.
3. If the s_i field in the table is the same as the symbol being retrieved, then the v_i field in the table is extracted.
4. If the s_i field in the table is different from the symbol being retrieved, then the index is increased by one entry, and steps 2 through 4 are repeated. Again, table wraparound can occur. If it is determined that the symbol does not exist in the table, by returning to the starting index value, then an "undefined symbol" condition is returned.

Linear hashing (see Figure 13.16) is an efficient method; the primary disadvantage to this method is that the table is normally fixed in size.

Nonlinear hashing is a technique that uses a hashing function to partition the symbols into equivalence classes; symbols in each equivalence class are stored as a linked list, in either sorted or unsorted order. Nonlinear hashing is depicted in Figure 13.17. The hash table is a list of addresses stored consecutively, and the hashing function computes an index to the list. Each address in the list serves as the head of a linked list used to store the entries in the corresponding equivalence class.

The posting operation involves the following steps:

1. The hashing function is applied to the symbol being posted and is used to establish a pointer to a position i in the hash table H. (More specifically, the hashing function provides the index to a position in the table of addresses.)

Posting of the entry: ⟨LOOP, 6381⟩

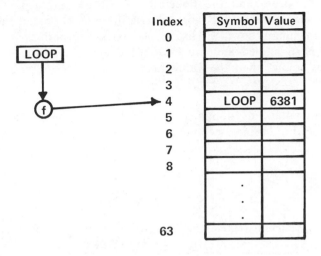

Key: ⓕ is a hashing function that maps the bits that comprise the symbol into a value in the range 0-63

Figure 13.16 Linear hashing.

2. If H_i is null, then no symbol in that equivalence class exists. A node is created and the table entries are inserted. H_i is set to point to the new node.

3. If H_i is not null, then symbols exist in that equivalence class and the linked list must be searched. The symbol being posted is compared with the symbol field of each node by chaining down the list. If no match is found, a node is created, the table entries are inserted, and the new node is added to the linked list. If a match is found, then a duplicate symbol exists and an appropriate condition is returned.

The retrieval process essentially reverses the process, as follows:

1. The hashing function is applied to the symbol serving as a key and is used to establish a pointer i in the hash table H.

2. If H_i is null, no symbol exists in that equivalence class and the symbol being retrieved is undefined.

3. If H_i is not null, then at least one symbol exists in that equivalence class and the linked list must be searched. The symbol being retrieved is compared with the symbol field of each node by chaining down the list. If no match is found, then the symbol is undefined and an appropriate return is made. If a match is found, then the value field of the matched node is returned.

The primary advantage of nonlinear hashing is that the technique combines the speed of hashing techniques with the flexibility of a linked list. Nonlinear hashing is used frequently in modern language processors.

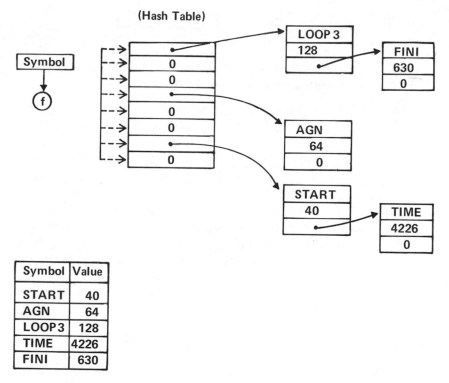

Figure 13.17   Nonlinear hashing.

13.5 OTHER CONCEPTS

Advanced topics in the area of data structures include compound lists, where a node can represent another list, tree structures, threaded lists, the mathematical theory of graphs, recursive techniques, and storage management. As with many other topics in computer science, the topic of data structures is an area of study in its own right. The reader is encouraged to explore the Selected Readings on this fundamental topic in computer science.

PROBLEMS

1. Select a method of storing *strings* in a given programming language. Use either the string-terminator, length-string, or the contiguous-string method given in Figure 13.2. Write subprograms for the *concatenation, pattern matching and replacement*, and *substring* operations.
2. Select a method of storing lists in a given programming language. Use one of the methods given in the chapter. (With FORTRAN, consecutive allocation with index pointers might be most appropriate. With PL/I, linked allocation might be most appropriate.) Write subprograms for the *addition, deletion*, and *insertion* operations.
3. Develop a *deque* routine that will serve as either a stack or a queue.
4. Develop a flow diagram of the posting and retrieval operations for either of the following symbol table methods:

  a. Linear hashing
  b. Nonlinear hashing

5. Implement as a subprogram two of the following symbol table methods:

  a. Linear accumulation and search
  b. Linear hashing
  c. Nonlinear hashing

Three aspects must be considered: storage management, posting, and retrieval.

SELECTED READINGS

Gear, C. W., *Introduction to Computer Science*, chap. 7—"Data Structures," Science Research Associates, Chicago, 1973.

Katzan, H., *Advanced Programming: Programming and Operating Systems*, chap. 2— "Assembler Programs and Symbol Tables," chap. 6—"List Processing," Van Nostrand-Reinhold, New York, 1970.

Knuth, D. E., *The Art of Computer Programming*, Vol. I, *Fundamental Algorithms*, chap. 2—"Information Structures," Addison-Wesley, Reading, Mass., 1968.

Walker, T. M., and W. W. Cotterman, *An Introduction to Computer Science and Algorithmic Processes*, chap. 3—"Introduction to Data Structures," Allyn and Bacon, Boston, 1970.

14

INTRODUCTION TO NUMERIC COMPUTING

14.1 INTRODUCTION

Numerical analysis is concerned with the development of techniques for the solution to mathematical problems for which an analytical solution does not exist or is difficult to obtain. As a result of the widespread use of computers, numerical analysis has become an important part of mathematics and computer science. *Numeric computing* is concerned with the computational aspects of numerical analysis.

The straightforward evaluation of equations is not generally regarded as numerical analysis or even numeric computing. For example, the solution to a quadratic equation of the form:

$$ax^2 + bx + c = 0$$

utilizes the quadratic formula, and its roots x_1 and x_2 are computed as follows:

$$x_1 = \frac{-b + \sqrt{b^2 - 4ac}}{2a}$$

$$x_2 = \frac{-b - \sqrt{b^2 - 4ac}}{2a}$$

Although the method requires a little mathematical training, it is generally regarded as an evaluation problem, since an analytical solution is known and is easily computed. A similar problem involves the evaluation of an nth degree polynomial of the form

411

$$p(x) = a_0 + a_1x + a_2x^2 + \ldots + a_nx^n$$

The number of computer operations can be reduced by using *nested multiplication*, as demonstrated in the evaluation of the example

$$p(x) = 5 + 16x + 32x^2 + .01x^3 + 4.5x^4$$

in a programming language, as follows:

$$P = 5 + X*(16 + X*(32 + X*(.01 + 4.5*X)))$$

Computational conveniences, such as this, are commonly regarded as "programming techniques."

Looping and iteration were covered in earlier chapters and the distinction between a numerical analysis technique and a simple computational method is indeed a fine line. For example, one method for computing the square root x of a number a is given in the following steps (where ϵ is a small value):

1. $x \leftarrow 1$
2. *if* $|x^2 - a| < \epsilon$ *then* the current value of x is the result
3. $x \leftarrow \frac{1}{2}\left(x + \frac{a}{x}\right)$
4. *goto* step 2

This is a brute-force method that contains very little, if any, mathematical refinement. This is obviously a value judgment, but the author prefers to limit numerical analysis to cases where mathematical methodology serves as a distinct aid in obtaining a solution to a problem.

14.2 ERRORS

Error analysis is of prime concern in numerical analysis for reasons that are not obvious to persons engaged in everyday processing. Perhaps the most significant aspect of error analysis is that arithmetic computations are performed on a fixed number of digits, usually the size of an arithmetic register. Thus, a partial result must be rounded or truncated when it exceeds the size of a register. Another important point is that because of the speed of modern computers, long sequences of calculations can be performed. Small errors tend to snowball, so that an acceptable deviation in the beginning may cause the end result to be "way off base." Finally, the relative values of numbers are used to make decisions during the course of execution of a program, and when the possibility of errors is not considered, the actual flow of a program can be altered. Another problem is that the binary representation of decimal numbers is not exact, especially in floating point format. Thus, the value 5 may be effectively stored as 4.9999999, which could affect the decision-making process.

The remainder of this section is concerned with different types of errors and relevant terminology.

Actual, Absolute, and Relative Error

Most measurements contain errors that are classed as being actual, absolute, or relative. Consider a number x and its approximation x^*. The difference $E = x - x^*$ is the *actual error*, and since there is usually no prior knowledge of whether E will be positive or negative, the absolute value of E is used and is referred to as the *absolute error*. The significance of an absolute error is frequently less valuable than the *relative error*, computed as $|E|/x$. For example, a measurement error of 10 feet in the distance between the earth and the moon would hardly be worth considering, whereas in the length of a football field, it would be significant.

Sources of Error

The science of numerical analysis strives to correct and compensate for errors, and a knowledge of the source of error is important in dealing with the problem. Errors usually arise in three ways: measurement or programming, as a result of methodology, or as a result of the characteristics of the computer. The types of errors are discussed without regard to their source.

Initial error results from variations in data recording or in taking measurements and is the most frequent type of error. If x is the true value of a data item and x^* is the value used in computation, then $x - x^*$ is the initial error. Initial errors are important because they affect the computed results regardless of how sophisticated the numerical analysis techniques are.

Truncation error results from the process of "chopping off" a number after a certain number of digits. For example, the number π, 3.14159265 ... , truncated after five significant digits would yield 3.1415. Another common truncation error occurs when the terms in an infinite expansion are dropped after a certain term. Dropping terms after the fourth in the series for e^x, that is,

$$e^x = 1 + x + \frac{x^2}{2!} + \frac{x^3}{3!}$$

gives a truncation error, sometimes called a *residual error*, for series approximations. Series expansions are covered later in the chapter.

Rounding error occurs when the less significant digits of a quantity are deleted and a rule of correction is applied to the remaining digits. For example, π rounded to five significant digits is 3.1416. An accepted rounding procedure is: If rounding is to take place in the nth digit, add 5 to the $(n + 1)$st digit (carrying a 1 to the nth digit, if necessary) and truncate after the nth digit.

Propagated errors are caused by the cumulative buildup of errors during computation. If x is the true value of a variable and x^* is used during computation, then $f(x) - f(x^*)$ is the propagated error built up during the computation of the function f.

Floating-point arithmetic with fixed-length registers is the cause of many errors because, by its very nature, it is inexact. Since many applications require only limited precision, many users are not concerned with the problem. Another task of numerical analysts is to determine the accuracy of computed results, regardless of what they are. A good rule of thumb is that floating-point multiplication and division do not significantly affect the accuracy of computed results, whereas floating-point addition and subtraction do affect the computed result, especially when x is nearly equal to $-y$ in the calculation of $x + y$ and x is nearly equal to y for $x - y$.

Numerical computations contain some surprises for the unwary user. A good example is the fact that the *associative law* of arithmetic, that is,

$$x + (y + z) = (x + y) + z$$

does not hold in the computer for certain values of x, y, and z. When truncating to four digits after each addition, for example, it is easily shown that

$$(31.58 + 9.348) + 8.763 \neq 31.58 + (9.348 + 8.763)$$

The same limitation exists for some values when rounding is performed after addition.

14.3 SERIES APPROXIMATION

A *transcendental function* is characterized by the fact that its equation is not a polynomial with integer coefficients. Typical transcendental functions are sin, log, and the exponential. From a computing point of view, a transcendental function cannot be evaluated for a given value by a finite number of arithmetic operations. Most transcendental functions have series expansions that are approximated to a given degree of accuracy by truncating the series expansion. Some common examples are

$$\sin x = x - \frac{x^3}{3!} + \frac{x^5}{5!} - \frac{x^7}{7!} + \cdots$$

$$\cos x = 1 - \frac{x^2}{2!} + \frac{x^4}{4!} - \frac{x^6}{6!} + \cdots$$

$$\exp x = 1 + x + \frac{x^2}{2!} + \frac{x^3}{3!} + \cdots$$

$$\log (1 + x) = x - \frac{x^2}{2} + \frac{x^3}{3} - \frac{x^4}{4} + \cdots \qquad \text{where } |x| < 1$$

Functions, such as these, are normally available to the user as library subprograms. The methodology used in the subprograms usually adjusts the argument in a manner so that a series of approximations is valid for a specified number of digits of precision.

In the development of the log function, for example, the fact that values are stored in floating-point notation aids in the computations and also in the description of the method. The logarithm of x can be written as

$$\log x = \log (a \times 10^b)$$

where x is represented in floating-point notation (or its equivalent in binary) as $a \times 10^b$ and where $0.1 \le a < 1.0$ by the properties of floating-point notation. Thus, we can write

$$\log x = \log a + \log 10^b$$
$$= \log [1 + (a - 1)] + b \times \log 10$$

The quantity of $a - 1$ is within the constraints of the log series, so that the series approximation is made to apply to a more extensive set of arguments.

The evaluation of the sine function involves an investigation of the error and the use of the fact that the function is periodic to control the number of terms in the series approximation. The complete Taylor-series expansion for the sine function is

$$\sin x = x - \frac{x^3}{3!} + \frac{x^5}{5!} - \frac{x^7}{7!} + \cdots = \sum_{n=1}^{\infty} \frac{(-1)^{n-1} x^{2n-1}}{(2n - 1)!}$$

for the argument $|x| < \infty$, where x is expressed in radians.* The number of terms needed in the expansion is dependent upon the error limitations. Suppose we carried the approximation to five terms. The absolute error E would be:

$$E = \left| \sin x - \sum_{n=1}^{5} \frac{(-1)^{n-1}x^{2n-1}}{(2n-1)!} \right| = \left| \sum_{n=6}^{\infty} \frac{(-1)^{n-1}x^{2n-1}}{(2n-1)!} \right|$$

From the right side of this equation we can see that the error for a five-term expansion is dependent upon the magnitude of x. (Clearly, if the expansion is carried beyond five terms, the error would be reduced.) The objective is to constrain the argument to a value such as $\pi/2$ and then compute the required number of terms in the expansion. The analysis uses a mathematical concept that states that the error is not larger in magnitude than the first neglected term in the truncation of an alternating series of decreasing terms.

The first step is to place limitations on the argument x of the sine function. We know two facts about the sine function:

$$\sin x = \sin (x + 2k\pi) \qquad \text{where } k \text{ is an integer}$$

and

$$\sin (x + \pi) = -\sin x$$

Thus, we can use

$$\sin x = (-1)^k \sin a$$

where $a = x + k\pi$. In the calculation of the function, the value of k is computed so that $-\pi/2 \le a \le \pi/2$, which is equivalent to $-1/2 - x/\pi \le k \le 1/2 - x/\pi$. Assume that four digits of accuracy is required, so that

$$\left| \frac{E}{\sin a} \right| \le 10^{-4}$$

From mathematics, $|\sin a| \ge 2a/\pi$ for $|a| \le \pi/2$. Thus, the value of the first neglected term must be less than

---

* $\pi r = 180°$, where r = radians; thus, one radian equals $180/\pi$ degrees.

$$E \leq 10^{-4}|\sin a|$$

and

$$E \leq 10^{-4}\frac{2}{\pi}|a|$$

The absolute value of the first negative term is $|a^{2n-1}/(2n-1)!|$ so that the relation

$$\frac{a^{2n-1}}{(2n-1)!} < 10^{-4}\frac{2}{\pi}|a|$$

holds when $|a| \leq \pi/2$. Thus, for the constraint $|a| \leq \pi/2$, the relation becomes

$$\frac{(\pi/2)^{2n-1}}{(2n-1)!} < 10^{-4}$$

which is satisfied by $n = 6$. Therefore the sine function can be approximated to four digits of precision by

$$\sin x = (-1)^k\left(a - \frac{a^3}{3!} + \frac{a^5}{5!} - \frac{a^7}{7!} + \frac{a^9}{9!} - \frac{a^{11}}{11!}\right)$$

where $a = x + k\pi$ and k is the largest integer that is less than $1/2 - x/\pi$.*

14.4 ROOTS OF NONLINEAR EQUATIONS

An area of study that applies computer methods to conventional mathematical problems involves the solution to nonlinear equations,† of the form

$$f(x) = 0$$

where f is a continuous function of a single variable x. A solution to the

---

* The "floor" function is the largest integer that does not exceed a given argument, so that $k = \text{floor}(1/2 - x/\pi)$.

†A nonlinear equation is one in which the independent variable, say x, does not appear linearly, such as $ax + b$, so that the roots of the equation cannot be solved explicitly by arithmetic operations.

equation is a number α, called the *root* of the equation, such that $f(\alpha) = 0$. Real roots occur at points where the function crosses the x axis, as shown in Figure 14.1, since these are the points where $f(x) = 0$.

In a general sense, the problem is not a simple one, since various equations have a finite or infinite number of roots, which may be real or complex.* Normally, a root-finding problem is presented in either of the following contexts:

1. A rough estimate of a root is given and it is necessary to find an actual root within a given tolerance of error.
2. Find all roots of the equation in a restricted domain of the independent variable x.

The most common approach to root finding is to graph the function, estimate the roots in the area of interest, and then construct a computer program that computes the roots to the desired accuracy. Four techniques for finding the roots of an equation are presented here: interval bisection, linear interpolation, the Newton-Raphson method, and the secant rule. In applied numerical analysis, some of the methods are combined to reduce the number of iterations necessary for finding a solution. Numerical analysts are also concerned with limiting precision and the location of multiple roots; these are more advanced topics that are not covered here.

Interval Bisection

The fact that a function $f(x)$ is continuous in the interval x_1 to x_2 and that $f(x_1)$ and $f(x_2)$ have different signs means that a root of the equation exists in the interval. The interval-bisection method is simple and involves bisecting the interval and selecting the half that contains the sign change. If x_1 and x_2 are the endpoints of the interval, then the procedure is summarized as follows:

1. If $f(x_1)f(x_2) < 0$, then evaluate the function $f(x)$ at the midpoint $x_3 = (x_1 + x_2)/2$.
2. If $f(x_3) = 0$, then x_3 is the desired root.
3. If $f(x_1)f(x_3) < 0$, then the root lies in the interval (x_1, x_3) and the process is repeated with x_2 replaced by the computed x_3.
4. If $f(x_3)f(x_2) < 0$, then the root lies in the interval (x_3, x_2) and the process is repeated with x_1 replaced by the computed x_3.

---

* That is, the equation may be either a polynomial or a transcendental equation.

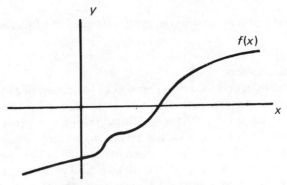

(A) An equation with one real root

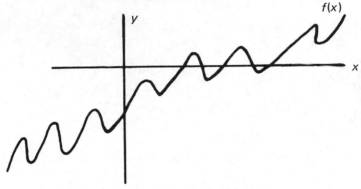

(B) An equation with several real roots

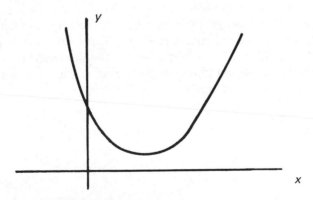

(C) An equation with no real roots

Figure 14.1   A real root to an equation occurs where the graph of the equation crosses the *x* axis.

The interval bisection method is summarized in the flowchart of Figure 14.2.

Linear Interpolation

Interval bisection uses only the sign of the function at the endpoints of the interval. An alternate approach is to take into consideration the size of the function at the endpoints, through a process of linear interpolation. If the curve of the equation is fairly straight, then the intersection of the line joining the two endpoints on the curve is a better approximation to the root of the equation than the midpoint of the interval, as shown in Figure 14.3. A new midpoint x_3 is computed in linear interpolation, as in interval bisection, as follows:

$$\frac{f(x_2) - f(x_1)}{x_2 - x_1} = \frac{-f(x_1)}{x_3 - x_1}$$

and

$$x_3 = x_1 - \frac{f(x_1)(x_2 - x_1)}{f(x_2) - f(x_1)}$$

The process of linear interpolation is summarized in the flowchart of Figure 14.4.

The Newton-Raphson Method

A method that converges rapidly for finding the root of an equation is known as the Newton-Raphson method. The method requires a close first approximation and consists of the construction of a tangent to the curve $f(x)$ at the latest approximation x_i. The next approximation is the point where the tangent intersects the x axis, as depicted in Figure 14.5. The slope of the tangent m is

$$m = \frac{f(x_i)}{x_i - x_{i+1}}$$

$$x_{i+1} = x_i - \frac{f(x_i)}{m}$$

The slope is simply the first derivative of the equation $f(x)$ at the point x_i, so that the Newton-Raphson formula is

$$x_{i+1} = x_i - \frac{f(x_i)}{f'(x_i)}$$

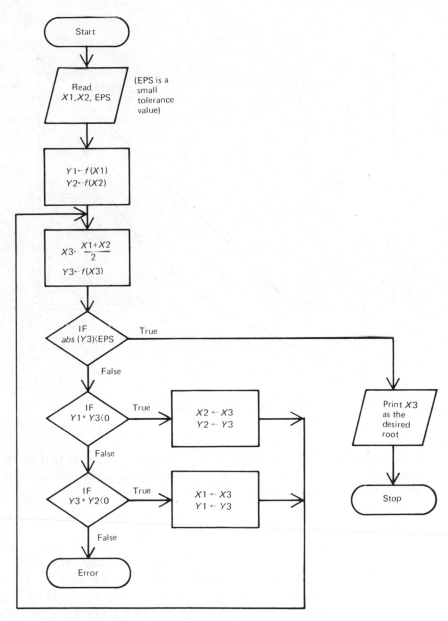

Figure 14.2   Flowchart of the interval bisection process.

421

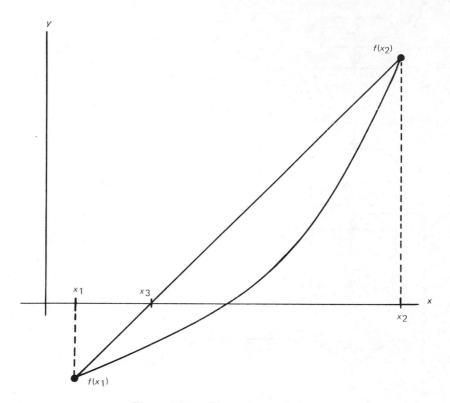

Figure 14.3   Linear interpolation.

The Newton-Raphson method does not always converge, so that when programming the method, it is a good idea to put an upper limit on the number of iterations.

The Secant Rule

A requirement of the Newton-Raphson method is that the equation $f(x)$ be differentiable in the domain of the required root. If it is impossible to evaluate the derivative $f'(x)$ or it is cumbersome or expensive to compute it, the secant of the equation $f(x)$ can be used to approximate the Newton-Raphson method. (See Figure 14.6.) The secant rule uses only values of $f(x)$ and uses two approximations, x_{i-1} and x_i, to find the closer approximation x_{i+1}. The secant of $f(x)$ is used to approximate the slope m, as follows:

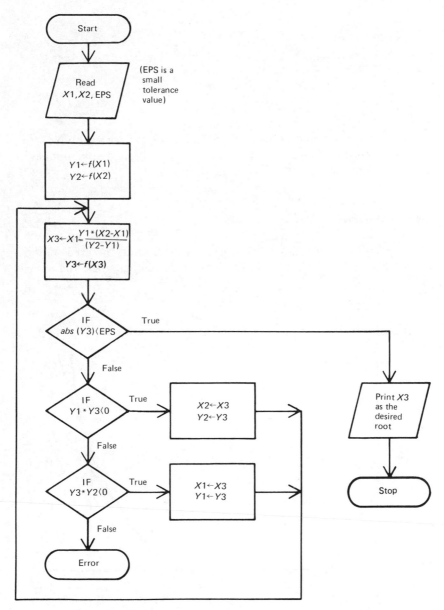

Figure 14.4 Flowchart of the linear interpolation process.

423

$$m = \frac{f(x_i)}{x_i - x_{i+1}}$$

$$\frac{f(x_{i-1}) - f(x_i)}{x_{i-1} - x_i} = \frac{f(x_i)}{x_i - x_{i+1}}$$

$$x_{i+1} = x_i - \frac{f(x_i)(x_{i-1} - x_i)}{f(x_{i-1}) - f(x_i)}$$

A more refined method of approximating the derivative in the Newton-Raphson method is available through divided difference techniques, a topic included in the area of numerical analysis.

14.5 NUMERICAL INTEGRATION

Numerical integration is concerned with finding the area under a curve, depicted in Figure 14.7. In elementary mathematics, the area is

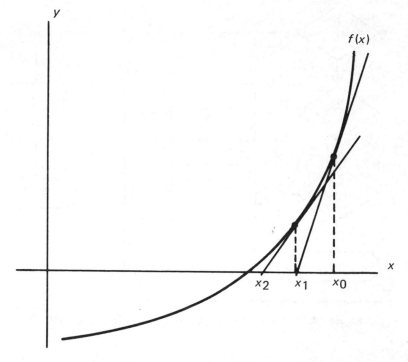

Figure 14.5   The Newton-Raphson method.

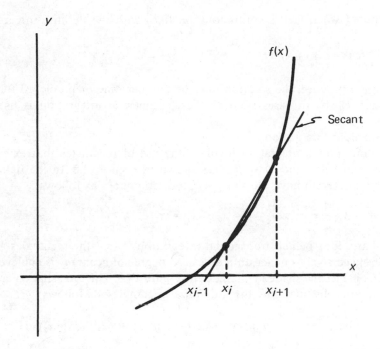

Figure 14.6   The secant rule can be used to approximate the Newton-Raphson method.

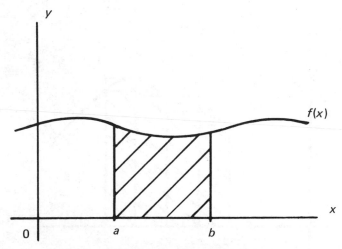

Figure 14.7   Numerical integration is concerned with finding the area under a curve $f(x)$.

425

computed when $f(x)$ is continuous on (a,b) with the definite integral

$$\text{Area} = \int_a^b f(x)\ dx$$

In actual practice, the solution may be cumbersome or no closed-form solution exists. In cases such as these, numerical integration is used.

Trapezoidal Integration

Trapezoidal integration involves the use of rectangles that extend above and below the curve $f(x)$, as shown in Figure 14.8. In the figure, the rectangles all have the same width h, computed as follows:

$$h = x_4 - x_3 = x_3 - x_2 = x_2 - x_1 = x_1 - x_0$$

The basic idea behind trapezoidal integration is that the rectangles are made successively smaller until a desired degree of accuracy is achieved.

Consider the shaded rectangles in Figure 14.8. The total shaded area is computed by summing the individual rectangles, as follows:

$$\begin{aligned}
\text{Littlearea} &= (x_1 - x_0)f(x_0) + (x_2 - x_1)f(x_1) + (x_3 - x_2)f(x_2) \\
&\quad + (x_4 - x_3)f(x_3) \\
&= h[f(x_0) + f(x_1) + f(x_2) + f(x_3)]
\end{aligned}$$

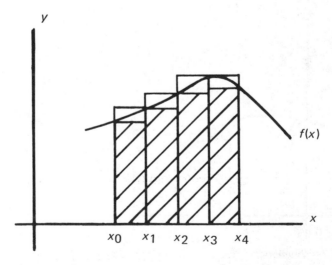

Figure 14.8   Trapezoidal integration is based on the use of rectangles.

This area is obviously less than the area under the curve. Next, consider the larger rectangles formed from shaded and nonshaded areas that extend above the curve. The total area is computed by summing the larger rectangles, as follows:

$$\begin{aligned} \text{Bigarea} &= (x_1 - x_0)f(x_1) + (x_2 - x_1)f(x_2) + (x_3 - x_2)f(x_3) \\ &\quad + (x_4 - x_3)f(x_4) \\ &= h[f(x_1) + f(x_2) + f(x_3) + f(x_4)] \end{aligned}$$

This area is obviously larger than the area under the curve. A more precise approximation is made of the area under the curve by taking the average of the big and little areas, as follows:

$$\begin{aligned} \text{Area} &= \frac{1}{2} \{h[f(x_0) + f(x_1) + f(x_2) + f(x_3)] + h[f(x_1) + f(x_2) + f(x_3) + f(x_4)]\} \\ &= \frac{h}{2} [f(x_0) + 2f(x_1) + 2f(x_2) + 2f(x_3) + f(x_4)] \end{aligned}$$

Essentially, the averaging technique is the same as computing the area of the trapezoid shown in Figure 14.9 for each width $x_i - x_{i-1}$ and summing the results.

In summary, the method of trapezoidal integration consists of dividing the domain of integration (a,b) into n equal subdivisions of width:

$$h = \frac{b - a}{n}$$

and computing the area with the formula

$$\text{Area} = \frac{h}{2} [f(x_0) + 2f(x_1) + 2f(x_2) + \cdots + 2f(x_{n-1}) + f(x_n)]$$

Most programs that use trapezoidal integration adjust n automatically. A desired accuracy and a guess at the number of subintervals is used as input. The program iterates, increasing values of n, until the desired accuracy is achieved.

Example. The area under the polynomial $f(x) = x^2 - 5x + 7$ from $x = 1$ to $x = 7$ is computed using $h = 1$. The values of $f(x)$ are

x	1	2	3	4	5	6	7
$f(x)$	3	1	1	3	7	13	21

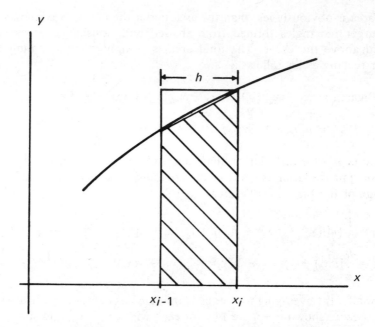

Figure 14.9   Trapezoidal integration is essentially the process of computing the
area of trapezoids and summing them. By making h smaller, the
true area can be approximated to a desired accuracy.

and the area is computed as

$$\text{Area} = \frac{h}{2}[f(1) + 2f(2) + 2f(3) + 2f(4) + 2f(5) + 2f(6) + f(7)]$$
$$= \tfrac{1}{2}(3 + 2 \times 1 + 2 \times 1 + 2 \times 3 + 2 \times 7 + 2 \times 13 + 2 \times 21)$$
$$= \tfrac{1}{2}(3 + 2 + 2 + 6 + 14 + 26 + 42)$$
$$= 47.5$$

The area is not accurate, since the true area is

$$\int_{1}^{7} (x^2 - 5x + 7)\, dx = 36.$$

Using the smaller subinterval $h = 0.5$ and the following values of $f(x)$:

x	1	1.5	2	2.5	3	3.5	4	4.5	5	5.5	6	6.5	7
$f(x)$	1.5	1.75	1	0.75	1	1.75	3	4.75	7	9.75	13	16.75	21

the area is computed as

$$\text{Area} = \frac{0.5}{2}[f(1) + 2f(1.5) + 2f(2) + 2f(2.5) + 2f(3) + 2f(3.5) + 2f(4)$$
$$+ 2f(4.5) + 2f(5) + 2f(5.5) + 2f(6) + 2f(6.5) + f(7)]$$
$$= 0.25[3 + 2(1.75 + 1 + 0.75 + 1 + 1.75 + 3 + 4.75 + 7$$
$$+ 9.75 + 13 + 16.75) + 21]$$
$$= 36.25$$

Thus, trapezoidal integration can give a credible answer with an interval as large as $h = 0.5$.

Simpson's Rule

Simpson's rule is a more sophisticated method of numerically computing the area under a curve and converges more rapidly to a desired degree of accuracy. The method is summarized here and procedures for using it are given. The derivation is more complicated and can be found in most books on numerical analysis.

Instead of passing a straight line through the endpoints of an interval, as in the trapezoidal rule, Simpson's rule passes a quadratic equation through the endpoints and it results in a more accurate approximation, as shown in Figure 14.10. Given a domain (x_0, x_2), as shown in the figure, Simpson's rule computes the area as

$$\text{Area} = \frac{x_2 - x_0}{6}[f(x_0) + 4f(x_1) + f(x_2)]$$

Simpson's rule requires an even number of subintervals, so that if the domain of integration is (a,b), then

$$h = \frac{b - a}{n}$$

$$x_i - x_{i-1} = \frac{h}{2}$$

where $x_0 = a$ and $x_{2n} = b$. Since the distance between subintervals is automatically halved, that is, $h/2$, the number of major divisions n to which Simpson's rule is applied need not be even.

Given a set of subintervals x_0 to x_{2n} as outlined above, Simpson's rule computes the area as:

$$\text{Area} = \frac{h}{6} [f(x_0) + 4f(x_1) + f(x_2)]$$

$$+ \frac{h}{6} [f(x_2) + 4f(x_3) + f(x_4)]$$

$$+ \frac{h}{6} [f(x_4) + 4f(x_5) + f(x_6)]$$

$$+ \cdots +$$

$$+ \frac{h}{6} [f(x_{2n-2}) + 4f(x_{2n-1}) + f(x_{2n})]$$

$$= \frac{h}{6} [f(x_0) + 4f(x_1) + 2f(x_2) + 4f(x_3) + 2f(x_4) + \cdots$$

$$+ 2f(x_{2n-2}) + 4f(x_{2n-1}) + f(x_{2n})]$$

Thus, when the subscripts run from 0 to $2n$, the first and last terms have a coefficient of 1, terms with odd subscripts have coefficients of 4, and terms with even subscripts have coefficients of 2.

Example. The area under the polynomial $f(x = x^2) - 5x + 7$ from $x = 1$ to $x = 7$ is computed using $h = 2$. The values of $f(x)$ are those given for the example for trapezoidal integration on page 427. The area is computed as

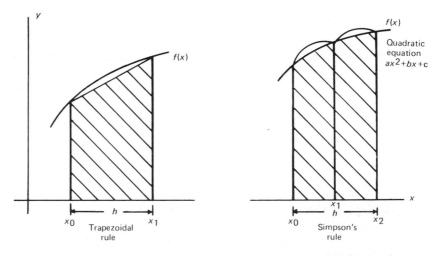

Figure 14.10 Simpson's rule gives a more accurate approximation to the true area than the trapezoid rule.

$$\text{Area} = \frac{h}{6}[f(1) + 4f(2) + 2f(3) + 4f(4) + 2f(5) + 4f(6) + f(7)]$$
$$= \frac{1}{3}(3 + 4\times1 + 2\times1 + 4\times3 + 2\times7 + 4\times13 + 21)$$
$$= \frac{1}{3}(3 + 4 + 2 + 12 + 14 + 52 + 21)$$
$$= 36$$

which is an excellent answer. However, the accuracy of Simpson's rule is not surprising in this case, since a quadratic equation is being approximated by the quadratic equation inherent in the methodology.

14.6 OTHER NUMERICAL METHODS

If the computer is the "king," then numerical computing is the "queen." Most of the early work in computer science involved the solution to numerical problems on the computer. In fact, several colleges and universities had programs in numerical analysis before the first computer science programs were developed. The methodology of numerical analysis is well developed and includes techniques for the following types of problems:

1. Interpolation and approximation
2. Integration
3. Roots of equations
4. Solution to ordinary and partial differential equations
5. Matrices, eigenvalences, and eigenvectors
6. Mathematical programming
7. Error analysis

The literature of numerical analysis is extensive. The Selected Readings for this chapter include some of the more readable works in this area.

PROBLEMS

1. Select an nth degree polynomial, where n is relatively large, such as 20 or more. Write two programs in a numerically oriented programming language (such as ALGOL, BASIC, FORTRAN, or PL/1) to evaluate the polynomial using the following techniques:

   a. The brute force method using exponentiation, multiplication, and the additive operators
   b. Using nested multiplication

The objective is to test the speed of the methods, so that you should insert the algorithm in a DO or FOR loop and execute it repetitively a large number of times, say 10,000. Compare the times taking into consideration the overhead time involved. Next, do the problem for several values of n, such as 5, 10, 15, 20, 25, 30, 35, and plot the results. Your graph should look somewhat as follows:

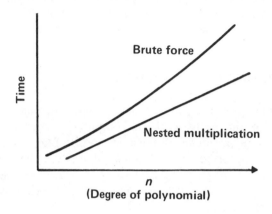

Or, should it?
2. Develop a subprogram to round a floating-point value to n places, where n is an argument to the subprogram.
3. Develop a function subprogram for computing one of the following:

    a. sqrt x
    b. sin x
    c. tan x

4. Using the method of interval bisection, compute the root of the equation $x^2 - 5 = 0$ in the interval [2,3] to three decimal places. Do the calculations by hand and count the number of iterations.
5. Write a general program to find the root of an equation by the method of interval bisection. Have the program call a function subprogram, supplied by the user, that computes the function for a given argument. Input to the program should be interval, tolerance, and the maximum number of iterations. Try the program on the following equations:

    a. $f(x) = x^3 - 3x + 1$ (real root)

    b. $f(x) = -x + \dfrac{5}{6}(2x - 3) - 2\sqrt{2x - 3} - (0.947)$

    $\log^2 (2x - 3) - (5.64) \log (2x - 3) - 4.54$

    Interval [159,160]

6. Using linear interpolation, sketch the various approximations for the calculation of the root(s) to the following equations: [Gerald, p. 27]

    a. $x^3 + x^2 - 3x = 0$
    b. $e^x - 3x^2 = 0$

7. Develop a program to compute the root of the following equation (problem 5) using the Newton-Raphson method:

$$f(x) = -x + \frac{5}{6}(2x - 3) - 2\sqrt{2x - 3} - (0.947)\log^2(2x - 3)$$
$$- (5.64)\log(2x - 3) - 4.54$$

where

$$f'(x) = \frac{2}{3} - \frac{2}{\sqrt{2x - 3}} - \frac{4(0.947)\log(2x - 3)}{2x - 3} - \frac{2(5.64)}{2x - 3}$$

8. Using trapezoidal integration, develop a program to compute the value of

$$\int_{2.2}^{4.2} e^x \, dx$$

using $h = 0.1$, $h = 0.2$, and $h = 0.4$.
9. Do problem 8 using Simpson's rule.
10. Given the following values:

x	1.0	1.1	1.2	1.3	1.4	1.5	1.6	1.7	1.8	1.9	2.0	2.1	2.2
$f(x)$	2.053	2.248	2.352	2.400	2.536	2.618	2.743	2.800	2.812	2.836	2.754	2.700	2.685

Develop a program to compute

$$\int_{1.0}^{2.2} f(x) \, dx$$

using trapezoidal integration and Simpson's rule for $h = 0.1$ and $h = 0.2$.

SELECTED READINGS

Gear, C. W., *Introduction to Computer Science*, chapter 9—"Numerical Methods," Science Research Associates, Chicago, 1973.

Gerald, C. F., *Applied Numerical Analysis*, Addison-Wesley, Reading, Mass., 1970.

Jacquez, J. A., *A First Course in Computing and Numerical Analysis*, Addison-Wesley, Reading, Mass., 1970.

Katzan, H., *APL Programming and Computer Techniques*, Van Nostrand-Reinhold, New York, 1970.

Nielsen, K. L., *Methods in Numerical Analysis*, Macmillan, New York, 1956.

Price, W. T., and M. Miller, *Elements of Data Processing Mathematics* (2d ed.), Rinehart Press, San Francisco, 1970.

Shampine, L. F., and R. C. Allen, Jr., *Numerical Computing: An Introduction*, Saunders, Philadelphia, 1973.

Walker, T. M., and W. W. Cotterman, *An Introduction to Computer Science and Algorithmic Processes*, chap. 7—"Numeric Algorithms," Allyn and Bacon, Boston, 1970.

15

INTRODUCTION TO AUTOMATA

15.1 INTRODUCTION

Automata theory deals with the notion of an abstract machine, that is, a computing machine in which considerations of space and time have been subordinated to a discussion of basic mathematical structure, and with the class of functions that can be computed by it. Quite naturally, the properties of any given abstract machine are related to the processes being modeled. Classical problems studied with the aid of these machines include: (1) the logic of sequential circuits; (2) mechanical language translation; (3) pattern recognition; (4) analysis of neural nets; (5) the structure of formal languages; (6) the theory of self-reproducing and growing systems; and (7) the determination of computable functions. This chapter presents a collection of basic topics necessary for the understanding of progress that has been made thus far in this area of computer science. A certain amount of mathematical notation is required for a discussion of *basic automata.*

It is possible to separate the uses of mathematics in computer science into four distinct categories: discursive, normative, functional, and structural. The *discursive* category uses mathematical notation as a convenient extension of natural language. *Normative* applications use mathematics to discover or demonstrate the optimum way to achieve desired results. The remaining two categories fall into the general area of descriptive mathematics. A *functional* description is an attempt to describe the operability of a system, subsystem, or component. It should be distinguished from a procedural description that explicitly recognizes the sequential nature of many processes. *Structural* descriptions, on the other hand, are used to describe the relationships among components, without regard to the utilization or functioning of the components.

435

In describing automata, natural language is frequently inefficient or even inadequate for expressing a complex idea. A symbol or a mathematical expression can often summarize what would take many qualifying phrases. This is an application of the discursive use of mathematics; it is required for this chapter and is introduced in the next section.

15.2 DISCURSIVE MATHEMATICS

Statements and Predicates

Basic to mathematical representation is the concept of a statement. A *statement* is an expression that can assume the value true or false. For example, the expressions: $10 > 5$, "the earth is a planet," and $25 = 6$ are statements assuming the values *true*, *true*, and *false*, respectively. Other expressions such as $x > 100$ are meaningless, since they contain unknown variables. Expressions in which the replacement of variables with literal quantities results in a statement are called *predicates*.

The concept of a statement can be extended by prefixing a predicate with a universal or existential quantifier. The *universal quantifier* is symbolized as $(\forall x)$, where x is a variable; it should be interpreted to read, "for all $x, \ldots$," or "for every $x, \ldots$." For example, the statements $(\forall x)(x > 5)$ and $(\forall x)(\forall y)(x > y)$ are false. The *existential quantifier*, written $(\exists x)$, is similar and is defined as, "there is an x such that $\ldots$," or "there exists an x such that $\ldots$." In this instance, the statement $(\exists x)(x > 5)$ is *true*.

Using the connectives: *and* ($\wedge$), *or* ($\vee$), *implies* ($\Rightarrow$), *if and only if* ($\Leftrightarrow$), and *not* ($\sim$), statements or predicates may be combined with other statements or predicates to form new ones.

Sets

A *set* is a collection of objects denoted by listing the elements, as in

$$E = \{ e_1, e_2, e_3, \ldots, e_n \}$$

or characterized by a predicate which is said to define the set, as in

$$E = \{ e : P(e) \}$$

where e is an object-variable and P is a predicate. In the latter case, E is the collection of objects e for which $P(e)$ is true. Similar to the former definition, sets may be arbitrary collections of objects, defined as follows:

$$\{ \, e : (e = a) \lor (e = b) \, \}$$

which is the same set as

$$\{ \, a, b \, \}$$

Subsets may be specified in a similar manner. Again, given the set S with elements e_i and the predicate P,

$$\{ \, e : (e \, \epsilon \, S) \text{ and } P(e) \, \}$$

or more concisely,

$$\{ \, e \, \epsilon \, S : P(e) \, \}$$

denotes a subset of S. Here, the symbol ϵ denotes "an element of." Whenever $P(e)$ is undefined, the corresponding element is excluded just as though $P(e)$ had the value false. Therefore, the set remains well defined even though the selecting predicate P is a partial function* relative to S. A is a subset of B if every element of A is also an element of B; that is,

$$A \subseteq B \Leftrightarrow (\forall x)[(x \, \epsilon \, A) \Rightarrow (x \, \epsilon \, B)]$$

Conceptually, the idea that one set A is a subset of another B may be viewed as A being "included in" B. The symbol $\subseteq$ is used to represent this notion symbolically. The notion of *inclusion* leads to a definition of set equality. By the above definition, a set B could be a subset of itself, since the following definition holds:

$$B \subseteq B \Leftrightarrow (\forall x)[(x \, \epsilon \, B) \Rightarrow (x \, \epsilon \, B)]$$

Intuitively, two sets are equal if they contain the same elements; thus,

$$A = B \Leftrightarrow (A \subseteq B) \land (B \subseteq A)$$

It follows that A is a *proper subset* of B (denoted by $A \subset B$) if $A \subseteq B$ is true but $B \subseteq A$ is not, or

$$A \subset B \Leftrightarrow (A \subseteq B) \land (A \neq B)$$

---

* A *partial function* is one that is defined on part of its domain. For example, the square-root function, in ordinary computing, is not defined for negative numbers.

In arithmetic, an operation can be performed on two numbers to yield a third number as a result. Similarly, operations can be performed on two sets that yield a third set as a result. The operations are union, intersection, and complement; each generates a set as a result, which in some cases may not contain any elements.

The *union* of two sets A and B is written

$$A \cup B$$

and is defined as

$$A \cup B = \{ x : (x \in A) \lor (x \in B) \}$$

For example, if

$$A = \{ a, b, c \}$$

and

$$B = \{ c, d, e \}$$

then

$$A \cup B = \{ a, b, c, d, e \}$$

Similarly, the *intersection* of sets A and B is written

$$A \cap B$$

and defined as

$$A \cap B = \{ x : (x \in A) \land (x \in B) \}$$

Thus, if A and B were defined as in the preceding example, then

$$A \cap B = \{ c \}$$

The *complement* of a set B with respect to a set A is denoted by

$$A - B$$

where

$$A - B = \{ x : (x \in A) \wedge (x \notin B) \}$$

Two sets are said to be *disjoint* if $A \cap B = \phi$, where ϕ represents the empty set. An empty set is said to be *void* and is sometimes called the *null set*.

Functions, Mapping, and Cartesian Product

A *function* or a *mapping* is a rule that associates with each element of a set A an element of a set B. Given a function f, the rule is expressed as

$$a \in A \xrightarrow{f} b \in B$$

or in functional notation,

$$f: A \rightarrow B$$

A is called the *domain* of the function and B is called the *co-domain*. The set of values $f(a)$ is called the *range* of the function for the *argument a*. Let the range of the function f be denoted by B'. Then

$$B' \subseteq B$$

If $B' \subseteq B$, then f is a mapping of A *into* B; if $B' = B$, then f is a mapping *onto* B. Moreover, the function is *one-to-one* if when $a_1 \neq a_2$, then

$$f(a_1) \neq f(a_2) \qquad \text{for all } a_i \in A$$

Let A and B be sets. The set of all pairs $<x,y>$ such that $x \in A$ and $y \in B$ is called the cartesian product of A and B and is written $A \times B$. More formally,

$$A \times B = \{ <x,y> : (x \in A) \wedge (y \in B) \}$$

For example, if $A = \{ a, b \}$ and $B = \{ 1, 2, 3 \}$, then

$$A \times B = \{ <a,1>, <a,2>, <a,3>, <b,1>, <b,2>, <b,3> \}.$$

15.3 SEQUENTIAL MACHINES

The term *sequential machine* implies a discrete, deterministic computing device with a finite memory. Clearly, this definition includes the standard digital computer as well as a variety of digital control devices. It is modeled by an abstract machine with the following properties:

1. A finite set of inputs that can be applied to the machine in a sequential fashion
2. A finite set of internal states that the machine can be in
3. A next-state function uniquely determined by the present input and present state
4. A finite set of outputs that can be generated

It follows that a sequential machine maps elements from the set of inputs to elements of the output set; the output is dependent upon the past history of inputs as well as the present input.

Moore Machines

A *Moore*-type sequential machine is described mathematically as a quintuple

$$M = (S,I,O,\delta,\lambda)$$

where

S is a finite nonempty set of internal states
I is a finite nonempty set of inputs
O is a finite nonempty set of outputs
$\delta: S \times I \to S$ is the next-state function
$\lambda: S \to O$ is the next-output function

A Moore machine can be represented in three ways: (1) by a collection of sets and functions, (2) by a state table, and (3) by a transition diagram. Consider a set-theoretic representation of the Moore machine:

$$M = (S,I,O,\delta,\lambda)$$

where

$S = \{ x, y, z \}$
$I = \{ 0, 1 \}$
$O = \{ a, b, c \}$
$\delta: \quad \delta(x,0) = y, \quad \delta(x,1) = z, \quad \delta(y,0) = z, \quad \delta(y,1) = x, \quad \delta(z,0) = x,$
$\quad\quad \delta(z,1) = z$
$\lambda: \quad \lambda(x) = a, \lambda(y) = b, \lambda(z) = c$

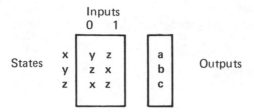

Figure 15.1   Representation of a Moore machine by a state table.

The Moore machine is represented as a *state table* in Figure 15.1 and as a *transition diagram* in Figure 15.2. For example, the arrow pointing from node z to node x indicates that $\delta(z,0) = x$, while the character below the horizontal line in each node indicates the output, that is, $\lambda(y) = b$. Obviously, the output of the machine for each state is fixed. The concept is generalized in the Mealy machine, which follows.

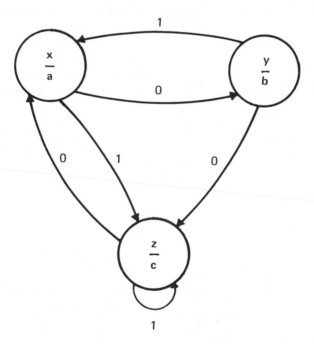

Figure 15.2   Representation of a Moore machine by a transition diagram.

Mealy Machines

A *Mealy*-type sequential machine is represented similarly as a quintuple

$$M = (S,I,O,\delta,\beta)$$

where

> S is a finite nonempty set of internal states
> I is a finite nonempty set of inputs
> O is a finite nonempty set of outputs
> $\delta : S \times I \to S$ is the next-state function
> $\beta : S \times I \to O$ is the next-output function

The definition is the same as for the Moore machine except for the next-output function, which is dependent upon the present input. Consider the state table and transition diagram for a Mealy machine, given in Figures 15.3 and 15.4. In the state table, there is an output column for each input, as compared to the Moore machine, which contains only one output column. In the corresponding transition diagram, the output occurs along with the indication of input.

State Machines

In many applications of sequential machines, the major concern is with the properties of the state transition function and the outputs are of little or no interest. For these purposes, a *state machine* is defined as follows:

$$M = (S,I,\delta)$$

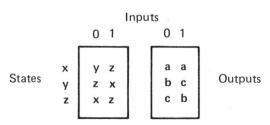

Figure 15.3   Representation of a Mealy machine by a state table.

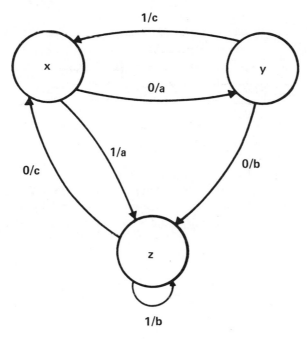

Figure 15.4   Representation of a Mealy machine by a transition diagram.

where

S is a finite nonempty set of states
I is a finite nonempty set of inputs
$\delta: S \times I \to S$ is the next-state function

Clearly, a state machine is a special case of either a Moore machine or a Mealy machine. State machines are particularly useful for modeling sophisticated routines that perform *control functions*. A process control monitor program or the supervisor program of a time-sharing system are good examples of processes to which state machines could be applied.

Elementary Properties of Sequential Machines

For those accustomed to thinking about machines as circuits, it is convenient to picture the Mealy machine as shown in Figure 15.5. For a Moore machine, the input connection to the output box is omitted; for

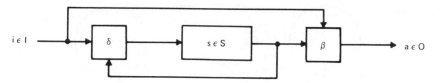

Figure 15.5   A Mealy machine represented as a circuit.

the state machine, the entire output logic is removed, as well.

Two sequential machines are *isomorphic* if and only if they are identical except for the naming of the inputs, outputs, and internal states. More formally, two machines of the same type, that is,

$$M = (S,I,O,\delta,\lambda)$$

and

$$M' = (S',I',O',\delta',\lambda')$$

are isomorphic if and only if there exist one-to-one onto mappings

$$g_1: S \to S'$$
$$g_2: I \to I'$$
$$g_3: O \to O'$$

such that

$$g_1(\delta(s,i)) = \delta'(g_1(s),g_2(i))$$
$$g_3(\lambda(s,i)) = \lambda'(g_1(s),g_2(i))$$

Two machines that are isomorphic may imitate each other through the use of appropriate circuits to perform the input and output conversions. As shown in Figure 15.6, machine M' is made to behave like machine M by placing the g_2 circuit, which maps $I' \to I$, in front and by placing the g_3^{-1} circuit, which maps $O' \to O$, in back.

Intuitively, two machines that generate the same output when started in equivalent states with the same input are considered to be equivalent.* Let the function $N_M(s,i)$ denote the output generated by

* Sequences of characters from the input and output alphabets are termed *words*. They are denoted i and o, respectively.

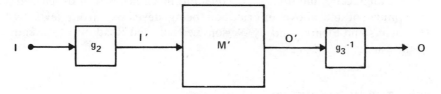

Figure 15.6   Imitating the behavior of machine *M* with machine *M'*.

machine *M* when started in state *s* with input *i*. For any two machines *M* and *M'* (not necessarily distinct), state *s* is said to be equivalent to state *s'* if and only if $N_M(s,i) = N_{M'}(s',i)$; it is written $s \equiv s'$. Thus two machines

$$M = (S,I,O,\delta,\lambda)$$

and

$$M' = (S',I',O',\delta',\lambda')$$

are equivalent if and only if the following conditions hold:

1. $I = I'$
2. $O = O'$
3. $(\forall s \in S)[(\exists s' \in S')(s \equiv s')]$
4. $(\forall s' \in S')[(\exists s \in S)(s' \equiv s)]$

Figure 15.7 gives transition diagrams for two equivalent machines, *A* and *B*. Casual inspection indicates that $x \equiv s$ and $y \equiv z \equiv t$.

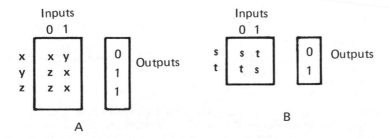

Figure 15.7   Two equivalent machines.

Academically, the theory of sequential machines is well developed, with much of the above information being developed from texts by Hartmanis and Stearns and by Nelson (see Selected Readings at the end of the chapter).

15.4 TURING MACHINES

Although sequential machines, as presented thus far, are adequate for a limited class of problems, they are inadequate for representing digital systems with even a small amount of memory. For example, a sequential machine with $2^{32,768}$ states would be required to represent a machine with 32,768 bits of main storage. Yet 32,768 bits is equivalent to only 4096 8-bit bytes or 512 64-bit words.* It would be convenient, therefore, to append an external storage device to the basic concept of a sequential machine. Fortunately, such a machine has been considered and is named a Turing machine in honor of A. M. Turing, who first proposed it in 1936.

Conceptually, a Turing machine is composed of a sequential machine (which is the control element), a read-write head, and a finite unbounded tape. Thus, the fact that a major component of a Turing machine is a sequential machine would indicate that there is a certain amount of similarity between them, especially at the basic level. The tape, which represents the mechanism by which data is stored externally, can be visualized as a linear sequence of tape squares (or character positions), with each square containing a blank character or character from a finite alphabet. Only one tape square can be scanned by the read-write head at any one time. During each cycle of operation, the tape square under the read-write head is scanned to determine the character that is recorded there. Depending upon its internal state and the character read, the control element executes one of the following operations:

1. A new character is written in the tape square under the read-write head.
2. The read-write head is positioned over the tape square to the right of the current square.

---

* It should be pointed out that the fact that an event B has occurred can be recorded in two ways: (1) by setting an indicator of some kind in storage; and (2) by transferring to an internal state that can be reached only if event B has occurred. It is in this sense that a sequential machine can represent a classical digital computer.

3. The read-write head is positioned over the tape square to the left of the current square.
4. The operation of the machine is halted.

After each machine operation, the machine progresses to the next state that is indicated in the instruction. When an instruction is reached that does not exist, then the machine automatically "halts."

Formal Definition of a Turing Machine

In the definition that follows, the symbols $s_0, s_1, s_2, \ldots$, are regarded as denoting internal configurations or states; $A_0, A_1, A_2, \ldots$ are the characters which the machine is capable of reading or recording; and the symbols R and L represent a move of one square to the right and one square to the left. An *expression* is a finite sequence of symbols and characters chosen from the list: $s_0, s_1, s_2, \ldots, A_0, A_1, A_2, \ldots$, R,L. A *quadruple*, then, is an expression that has one of the following forms:

1. $s_i A_j A_k s_l$
2. $s_i A_j R s_l$
3. $s_i A_j L s_l$

The operation of a Turing machine is described by a set of quadruples, where each specifies the *next operation* when in state s_i and when the tape square under the read-write head contains the character A_j. Thus, quadruple 1 specifies that the next operation is to replace A_j by A_k in the square being scanned and to enter state s_l. Quadruple 2 specifies tape motion of one square to the right followed by an entry into state s_l. Quadruple 3 specifies a similar motion to the left.

A *Turing machine* is a finite nonempty set of quadruples that contains no two quadruples whose first two symbols are identical. The s_i's are termed its *states* and the A_j's are called its *alphabet*.

The character A_0 has special significance as the blank symbol and will sometimes be written B. Replacing a character with B is tantamount to erasing it.

Instantaneous Description of a Turing Machine

It is desired to capture, in one expression, the entire current state of a Turing machine. Such a description would necessarily include the following information: (1) the tape expression, (2) the present state of the machine, and (3) the tape square currently positioned under the read-write head.

An *instantaneous description*, α, of a Turing machine T is thus an expression that contains exactly one s_i that is not the rightmost symbol of a quadruple, and neither of the characters R or L, such that s_i is a state of T and the A_j's that occur in the α are contained in the alphabet of T. Given a Turing machine T with instantaneous description α, such that s_i occurs in α followed immediately by the symbol A_j, then s_i is called the *internal state* of T at α and A_j is the *character scanned* by T at α. The characters remaining in α after removing s_i are the contents of the tape at α.

It is now possible to indicate the operation of a Turing machine as it progresses from one instantaneous description to another. Consider a Turing machine T with instantaneous descriptions α and β. The statement $\alpha \rightarrow \beta$ is defined to mean that one of the following alternatives holds (where P and Q represent sequences of tape characters):

1. $Ps_iA_jQ \rightarrow Ps_iA_kQ$; that is, T contains the quadruple $s_iA_jA_ks_l$.
2. $Ps_iA_jA_kQ \rightarrow PA_js_iA_kQ$; that is, T contains the quadruple s_iA_jRs_l.
3. $Ps_iA_j \rightarrow PA_js_iA_0$; that is, T contains the quadruple s_iA_jRs_l.
4. $PA_ks_iA_jQ \rightarrow Ps_iA_kA_jQ$; that is, T contains the quadruple s_iA_jLs_l.
5. $s_iA_jQ \rightarrow s_iA_0A_jQ$; that is, T contains the quadruple s_iA_jLs_l.

Lastly, the instantaneous description α is *terminal* if no β exists for which $\alpha \rightarrow \beta$.

Computation of a Turing Machine

The control element of a Turing machine, under control of a series of quadruples as described above, completely determines the computation performed by that machine. More formally, a *computation of a Turing machine* is a finite sequence $\alpha_1, \alpha_2, \ldots, \alpha_p$ of instantaneous descriptions such that $\alpha_i \rightarrow \alpha_{i+1}$ for $1 \leq i < p$ and α_p is terminal with respect to the machine T. In order to program a Turing machine effectively, therefore, a complete list of the required operations and their sequence must be specified.

Consider, for example, an algorithm to add two numbers, on tape, and replace the numbers with their sum. By convention, the number n is represented on tape by $n + 1$ consecutive I's ($4 = $ IIIII), followed by a blank character. Hence, the sum of 3 (represented by IIII) and 4 (represented by IIIII) is 7 (represented by IIIIIIII). The following algorithm will compute $f(X_1, X_2) = X_1 + X_2$ (the read-write head is positioned at the first digit of the leftmost number):

1. Move right along the tape until a blank (B) is reached (this blank separates the numbers).

2. Write a | in place of the blank.
3. Move right until a blank is reached.
4. Move left one square.
5. Write a blank.
6. Move left along the tape one more square.
7. Write a blank.
8. Halt.

A machine to compute this function would consist of the following quadruples:

$$
\begin{array}{cccc}
s_1 & | & R & s_1 \\
s_1 & B & | & s_2
\end{array}
\quad \text{(steps 1 and 2)}
$$

$$
\begin{array}{cccc}
s_2 & | & R & s_2 \\
s_2 & B & L & s_3
\end{array}
\quad \text{(steps 3 and 4)}
$$

$$
\begin{array}{cccc}
s_3 & | & B & s_3 \\
s_3 & B & L & s_4
\end{array}
\quad \text{(steps 5 and 6)}
$$

$$
\begin{array}{cccc}
s_4 & | & B & s_5
\end{array}
\quad \text{(steps 7 and 8)}
$$

Consider another function $f(X_1,X_2) = X_1 - X_2$; a Turing machine to calculate this function operates by successively cancelling |'s from both ends of the tape until one number is exhausted. The following set of annotated quadruples describes the required Turing machine:

$$
\begin{array}{cccc}
s_1 & | & B & s_1 \\
s_1 & B & R & s_2
\end{array}
\quad \text{(erase | on the left)}
$$

$$
\begin{array}{cccc}
s_2 & | & R & s_2 \\
s_2 & B & R & s_3
\end{array}
\quad \text{(locate separating blank)}
$$

$$
\begin{array}{cccc}
s_3 & | & R & s_3 \\
s_3 & B & L & s_4
\end{array}
\quad \text{(locate right end)}
$$

$$
\begin{array}{cccc}
s_4 & | & B & s_4 \\
s_4 & B & L & s_5
\end{array}
\quad \text{(erase | on the right)}
$$

$$
\begin{array}{cccc}
s_5 & | & L & s_6
\end{array}
\quad \text{(halt if } m_2 \text{ has been exhausted)}
$$

$$
\begin{array}{cccc}
s_6 & | & L & s_6 \\
s_6 & B & L & s_7
\end{array}
\quad \text{(locate separating blank)}
$$

s_7 | L s_8 (halt if m_1 has been exhausted)

s_8 | L s_8
s_8 B   R s_1 (locate left end and return to s_1)

As in any program, primitive Turing submachines are defined which provide basic functions needed for complex calculations. A complete treatment of the subject matter can be found from the Selected Readings.

15.5 COMPUTABILITY

One of the branches of abstract mathematics related to computer science deals with the theory of computability, a topic that concerns computations in which the limitations of space and time are not considered. The subject is of interest for two reasons: (1) Various aspects of computability can be demonstrated with the use of Turing machines; and (2) the intuitive notion of computability can be introduced with the use of red-light-green-light machines (see below), which provide a conceptual background for much of computer theory.

A function $f(x_1, x_2, \ldots, x_n)$ is said to be *computable* if there exists a Turing machine that will evaluate this function in a finite number of steps. If the function is not computable over every element of its domain, then it is defined to be *partially computable*. As was shown previously, the function $f(x_1, x_2) = x_1 + x_2$ is defined for the set of nonnegative integers. The function $f(x) = \text{sqrt}(x)$, however, is *partially computable*, since it is defined for those integers that are perfect squares. Conversely, a Turing machine can be viewed as a device that maps input sequences into output sequences. If the mapping can be described by a computable function, then a Turing machine exists that will perform the required calculations in a finite number of steps.

Red-Light-Green-Light Machines

The notion of a red-light-green-light machine (see Figures 15.8 and 15.9) draws its intuitive appeal from the fact that most of the detail ordinarily associated with sequential or Turing machines is eliminated. This general type of machine is used to demonstrate the concepts of recursive sets* and recursively enumerable sets. †

---

* A set is said to be a *recursive set* if an algorithm exists for determining whether or not a given element belongs to that set. The algorithm is termed a *decision procedure* for that set.
† A set is said to be *recursively enumerable* if given an element of that set y, a function that enumerates that set eventually turns up y.

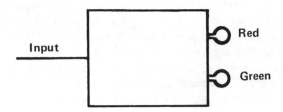

Figure 15.8   Red-light-green-light machine.

It is assumed that input to a red-light-green-light machine (Figure 15.8) is a positive integer, regardless of its actual representation, and that the machine operates in a deterministic fashion once the number has entered the machine. The result of the computation is that either the *green light* (representing "yes") or the red light (representing "no") lights up, for each integer that is entered. The machine is deterministic in the sense that repetition of a computation with the same input will generate the same result.

Associated with each red-light-green-light machine is a set of integers, S, for which the machine lights up green when an integer $s \in S$ is input. Given a set of integers with a specific property (the set of even numbers or the set of perfect squares, for example), a basic question is whether or not a red-light-green-light machine can be constructed so that it will light up green when a member of this specific set is input but light up red if the input is not a member of this set. If one can be constructed, then the set is said to be a *computable set* or a *recursive set*. Consider, on the other hand, a much more simple machine (on the surface, at least), called a green-light machine (see Figure 15.9). This type of machine is just like the red-light-green-light machine except that there exists only one light. A set of integers is also associated with this machine. A green-light machine differs from its predecessor, however, in one major

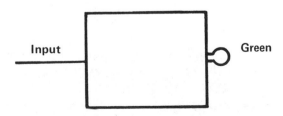

Figure 15.9   Green-light machine.

respect: With the first machine, the computation always comes to a halt and one of the lights lights up, but with a green-light machine, the green light lights up only when the input is a member of the associated set. Thus, it is never known whether or not the machine will eventually light up; it may be that a long computation is involved or it may be that the given number is not a member of the set. Sets that can be determined by green-light machines are called *recursively enumerable sets*. The following relationship may now be stated: A set S is recursive if and only if S and S' are recursively enumerable, where S' is the set of integers that does not belong to S. This fact is intuitively obvious, since a green-light machine can be built for S and for S' and then the machines can be connected, with a change of bulb, to form a red-light-green-light machine.

Regular and Realizable Events

Closely related to the computations performed by the red-light-green-light machines are the definitions of realizable and regular events. An *event* (E) is a subset of the set of all possible input sequences from some finite alphabet. An element of that subset is denoted by $a_1 a_2 \ldots a_n$, where a_1 precedes a_2, a_2 precedes a_3, and so on; an event E is said to be *realizable* if there exists a Turing machine T that generates output x (denoting "yes") and y (denoting "no") such that T generates x if and only if the input sequences $a_1 a_2 \ldots a_n$ belongs to E and generates y otherwise.

Three operations are defined on two events (i.e., sets of sequences) E and F:

1. $E \cup F = \{ e : e \epsilon E \text{ or } e \epsilon F \}$
2. $E \cdot F = \{ ef : e \epsilon E \text{ and } f \epsilon F \}$, that is, a sequence from E followed by a sequence from F
3. $E^* = \{ e : e \epsilon (E \cup E^2 \cup E^3 \ldots) \}$, where $E^{n+1} = E^n \cdot E$ and $E^1 = E$

A set E of sequences is *regular*, therefore, if

1. E is empty or contains one member, or
2. E can be generated from such a set by a finite number of applications of the *union, dot*, and *star* operations defined above.

A mathematical expression used to generate a regular event is called a *regular expression*. Regular expressions are used when designing a sequential machine to carry out a given set of operations. If the required operations can be expressed as a set of regular expressions, then these expressions can be used to develop the transition diagram of the desired sequential machine. If, however, the operations cannot be defined by regular expressions, then the desired machine cannot be specified.

15.6 NORMAL ALGORITHMS

Normal algorithms were developed in the 1950s by the Russian mathematician A. A. Markov for transforming strings of symbols from a given alphabet, which does not contain the symbols "→" and ".", in a mechanical way. A *normal statement* or *production* over the string S is a sequence of symbols of the form

$$\alpha \to \beta$$

which denotes that the first occurrence of string α in S should be replaced by string β. Here α is termed the *antecedent* and β the *consequent*. If there is at least one occurrence of α in S, then the production $\alpha \to \beta$ is said to be *applicable* to S. If the production is written as

$$\alpha \to . \beta$$

then it is termed *conclusive*, with the "." meaning that the computations stop after the application of this production. The null string Λ is also of interest. Λ is defined to have $n + 1$ occurrences in an arbitrary string γ of length n as follows: before the first symbol, after the last symbol, and between every two adjacent symbols.

A *normal algorithm* (or *Markov algorithm*, as it is sometimes called) is a finite sequence $P_1, P_2, \ldots, P_n$ of normal productions to be applied to a string S over a given alphabet according to the following rules:

1. The sequence (of productions) is searched to find the first production P_i whose antecedent occurs in S.
2. If no such production exists, the algorithm terminates.
3. Otherwise, this production is applied to S to form an intermediate string S'.
4. If the applicable production was conclusive, then the algorithm terminates. Otherwise, the normal algorithm continues with step (1).

The value of string S when the algorithm finally terminates is called the *result* of applying P to S.

In the examples that follow, productions are numbered for reference and the numbers are used to indicate the production used when transforming the input string: for example, the sequence of symbols

$$(4)$$
$$S \Rightarrow S'$$

indicates that production (4) was used in transforming S to S'.

Consider the string $S = \text{'}abcdcba\text{'}$ with simple productions

(1) $bc \rightarrow a$
(2) $ad \rightarrow .xy$

which would perform the following transformations in sequence:

$$\qquad (1) \qquad\quad (2)$$
$$abcdcba \Rightarrow aadcba \Rightarrow axycba$$

The manner in which the null string is treated is also of note. Consider $S = \text{'}at\text{'}$ and productions

(1) $ey \rightarrow .\Lambda$
(2) $cat \rightarrow dogey$
(3) $\Lambda \rightarrow c$

that generates the following sequence:

$$\quad (3) \qquad (2) \qquad\quad (1)$$
$$at \Rightarrow cat \Rightarrow dogey \Rightarrow dog$$

The power of normal algorithms is extended with a *marker symbol*, α, not contained in the given alphabet, and a *string variable* μ that can denote any symbol of the alphabet. Given an alphabet A, for example, the production (or algorithm containing one production)

$$\mu \rightarrow \Lambda$$

transforms every string into the empty string. The production successively deletes the first symbol of the string until it is empty, at which time the algorithm terminates. Similarly, the following algorithm deletes the first character of a nonempty string and leaves the empty string unchanged:

(1) $\alpha\mu \to .\,\Lambda$
(2) $\alpha \to .\,\Lambda$
(3) $\Lambda \to \alpha$

Another common application is to delete all characters to the left of a given symbol; the following algorithm does that and then removes the marker α:

(1) $\mu \to \Lambda$
(2) $\alpha \to .\,\Lambda$

The work of Markov is probably more significant than one might suspect, especially after an elementary treatment such as this. The problem of adding two numbers a and b, for example, can be considered a problem of transforming the string '$a + b$' into the string c that represents the sum. The most important use of normal algorithms, however, stems from the fact that they have led to the development of theoretical concepts that have been proved to be invaluable in language research and symbol manipulation techniques.

15.7 ARTIFICIAL LANGUAGES

Much of computer science is dependent upon a language of one kind or another. For example, regular expressions, as introduced above, are used to describe sets of sequences; the vast majority of computer programs are written in a higher-level programming language, and many applications such as machine translation or information retrieval utilize a language of some type. In other cases, it is desired to manipulate the statements of a language in a prescribed manner. It is necessary, therefore, to have a language free from ambiguity and one that can be described by formal rules. Artificial languages, as compared to natural languages, meet these needs, since they are limited to statements (or sequences of characters or symbols) that have particular attributes.

Basic Definitions
A *vocabulary* V of an artificial language L is a finite nonempty set of words. A finite sequence of words is termed a *sentence*, including the null sequence λ. The length of a sentence α, denoted by $l(\alpha)$, corresponds to

the number of words in the sentence; clearly $l(\lambda) = 0$. As with regular events, operations can be performed on sentences to form new sentences. Given the sentences $\alpha = \alpha_1\alpha_2\alpha_3 \ldots \alpha_m$ and $\beta = \beta_1\beta_2\beta_3 \ldots \beta_n$ of a vocabulary V, then the following primitive operations are defined:

1. *Equality*: $\alpha = \beta \Leftrightarrow l(\alpha) = l(\beta)$ and $\alpha_i = \beta_i$ for $i = 1, 2, \ldots, l(\alpha)$.
2. *Reflection*: $\alpha^\mathsf{T} = \alpha_m\alpha_{m-1} \ldots \alpha_1$
3. *Concatenation*: $\alpha\beta = \alpha_1\alpha_2 \ldots \alpha_m\beta, \beta_2 \ldots \beta_n$
4. *Powers*: $\alpha^\circ = \lambda; \alpha^1 = \alpha, \alpha^2 = \alpha\alpha, \alpha^n = \alpha\alpha^{n-1}$

Lastly, a sentence α is a subsentence of the sentence β if and only if there exist two sentences ϕ and θ such that

$$\beta = \phi\alpha\theta$$

Languages and Grammars

A set of sentences S over a vocabulary V is termed an artificial language L, that is, $L = \{ S, V \}$. If S is a finite set, then L is a *finite language*. If S is an infinite set, then L is an *infinite language*. Examples of each type over the vocabulary $V = \{ a, b \}$ are

$$S' = \{ a, aa, ab, aba, abab \}$$

and

$$S'' = \{ a^ib^j : i,j = 0, 1, \ldots \}$$

A *grammar* is a set of rules that defines how the sentences of a language can be formed. Formally, a *grammar* G is a quadruple $G = (V_n, V_i, P, \sigma)$, where

1. V_n is the nonterminal vocabulary of the language.
2. V_i is the terminal vocabulary of the language, that is, the words of the language.
3. P is a finite set of ordered pairs (α, β) over $V_n \cup V_i$ where α contains at least one word (symbol) of V_n.
4. σ, ϵ, V_n is a special symbol denoting a sentence.

The set P needs further explanation. It is the set of *productions* or *rewriting rules* of the language. Given the sentence $\mu_1 = \phi\alpha\theta$, the production (α, β) indicates that sentence α can be replaced by sentence β such that $\mu_2 = \phi\beta\theta$. This substitution is indicated by

$\mu_1 \rightarrow \mu_2$

where the arrow is read "can be rewritten as." For example, consider the grammar $G = (N,T,P,\sigma)$, where

$N = \{ \sigma, X \}$
$T = \{ x, y \}$
$P = \{ (\sigma,xXy), (X,yXx), (X,y) \}$

A valid sentence, according to G, would be generated as follows:

$(P_1) \qquad (P_2) \qquad (P_2) \qquad (P_3)$
$\sigma \rightarrow xXy \rightarrow xyXxy \rightarrow xyyXxxy \rightarrow xyyyxxy$

Thus, the sentence '*xyyyxxy*' is a valid sentence of the language denoted by $L(G)$. A grammar G is said to be *ambiguous* if there is a sentence $s \in L(G)$ that can be produced with productions P in at least two different ways. If a sentence can be produced in only one way, using a given grammar, then it is termed *unambiguous*.

Historically, the theory of language was developed independently of automata theory. As linguists began using the computer and as computer scientists began using formal languages, the two fields have gradually merged, to some extent. Currently, certain topics in language theory are considered bona fide extensions to what is known as automata theory.

15.8 CONCLUSIONS

Automata theory provides the computer scientist interested in formal concepts with a foundation for much of computer theory. Because of the procedural nature of computing machines and most programming languages, the mathematical and structural techniques of automata theory provide a means of describing algorithmic processes as well.

But there is a more practical reason for studying automata and its theory. Many of the technological innovations of today are an outgrowth of mathematical advances of 10 or even 50 years ago. Statistical mechanics, operations research, and decision analysis are a few of many examples that could be named. It seems reasonable to conjecture, therefore, that the computing system of the future will be an outgrowth of the automata of the present.

PROBLEMS

1. For arbitrary sets A, B, and C, show that the following identities are true:

    a. $\phi \cup A = A$
    b. $\phi \cap A = \phi$
    c. $A \cup (B \cap C) = (A \cup B) \cap (B \cup C)$

2. Give the equivalent phrase in English for the following definitions:

    a. $A = \{$ cereal, eggs, toast $\}$
    b. $R = \{ r : (\forall r \in R) \wedge (\exists s \in R) \wedge (r = \frac{1}{s}) \}$

3. Define the following sets using set notation:
    a. The set of all positive integers greater than 43
    b. The set of all real numbers a for which the absolute value of the sine (i.e., $|\sin a|$) is greater than or equal to $2a/\pi$, for $|a| \leq \pi/2$. (See section 14.3)
    c. The set of perfect squares less than 200.
4. Draw a transition diagram of the following Moore machine:

	Inputs		
	0	1	
x	x y	0	
States y	z x	1	Outputs
z	y x	1	

5. Give a set-theoretic representation of the Moore machine in problem 4.
6. Give a state table for the Mealy machine illustrated on the next page.
7. Give a set-theoretic representation of the Mealy machine in problem 6.
8. Verify that the Turing-machine actions for the quadruples given in the chapter compute $f(x_1,x_2) = x_1 + x_2$ and $f(x_1,x_2) = x_1 - x_2$.
9. Develop a set-theoretic definition of a Turing machine. Use one of the readings if necessary.
10. Write a Turing-machine program to compute $(x + 1)(y + 1)$, using the fact that:

$$(x + 1)(y + 1) = \underbrace{(y + 1) + (y + 1) + (y + 1) + \cdots + (y + 1)}_{x + 1 \text{ times}}$$

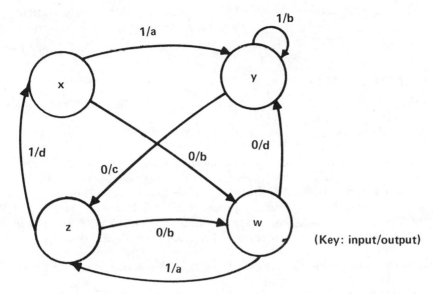

(Key: input/output)

11. Develop a state machine (Moore or Mcaly) that will perform the following recognition problems:
    a. Recognize a set of sequences that contains an even number of 1's and no 0's.
    b. Recognize a set of sequences that contains an even number of 1's with embedded 0's.

    The machine should start in a given state and generate a 1 when a correct sequence is received. It should generate a 0 for invalid sequences.

12. Discuss the stopping problem for problem 11.

13. Develop a machine for recognizing the following constructs in a programming language:
    a. Identifier
    b. Integer
    c. Decimal number

14. For regular events A, B, and C, demonstrate that the following are true:
    a. $(A*)* = A*$
    b. $A . (B \cup C) = A . B \cup A . C$

15. Develop a normal algorithm to perform the following algorithms:
    a. Correct the number of symbols in a string by replacing each symbol by a tally mark—such as a 1.
    b. Give a string S. Replace all occurrences of the symbol L with the symbols LA.

    c. Duplicate a string. (This algorithm is deceptively difficult
because of the problem of destroying the original string.
Korfhage [p. 105] contains a solution.)

SELECTED READINGS

Arbib, M. A., *Brains, Machines, and Mathematics*, McGraw-Hill, New York,
    1964.

Arbib, M. A., *Theories of Abstract Automata*, Prentice-Hall, Englewood Cliffs,
    N.J., 1969.

Booth, T. L., *Sequential Machines and Automata Theory*, Wiley, New York, 1967.

Davis, M., *Computability and Unsolvability*, McGraw-Hill, New York, 1958.

Davis, M., "Computability," in *Proceedings of the Symposium on Systems Theory*,
    Polytechnic Press, Polytechnic Institute of Booklyn, New York, 1965, p. 127.

Davis, M. D., "A note on universal Turing machines," in Shannon and
    McCarthy (eds.), *Automata Studies*, Princeton Univ. Press, Princeton, N.J.,
    1956.

Gill, A., *Introduction to the Theory of Finite State Machines*, McGraw-Hill, New
    York, 1962.

Harrison, M. A., *Introduction to Switching and Automata Theory*, McGraw-Hill,
    New York, 1965.

Hartmanis, J., and R. E. Stearns, *Algebraic Structure Theory of Sequential
    Machines*, Prentice-Hall, Englewood Cliffs, N.J., 1966.

Hopcroft, J. E., and J. D. Ullman, *Formal Languages and Their Relation to
    Automata*, Addison-Wesley, Reading, Mass., 1969.

Korfhage, R. R., *Logic and Algorithms*, Wiley, New York, 1966.

Miller, G. A., *Mathematics and Psychology*, Wiley, New York, 1964.

Minsky, M. L., *Computation: Finite and Infinite Machines*, Prentice-Hall,
    Englewood Cliffs, N.J., 1967.

Nelson, R. J., *Introduction to Automata*, Wiley, New York, 1968.

Singh, J., *Great Ideas in Information Theory, Language and Cybernetics*, Dover,
    New York, 1966.

Stone, H. S., *Discrete Mathematical Structures and Their Applications*, Science
    Research Associates, Chicago, 1973.

16

COMPUTERS AND SOCIETY

16.1 INTRODUCTION

In its broadest sense, *society* is defined as the totality of social relationships among human beings. To the individual, however, society is not a "sea of humanity" because of the structural constraints adopted for organizations and because of the finiteness of human existence. We participate in society as individuals and through the organizations to which we belong. Organizations can accomplish tasks that are impossible for the individual to perform—in any time frame—and, in an analogous fashion, individuals can do things that are very cumbersome to accomplish in an organizational environment. Organizations depend upon people and people depend upon organizations.

A similar situation exists with the computer. It can perform computational tasks that would be impossible for an individual or an organization to perform in a lifetime. As a simple example, it can compute the payroll more reliably, more accurately, and more economically than a multitude of payroll clerks. It has been said that information is power, but in spite of its power, the computer is dependent upon the organization and the individual for its very existence.

The fact that we, as a society, have entered into a working relationship with the computer has serious implications. It means that the computer affects our everyday lives and if we are to benefit from this relationship, we must understand the partnership.

The Organization

We live in a society dominated by organizations, such as businesses, governmental agencies, schools, churches, hospitals, and various social

461

groups. Most of us belong to more than one organization. An organization is a system; the resources of the system are people, capital, machines, buildings, and so forth. Thus, the resources of an organization are analogous to the components of a system. The various components of the system communicate through information.

Organizations are the primary users of computers. Historically, business has led the way in the use of computers because of the profit motive and because some businesses, such as banks and insurance companies, are essentially information processing organizations. Currently, most organization, large or small, use computers. If an organization lacks qualified personnel or finances, it can now share common computing facilities with another organization or have its computing services performed by a computer service company. Many banks, for example, perform payroll services for their customers on a regular basis.

The advantages of computers to the organization are significant and are summarized as follows:

1. Additional information becomes available.
2. Information can be made available more quickly.
3. Information is more inclusive and accurate.
4. Information can be presented in a form that is more useful to the decision maker or the administrator.

Other than problem-solving activities performed by scientists, engineers, and analysts and routine data processing, the greatest benefit of computers to organizations occurs in three areas: planning, decision-making, and controlling. The precise techniques tend to vary between organizations but generally involve optimization, simulation, prediction, scheduling, and measurement of organizational performance.

When computers are used extensively in organizations, there seems to be a tendency toward centralization of authority. Centralization or decentralization is a matter of degree rather than an absolute concept. In organizations that employ decentralization as an operating technique, decisions are made by lower-level administrative or management personnel because of time, distance, and familiarity with the factors affecting the decision. Through the effective use of computer facilities, higher administrative and management personnel can participate in local decision making to a greater extent because they can be supplied with appropriate information in a shorter period of time.

The use of computers does not imply centralization, and the lack of computers does not imply decentralization. Other factors affecting the situation are the size of the organization, management philosophy, physical facilities, the organization growth, and the type of business the company is in. To sum up, the use of computers provides the practical means for centralization, regardless of whether or not an organization decides to go in that direction. However, the use of computers does require organizational changes in both structure and everyday operation. Changes normally occur in the following areas:

1. Departments engaged in data processing
2. Departments engaged in informational services
3. Service departments using computer services
4. Organization and training departments
5. The computer department itself
6. Higher administrative levels that support the computer function

The computer department is and will continue to be a problem to most organizations, since operators, programmers, analysts, and capable managers are presently in short supply. On the other side of the coin, the computer department is a good source of quality personnel for the organization. The perseverence necessary to become a good programmer is a valuable trait that is applied well to other organizational occupations. The typical systems analyst knows a great deal about an organization and is always a prime candidate for promotion into administrative or management positions. The computer installation manager, because of his managerial and technical background, is frequently tapped for an executive position.

Another benefit of computers to organizations is standardization. In many cases, the interface between departments is ill defined and the organization essentially operates through informal organizational procedures. Before a computer can be used in a system, that system is usually described in detail and subsequently formalized. Many organizations have benefited considerably from the process of studying how they actually operate. The standardization of reports and time schedules has also helped organizations realize the scope of information that is and can be made available to them.

The Individual

The use of computers has changed organizations to the extent that the lives of individuals, both in and out of those organizations have been markedly influenced. The subject has been treated as an emotional issue by social scientists and journalists and has aroused the fears of society in general. The following quotations from William Rodgers' celebrated book *Think*, a biography of the Watsons and IBM, demonstrate some modern points of view:

> E. B. White, a serious humorist and essayist, wrote that he did not believe in computers very much, since the convenience they afforded some people was regarded as more important than the inconvenience they caused to all. 'In short,' he wrote in *The New York Times*, 'I don't think computers should wear the pants or make the decisions. They are deficient in humor ... The men who feed them seem to believe that everything is made out of ponderables, which isn't the case, I read a poem once that a computer had written, but didn't care much for it. It seemed to me I could write a better one myself, if I put my mind to it (p. 291)

> Tom Watson at IBM, like Howard Aiken, the designer of the original Mark I, has assured the world that the computer is no more than a tool, a view held by most people who profit by, or in, this field of technology. Others are certain that it is already something of a monster, corrupting values and causing distortion of viewpoints. Some fear it is an instrument that, by compiling a lifetime accumulation of details about each person's live, will doom human beings to a loss of privacy. (p. 294)

It is generally felt that fear of computers is diminished through knowledge of the subject matter. A certain amount of apprehension always accompanies a new technology. For example: the automobile was disliked because engines were noisy and dirty; and the telephone was initially regarded as an invasion of privacy. However, there are some valid concerns over the computer revolution, which many people feel we are now experiencing. Some of the key issues are:

1. *Automation and Jobs.* Does automation eliminate job opportunities? What kind of jobs exist in a computerized society? Will organizational structure change with an increase in the use of computers? Do we live in a society of specialists?
2. *Personal Issues.* Are information systems destroying our privacy? Is dehumanization a fact or a myth? Are people victims of computers or are computers victims of people? Can we ensure the confidentiality of information?
3. *The Future.* What does the future hold in a computerized society?

Will we still use books in the year 2000? What about leisure time? Specialization? Changing careers? OLIVER—the everyday computer.

The computer is here to stay. Let there be no doubt about that. It has changed the way we look at the world to such an extent that we could never retreat back to an earlier way of life. Moreover, we have adapted to the pace of change so that we continually expect new and better products, increased productivity, more leisure time—items that the computer has helped to bring about. Like practically everything else in society, it is necessary to take the bad with the good. Perhaps the lack of privacy or depersonalized education systems, for example, are the price we must pay for the benefits of computers. This and other topics are explored in this chapter.

16.2 BUSINESS

The biggest use of computers in business is in the areas of problem solving and data processing. This fact has been mentioned previously. Analysts, scientists, and engineers are able to use the computer for numerical calculations and have expanded their functional capabilities to a considerable degree. Data processing is used for operations that involve routine logic and mathematics but require the same processing to be applied to a great many similar transactions. Utility billing, payroll, dividend checks, and inventory records are examples of areas that utilize data processing methods. In addition, many information-service companies use computers to provide immediate service to their customers. For example, service companies now exist that will verify the validity of a credit card. To verify a credit card, the businessman makes a toll-free call to the service company, which verifies that the card is neither lost, stolen, nor expired. If the card turns out to be "bad," then the service company is held responsible for the charges. Without verification, the acceptance of a bad credit card becomes the responsibility of the businessman. Other services, called "information banks," store large amounts of information for use by customers on a demand basis via telecommunications facilities. Computer service companies are regarded as special cases, since their product is essentially the computer.

Businesses that limit their use of the computer to problem solving and data processing, however, tend to gain less from their computer than those that attempt to integrate the computer into the total business system. In other words, information systems should not be justified solely on the basis of cost-reduction grounds, but also on the basis of how management can benefit from the increased information.

Essentially, we are talking about a *management information system*, frequently referred to as an MIS. The objective of an MIS is to provide a means for the information of a business to be integrated and dynamically updated so that it can be used for planning, decision making, and control purposes. Conceptually, an MIS is an on-line real-time information system consisting of the following components, facilities, or resources:

1. A centralized *data line* consisting of an integrated set (or subset) of company files
2. A comprehensive set of data on the company, its operating structure, and the competitive environment
3. The capability for retrieving data from the data base for analysis and reporting
4. A set of planning models for use in prediction and planning activities
5. A set of control models that can be used to monitor performance of the company
6. A set of decision models to be used for decision making, using the information in the data base

No one attribute or collection of attributes defines a management information system, which seems to be more of a commitment to the concept of an integrated business system than a set of physical facilities.

Planning is the most widely developed area in which management information systems are used. Planning is known to exist at three organization levels:

1. *Long-range planning* to develop organizational objectives, establish corporate goals, and set corporate policies
2. *Tactical planning* to make efficient use of resources, such as money, machines, and personnel
3. *Operational planning* to develop alternatives for specific functions or products

The information necessary for planning is derived from competitive analysis, market research, and internal statistics, and from known operational characteristics of the company.

Long-range planning frequently involves the financial status of the organization and its relationship to the business environment. National economic forecasts and political information are frequently used at this level to establish a sound basis for decisions. Information is usually made available to executives in the form of reports.

Tactical planning is analogous to what is generally known as management control and utilizes cybernetic principles and control systems to determine how resources are acquired, organized, and employed. Exception reporting is frequently used.

Operational planning usually involves optimization and data analysis techniques to organize daily activities. Delivery schedules, trucking routes, and purchase orders are frequently developed by computer, because of the number of independent variables involved.

Operational planning is closely related to *decision making*, which uses the computer to develop and evaluate alternatives. Statistics and simulation are frequently used for selecting courses of action for the business to follow at each of the above levels of planning.

Computers serve control purposes in businesses in two principal ways: (1) as a means of controlling how the company operates, such as savings bank, credit, and inventory systems; and (2) as a means of measuring performance and alerting appropriate people to unusual conditions that need attention. Operation of an organization has been discussed previously. Performance measurement is usually achieved through periodic reports and specific informational requests. This is an area in which a management information system is invaluable. When information is needed for a decision at one of the planning levels, an analysis can be made from the central data base, often within hours when an on-line real-time system is used.

Systems that alert man against unusual conditions are still in their infancy but offer great potential for the future. The basic idea is this: A *business information and control system* is used, into which all planning, operational, environmental, and competitive data are entered and maintained on a continual basis, day-to-day or hour-to-hour. Routine decisions, such as when to reorder supplies or raw materials, are made by the computer and the departments involved are informed automatically. The computer essentially operates the business by keeping track of *all* information and by making routine decisions. Since the computer serves only a control function, the outward appearance of the business is the same. Many routine clerical jobs, such as ordering pencils, are eliminated and the people are moved into information-gathering positions. Top management has more time to allocate to planning and less time is needed for day-to-day operations. Thus, the human is doing what he can do best—planning—and the computer is employed in its best capacity —routine operations. The use of this type of control system may be accompanied by a gradual shift in middle management from managing people to managing products and resources.

One of the key features in a business information and control system is that at any point in time, any item of information worth knowing about business is stored in the computer, and it can be accessed by authorized people.

16.3 GOVERNMENT AND LAW

One of the major functions of government is to meet the needs of society, whatever they are, and most governmental officials can attest to the fact that it is impossible to please everyone. However, the problems are deeper than that. First, it is difficult to determine what programs are needed and to assess appropriate priorities. Second, it is difficult to determine what has been done. Third, it is impossible to tell if a program is successful until it is past "the point of no return" in terms of finances and time. And last, it is difficult to manage a governmental agency that is characteristically understaffed and underfinanced. In the past, governmental officials frequently used the method of "incremental change" for decision making. The *method of incremental change* involves making a small change in a given direction. If the reaction to it is favorable, then another small change in the same direction is made, and so forth. If the reaction to the incremental change is not favorable or if funds for the project "dry up," then it is relatively easy to back up and make an effort in a different direction. This description is overly simplified, obviously, but it illustrates an important point. Significant changes often extend over unreasonably long periods of time, which is frustrating to the populus and to the administrator himself. The use of the computer in government has helped alleviate this problem somewhat.

The single biggest user of computers in the United States is the federal government. The objective of most computers installed in the government is increased productivity through information systems. The benefits of information systems to government planners are summarized as the capability with which:

1. To make better plans and decisions
2. To improve operating efficiency
3. To better serve society

There are also some fringe benefits of computers in government. Computers are often regarded as capital expenditures by the government and are not charged to the budget of a particular agency. Thus, the administrator of that agency is given the capability of doing a better job without additional expenditures if he decides to utilize computers. The computer has also helped many administrators with their human relations. We live in a socially conscious society, similar in concept to the economically conscious society that existed after the depression of the 1930s. In economics, we have developed a variety of economic indicators, such as the gross national product, that give us an idea of the health of the economy. Although social indicators are not in widespread use among the citizenry, statistical data, available through information systems, has aided many governmental agencies in assessing how well they are serving the needs of society.

Federal Government

It is practically impossible and certainly impractical to list all of the uses of computers in the federal government. Moreover, many of the applications are either classified for national security or generally not available to the general public. A sampling of computer applications is given in the following paragraphs.

Internal Revenue Service. The agency best known to the average citizen for its computer capability is the IRS. Through the years, the use of computers has reduced the occurrences of "tax cheating" and has substantially increased revenues. The IRS has a network of regional centers and a national center that employ computers. Computers are used to verify the arithmetic on returns and to crosscheck reports from employers and banks on income, withholdings, interest, and dividends with actual declarations. Estimated tax as well as name changes, moves from one region to another, and so forth are also processed. Most IRS regional centers use key-to-tape or key-to-disk systems for data entry from returns and reports and information is normally available to auditing personnel through CRT-type terminal devices. Regional centers submit tax records to the national center, where a record is kept for each taxpayer. (There are 80 million taxpayers and tax-paying entities in the United States.) Tax refunds, delinquent notices, and bills are made through the national center. The computer is also used for auditing purposes. Through the years, IRS personnel have developed criteria with the greatest audit potential. For example, if medical deductions were greater than 70 percent of a taxpayer's income, the computer might signal that the return might be worth looking into. (This, by the way, is an example that is made purposefully ridiculous so as not to be interpreted as a fact.) It has been conjectured, but by no means substantiated, that one of the benefits of tax preparation firms is that they supposedly know the limits that can be deducted, and so forth, in each category. (It has also been conjectured that these same companies use their customers as guinea pigs to determine what these limits are.)

Census Bureau. In the most recent census (1970), the U.S. Census Bureau collected and processed information on 205 million people living in the United States. Although the 1970 census resulted in minor criticism because of the personal questions involved, the facts are used to allocate Federal funds and to realign the boundaries of congressional districts. The Census Bureau has elaborate procedures to ensure the privacy of individual data—even to the extent that they ensure that the number of people involved in a sample is large enough to ensure individual privacy. Census data is available to researchers, but only after it is processed to remove any personal information.

Military. The military is another relatively large user of computers, in five general areas: The Defense Supply Agency, in space observations (i.e., satellites), weapon systems, command and control systems, and strategic decision making. The Defense Supply Agency, which is a consolidated source of supplies for all of the services, maintains centralized records on 1.5 million different items. It has been called the world's biggest supermarket. The Air Force SPADATA program, for Space Detection and Tracking System, keeps track of all man-made objects in space. It uses a network of observation stations to detect new objects and verify the existence of old ones. Computers are used in most weapon systems for guidance and trajectory computations. Moreover, once a ballistic missile is launched, a computer keeps track of its location. Command and control systems use a vast network of radars and computers to ensure the integrity of the United States airspace. Radar data from observed aircraft are entered directly into computers for comparison against flight patterns. Unusual events are detected and strategic forces are alerted. In the area of decision making, computers are used to keep track of ships, planes, and men, and to perform complex statistical analyses regarding military actions. Mobile computers are used in the field, on board ships, and in planes, whenever computational power is needed. Push-button war is largely fiction and local commanders are incorporated into the decision-making loop whenever possible. Simulation techniques are widely used in the military for gaining analytical and decision-making experience through the use of war games, which include both tactical and logistic aspects of military conflict.

Computers are also used in: the *Veterans Administration* to process the paperwork associated with hospital, educational, and insurance benefits; the *Treasury Department* to issue government checks; the *Food and Drug Administration* to process new drug applications; the *Labor Department* to assist in the job placement; the *Weather Bureau* for forecasts of periods up to 30 days; the *U.S. Postal Service* to speed up postal service with automatic scanners and sorters; and the *Social Security Administration* for processing earning records and deductions, routine monthly payments, and Medicare and Medicaid systems. The Social Security Administration uses at least 27 computers and is the largest single computer installation in the world.

Congress

One of the areas of the government that is suffering most from "information overload" is the legislative branch. The computer is needed by legislators to keep track of pending legislation and to assess the needs of their constituents. For example, the 89th Congress considered over 26,000 bills, and in the 90th Congress, over 29,000 pieces of legislation were introduced. Legislation has been introduced in the U.S. Congress for an information system for Congress. Other proposals include an electronic voting system and an on-line real-time system that would have access to all federal data bases. At this time, at least five state legislatures (Florida, Hawaii, New York, North Carolina, and Pennsylvania) provide their members with computerized reports on pending bills and other legislative data.

Courts and Law

A major problem that has accompanied the increasing crime rate in the country is the backlog of pending court cases. Persons accused of crimes often have to wait in jail for years, when bail is not available, and in addition to the personal injustices involved, these cases cause overcrowding of jails and a burden to the taxpayers. In both criminal and civil cases, details of the cases are often forgotten by witnesses before the cases come to court. Several states and cities use computers for court administration to keep track of backlogged cases, prepare trial calendars, generate subpoenas and notices to prisoners, and prepare status reports so that lawyers can plan their own schedules accordingly. Another area in which computers have been successfully used is in the area of jury selection.

Although lawyers have been relatively slow to use the computer, many law firms now use computer services for billing, account, tax and estate computations, and for legal information retrieval. In the latter case, the computer is used to search for legal precedents. The lawyer, using a terminal device, enters data on his own case. The computer searches through voluminous information and generates referrals to specific cases that can be used as legal precedents.

Local Government

The computer has been a boon to state and local governments that are forced by their very nature to deal with messy social problems. Some typical state and local problems are: transportation planning, real-estate assessment and tax, water and air pollution, urban and land-use planning, social welfare management, and a variety of other "headaches" such as pest control, pet licenses, and road repair. Transportation, urban, and land-use planning activities frequently use simulation. Computers are also used to prepare land assessments and tax bills and to generate reminders and daily work lists for a variety of other state and local governmental functions.

Computers have helped several welfare programs considerably, especially in large municipalities where a welfare recipient can register at more than one regional center. In New York City, for example, one welfare recipient was eventually caught after receiving welfare checks for several years from different welfare centers in three of New York's five boroughs.

With the current concern over pollution, control computers have been used to improve on the efficiency of various facilities. Recent applications involve the monitoring of a power generating station, controlling a sewage treatment plant, and controlling traffic lights. Traffic control by computer has great potential for the years to come. By controlling traffic lights to meet the needs of the traffic at any point in time, congestion, travel times, and air pollutants are reduced.

Police and Criminal Systems

We live in a mobile society through the use of automobiles, airplanes, trains, and buses. Criminals also benefit from the same advantages, and in the past all one had to do was "blow town" and he was relatively free. The Federal Bureau of Investigation has reduced the problem considerably with its National Crime Information Center (NCIC), which is an on-line real-time computerized information network. The NCIC system stores the arrest records of persons and information on wanted persons and stolen property. Local and state law-enforcement personnel can query the NCIC system to obtain information on a subject that warrants further investigation.

The Justice Department has also gotten into the act through its Law Enforcement Assistance Administration (LEAA). LEAA has a $7 million research project, called project SEARCH (System for Electronic Analysis and Retrieval of Criminal Histories), to produce a nationwide on-line information network for exchanging criminal histories. Eventually, local, state, and federal agencies are expected to use the SEARCH system.

Many states have now computerized their motor vehicle registration and driver's license facilities so that they can be accessed by state agencies and local police to obtain the name of the owner of an automobile and verify the validity of a registration or a driver's license.

In addition to being connected to the NCIC information system, many state, county, and local law enforcement agencies have information systems of their own. Notable examples of systems that have achieved some degree of success are the Law Enforcement Information Network (LEIN) at Michigan state headquarters in East Lansing, the California Law Enforcement Telecommunications System (CLETS), the Chicago "hot-desk" system, the New York State Identification and Intelligence System, and the County Law Enforcement Applied Regionally (CLEAR) system, developed in Cincinnati and Hamilton counties of Ohio and adopted elsewhere. Law enforcement systems of this type are accessed via telecommunications facilities in the station house, the patrol car, or both. From a patrol car, requests are normally radioed to an operator manning a terminal device. The operator, who is experienced at querying the information system, can normally respond in less than a minute to the police officer. Terminals in patrol cars have been implemented for some systems, but it is difficult to tell at this point whether they were installed after a thorough systems analysis or as the result of an aggressive equipment salesman.

Politics

Computers have even been used in political campaigns, vote counting, and election-night broadcasting. The first major political figure who used computers was John F. Kennedy, prior to the 1960 presidential election. The Kennedy campaign staff built a model of the voting public from sample data obtained from a public opinion polling company. The model was used to evaluate strategies for dealing with campaign issues—one of which was the fact that Kennedy, if elected, would be the country's first Catholic president. The eventual strategy worked out with the aid of the model was to approach the problem "head-on" rather than sidestepping the issue.

In general, computers are used in political campaigning in two principal ways: (1) as a means of doing routine clerical operations; and (2) as a means of analyzing voter characteristics. In the first category, typical operations are:

1. The compilation and maintenance of voter names, addresses, and voting preferences
2. The preparation of address labels for mailing campaign literature
3. The preparation of special appearance letters—generated by computer
4. Selection of voters from the mailing list (operation 1) that are sensitive to a particular campaign issue so that they can be sent special campaign literature or so that they can be omitted from the mailing of literature sensitive to them
5. The management of contributors, potential and actual, of campaign funds

Typical operations in the second category are:

1. Analysis of voters by geographical area, taking into consideration income level, ethnic group, past voting habits, race, religion, and a variety of other political factors
2. Correlations of political issues with geographical areas identified in operation 1
3. Assessment and prediction of voter behavior through simulation and other modeling techniques

These and similar techniques were used in Winthrop Rockefeller's campaign for governor of Arkansas in 1966 and in Robert Griffin's campaign for senator from Michigan in the same year.

Vote counting is an area in which computers have fared rather poorly. The basic objective, of course, is to have complete election results shortly after the polls close in a voting district. In fact, IBM formerly marketed a vote-counting machine that accepted specially punched cards as input. However, late and controversial tabulations in several localities have caused computerized vote counting to be viewed with distrust, and at least 11 states have outlawed the concept completely.

Most of us are familiar with election-night TV reporting, wherein a candidate is declared the winner by the computer after only a small percentage of the vote is in. Almost without exception, the eventual vote count proves the computer to be correct. How is it done? Primarily, predictions are made with statistical techniques and historical voting patterns of that district. The basic thinking behind the methods goes somewhat as follows: if a certain percentage of the voters vote a certain way, there is a given probability that the remaining voters will vote that way also; the prediction is made by putting the two percentages together.

16.4 MEDICINE

As a society, we are entering a crisis period as far as medical and health care are concerned; perhaps we are already in one. Services are becoming increasingly expensive, and as an affluent society, we have come to expect better and better care. In addition, the medical sciences have become exceedingly complex to the extent that available knowledge doubles every five to ten years. Thus, medical people must know more, we expect more, and services in general are expected to cost more. Increased medical costs are not limited to medical treatment, per se, but are also the result of expanded administrative services, such as hospital drug control, blood-bank inventory control, and the control of laboratory tests. It is expected that the effective use of computers in medicine will help reduce or at least help control rising costs and aid medical people in providing better medical and health care.

The primary applications of computers in the field of medicine and health services are:

1. Monitoring a patient's condition
2. Storing a patient's medical records
3. Assisting in the diagnosis of diseases
4. Maintaining central information systems

It is important to add to this list the widespread use of computers in medical education and research and in hospital administration.

Patient Monitoring

The most dramatic use of computers in medicine is in the area of patient monitoring. Control computers are frequently used in intensive care units to monitor the condition of patients after a severe operation, such as open-heart surgery. The computer monitors and records the patient's heart rate, blood pressure, temperature, and fluid drainage. Obviously, the computer does not perform the monitoring, per se, but controls a variety of sensing and recording equipment that perform the required services. A single computer can monitor hundreds of post-operative patients. The computer is programmed to detect unusual conditions and to administer medication and blood infusions.

Control computers are also used to screen electrocardiograms, so that a patient can receive an electrocardiogram and have it analyzed in less than a minute. Normally, the computer can screen several electro-cardiograms at one time.

Medical Records

Physicians are notoriously good at doctoring and notoriously bad at paperwork (and writing). The fact that people move frequently and change doctors only compounds the problem. The information about a patient is recorded, either from written records or with a terminal device, in a centralized medical information system. Medical personnel with the proper authority can retrieve specific facts about a patient or his entire medical profile. In today's age of specialization, a patient's records could be scattered among several doctors' offices. With the centralized system, a complete medical history of a patient is available to allow doctors to provide more effective medical treatment.

A recent innovation in medical recording is referred to as *automated medical recording*. The method uses computer-administered questioning so that an examination can be tailored to the characteristics of the patient. The physician uses a CRT-type terminal device. Questions are presented on the screen; depending upon the question, either the physician, the nurse, or the patient can respond.

Some of the advantages of a centralized medical information system are that records can be analyzed for diseases without outward symptoms that might go unrecognized by doctor or patient and for the early detection of epidemics.

Clinical Decision Making and Treatment

In a book on statistical decision analysis, Howard Raiffa gives a "simple" decision that must be made by a doctor. The doctor does not know whether a patient's sore throat is caused by strep or a virus. If he knew it were strep, he would prescribe penicillin; if he knew it were caused by a virus, he would prescribe rest, gargle, and aspirin. Failure to treat a strep throat with medication might result in a serious disease, such as rheumatic heart disease. On the other hand, penicillin should not be prescribed indiscriminately because of a possible reaction or the development of pencillin-resistant bacteria. The doctor should take a throat culture; however, the bacteria could die before the analysis is complete and the presence of strep does not guarantee that it is causing the sore throat. The doctor has several possibilities:

1. Take no culture; treat sore throat as viral.
2. Take no culture; treat sore throat as strep.
3. Take no culture; prescribe penicillin for 10 days.
4. Take culture; prescribe penicillin if positive.
5. Take culture and prescribe penicillin; continue penicillin if positive and discontinue pills if negative.

And, a sore throat is regarded as a simple problem.

The three basic steps in diagnosis are listed by Richard Dorf as:

1. Obtain patient's condition through examination and history.
2. Evaluate the relative importance of the various symptoms.
3. Consider all diseases with similar symptoms and systematically eliminate diseases until an appropriate disease category is found.

The computer is used to store all diseases and their symptoms, thereby eliminating one of the sources of possible error. In a *clinical decision support system*, the physician uses the computer in an interactive mode for systematically analyzing a decision tree that is constructed from a particular set of symptoms. In the event of multiple diseases, the computer can assist the physician, through modeling and optimization techniques, to determine the best treatment plan.

Clinical support systems are not in widespread use, but it is difficult to determine if the situation is a result of the fact that few systems exist, or because physicians do not want to use them.

Medical Information Systems

Medical information systems encompass two functions: medical record keeping, mentioned previously, and hospital accounting and control systems. It is estimated that approximately 25 percent of all hospital costs are for accounting, billing, medicare and medicaid systems, and a variety of other clerical and administrative functions. Conventional data processing facilities are usually sufficient for patient accounting; however, many hospitals have gone to on-line real-time systems. Small hospitals frequently share a common hospital accounting system.

Computers have helped enormously in the administration of hospitals and medical centers. Problems of these institutions are unique in the sense that advanced technology is applied whenever possible —meaning obviously, staff and equipment. Within a given operational budget, administrators usually prefer to minimize clerical expenditures and maximize expenditures on staff and equipment to provide the best possible medical care. The use of computers has reduced the "per patient" cost of clerical services and has generally improved medical care.

Other Medical Applications

Other uses of the computer in medicine by hospitals and physicians are:

1. Patient billing by physicians, usually through a computer service bureau
2. Menu planning in hospitals
3. Scheduling in clinics and wards
4. Inventory and drug control
5. Blood bank management
6. Control of laboratory tests

In medical research, computers are used to model the brain, the circulatory system, the side effects of various drug treatments, and for physiological simulation in medical training. In fact, the University of Southern California medical school has a computer-controlled mannequin, complete with heartbeat, blood pressure, breathing action, jaws, eyes, and muscles, for the training of resident doctors. The computer-controlled mannequin can suffer from a variety of diseases and even die. However, this patient prepares a printed report of how well the attending physician performed.

16.5 EDUCATION

One of our biggest disappointments has been the use of computers in education, although it may turn out that our original expectations were too great. In our economic society, a good rule of thumb is that "increased productivity accompanies increased costs." This has been true in manufacturing, government, marketing, banking, and even medicine. Characteristically, it has not been true in education. The cost of education has skyrocketed, but we continue to be constrained by the traditional teacher-student relationship. It was hoped by many that computers would help in this regard, but substantial results have been slow to arrive. From a performance point of view, most computer-based educational systems and techniques have been successful. The costs of computerized systems are high, perhaps as high as 10 to 1 over conventional methods.

The uses of computers in education can logically be placed into three categories:

1. For clerical operations in educational administration
2. As a technique and/or tool for use in the educational process
3. As a field of study—computer science and data processing

This section is concerned with items 1 and 2.

Administration

One area in which computers *have* reduced educational costs is in the area of administration and control. Many school systems have replaced manual record keeping with a computerized version using conventional data processing methods. Computerized systems are more reliable and accurate, and can be programmed to produce a variety of reports useful for school administration. Many systems also include medical records so that the data can be used for a variety of analyses. Centralized record keeping is useful when students frequently are moved from school to school, as is the case with the children of migrant farm workers. When a student in this category enters a new school, his complete record can be received in hours and he can be placed immediately. Most school systems currently require medical examinations and inoculations for the various communicable diseases. Students who are transferred are frequently given the same shots, over and over again. With a computerized system, the whole process of changing schools can be made less traumatic to the child involved.

Computers are commonly used for class scheduling, for curriculum planning, and for the grading of examinations. Class scheduling is a cumbersome and time-consuming process. Computer programs are now available for scheduling that optimize the use of classrooms and institutional personnel. Curriculum planning is a recent concept that has great potential in the areas of staffing and physical facilities. It has been shown that future needs of a school can be reliably predicted on the basis of current class enrollments, student aptitudes, and student interests. Because of the newness of this area, sufficient time has not elapsed for results to be achieved and reported. Computer facilities for grading examinations are a welcome resource to teachers at all levels of instruction. The key point is that it frees them for more productive activities.

Instruction

Computers are used in instruction in three principal ways:

1. As a means of testing skills, such as in the areas of arithmetic and language
2. As part of a programmed learning program
3. As an analysis and problem-solving tool

As a means of testing skills, a computer system is programmed to present the student with exercises. The student is seated at a terminal device. (The specific type of device is not important.) If the student responds correctly, he is presented with another exercise. If he responds incorrectly, he is given the answer and the session continues with another exercise. The length of the session is usually dependent upon achieving a prespecified number of correct answers. (A student pointed out a danger in this method: playing with the computer terminal is so much fun that it is conjectured that many students make mistakes to prolong the session.)

Programmed instruction (frequently called computer-aided instruction or CAI) is more complicated and requires that a course be synthesized as a set of programmed steps. CAI systems are available for assisting the teacher in "course writing." The student sits at a CAI terminal (usually a CRT-type device) and is presented textual material, which he reads. He is then asked questions. If he responds correctly, the CAI system goes on to the next topic. If he responds incorrectly, he is given the answer and a brief review of the subject matter. The depth to which this process can go is dependent upon the course author and the CAI system.

CAI systems are primarily on-line systems that can usually service hundreds of students. The CAI programs take care of sequencing and terminal control. The course author takes care of the course content, which may vary among students using the system at any one time.

The advantage of CAI is that it allows the student to proceed at his own pace and gives him individual attention (note that the word *personal* was not used) that is not available in many classroom situations. CAI costs are very high, ranging from $200 to $2000 per instructional hour.

The use of the computer as a problem-solving and an analysis tool in mathematics, science, engineering, and business has been well demonstrated. It has also been used successfully in the social sciences, the humanities, and the arts. Applications range from a simple computer program to generate random poetry to an extensive system for language translation. A few sample uses of the computer in these areas are listed below:

Study of linguistics
Language translation
Concordance generation
Literary analysis
Poetry writing
Attribution study (authorship problem)
Music analysis
Programs that solve problems
Symbolic mathematics
Simulation of a neurotic person (behavioral science)

    Analysis of census data
    Political simulation
    Simulation of a cell (biology)
    Game plan analysis (football)

In the creative arts, there are:

    Computer generated art forms
    Music composition
    Creating motion pictures
    Choreographic description
    Fiction writing

Computers have even been used to generate horoscopes and para-psychological experiments.

    This situation with computers in education is well summarized by Donald Sanders:

> A primary purpose of using computers as an instructional tool in the classroom should be to *provide insight* and not merely compute numbers or process documents.

In this regard, we have hardly begun, but in the application of systematic thinking and problem-solving methods, computer training provides a valuable learning experience.

16.6 AUTOMATION AND JOBS

    It *is* true that the computer has displaced some people. Automation always does. It is difficult to generalize about automation because each situation is different and research data is often conflicting. Displaced persons are often absorbed into other units or leave the labor force, through retirement, pregnancy, or for other reasons. In spite of the negative aspects of automation, economists agree that the concept is beneficial to society in the long run and that displacement should not be prevented. It is difficult for the employee being displaced to be philosophical about the matter, and reeducation and retraining are frequently necessary. This should be part of the planning process.

Management and Organization

    The effects of automation on management and organization are summarized as follows:

1. Centralization of planning and control at a higher level of the organization.
2. It has made the middle manager's job more complex. (It was predicted that automation would reduce the number and status of middle-management jobs. This prediction never materialized.)
3. It has increased the middle manager's and supervisor's needs for human-relations skills.
4. It has reduced the span of supervision, that is, the number of employees a supervisor can effectively manage.

Item 4 is particularly significant in the computer field, where a typical first-line manager may have five to eight programmers or systems analysts reporting to him.

As computers are assigned to routine tasks, more of the energy of the organization is devoted to the solution of nonroutine problems. This requires a certain amount of imagination and creativity that the typical bureaucratic organization, with its rigid structure and personnel pigeonholing, is not designed to cope with. Therefore, a decline of bureaucratic organizational characteristics tends to accompany a computerized organization. It could be that The Peter Principle, which states that "in a hierarchy every employee tends to rise to his level of incompetence," will finally be refuted. In the same book (i.e., *The Peter Principle*), the authors mention a type of behavior referred to as *professional automatism*, wherein means are more important than ends. More specifically, the paperwork is more important than the purpose for which it was originally designed.

Overall, information systems and decision-making models have enabled executives to reassume many of the decision-making functions that were subordinated to middle management in the previous generation of decentralized organizations. More time can be spent on policy matters and less time "fighting fires." Middle management has more time for planning and control, and lower-level management can devote needed time to the human-relations problems associated with a changing society.

Education, Specialization, and the Professions

Automation requires more professional and scientific employees to manage and control the complex systems involved. Clerical workers are moved into more responsible positions; blue-collar workers are upgraded to white-collar jobs. The people who suffer most from automation are the ones lacking in basic education, intelligence, or aptitude for retraining, because it is difficult to place them in other jobs in the organization. Large organizations tend to be better in this regard for the simple reason that they possess the resources and the job opportunities to do it. In smaller organizations, displaced employees are more likely to be laid off.

The computer revolution has brought about a special breed of "professional specialist," uncommitted to an organization. This modern technocrat is described by Alvin Toffler in *Future Shock* as follows: "He is willing to employ his skills and creative energies to solve problems with equipment provided by the organization, and within temporary groups established by it. But he does so only so long as the problems interest *him*. He is committed to his own career, his own self-fulfillment." Thus, it can be said that the loyalty of the professional man of the new technology is to his profession and not to the organization that is employing him at any point in time. Specialization increases the number of different occupations and dissolves the traditional boundaries of the bureaucratic organization. On any given team, several levels within the organization may be represented.

Planning and Implementation

The people problem is solved through effective planning and careful implementation. People resist change for obvious reasons:

1. Possible loss of job
2. Change in working environment (new friends, etc.)
3. Fear of not being able to learn the new skill required
4. Possible loss of status in the community

But, people faced with the above fears do not simply say, "I resist." The resistance is manifested in what can be regarded as seemingly irrational behavior, such as forgetting to enter data, withholding output, low morale, and ignoring computer facilities. Many organizations solve the problem by keeping the employees informed of developments and allowing the employees to participate in the new system, and by careful timing of the implementation cycle. Some organizations have even gone so far as to guarantee in writing that the employee will not be displaced when the new equipment (or facilities) is installed.

16.7 PERSONAL ISSUES

The "popular" way to feel about computers and information is expressed by McLuhan and Watson in *From Cliche to Archetype* as follows: "As information itself becomes the largest business in the world, data banks know more about individual people than the people do themselves. The more the data banks record about each one of us, the less we exist." Many other writers in the social arena have expressed similar concerns. Lewis Mumford is concerned with the dehumanizing aspect of computers when he writes: "The process of automation has produced imprisoned minds that have no capacity for appraising the results of their process, except by the archaic criteria of power and prestige, property, productivity and profit, segregated from any more vital human goals." There are, of course, differing opinions. For example, Alvin Toffler in *Future Shock* believes that the new technology has provided us with too many options at too great a rate. He attributes much of what is bad in our society to this rate of change and not to the change itself.

The Number Game

One of the biggest complaints heard from students, customers of a public utility, credit-card holders, and so forth, is, "I'm just a number to them. They don't know who I am." The problem is actually a matter of necessity, rather than a disregard for human dignity. If it is necessary to record information on thousands of persons, it is simply more efficient to code them by number than by name. Moreover, names are frequently misspelled and abbreviated, and sometimes initials and nicknames are used. Therefore, it is not altogether unreasonable to use numbers inside of the computer. The problem arises when a person is forced to memorize the number. The use of identification numbers is also an outgrowth of traditional batch processing systems in which the respondent has no means of interacting with the computer. With the widespread use of modern on-line interactive systems, the situation will probably change somewhat, since the computer can communicate with the respondent to remove any ambiguities. There are more pressing issues.

Computer Victims

Most Americans have either a credit card, a utility account, a checking account, or a magazine subscription—the average citizen has at least one of each. Many people have experienced the helpless feeling associated with the following sequence of events:

1. The person receives a bill for $0.00 and ignores it.
2. Next month a dunning letter arrives.
3. The person consults with friends and finally sends a check for $0.00.

4. The computer responds by stating it doesn't accept checks for $0.00.

Another recurring case goes somewhat as follows. A person has dinner at a restaurant and uses a credit card. He is never billed. He inquires of the company and is informed, "Be patient, the bill will arrive." Perhaps he does nothing. Subsequently, he tries to use the same credit card. The validity of the card is verified with one of the service companies (mentioned earlier in this chapter) and he is told that a bill is outstanding and credit will not be accepted.

The person's credit rating may be ruined. (It is also computerized.) However, this is not known until credit is refused and the person investigates the reason why. There are numerous documented cases of persons who have even been turned down for jobs because of poor credit ratings that they didn't even know about.

The individual is practically helpless. He may have a dispute, for example, with a department store for an erroneous charge. He is given a poor credit rating. The dispute is finally resolved and the erroneous charge is cancelled. The store never bothers to inform the credit company, which acts as an information handling company and takes no responsibility for the accuracy of the data. The individual could consult a lawyer, but that could eventually cost him thousands of dollars. It is no wonder that many people wish the computer would go away.

Things are even worse than meets the eye at first glance. Credit-card companies, department stores, and the like are profit-making organizations, and they do make a profit regardless of who suffers. Consider the problem of straightening out a customer's account, and suppose the customer is right. There are two options open to the company:

1. Investigate the situation, answer the customer's letters, and seriously attempt to straighten out the matter.
2. Ignore the customer's letters. The customer will either pay the bill, or get angry and cancel his account. (By this time, he has probably said, "To heck with the credit rating.")

From a business point of view, the most profitable course of action might very well be the second one. Many customers will pay their bill, however erroneous, in order to preserve a good credit rating. If the customer does cancel his account, the cost of the advertising to get a new customer is usually far less than the cost of resolving the original problem.

The same reasoning holds true for the correcting of "programming bugs," such as the bill for $0.00 mentioned previously. The programming, checkout, and computer time necessary to correct a simple "bug" may cost thousands of dollars. In light of the situation, it is a wonder that most computerized systems operate as well as they do.

The problem obviously is not the problem of the computer. It is a people problem caused by poor systems design, poor programming, or sloppy input. Not only are people victimized by the computer, but the computer is also victimized by people.

Privacy and Confidential Information

Another area of concern to most people is "privacy." Alan F. Westin defines *privacy* as, "the claim of individuals, groups, or institutions to determine for themselves when, how, and to what extent information about them is communicated to others." The concern for privacy is nothing new and organizations have always collected information of various kinds. However, the problem has been brought to the public's eye in recent years with the widespread use of computers, information systems, and telecommunications facilities. The use of computers has not created the privacy problem but has enlarged the scope of information gathering. Privacy involves organizations, individuals, and society as a whole. Organizations need privacy to carry out their basic objective, whether it be business, politics, or government. There is a tendency for individuals to invade the privacy of other individuals, for reasons ranging from curiosity to criminal blackmail. Within societies, surveillance techniques are generally accepted when used by authorized agencies against enemies of that society. Thus, privacy is both desirable and undesirable, depending upon the factors involved.

From the individual's point of view, privacy is exceedingly important because it provides basic psychological and legal needs. Some of the more obvious of these needs are:

1. *Personal autonomy*—wherein a person's hopes, fears, shame, and aspirations are protected against public scrutiny
2. *Emotional release*—so that a person can "unwind," "let it all out," or show intimate feelings without fear of events being misinterpreted
3. *Self-evaluation*—so that a person can employ introspection, observation, and other means to improve himself
4. *Limited and protected communications*—so that a person can seek and utilize counsel (legal, clerical, etc.) without fear of incrimination

There are other reasons why privacy is important to the individual. First, organizations, such as the federal government, have files on people. Some of the agencies are the IRS, the FBI, the Social Security Administration, the Veterans Administration, the Department of Justice —to name only a few. Each agency generally has its own procedures for collecting data and ensuring its accuracy, value, and appropriateness. Usually, an agency's regulations for the release of information are developed in light of its collection procedures. This is also true of credit companies. But what about when information is shared, as in a data bank? It is also less expensive to obtain information from another agency than to collect it yourself. Once information systems are integrated, the regulations of the collecting agency do not necessarily apply to the agency that is using it.

Another concern about information systems is that the past can very easily get in the way of the future. What does this mean? Suppose a first-grade teacher subjectively remarks in a child's record that he is "hyperactive" or has a "short attention span." It is unlikely that anyone who might see the child's record could accurately interpret the significance of the remark. But, what about 20 years later when that person is seeking employment. Who knows how a prospective employer might respond to a subjective remark? More importantly, the terms *hyperactive* and *short attention span* might have entirely different meanings in 20 years. Arthur R. Miller has this to say about the situation: "In the past, there was a limited risk that subjective appraisals by individual teachers would be widely circulated. Now, with missionary zeal our well-intentioned information handlers are ready to offer their files 'to anyone who had access to individual school records' as well as to 'prospective employers.'"

In short, we do not have control over information that can and is released about ourselves. There has been extensive legal consideration of the subject and Miller's book* is recommended to the reader for an introduction to what has been accomplished in this regard. Personal factors are just as important. Miller has the following to say about the protection of individual privacy: "The objective of protecting the individual privacy is to safeguard emotional and psychological tranquility by remedying an injurious dissemination of personal information …"

To complicate the situation, there is even some debate over exactly what constitutes "private" information. In a research study performed

---

* *The Assault on Privacy* by A. R. Miller.

by E. V. Comber, the following factors were given that may apply in determining when an informational item is private:

1. The context within which the specific information is embedded
2. The amount of information assembled and accessible
3. The intrinsic nature of the information
4. The sophistication of the social values held by the individuals concerned
5. The character and scope of the subculture
6. Significance of personal attributes such as age, ancestry, social status, race, and so forth.

The conclusion to our discussion of privacy must necessarily be that the problem does not lie with computers, but with the discipline and conduct of man, who is the designer and user of the information system.

16.8 THE FUTURE

In attempting to assess the immediate future of computer technology, it is always wise to look at other technological innovations to determine how they were absorbed into society. We do not have to go far. The telephone and electric power are far enough. Neither would be in widespread use today if national (and international) networks did not exist, allowing people and organizations to "tie in" to satisfy their particular needs. Fortunately, the same telephone network we use for telephone calls can be used for the computer networks of tomorrow.

John Kemeny, President of Dartmouth College and co-inventor of the BASIC language, has stated we are likely to see the development of huge computer networks in the next decade, similar to airline reservation systems and the time-sharing networks operated by several service companies.

In his "Man and Nature" lectures given at the Museum of Natural History in New York City in the fall of 1971, Dr. Kemeny outlined a network of nine regional centers that would service the 80 cities in the United States with populations of 150,000 or over. The nine centers are depicted in Figure 16.1. None of the 80 cities would be more than 500 miles from a regional center and many suburbs and small cities would also be picked up by the system. In addition to providing service to their respective regions, the centers would be connected together via microwave or high-speed lines to balance the workload and provide emergency service in case of system failure. The regional centers would

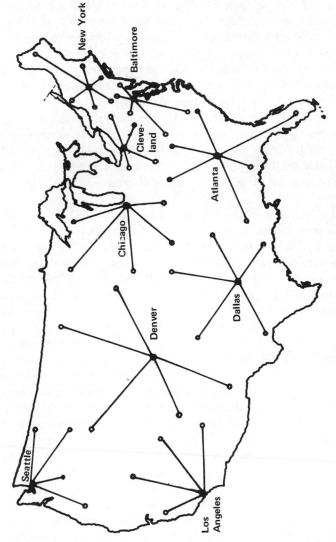

Figure 16.1 Proposed national computer network.

be used to provide time-sharing service, on-line information systems, and remote job entry facilities.

It is likely that each regional center will utilize a set of central processing units (a multiprocessing system) sharing the same main storage, direct-access storage, and peripheral input/output units. Systems of this type are in existence today, and network computer service is currently available at many colleges and universities.

In the next decade it is likely that the home terminal will come into widespread use. What will it be used for? The most obvious answer is for computation service and for computer-aided instruction (CAI) on a large-scale basis. Kemeny futher describes the future "library" system that will allow a person to access a large information system from his own home. With many persons vying for computer service, scheduling will be a problem. Complex operating systems will be used to control computer processing, terminal service, and the running of background jobs.

Kemeny's library of the future will be a complete library stored in the computer. It will be federally funded and maintained on a national basis. Although the costs would be staggering, there are many advantages. The growth rate of libraries in number of volumes doubles approximately every 30 years, and a high percentage of the books are never consulted. By providing access to heavily used information through the computer from the national library system, local library facilities (such as those in colleges and universities) could be reduced considerably. Storage large enough to hold this voluminous amount of information is viewed as a problem, and Kemeny sees books and journals stored as photographic images, similar to the microfilm storage mentioned in this book. Instead of publishing books, publishers will prepare photographable material suitable for entry in the computer. Royalties would be paid on usage and seldom-used publications would be removed from the system to provide faster access to the other information in the system. An added benefit of the concept is that the lead time for publication would be decreased so that available information to researchers and students would be more relevant and up-to-date.

Kemeny also foresees the day of the *personalized newspaper,* available through the home terminal. Instead of publishing thousands of copies, a newspaper such as *The New York Times* would store the information in a computer memory tied to a national computer network. The reporter could type his story directly into the computer, through the network, and the newspaper's staff could perform routine editing and make policy decisions on its contents. Each reader of the newspaper would have a profile, stored in the computer, of topics of interest to him. For example, the reader might be interested in business, sports, and the society section. (That's some combination.) The computer would display a list of the available news in each topic and the reader would choose the stories of interest to him – in much the same manner that a person scans the headlines while reading the paper in the conventional manner. The computer would then type the story at normal reading speed or display it on a CRT-type device. At any point in time, the reader could discontinue reading and go on to the next topic. The advantages are that the reader would be provided up-to-date news on topics of interest to him. What about advertising? Kemeny gives two possibilities: (1) displaying ads between pages of text; or (2) paying an extra fee for the option of eliminating advertisements.

If all of this sounds far-fetched, the following paragraphs will surprise you. Alvin Toffler reports in *Future Shock* that " ... in the mid sixties, Joseph Naughton, a mathematician and computer specialist at the University of Pittsburgh, suggested a system that would store a consumer's profile—data about his occupation and interests—in a central computer. Machines would then scan newspapers, magazines, video tapes, films and other material, match them against the individual's interest profile, and instantaneously notify him when something appears that concerns him. The system could be hitched to facsimile machines and TV transmitters that would actually display or print out the material in his own living room."

In *Computer Decisions*, Senior Editor Richard Laska reports that the information bank of *The New York Times* is about to go on-line. The information bank will enable users to access and display on their video terminals information appearing within the last three to five years in *The New York Times* or in some 35 other periodicals. All the user need do is establish a telephone link to the New York Times Information System, enter identifying information, and enter descriptive terms that the system can use to narrow its search. The cost of the service is a flat charge of $1,600 per month, which includes a video terminal, a printer, and unlimited use of the system.

The subject of personal or home computers continues to "pop up" every once in a while. Scientists at MIT are experimenting with a personal-computer concept, called OLIVER, for helping to deal with the decision and information overload. OLIVER, which is an acronym for On-Line Interactive Vicarious Expediter and Responder—chosen for Oliver Selfridge, is a computer programmed to store information for an individual, such as his anniversary and his wife's dress size, stock prices, and weather forecasts, and perform routine tasks such as paying bills and ordering food. OLIVER could store a multitude of professional details and serve as a handbook or question-answering device. Moreover, OLIVER could be programmed to identify with its owner to the extent that as its owner's attitudes, likes, and dislikes changed, OLIVER could modify itself accordingly. The MIT people even foresee groups of OLIVERs communicating among themselves to handle routine matters for their masters.

16.9 CONCLUSIONS

In conclusion, it is only fair to admit that it *is* difficult to put the impact of computers on society in perspective. Knowledge of the subject matter is ostensibly the solution to the dilemma, but once one "digs in" and learns about the field, he can honestly no longer be objective. The best medicine is to call on outside authority. First, a pessimistic quotation from Charles Reich in *The Greening of America*:*

> The American Corporate State today can be thought of as a single vast corporation, with every person as an involuntary member and employee. It consists primarily of large industrial organizations, plus nonprofit institutions such as foundations and the educational system, all related to the whole as divisions to a business corporation. Government is only a part of the state, but government coordinates it and provides a variety of needed services. The Corporate State is a complete reversal of the original American ideal and plan. The State, and not the market or the people or any abstract economic laws, determines what shall be produced, what shall be consumed, and how it shall be allocated. It determines, for example, that railroads shall decay while highways flourish; that coal miners shall be poor and advertising executives rich. Jobs and occupations in the society are rigidly defined and controlled, and arranged in a hierarchy of rewards, status, and authority. An individual can move from one position to another, but he gains little freedom thereby, for in each position he is subject to conditions imposed upon it; individuals have no protected area of liberty, privacy, or individual sovereignty beyond the reach of the State.

An appropriate way to end this chapter on computers and individuals is

* Reich, p. 93.

with a contrary opinion with a computer orientation from Donald H. Sanders in *Computers in Society*:*

> ... the optimists believe that the sophisticated computer systems of the future will permit a more human and personalized society that will further reduce the need for individual conformity. They argue that the complexity of our present society, the millions of people crowded into it, and the inadequacy of our present information systems act to encourage conformity and thus to restrict personalization and human freedom of choice. However, when sophisticated information systems are developed and widely used to handle routine transactions, it will then be possible to focus greater personal attention on exceptional transactions. Therefore, more humanistic attitudes will emerge.

SELECTED READINGS

Comber. E. V., "Management of confidential information," *Proceedings of the 1969 Fall Joint Computer Conference*, AFIPS Vol. 34, pp. 135–143.

Davis, K., *Human Relations at Work*, McGraw-Hill, New York, 1967.

Dorf, R. C., *Introduction to Computers and Computer Science*, Boyd and Fraser, San Francisco, 1972.

Hamming, R. W., *Computers and Society*, McGraw-Hill, New York, 1972.

Katzan, H., *Computer Data Security*, Van Nostrand-Reinhold, New York, 1973.

Kemeny, J. G., *Man and the Computer*, Scribner, New York, 1972.

Laska, R. M., "All the news that's fit to retrieve," *Computer Decisions* 4, No. 8 (Aug. 1972), 18–22.

Martin, J., and A. R. D. Norman, *The Computerized Society*, Prentice-Hall, Englewood Cliffs, N.J., 1970.

McLuhan, M., and W. Watson, *From Cliche to Archetype*, Viking, New York, 1970.

Miller, A. R., *The Assault on Privacy*, Univ. of Michigan Press, Ann Arbor, 1971.

Mumford, L., *The Myth of the Machine: The Pentagon of Power*, Harcourt, Brace, Jovanovich, New York, 1970.

Peter, L. J., and R. Hull, *The Peter Principle*, William Morrow, New York, 1969.

Raiffa, H., *Design Analysis: Introductory Lectures on Choices under Uncertainty*, Addison-Wesley, Reading, Mass., 1968.

Reich, C. A., *The Greening of America*, Bantam, New York, 1970.

Rodgers, W., *Think: A Biography of the Watsons and IBM*, Stein and Day, New York, 1969.

* Sanders, p. 252.

Rothman, S., and C. Mosmann, *Computers and Society*, Science Research
    Associates, Chicago, 1972.
Sanders, D. H., *Computers in Society: An Introduction to Information Processing*,
    McGraw-Hill, New York, 1973.
Toffler, A., *Future Shock*, Random House, New York, 1970.
Westin, A. F., *Privacy and Freedom*, Atheneum, New York, 1967.

INDEX